NUFFIELD EUROPEAN STUDIES

INDUSTRIAL ENTERPRISE
AND EUROPEAN INTEGRATION

NUFFIELD EUROPEAN STUDIES

The purpose of the Nuffield European Studies series is to provide, for students and teachers in the social sciences and related disciplines, works of an interdisciplinary and comparative nature dealing with significant political, economic, legal, and social problems confronting European nation-states and the European Community. It will comprise research monographs as well as the edited proceedings of conferences organized by the Centre for European Studies at Nuffield College, Oxford. The general editors of the series are Joachim Jens Hesse, Ford-Monnet Professor of European Politics and Comparative Government in the University of Oxford, and Vincent Wright, Official Fellow of Nuffield College and Director of the Centre for European Studies.

INDUSTRIAL ENTERPRISE
AND
EUROPEAN INTEGRATION

*From National to International Champions
in Western Europe*

Edited by
JACK HAYWARD

OXFORD UNIVERSITY PRESS
1995

Oxford University Press, Walton Street, Oxford OX2 6DP

Oxford New York
Athens Auckland Bangkok Bombay
Calcutta Cape Town Dar es Salaam Delhi
Florence Hong Kong Istanbul Karachi
Kuala Lumpur Madras Madrid Melbourne
Mexico City Nairobi Paris Singapore
Taipei Tokyo Toronto
and associated companies in
Berlin Ibadan

Oxford is a trade mark of Oxford University Press

Published in the United States
by Oxford University Press Inc., New York

British Library Cataloguing in Publication Data
Data available

Library of Congress Cataloging in Publication Data
Industrial enterprise and European integration: from national to
international champions in Western Europe/edited by Jack Hayward.
— (Nuffield European studies)
1. Business enterprises—Government policy—European Economic
Community countries.   2. Industrial policy—European Economic
Community countries.   3. Industries—European Economic Community
countries.   I. Hayward, Jack Ernest Shalom.   II. Series.
HD2844.5.I565   1995   338.7'094—dc20   94-43370
ISBN 0-19-827972-8

1 3 5 7 9 10 8 6 4 2

Typeset by Best-set Typesetter Ltd., Hong Kong
Printed in Great Britain
on acid-free paper by
Biddles Ltd., Guildford and King's Lynn

Preface

In 1991, while spending a year teaching at Sciences Po in Paris, I was approached by an old friend and co-researcher, Vincent Wright, to organize a workshop at the newly established Centre for European Studies at Nuffield College, Oxford. We agreed on the theme 'National Enterprise and the International Environment in West Europe'. Having recruited a team of contributors who prepared draft papers, we duly met in Oxford in mid-May 1992. A grant from the Nuffield Foundation covered most of the expenses and I would like to express my gratitude for this support.

Most of the initial papers have survived, in more or less heavily redrafted form, in this book. Several of the chapters have been added by people (Cox and Watson, Kassim, McGowan and Wright) most of whom attended the workshop but did not at the time contribute a paper. Thus enriched, the results of our individual efforts and collective deliberations are before you. Given the complex and fast-moving nature of the relations of firms, governments, and European Community, one cannot hope to provide more than a partial and time-bound analysis of a process that has been drastically modified by the political and economic changes that have occurred, especially since the end of the 1980s. The ambiguity of the initial term 'national enterprise' led us to adopt instead, as our focus, the transition from firms as national champions to the search for Euro-champion and international champion status.

In a book that takes as its centre-piece the major firms operating within four policy sectors (electricity, aerospace, air transport, and telecommunications) and a binational collaborative project (the Channel Tunnel), it is also indispensable to place their activities within both their national and European Community-wide contexts. As Alan Milward has convincingly argued in *The European Rescue of the Nation State*, postwar political economy has been characterized by *both* the reassertion of the state and the resort to collective action through the European Community. The latter has been an indispensable complement to attempts by states to grapple with industrial problems that they could no longer manage effectively on their own. Just as the newly liberated nation states of central East Europe have wished both to assert their independence and to join the European Union, so in Western Europe we cannot understand the behaviour of industrial champion firms without placing them in their national habitats and within the European Community.

Both state and community contexts have involved constraints as well as providing firms with the capacity to expand. However, these constraints and capacities have impinged on the firms differently in the case of France, Germany, Britain, and Italy, just as the actions of the European Community have affected particular industrial sectors in contrasting ways. In the early 1990s, France slumped into a record unemployment (12.5%), despite trying to meet its public borrowing requirement and boost its flagging economy by recourse to the privatization nostrum. Britain, having already largely exhausted its saleable public assets, sank into the European Community's slow stream, while running its economy on cheap labour and low investment. Germany, having absorbed its reunited Eastern brethren—partly by a rapid privatization of its industries—was openly assuming its *de facto* position of economic leadership within the European Community but struggling to preserve the social features of its social market economy. Meanwhile, Italy, having at last appeared ready to clean up its corrupt politico-industrial complex as well as reduce its crippling burden of public debt, electorally handed its government over to a businessman who seemed more concerned to rescue his own business and his friends than to pursue the overdue task of reform.

More generally, the attempts by both states and the European Community to impose their will upon firms in the name of industrial patriotism or communitarian preference have come to grief in the face of an increasingly intractable global market economy. So, even if the European community has supplemented the deficiencies of its member nation states, both rescuer and rescued have had to accept their increasing incapacity to bend international markets to their will. They have all pursued policies of competitive disinflation.

Subsequent to this project's conception, I myself moved to a sister-centre of the one under whose auspices it was prepared. The friendly co-operation which has since marked our research and teaching activities was inadvertently inaugurated at the workshop out of which this book emerged. It is my firm intention that this initiative will be sustained in the future.

J.H.

Contents

Figures

Tables

Abbreviations

BR	British Rail
CDU	German Christian Democratic Union
CEC	Commission of the European Community
CEGB	UK Central Electricity Generating Board
CPE	customer premises equipment
CSU	German Christian Social Union
DBP	Deutsche Bundespost
DC	Italian Christian Democratic Party
DG	Directorate General (EC)
ECJ	European Court of Justice
EdF	Electricité de France
EFTA	European Free Trade Area
EMU	European Monetary Union
ENEL	Ente Nazionale per l'Energia Elettrica (Italy)
ESI	electricity supply industry
ESPRIT	European Strategic Programme for Research and Development in Information Technologies
EUREKA	the European Research Co-ordinating Agency
FDR	Federal Democratic Republic (the new united Germany)
FRG	Federal Republic of Germany (West Germany)
FDP	German Free Democratic Party
GDR	German Democratic Republic (East Germany)
IATA	International Air Transportation Association
ICAO	International Civil Aviation Organization
ISDN	Integrated Service Digital Network
OFGAS	Office of Gas Supply (UK)
OFTEL	Office of Telecommunications (UK)
PSI	Italian Socialist Party
PTOs	public telecommunications operators
RACE	Research in Advanced Communications for Europe
SPD	German Social Democratic Party
VANS	value added network services

Contributors

PATRIZIO BIANCHI is Professor of Economics, University of Bologna.

ELIE COHEN is Director of Research, Centre National de la Recherche Scientifique, Groupe d'Analyse des Politiques Publiques.

ANDREW COX is Professor of Political Science, University of Birmingham.

JOSEF ESSER is Professor of Political Science, Goethe University, Frankfurt.

WYN GRANT is Professor of Politics, University of Warwick.

JACK HAYWARD is Professor and Director, Institute of European Studies, University of Oxford.

IAN HOLLIDAY is Lecturer in Government, University of Manchester.

HUSSEIN KASSIM is Lecturer in Politics, Birkbeck College, University of London.

FRANCIS MCGOWAN is Lecturer in Politics, School of European Studies, University of Sussex.

PIERRE MULLER is affiliated with the Centre de Recherches Administratives, Paris.

MARK THATCHER is Leverhulme Research Fellow, Ecole Nationale Supérieure de Télécommunications, Paris.

HELEN WALLACE is Professor and Director, Sussex European Institute.

GLYN WATSON is Research Assistant, Political Economy Research Unit, University of Birmingham.

STEPHEN WOOLCOCK is Senior Research Fellow, London School of Economics.

VINCENT WRIGHT is Official Fellow and Director, Centre of European Studies, Nuffield College, Oxford.

Introduction

Europe's Endangered Industrial Champions

JACK HAYWARD

Within the ever-widening expanse of comparative political economy, the comparative study of industrial policy has been very susceptible to fashion. After the Second World War, and especially in France, it was associated with national economic planning and with macro-economic policy. In the 1960s, it was more specifically linked with the merger mania that took the specific form of developing firms that could carry the national flag into the internationally competitive arena. What had been seen as government–industry relations, regarded as a sectoral activity, became increasingly focused upon particular firms, although it took quite a while for this to be appreciated by external observers. It was so much more convenient for government economic ministries to aggregate their interventionist activities, dealing with trade associations and peak organizations rather than operating on a firm-by-firm basis. The shift to a national champions emphasis can also be seen as a way of simplifying the task of public intervention, quite separate from the economic rationale based upon arguments from competitive efficiency which were to the fore. As protectionism receded in the wake of technology-driven changes that imposed a globalization of industrial activity, intergovernmental relations and non-national firms impinged ever more upon industrial policies. This book's distinctive contribution to the industrial policy debate is to place the champion firm at the centre of its political and economic analysis, conducted with reference to the national and sectoral, the European and international contexts within which firms engage in their business.

Firms and governments have been increasingly forced to deal with the political and economic consequences of the globalization of economic activity. The context in which major European firms have operated has changed in at least five significant ways. First, irrespective of whether they are publicly owned or not, national firms have increasingly lost their *de facto* market monopoly or semi-monopoly. The increased permeability of national frontiers has deprived them of their protection from foreign competition. Second, these firms have been increasingly compelled to have recourse to international capital markets because national banks and governments have been unable or unwilling to satisfy their needs. Third, when these firms have been in deficit, they could overtly or covertly be subsidized. They are now increasingly required to be self-sustaining. Fourth, these firms have been increasingly compelled to adopt an international strategy by contracting transnational alliances or engaging in direct foreign investment. These alliances take various forms, such as joint ventures, collaboration in marketing, research and development, or the establishment of foreign subsidiaries. Finally, these firms no longer feel the need to act as though they were serving the national interest, whether or not their governments were accepted as the judges of what action this principle required in particular cases. Instead, such firms have few inhibitions about acting to promote their own security, profitability, and bargaining power. They are no longer the industrial projections of national identity, so that the sometime national champions of the 1960s have perforce tended to acquire a transnational identity.

A discussion of national industrial champions is bound to give pride of place to France. It was in that country, for both historical and institutional reasons, that the phenomenon acquired its most explicit, assertive, continuous, and comprehensive characteristics. State promotion of industrial activity was not merely of long standing. It was believed that recourse had to be made to public intervention, financial support, and official guidance because of France's industrial backwardness. The chosen instruments of a policy of industrial patriotism could not be independent firms left to fend for themselves in a competitive market. They had to enjoy a special relationship with the state, thanks to their management (usually derived by *pantouflage* from the state-trained public service); privileged access to funds for investment, research, and development expenditure; guaranteed markets through public procurement; and protection from foreign competition. Although attempts were made to extend this French industrial policy style through the European Community, and despite more piecemeal, episodic, and implicit ventures in this direction in other West European countries, the national industrial champion has in non-French eyes been afflicted with the original guilt by association with France's predilection for state protection and promotion. This fact must be borne in mind in tracing the fortunes and misfortunes of a high-profile industrial exercise in heroic policy making.

To see what has changed since the heyday of the national champions policy, we need to consider the context in which it developed. The increase in international competition as a consequence of trade liberalization exposed European firms to 'the American Challenge', to which Jean-Jacques Servan-Schreiber drew attention in 1967 with the intention of alarming the French Government in particular into taking corrective action. It was this French journalist, with an exceptional gift for quickly appreciating the developments in train and for expressing his views in clear and arresting language, who put the industrial 'assault on Europe' firmly on the 1960s political agenda. In *The American Challenge*, Servan-Schreiber used forceful phrases about the American '*seizure of power* within the European economy' and the 'capture' of the high growth, technologically advanced industries to dramatize the predicament faced by European firms.[1] However, he rejected the policy of Euro-protectionism against industrial annexation or satellization by American multinational corporations. Instead he recommended that European firms—'a few global corporations and a great number of tradition-bound small businesses'—become competitive on the world market. Because they could not do so without financial assistance, this should be provided by governments 'particularly in such areas as electronics, data processing, space research and atomic energy'.[2] Nevertheless, Servan-Schreiber had the prescience to leapfrog over the 'national champion' response to the problem he highlighted, moving directly to the need for a Eurochampion strategy.

At about the same time as *The American Challenge*, a number of other manifestations of the need for a micro-industrial policy appeared in France, spearheaded by a few select, national champions, created by restructuring firms where they did not already exist. We may notice three such calls to action in particular: the 1967 Nora Report on Public Enterprises, invited to model themselves on the menacingly intrusive multinational firms; the 1968 Montjoie Report from the Planning Commissariat on Industrial Development; the 1969 book by the planner and future minister Lionel Stoléru, *L'Impératif industriel*.[3] The mid-1960s was a period when the restructuring of industry by government or its agencies was fashionable. In Britain, this took the form of the Industrial Reorganization Corporation, created by the Labour Government in 1966 at a time when national economic planning enjoyed a brief popularity. In France, where it had been successfully pursued for twenty years, the Fifth Plan, covering 1966–70, anticipated the Servan-Schreiber analysis but confined itself to a national solution. It fixed as the main objective for French industry the 'reinforcement of its European and world competitive position' by creating or consolidating one or two firms or groups of international dimensions capable of sustaining foreign competition.[4] Despite the fact that it might have been expected that the heroic language of 'national champions' would have been used in the Gaullist 1960s to express the French response to the American challenge, the assertive strategy of industrial counter-attack had not yet acquired its defensively bellicose designation.

It was from the United States that the phenomenon advocated in the French Fifth Plan acquired its appellation. In their percipient 1969 study of French industrial planning, McArthur and Scott seem to be consciously innovating when they refer to 'the creation of a French "champion" in each industry . . . Such a champion would represent the nation in international competition, and would probably assume the aura of a public servant, a company operating in the interests of the nation as well as its owners and managers.'[5] They went on to argue: 'If the French desire to create industrial champions can be understood as a largely defensive response to the threat of American economic domination, and if an international escalation of mergers is to be predicted as a likely consequence, one may question whether the creation of champions is really the best defensive prescription for France to follow at this time.' They admit that the French may have little choice as their mainly US competitors 'appear as "national champions" already', although there were 'many champions' in industries like cars, chemicals, oil, and electronics.[6] However, they expressed the fear that French policy might provoke other states to create industrial champions of their own on the model of ELF-ERAP, the 'French oil champion determined to muscle its way into world markets with the backing of the State', encouraging increased industrial concentration and state regulation.[7] The stage is set for the battle between Anglo-American and Continental European views of industrial strategy.

In 1974 Raymond Vernon, McArthur and Scott's Harvard Business School colleague, followed up a pioneering study of US multinational corporations by editing a study of the relations between big firms and governments in Europe. He noted 'a growing tendency to use large national enterprises in an effort to solve specific problems, as if they were agencies of the state'.[8] While such a public policy in small countries often amounted to influencing a single firm, even in large countries, as a result of the tendency to equate size with being technologically advanced and efficient, the number of such firms could be reduced to one or two. Thus 'the idea of developing a national champion—an enterprise responsive to its national government's needs and entitled to its national government's support—began to take root'.[9] Where France led others followed, tending to use the same policy instruments. 'Providing capital on favoured terms was one typical device; discriminating in government procurement policies was a second; subsidizing research programmes a third. Whatever the method, it implicitly or explicitly embodied one important factor: the exercise of public power to discriminate in favour of chosen national champions.'[10] However, while these firms were, in the Servan-Schreiber manner, meant to carry the industrial flag into the dynamic fields of advanced technology, short-term political expediency distorted this principle into supporting declining traditional industries such as coal and shipbuilding.

As well as anticipating a propensity to support lame ducks, Vernon also spotted reasons for the reluctance to develop Eurochampions as advocated by Servan-Schreiber. 'As long as the buyers were largely from the public sector, the markets were cut up in watertight national units.' Even when this was not the case, firms were 'quite unwilling to merge their identity with European enterprises of another nationality', preferring alliance with a stronger American partner of a more piecemeal and improvised kind.[11] As early as 1974, Vernon predicted:

the time may well have passed when policies can any longer be made effectively at the European level without taking into account Europe's deep interdependencies with other parts of the world . . . Anything less than a global approach to industrial policy can generate consequences that may defeat the purpose of the policy . . . Europe's pace and style in creating a European technology policy have been so slow and so inhibited that few European enterprises are likely to count upon such a policy for strong sustenance and support. Besides, the nature of modern technology often demands networks larger than Europe can provide: a network for the assembly of relevant information on design and production; and a network of market outlets sufficiently large to absorb the development costs of the product.[12]

What was already apparent to an acute observer in the early 1970s—the increasing impracticality of both the national and Eurochampion strategies in an ever more globalized market— became much more evident by the 1980s.

The French, equipped by a long-standing national tradition of state interventionism, were naturally in the forefront of this trend. They responded to increased international competition—first mainly American, later increasingly Japanese—by discriminatory merger credit, fiscal, and public procurement policies in support of their public or private national champions. Whilst these policies were supposed to be directed primarily towards the high technology sectors, in fact short-term political pressures pushed governments into supporting the servile, palaeo-industrial sectors destined for the scrap yard. All too often, proud governments which claimed to be asserting their sovereign will ended up as humble instruments of a 'stretcher bearer state' supporting lame ducks, prisoners of firms that were unlikely ever to become internationally competitive.[13] This was as true of France and Britain as of less pretentious governments in Italy and Germany, although the smaller, even more exposed European states were less able to succumb to such defeatist temptations.

While state intervention has in practice been more attracted by failure than success, at the risk of being unfairly identified with a lack of success of which it is not the prime cause, the competitive capacity of firms is for good or ill inescapably related to their national environment. Although it is firms and not states that compete internationally, a justification for considering not merely the champion firms but their parent states in this book is that some nations achieve competitive success much more frequently and for longer periods than others. According to Michael Porter, this is because 'competitive advantage is created and sustained through a highly localized process. Differences in national economic structures, values, cultures, institutions, and histories contribute profoundly to competitive success. The role of the home nation seems to be as strong or stronger than ever. While the globalization of competition might appear to make the nation less important, instead it seems to make it more so. With fewer impediments to trade to shelter non-competitive domestic firms and industries, the home nation takes on growing significance because it is the source of the skills and technology that underpin competitive advantage.[14]

Porter goes on to argue that few national champions succeed in isolation; what is necessary, as shown notably in Germany and Italy, is a cluster of vertically and horizontally related firms, 'toughened by domestic rivalry'.[15]

The inability of a narrow national champion industrial policy to allow European firms to take advantage of the single 'domestic' market in the 1980s required a change of strategy if its benefits were not to accrue predominantly to their American or Japanese competitor firms. Once again, France—now under Socialist not Gaullist management—took the lead by trying to project its national policy onto the EC plane. In a September 1983 memorandum to the European Council, the French argued in favour of a Euro-protectionist industrial policy to constitute European champion firms and enable them to catch up on their American and Japanese competitors, who frequently enjoyed a duopoly in the advanced technology industries. By raising external and lowering internal trade barriers, revising company law through tightening the definition of an EC firm and product, changing public purchasing regulation, and encouraging research and development co-operation in advanced technology products with financial incentives, it might be possible to counteract the temptation to ally with American or Japanese firms. Eurochampions could *subsequently* engage in joint ventures with non-European firms, 'whereas premature external alliances could lead to European firms sliding into a subcontracting role'.[16] While this ambitious policy occasionally succeeded (as we see in Chapter 6 in the case of Airbus) it remained confined to a few areas, such as the ESPRIT-style R&D co-operation into other areas, with the launching of RACE (Research in Advanced Communications for Europe) and the European Research Co-ordination Agency, EUREKA.[17] Although there was a marked increase in the total number of mergers and acquisitions, especially in the expansionist years 1989–90 and in the share going to EC firms, even in the exceptional year 1989–90 53.1 per cent of them were national, 27.5 per cent were EC, and 19.4 per cent involved non-EC firms from EFTA countries as well as the USA and Japan.[18]

Disenchanted with the failure of the EC to follow the French Government's *dirigiste* lead because of opposition, notably from the governments of Britain and Germany, the Eurochampions policy was abandoned in practice. The consequences rapidly materialized. 'In the first half of 1984, there were a spate of deals between French nationalized companies and US companies in the form of direct investment, joint ventures, or collaboration in marketing and research, in sectors which included computers, telecommunications, integrated circuits, biotechnology, medical equipment, and energy,'[19] a veritable roll-call of advanced technology sectors. This coincided with a switch to a more liberal economic policy in France, which encouraged the change in EC emphasis from industrial to competition policy.

The 1988 Cecchini Report on behalf of the EC, anticipating 'The Economics of 1992', reflected the ambiguity of a compromise that combined a flexible industrial policy with an oligopolistic conception of competition as 'strategic rivalry between a limited number of firms'.[20] The main reason for this equivocation is that the major EC countries fundamentally disagree, with Germany being intermediate between a dogmatically pro-competition Britain welcoming direct investment from American and Japanese firms, while France clings to the attempts at co-ordinating joint projects and insisting that competitive regulation should consider competition in the world market and not simply the EC. Matters came to a head with the 1992 de Havilland case, in which the British Commissioner Leon Brittan blocked the takeover of the Canadian firm by a Franco-Italian joint venture. The new EC regulatory approach to mergers has reflected an American-cum-German anti-trust emphasis on preserving competition. In practice, pursuing an active industrial policy is increasingly difficult because 'national governments become increasingly unable to perform such a role, while EC institutions lack the legitimacy and political power to fill the vacuum'.[21]

Because this study of the transformation of national champions is focused on the larger states of Western Europe, we should note that the smaller states were always more exposed to competition in the world market. Nor did they have a government capacity to impose its will, so they were induced to develop political mechanisms to deal with external and internal market forces through bargaining and compromise. Diminutive domestic markets have led 'the small European states to seek their specialization and economies of scale in export markets'.[22] Katzenstein has convincingly argued that 'the small European states are clear exceptions to the generalization that liberalism in the international economy and intervention in the domestic economy are incompatible. The experience of the small European states suggests instead that political intervention in the domestic economy in the interest of domestic compensation does not constrain international liberalization, it is its necessary concomitant.'[23] He contrasts the liberal corporatism of Switzerland, the Netherlands, and Belgium with the social corporatism of Austria, Norway, and in some respects Sweden, with the latter states being more inclined to pursue a merger policy to constitute national champions. These might be more defensive, as in Norway, or more offensive as in Sweden, whose multinationals were in certain sectors competitors to be reckoned with in the international market. States like Britain, which hitherto regarded themselves as large, have had to accept that for practical purposes they have been reduced to smallness, with its economic consequences.

A more useful distinction for our purposes than the Katzenstein contrast between small, open economies characterized by liberal or social corporatism, is the contrast between countries whose major firms are linked closely to foreign capital and those which are not. Thus, quite apart from their membership of the EC, 'Dutch and Belgian firms have by far wider involvement in numerous global networks of manufacturing, marketing, and distribution than Austrian and Swedish firms'.[24] As a result, the investment decisions of Dutch and Belgian firms were not much influenced by their governments' policies, while Austrian industrial subsidies to state enterprises and Swedish exchange and capital controls ensured, until their late 1980s switch to internationalization and EC membership, greater weight to national policies. Furthermore, given the importance of holding companies in the Austrian and Belgian economies—especially OIAG in Austria, with its 400 firms within the group, and the Société Générale de Belgique with its 1,200 firms—the balance of power has shifted from the government to the conglomerate groups. Dutch champion firms on the scale of

Philips, Shell, and Unilever have, for their part, always been so international in their nature that they have not felt the need to defer to the government. As non-EC Austria and Sweden prepared to join the Community, the initial contrast with Belgium and the Netherlands receded.

In a context where international capital mobility makes it increasingly difficult to identify what is a Eurochampion firm, there seems to be no stable intermediate position between those of national and international champion. This hypothesis provides a suitable starting point for the successive examination of the role of French, German, British, and Italian governments operating in their national policy contexts, of firms in selected industrial sectors, and of the role of the EC in their regulation and restructuring. However, we must first place the tension between the competitiveness and independence of firms and of states within a comparative framework by raising some of the conceptual problems it poses.

FIRMS, FINANCIAL INSTITUTIONS, AND GOVERNMENTS

Rather than retraversing the well-trodden terrain of 'new-functionalist' and 'intergovernmental' interpretations of how the European political economy has been evolving in recent years, we shall seek to identify the major national and transnational actors as they relate to each other in the policy networks which they form. Emphasis is placed upon the role of the firms that have acquired the status of national or internationalized champions, the public or private financial institutions with which they are connected, and the governments operating either individually or increasingly in the EC and in various international summit contexts. Care has to be taken to allow the distinctive national and actual features of each case study to emerge, whilst preserving the comparative conceptual framework that allows one to relate their specific findings.

What do we mean by a 'national champion', as the point of departure for our investigation? If we select too tight a definition, which might fit France particularly well—that is, a definition emphasizing a deliberate and systematic state promotion of public or private national firms, supported by protectionism in merger, public procurement, trade, and research and development policies, as well as by discretionary intervention (e.g. financial subsidies) by an élite subscribing to a public service ideology culminating in 'big projects',[25]—we will find that it does not fit other countries, such as Germany. There, a much more informal, less obtrusively state-centred and more bank-related set of practices that go beyond 'infrastructure politics' to include piecemeal state or bank intervention, e.g. in matters of merger or public procurement policy, also amount in fact to the defence and promotion of national champion firms. In France itself, the shift from direct state financial intervention to institutional investors (the *Zinzins*) as a better way of protecting national firms from foreign takeover marks a move in the German direction. Rather than attempting to formulate a definition that will foreclose the exploration of instructive contrasts as well as the convergence to be observed between countries and policy sectors, it would be preferable to adopt a relatively non-exclusive usage that enables us to deal with British Petroleum and ENI, as well as France Télécom and Siemens.

Does the paradoxical formula of an 'internationalized national champion' encapsulate a flagrant contradiction in terms? Does 'international' mean globalization or 'triadization', with European firms facing competition primarily from American or Japanese firms? What residual roles do national governments still play in relation to firms that are regarded as having a strategic place in the national economy? Do the firms regard themselves as stateless, rootless world actors who are not tied to a particular national territory? To what extent are the rapidly changing international economic and technological pressures privatizing 'public goods' in ways that curb the capacity of national governments to treat infrastructures as traditional public utilities? More generally, can we find ways of comparing the country and sector solutions to the tension between the competitiveness and independence of firms and the competitiveness and independence of states? We should bear in mind four features of this tension in trying to understand the ways in which governments and firms have accommodated themselves to it.

1. The term 'industrial policy' is now generally recognized as imparting a spurious unity to public action which 'consists of an improvised amalgam of *ad hoc* instruments and inconsistent objectives intended to influence firms to behave in ways that would not

have spontaneously occurred in a market context'.[26] Nevertheless, governments do set explicit or implicit priorities, the normative objectives of macro and micro economic policy that influence their behaviour and those of major national firms. Whereas national security used to be a major imperative in public industrial intervention, there has been a shift—accentuated by the end of the Cold War—towards the norm of profitability. This is true not merely of the defence-related firms of the military–industrial complex but more generally of the public monopolies that operated according to a semi-military model that has its roots in the state-building origins of modern government. What heed do international champion firms pay to national priorities and how have governments adapted to this new context? We shall return to this question.

2. Firms and governments have had to select tactics and a strategy for dealing with the shift in emphasis from the capacity of states to impose their will to their increasing resignation to the constraints of market forces. The pursuit of long-term, comprehensive strategies, based upon bold and ambitious projects, initially to catch up on comparative backwardness and then, when the 'infant industries' have become mature adults, avoid them degenerating into senile industries, has proved increasingly difficult. National champions of the past are often the lame ducks of the presents. So, instead, short-term, piecemeal, 'muddling through' tactics of incrementalist market improvisation have become the order of the day. French governments have been faced with the biggest problem of adaptation, whilst British governments—which never felt comfortable with the more assertive and ambitious style that was fashionable in the 1960s—have reverted to a more congenial arm's-length style that does not exclude case-by-case intervention, overt or surreptitious. However, both governments and firms have behaved differently according to the special sectoral circumstances, as we shall mention more fully later.

3. The changing public/private balance in economic management posed by the general shift from nationalization to privatization and from regulation to deregulation (or more accurately, from forms of regulation that seek generally to master market forces to those forms of regulation that work specifically to correct some of their consequences) is another major source of tension. The new types of American-inspired regulation are subsidiary to rather than in substitution for market forces, particularly where competi-

tion is absent or incapable of preventing the abuse of dominant positions of power by privatized firms. The contrasting motivations and modalities of privatization by country and sector will help us to understand why governments have adopted different regulatory arrangements and how the firms concerned have adapted to this new context. In France, the Balladur Government has resumed the unfinished business of the mid-1980s Chirac Government, while in Italy the delegitimization through pervasive corruption of the public sector has given a powerful new impetus to privatization. The special problems posed by German reunification, both in terms of massive privatization and the regulatory issues that arise, as well as the particular case of Franco-British collaboration in the Channel Tunnel project, are especially instructive in their different ways. They both illustrate the difficulties of combining two very different types of public/private forms of economic management. The constraints imposed by British insistence upon reliance on private capital to finance the Channel Tunnel led initially to a loose regulatory framework but will doubtless result in a panoply of subsequent regulations as the emphasis shifts from the hazards of attracting private funds to build the Tunnel to dealing with the practical consequences of using it. At that point, the French emphasis upon public regulation may partially correct the public/private imbalance.

4. This reference to finance brings us to the need to consider the sources and destination of investment capital for the internationalized champions. The Channel Tunnel study will show how reliance upon private finance shifted control over a project that was initially dominated by two governments first to TML, the Tunnel's builder, then to its operator Eurotunnel, and finally to a consortium of mainly British, French, and Japanese banks. Governments have been a major source of capital through budgetary subsidies. What Elie Cohen has called the 'inflationary social compromise' has taken an extreme form in Italy, whilst in all four countries government has played the part of a 'stretcher bearer state', bringing succour to sundry lame ducks.[27] There has been an increasing tendency, notably in Britain and France, to 'de-budgetize' and reduce this form of public support, which has proved less acceptable to the EC Commission than German-style private banking arrangements. As well as offering protection from foreign predators, the *Hausbank* nexus between firms and 'their' banks pro-

vides industrial funds as part of the German anti-inflation financial compromise, operating within the regulatory framework set by the central bank and finance ministry. A major French bank, the Crédit Lyonnais, has moved in the German direction by an exchange of shares with industrial firms such as Aérospatiale, Thomson, Rhône-Poulenc and Usinor-Sacilor. Finance ministries play a much more important role when the budget is the source of funds but continues, in any event, to exercise influence over interest rates. The final and increasingly important sources of capital—especially in Britain and France—are the international financial markets, while the Stock Exchanges and merchant banks—historically important in Britain but only recently becoming of great significance in France—are filling the gap left by the retreat of state financing. However, public financing, directly by a debt-ridden state and through discredited public holding companies, remains of great importance in Italy, with all the problems this creates for convergence within the European Monetary System.

The tension between governments and firms is also of great comparative interest, nationally and sectorally, in the destination of investment capital. Foreign investment, both inward and outward, has been restricted, tolerated, or encouraged by national governments. Furthermore, the forms it takes (passive portfolio investment, the establishment or acquisition of subsidiaries, launching takeovers or negotiating mergers) usually are the subject of regulation or direct government intervention. Clearly, this financial dimension will need to be brought fully into a discussion of the way international champion firms steer between the recourse to incentives and coercion by states and the attractions and constraints represented by the markets. Deference to the former may lead to difficulties in the latter and vice versa.

If we are to bear in mind the three main clusters of actors, it may be useful to see their relationship in the simplistic terms of an 'iron triangle' that assumes different forms in the four countries and operates differently according to the sector studied.

At the national level, each cluster is highly complex, though in the case of any particular sector, matters are usually much simpler. Further complexity arises from the fact that it is necessary to consider the European Community and international levels, in which additional actors are involved. However, the 'iron triangle'

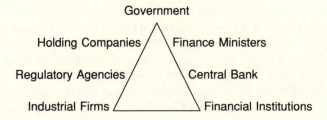

directs our need, in the case of each country and each sector, to identify the specific political and administrative executives, the managers of specific firms and financial institutions, who play an active part in the processes by which the measure of competitiveness and independence which both interacting states and firms can sustain are decided. For the purpose of contrasting the emphasis which different countries place upon particular clusters of actors, we may stress the leading role given to government in the French case, discussed more fully in Chapter 1. The financial institutions and industrial firms were usually prepared to take their lead from the government, partly because many of them were in public ownership. Even more important were practices and norms that long predated nationalization, so that the national champion firms have been particularly identified with the interventionist state. They were accustomed to accept state guidance in terms of their objectives rather than follow market signals, and they were inclined to look to public sources for finance. Even before changes since the 1980s, which have shifted the initiative away from the government towards industrial firms and financial institutions, there was a wide spectrum of relationships, ranging from the government taking direct entrepreneurial action to achieve its objectives to attempts to regenerate or nurse declining or bankrupt firms back to health. Increasingly 'national solutions' have proved impractical, so the French government has played its part in negotiating alliances with foreign firms to create international champions that preserve national interests as far as it is possible to do so. However, one must be careful to distinguish between the pretentious rhetoric of national assertion, the modest resources deployed to implement it and the limited results actually attained.

Italy has been noted for its state holding companies, notably the diversified IRI conglomerate and the ENI oil and chemicals combine which are more fully discussed in Chapter 4. Because Italy, unlike France, is not noted for the effectiveness of state action (to put it mildly), it was considered expedient to resort to more businesslike organizations to performs the role of rescuing industrial failures and resuscitating them. Although intended to be at arm's length from government, these national champions were infected by the pervasive politicization of Italian public life. Their utilization both for the development of southern Italy and for party finance had much more to do with expediency than with industrial logic, compared with the Austrian (OIAG), Spanish (INI and INH), Swedish (Procordia) or the private Belgian (Société Nationale d'Investissement) holding companies. These Italian champion firms concentrated upon becoming the national leader in their own country, resulting in their relative isolation in the international market. Initial success with developing its own cheap energy subsequently led ENI into severe financial straits, whilst its involvement with the Montedison Chemicals group in the Enimont financial scandal contributed to the discredit of the public holding formula and the switch to privatization.

It was the British pioneering role in privatization that led to European adoption of an American-style recourse to regulatory agencies. Because privatization did not necessarily result in competition, it was essential to safeguard the interests of the consumer by establishing regulatory bodies to ensure that the new firms did not abuse their monopoly or oligopoly power. Thus, at the same time that in areas such as the financial sector deregulation was the order of the day, in the former public utilities a process of re-regulation took place. However, as we shall see later, notably in Chapter 9 on Telecommunications and in Chapter 10 on the European Community, a process of re-regulation has led to a major extension of EC power to compensate for the reduced role of the member nation states. This has been rendered necessary by the industrial internationalization that has shifted power from governments to the major firms, whose interests displace those of the nation when they are not synonymous with them.

We have already referred to the German phenomenon of the *Hausbank*, which has become an increasingly popular formula in countries such as France that have moved away from the close link between firms and governments as a source of finance. There is also the fact that this side of the 'iron triangle' also offers a different and less obvious means of protecting national firms from British-style

takeover than either French public ownership or Italian state holding companies. The French in particular are using the new phase of
privatization from 1993 to set up interlocking directorates between
privatized banks and privatized firms as a more effective mechanism than the 'golden share' to prevent foreign takeovers that can
no longer be prevented because of the EC rules. As a result, the shift
from public to private ownership may not significantly reduce the
'national' control over key firms, even if some of the shares are
owned by foreigners. The role of the Bundesbank as a model for
independent control of monetary policy is another powerful mani-
festation of Germany setting a pattern for other EC states and for
the EC itself in reducing the intervention of national governments.
However, the prominence given to the Bundesbank should not
obscure the fact that in industrial affairs it is the other banks which
are the major 'partners' in the triangle constituted with government
and firms. It is these major industrial firms that have emerged as the
senior partners.

INTERROGATIONS FOR THE EUROPEAN FUTURE

In seeking to ascertain the extent to which the shift from public
sector monopoly national champions to private sector oligopolistic
international champions have changed their relationship with their
national governments in our four countries, how do our case studies fit into Elie Cohen's distinction between three kinds of national
champion? First, there are the strong firms in relation to which the
government plays the marginal role appropriate to a *subsidiary,
auxiliary, spectator state*. The government is reduced to being a
commercial traveller, lobbyist, or briber, with all the deleterious
side effects this produces. Second, there are the lame duck firms.
The government's role takes two forms. It can either ease their
decline before burying them, what may be described as the *undertaker state*'; or it may invite a foreign firm to take it over, as was
done for automobiles in Britain by Mrs Thatcher in the instance of
Nissan. In the latter case, we may wish to talk of a *regenerator
state*', replacing the discredited nationalization of lame ducks,
characteristic of the early post-war period but surviving in France
into the early 1980s. Third, there are the 'big project' firms pro-

moted by government in sectors designated as vital for national independence or to face international competition, particularly in 'high technology' sectors. France has distinguished itself in particular in this role of '*entrepreneur state*', with France Télécom being an exemplar.[28] However, there is a variant of this 'big project', the Channel Tunnel, in which joint Franco-British collaboration led to a restriction of the role of the two governments. We are dealing here with the state as *guarantor* or *underwriter*.

We saw earlier how the inability of the old-style national champions strategy to survive into the 1990s has led to attempts at developing Eurochampions, it being clear that an EC industrial policy as something separate from an EC competition policy was unworkable, except perhaps to engage in a trade war with Japan or the USA. Airbus and the TGV have been examples of at least partially successful French attempts to move from a national to a European plane, but in other sectors, such as computers and semi-conductors, France has had to turn to American or Japanese partners. Public sector status becomes a source of difficulty both with the EC and in securing international collaboration, so the promotion of either Eurochampions or international champions provides a strong incentive to privatization. The internationally integrative function of the firm supersedes the nationally integrative function of the government ministry because only the firm is deemed to know what product can be competitively sold on the world market. Ironically, given the neo-liberal interventionism of the EC, stringent EC regulations would have prevented a project like Airbus emerging in the early 1990s. The scene is set for global competition between international champions.

Does the neo-liberal EC style of the 1990s condemn national governments to confine themselves to the indirect intervention of an auxiliary to market forces or the sombre modesty of necrological undertaker? Are the days of the heroic entrepreneurial state definitely over? Have the (mythical?) terrors of the single market compelled a greater measure of intergovernmental co-ordination and interfirm co-operation or have the expectations of what the international market has in store, over and above its present pressures, reduced the French heroic entrepreneurial state to surreptitious liberal auxiliary? If the French-administered market economy cannot cope with the intrusive EC environments and cannot be extended to it, what prospects of survival have the German-style social market economy or the Italian-style holding company market economy, even in a modified form? EC 'harmonization', which was originally intended to combine elements of a maximalist French-style industrial policy with a German-style social market economy, has been moving via regulatory mutual recognition as a way of eliminating non-tariff barriers, towards a minimalist British-style competition policy. In such a context, firms will have much greater independence from their national governments, justified by their need to have the freedom to take their decisions as required by competitive markets, presupposed but not always a reality. The international champion, with its private priorities, would have displaced the national champions of yesteryear.

Notes

1. Jean-Jacques Servan-Schreiber, *The American Challenge* (Pelican edn 1969), 22–3; cf. p. 33.
2. Ibid. 53, 93.
3. Lionel Stoléru, *L'Impératif industriel* (Paris, 1969).
4. *Cinquième Plan de développement économique et social, 1966–70*, (Paris, 1965), 68; cf. p. 69.
5. J. H. McArthur and B. R. Scott, *Industrial Planning in France* (Cambridge, Mass., 1969), 525. Loukas Tsoukalis, in *The New European Economy: The Politics and Economics of Integration*, 2nd edn (Oxford, 1993), 30 n., inadvertently attributes to Raymond Vernon the first use of the term 'national champion'.
6. McArthur and Scott, *Industrial Planning*, 526.
7. Ibid. 525.
8. Raymond Vernon (ed.), *Big Business and the State: Changing Relations in Western Europe* (Cambridge, Mass., 1974), 3; see pp. 11–12, 17–23. See also his *Sovereignty at Bay: The Multinational Spread of US Enterprises* (New York, 1971).
9. Vernon, *Big Business and the State*, 11; cf. p. 6.
10. Ibid. 12.
11. Ibid. 18; see also pp. 19–20.
12. Ibid. 23–4.
13. Elie Cohen, *L'État brancardier* (Paris, 1989). More generally, see Jack Hayward, *The State and the Market Economy: Industrial Patriotism and Economic Intervention in France* (Brighton, 1986).

14. Michael E. Porter, *The Competitive Advantage of Nations* (London, 1990), 19, cf. p. xii.
15. Ibid. 119; cf. pp. 73, 117–20, 152–5, 165. On Italy, see more generally pp. 421–53.
16. Joan Pearce and John Sutton, *Protection and Industrial Policy in Europe* (London, 1985), 155; see also pp. 5–7, 14–15, 71. French memorandum in *Europe Documents*, no. 1274, 16 Sept. 1983. See also Michel Richonnier, 'Europe's Decline is Not Irreversible', *Journal of Common Market Studies*, 20 (Mar. 1984), 227–43.
17 Tsoukalis, *The New European Economy*, 49–51.
18. Ibid. 103–5.
19. Pearce and Sutton, *Protection and Industrial Policy*, 72–3.
20. Cecchini Report quoted in Tsoukalis, *The New European Economy*, 89; cf. p. 112.
21. Ibid. 117; cf. p. 110 ff., 335. For a very sceptical view, see P. A. Geroski, 'European Industrial Policy and Industrial Policy in Europe', *Oxford Review of Economic Policy*, 2 (Summer, 1989), 20–36.
22. Peter J. Katzenstein, *Small States in World Markets: Industrial Policy in Europe* (Ithaca and London, 1985), 81; cf. p. 24.
23. Ibid. 57; see also pp. 113–15.
24. Paulette Kurzer, 'The Internationalisation of Business and Democratic Class Compromises', *West European Politics*, 14/4 (Oct. 1991), 4; cf. pp. 5–8.
25. Elie Cohen, *Le Colbertisme 'high tech'* (Paris, 1992), 383.
26. Jack Hayward, *The State and the Market Economy* (Brighton, 1986), 8.
27. Cohen, *L'État brancardier*.
28. Cohen, *Le Colbertisme 'high tech'*. See also Henry Ergas, 'France Telecom: Has the Model Worked?', mimeo, paper given to the Oslo conference on 'The Interplay of Government, Industry, and Research in France', 1992.

PART I
GOVERNMENTS AND THEIR NATIONAL POLICY CONTEXTS

1

France: National Champions
in Search of a Mission

ELIE COHEN

The Maastricht Treaty,[1] which has included industrial policy
amongst the functions of the Commission, the return to big industrial projects in France, the conclusions of the Bergsten commission,[2] which were favourable to the defence of high technology
companies, and the industrialist plea made by *Business Week*[3] are
placing the question of industrial policy and notably the role of
'national champions' back on the agenda. This agreement over the
need for an industrial policy seems all the more enthusiastic since
it refers to realities that are completely conflicting. For Mr
Bangemann, the Industrial Commissioner of the EC, as for
American neo-industrialists, the policy of purely national champions has been a failure in every country where it has been implemented. Companies with protected markets, overflowing with
public funds, the initiators of fabulous projects, managed by civil
servants subject to the changing will of governments, can only
make things worse. A policy of national champions would be
economically inefficient, detrimental to markets, and a source of
decline for the countries that practise it.

On the other hand, the construction of a single market in Europe
and a rich scientific and technical environment in the United States
would contribute in a decisive manner to industrial recovery and a
return to periods of growth. However, France provides the obvious
example of industrial policies that have not brought about the
disasters predicted, and which have even contributed to a real
specialization of industry and an internationalization of national
champions. Oligarchic power, state property, and the requirements
of public service have apparently not altered the competitiveness of
national champions. It is, therefore, necessary both to understand

the French mystery and to pose questions about the development of national models.

Summarized briefly, our argument has three strands:

1. The exogenous effects of the post-war period, the economy of administered financing,[4] the inflationist social compromise, and major projects with a politico-military origin, rather than the structural policies or the statist ownership of certain large companies, were the source of the industrial great leap forward of the expansionist years (1954–74) and then of the relative decline of the years of crisis (1974–84). What has been labelled the policy of national champions was only the by-product of *grands projets* or the inadequate degree of concentration into larger firms.

2. In an open and diversified economy (mobility of factors of production, flexible production, extensive choice in the market-place, and organized knowledge as a key resource) integrated into a regional grouping (European Community), the state is culturally and institutionally incapable of playing a leading role in industry. The internationalization and the restructuring of national champions is the most recent example of the absence of a specific objective being given to nationalized companies other than during the immediate post-war period and the interventionist illusion of 1981–2.

3. The policy of 'neither . . . nor'[5] (*ni . . . ni*) pursued during the period 1988 to 1993 and which involved a freeze in both the nationalization and privatization of French companies, was nothing more than a set of techniques to disguise the impecuniousness of the state. It coincided with the moment when the logic of the industrial state and the shareholder state was freed from, or even came into contradiction with an institutional context (the EC) that has become hostile to so-called Colbertism. The deregulation of public services is completing the process of setting nationalized companies free from government control.

It therefore follows:

- that a competitive nation should concern itself with the quality of its infrastructures, its research system, its regulatory and fiscal conditions, and not with the promotion of national champions;

- that the rhythm at which the state is able to withdraw from the public sector is conditioned by budgetary priorities, the investment capacity of national savers, and the opportunity of providing temporary protection to competitive public companies.

1. *DIRIGISME* OR THE ECONOMY OF ADMINISTERED FINANCING

The notion of industrial policy that best seems to sum up the specificity of the French state's intervention in industry is also a source of serious confusion. It confuses policies designed to shape the environment in which the company operates (effects upon the industrial activity of all macro-economic and macro-social policies), sectoral policies (structuring, promotion of high-tech industries, aid to lame ducks), and the strategy of the shareholding state. Now aid to companies in difficulty is a form of social policy tacked on to the main elements of a sectoral policy (the innumerable plans for coal, steel, textiles, machine tools, shipbuilding yards . . .). The *grands projets* with politico-military origins which gave birth to national champions (Alcatel-Alsthom, Elf, Aérospatiale), to ambitious infrastructural programmes (rail, telecommunications, nuclear, etc.), and to powerful actors (the state-owned EdF, the state-owned telecom complex, the military-industrial complex, etc.) constituted the real heart of sectoral policies, even if they were largely outside the remit of the ministry supposedly in charge of industry. As for structural policies, which reveal in the most spectacular fashion the power of the state and which have been labelled derisively in France 'meccano policies', they have hardly had any effect in terms of industrial specialization and the shape of trade.

The most thorough studies have enabled us to establish that there has been no relation between the sectoral priorities of the French Plan and the selective policy of credit;[6] and that public financing has been directed towards housing, infrastructure throughout the country, and agriculture, with industry being only the fourth priority; that, finally, the major part of the Ministry of Industry's budget over the past 30 years has been spent upon subsidizing the rapidly declining French coal industry. Nor have state ownership and the French conception of public service increased industrial development or encouraged deliberate specialization. It is not its public or private character which has determined the success of a large project (see the role of Alcatel-Alsthom, Dassault or Schneider in the telecommunications, railways, aeronautical, and nuclear *grands projets*), but the aggregation, in the context of a closed economy, of public research, public procurement, and the industrialization through national champions. Moreover, such a strategy has costs: the poor performance in other sectors of nationalized industries (consumer electronics for Thomson or machine tools for Schneider).

Since the end of the 1960s, the passage from a national self-sufficiency strategy to that of a European partnership has not involved giving up the benefits of the national model. Rather it stems from the necessity to share development costs, to enlarge the marketplace and to favour strategies of the internationalization of national champions.

French industrial growth of the post-war period (1954–74) was not, therefore, a product of the enlightened despotism of the state. It was the result of an international environment sympathetic to a project shared by public élites, based upon national independence; of a statist strategy of the national-rational-equitable state; and of an inflationist social compromise which took the institutional form of the economy of administered financing.[7]

1.1. The Inflationist Social Compromise

The inflationist social compromise represented the consensual refusal of the state, the trade unions, and the employers to control nominal changes in incomes and prices. In this model, the inflationist expansion supported growth, self-financing, and the stifling of private investors. In accordance with Keynesian precepts, it encouraged above all painless and hidden transfers. From the moment that the economy was opened up to world competition, periodic devaluations became the sanction of this inflationist compromise; as such, it was accepted by the state's social partners. Recognition of the new role to be played by the trade unions was achieved by a major sharing of roles: a trade unionism based upon class struggle and employers who continued to be predominantly family-based and patriarchal could not work together. The sharing was done elsewhere, under the shadow of the state, by the extension of social policies and by a division of labour: for the companies, economic management in a market-driven environment; for the unions, social concessions (the management of social welfare by them); for the state, overall regulation and occasional substitution in cases where private initiatives were not forthcoming (the *grands projets*, the economy of administered financing).

Contrary to what has so often been alleged, what was essential was not so much the action of the state in economic affairs (the famous tools of the concerted economy: the Plan, public ownership, etc.) as the use of economic resources to accompany and facilitate social change. Indeed, the question was: how does one transform a rural country with a large peasantry and where small, private businesses proliferate around a modern industrial state, without destroying the fabric of society? Strong growth eased the pain of population shifts and allowed the financing of the infrastructural improvements of the country; when, finally, the state protected national capital from undesired incursions, everything was in place for the establishment of a 'capitalism without capital'.

Taken together, the economy of administered financing prompted extensive growth (mass production, underskilled manpower, weak privately funded R&D), the emergence of public and private national champions in the wake of the *grands projets*, and effective investment in infrastructure across the nation. The counterproductive character of administered financing did not come to light until interest rates took off and the lever effect transformed itself into a bludgeoning effect. Indeed, once interest rates in real terms reached 5 to 7 per cent, the weight of debt became unbearable, financial costs consumed most profit margins, and it became more profitable to pay off one's debts than to invest. It was at this point that one discovered that capitalism without capital was a major source of fragility for the industrial and financial structure. It is profoundly ironic that it was the Left that carried out nationalizations which had been made necessary by the failings of French private capital (the end of the Gillet dynasty at Rhône-Poulenc, of the Empains at Schneider, the crisis of internal

control in Pechiney, in Thomson, and so on) and of the administered economy, both being undertaken in the name of the
socialization of the means of production and as a strategy to
combat crisis. From 1984, French capital was subjected to the
double shock of imported deregulation and the policy of financial
innovation advocated by Pierre Bérégovoy, Socialist Finance
Minister.

Within the space of a few years, the French financial system
underwent profound change, as banks abandoned specialization,
credit became deregulated, and financial circuits specialized. The
distance between banks and companies began to increase once
again. At the same time the state began to bring to an end the
system of administrative intervention in industry (closing off of
various sources of subsidy, abandonment of sectoral plans, the
opening up of the French economy to foreign investment).

Driven by a euphoric stock exchange, French banks and companies were frogmarched into exceptional change and began to
recapitalize. It was in this context that Edouard Balladur, Finance
Minister in the Chirac Government of 1986–8, launched a round of
privatization. Knowing the risks for indigenous capital of liberal
privatization, worried by the political impact upon his inner circle
of political friends of selling off public companies, and concerned to
preserve the influence of the state, he invented a three-tiered structure: an inner circle at the summit consisting of a co-opted Board
of Directors, partial self-management through employee-share-
holders, and finally a popular shareholding base consisting in
reality of an easily manipulated mass.

The most decisive criticism of this construction was soon administered by the events. The crash of 1987 effectively opened a
'window of vulnerability' for French capital. Undercapitalized
companies strongly undermined by their crumbling centres and
their questionable legitimacy were the ideal prey for much more
powerful and better protected foreign groups. The liberal transition
devised by Pierre Bérégovoy and the Balladur-style privatizations
had, therefore, left unresolved the capitalist question, failed to
consolidate private industrial groups, and not managed to submit
the directors co-opted by the politicians to the sanction of the
market. From this point on, as was seen in the Compagnie du Midi
affair, the saviour came in the form of the state and a large
mutualized institutional investor.[8]

1.2. Industrial Policy or the Policy of Grands Projets

A distinction between three situations needs to be made. The conditions under which the state intervenes and the status of national champions are different according to whether the state is faced with powerful industrial actors whose structures it hopes to define; politically destabilizing lame ducks; or confronted by a complete absence of industrial actors in a sector seen as decisive for national independence—the most likely terrain for *grands projets*. In all three cases the means of intervention are formally comparable: sectoral plans, structural policies, direct subsidies or low-rate credits for modernization, investment or export, etc. In practice, the effect of these tools has been radically different.

Structural Policies   Over the past thirty years the state has never given up its desire to influence the industrial structures and orientations of its national champions. From the Ortoli–Montjoie Report and its sectoral counterparts such as the Clappier Report on the Chemical Industry (1966), to Edith Cresson's great restructuring ambitions (1991–2), the same idea has persisted: influence industrial structures in order to play a role in strategic decision making. This attempt has been in vain, even if it may have fooled casual observers. For example, the Clappier Plan is a slight document of about fifteen pages but whose long-lasting contribution has been the idea that the French chemical industry needs to concentrate around two public firms and two private firms. No attempt was made to carry out a strategic study, a study of industrial synergies, or suggest the financial networks involved. If concentration did come about, this did not occur according to the plans proposed by the report.

More fundamentally, faced with government needing to be re-elected, open to competing or even divergent political tendencies, dependent upon a fragmented civil service and jealous of its powers, working under the TV cameras and accountable for its acts to a changing public opinion, private governments were able to consolidate their power. They were able to impose a democratic centralist model, exert subtle control over the government machinery, and provide themselves with a plan which would apply to everyone, and thus earn themselves the monopoly of legitimate expertise. The state, through its company and company-support policies, certainly influenced the movement towards concentration but it did nothing to define its structures and predetermine their strategies. The case of *grands projets* should thus be considered separately.

The Policy for Lame Ducks   There seems little need to dwell upon the lame ducks—the second strand of sectoral industrial policy— other than to remind the reader that a national champion is mortal. The French state knew how to get rid of the heavyweights of its industry such as Boussac (textiles), Creusot Loire (steel, machine tools, and heavy equipment), and Normed (shipbuilding), a sign that national champions cannot escape the sanction of the market for long. The intervention of the state in this instance merely put off the inevitable, smoothed out the process of decline, and eased social and local tensions.

High-Tech Colbertism   Since the Second World War, high-tech Colbertism has been the historical form taken by the intervention of several nation states, armed with a monopoly of the general interest, in so-called industries of the future. Six characteristics summarize this model and call into question preconceived ideas about French interventionism. They allow us to understand the process through which embryonic hybrids of administration and private companies transformed themselves into national champions with world-wide aspirations free of public interference.

1. Offensive protectionism is the first condition of the success of a *grand projet*. The sovereign state creates the means of accumulation of scientific and financial resources. It provides future national champions with grants, secure markets through public procurement policies, and prevents foreign entry. The argument for doing so is always defence, national sovereignty, technological autonomy. But success in the international marketplace is the real goal.

2. Innovation is not by definition scientific or technical in nature, even in situations where the technical paradigm has been revolutionized in ways that favour the emergence of specialization. Nuclear power, space explorations, the railways, civil and military aeronautics, and telecommunications, all show that innovation is more important for the changes in operating procedures it brings, for the institutional forms invented, and

technical reappropriation, than for research into industries of the future. Strictly national technologies (graphite-gas in nuclear power, 'Diamant' for space exploration, 'Aerotrain' for the railways, etc.) were all abandoned under pressure from industrialists and public service users in order to guarantee the success of the sector as a whole.

3. The *grand projet* is possible only within the framework of a flexible state. The hybrid administration–enterprise embodies the two sides of a coin—tails, regalian authority, heads, the logic of an enterprise (BRP for oil, CNES for space research, DGT for telecommunications). The provision of financial support outside the annual budget, for example through a medium-term statutory programme, and above all the use of public procurement for national industrial ends, bear out this analysis.

4. The *grand projet* attracts capitalism without capital. This certainly means that the state has the upper hand over the industrialists at the beginning, but once there is a move away from the state-legitimized procurement logic, the latter are capable of freeing themselves.

5. The *grand projet* emerges only when the objectives of sectoral actors converge with those of overall policy. This explains the succession over time of long phases of underdevelopment followed by intense periods of intervention.

6. Finally, leaving aside the convenient abstraction of the state, the *grand projet* takes off only when a homogeneous élite is capable of mobilizing a workforce committed to the purposes of the state–entrepreneur and of national independence.

A state willing to bend the law, an absence of scientific breakthroughs, the reversibility of the state–enterprise relationship, and the capacity of actors to understand the context in which they are operating so as to get the backing of politicians for a sectoral project: these are the factors that have so complicated the application of planning or commercial points of reference.

The *grand projet* follows a sequence of logics: the 'arsenal' logic, the logic of public procurement, and the logic of the market which, when completed, enriches the national productive system with new, powerful actors who are sometimes rivals (with conflicts between technical agency, user, and industrialist). It is first of all based upon a technological challenge. It is promoted by an agency which may be specially created for this purpose. Its success then depends upon a transfer of results and close co-operation with industry. This relationship is only entirely fruitful because the state practises an aggressive protectionism, pre-finances the industrial development, transfers the results of public research, provides certain markets through public procurement, allows the depreciation of investment over a long period, and encourages development by putting the state's powers at the service of the national champion, be it public or private.[9] The success of the *grand projet* occurs when the state launches an infrastructural programme based upon the technologies developed and when the international market purchases the goods and services that are produced. Technical innovation, the emergence of new uses, oppressive protectionism, the development of a new industrial actor, and socio-political engineering are the five pillars of the *grand projet*.

Three types of arguments confirm that this model is reaching the end of its natural life: the first concerns the internal dynamics of the sectoral system; the second is that history reveals the exhaustion of this type of intervention; and the third argument relates to the already noted limits of national space as a venue for major technological ventures.

1. The success of the *grand projet* is the first source of its subsequent loss of power, since the national champions and the public users concerned tend to prefer establishing themselves in the international market above any other consideration. Elf-Aquitaine, Arianespace, Alcatel-Alsthom, France Télécom, EdF, Airbus Industrie, the Snecma, and Aérospatiale: all of these are industrial or service companies born or nurtured by the national *grand projet* and redeployed now on a European level, and which base their new legitimacy upon the market. In effect, during their nurturing phase these national champions benefited from the discretionary power of the nation state. Once they created a competitive advantage by mastering a technology (nuclear electricity or achieving a high level of productivity (telecoms) or gaining market share (aeronautics), these national champions began to see state intervention as a threat to their cash flow, to their own discretionary power and as an impediment to building international alliances. So the greater the success of the *grand projet*, the bolder was the determination of internationalized national champions to be

freed from state dependence and to be judged according to market criteria.

But success can also end in crisis. When the hybrid administration–enterprise is not in tune with economic reality, then high-tech Colbertism steadily turns in upon itself and becomes discretionary, parasitical interventionism. This introversion accentuates an already fragmented system and leads to the state losing the support of the sector's élite.

2. One of the last identifiable *grands projets* is that of telecommunications, with the catch-up plan dating from 1974. It belongs to the same period as the nuclear and railway plans, the first launched in 1969 and intensified in 1973, and the latter announced in 1976. However, in both these cases, the period of *logique d'arsenal* goes back longest. Since then, plans for telematics, satellites, and cable television have appeared, but have been added to the list of white elephants rather than given birth to powerful industries. Does this mean we can announce the death of *grands projets*? One cannot be completely sure. However, over the last few years the insistence with which the state has attempted to promote, without success, biotechnology, nuclear fusion, and oceanography provides sufficient grounds for suggesting that when the infrastructural dimension is absent (biotechnology and oceanography) or when the scientific object is ill-adapted to big technological agencies (biotechnology) or the industrial perspective becomes less feasible (fusion), it is difficult to see a future for the national model of the *grand projet*.

3. Finally, the *grands projets* with a national origin, such as Ariane, Airbus, or even the TGV, have become European. Of course, in each of these three cases, the technological and political initiator has been French. However, in order to succeed these projects have either become European or are in the process of so becoming (TGV–GEC–Alsthom–Fiat). Henceforth, the question has to be a different one: if high-tech Colbertism in one country is not feasible, does a European public institution exist that can pick up the baton?

If the French nation state acted in industrial matters mainly as a builder of *grands projets* designed to promote national sovereignty rather than as an active state seeking to develop the competitive advantage of national industry as a whole, what is the long-term balance-sheet of this strategy? Three answers can be suggested. In the first place, it is very difficult to imagine what would have happened if, after the Second World War, instead of building an economy of administered financing based on an inflationist compromise and industrial *grands projets*, the national élites had chosen to build a true market economy. Nevertheless, this basic choice, sustained by administrative organization and weak local institutions, had tremendous effects on the small and medium-size firms sector. Secondly, *grands projets* in the long run produce an industrial specialization: firms such as Schneider or Thomson or CGE deliberately abandoned the machine tool industry, the equipment industry, and consumer electronics and invested the money provided by the state in the nuclear power industry, military electronics, and telecoms. The total collapse of the machine tool industry and the weakness of private industrial R&D are the results of this policy. Finally, when compared with the performances of foreign firms in the same sector of France Télécom, EdF, Aérospatiale, Elf-Aquitaine, and others, the big public ventures were successful. Long-termism, shifts from national objectives to reliance upon international market sanctions, strong management, and weak political interference were the conditions of this relative success.

2. THE STATE AND THE ECONOMICS OF VARIETY

In the mid-1980s a new economic order arose. The developed countries were all faced simultaneously with a crisis of public funding. They undertook regional regrouping, and they were caught in a pincer movement between Japan and the newly industrialized countries of Asia, discovering at the same time the rules of a new art of production and marketing. The similarity of the diagnoses and the solutions put forward by European countries was, in itself, alarming. This reveals the shallowness of the transformation plans regarding the industrial specialization of open economies. Solutions were sought in the high-added-value sectors (biotechnology, robotics, new materials, etc.), in the cross-fertilization between research and industry and between product creation and consumption, in flexible specialization, in competitive deflation, and in quality control and zero stock.

For France, which was recovering from its errors of the 1979–83 period, rigour was the order of the day, as were a strong franc and policies aimed at a competitive environment for firms (fiscal, credit, research, and training). It was a time for profitability at all costs. The reawakening of the interventionists, frustrated by the new course of events, was to come about only with the advent of the 1990–1 recession. Poor industrial specialization, an absence of sufficiently competitive firms, and the weakness of the small and medium-sized company sector came to the fore once again. The state's easy-going foreign trade policy was condemned, the overvaluation of the franc was denounced, and the desirability of the state deficit re-evaluated.

However, realization that the situation had changed did not weaken the determination of the government. The Colbertist state had been fashioned to carry out grand technological projects to serve political ambitions. Everything was directed towards achieving this: its civil service organization, its élite selection, the need to provide infrastructures, the absence of profitability constraints, and the concentration of coercive power. This state could equally favour extensive growth by making cheap money available and providing protection for the home market and a supply of unskilled labour. Similarly, it can also find itself seriously disarmed when flexibility is required in production, when skilled workers and product quality are needed, and when its success in the hyper-choice market place depends on the judgement of the customer-who-is-always-right. Even if the state wished to reinvent a sector-based policy, it would be both institutionally and culturally impossible for it to succeed. Globalization, integration, and making the country industrially attractive have become the buzz-words.

Globalization is the term that was created to express a dual reality, the internationalization of markets and factors of production on the one hand and, on the other, the setting up of industrial firms capable of conceiving their development from the outset on a world scale, and deploying, to this effect, global production strategies (international division of the production process), marketing strategies (world standards, world brands, products launched simultaneously in the three major zones), management strategies (through externalization or integration of contributions from firms specialized in marketing, advertising, and financial or auditing accounts). Once goods, production factors, and capital become mobile, a country must justify the differentials in the cost of the least mobile production factor, labour, by the quality of its facilities and of its 'men'. This spatial competition is even more intense in Europe, where there is a similarity in the specializations and the free circulation of goods can transform a failed implantation into an import of unemployment and fiscal impoverishment.

What is at stake in the globalization of firms? The standard theory claims that in an economy where the costs of research and development are rising fast, or in which the life expectancy of products is growing ever shorter, where economies of scale can be attained only with significant market shares, and where no margins can be achieved without reducing the transaction costs, it follows that in a number of sectors (above all in electronics) no long-term survival is possible unless a triadic (EC, US, and Japan) strategy is adopted. This presupposes launching products simultaneously on the three major markets, a dense network of partners and subcontractors, local implantation, and world-wide management reconciling different quality demands, the capacity to respond to demands and political acceptability. This standard theory can be queried. One may especially look at the substance, the forms, and the rhythm of this globalization strategy. But it is even more important for us to question its meaning for nation states.

When a company goes global, does it, in so doing, participate in the power strategy of its country of origin? Might one even go so far as to say, using a military metaphor, that it projects its home country's power into the world? Is it either defending its own or its home country's interests, or should one merely postulate the identity of interests between a private power centre with an international vocation and a national home base?

Can the opposite be maintained, that is, that these groups contribute to the disintegration of national economic sovereignty, thus bringing about a new sharing out of the world between private power centres? In this way there would be an autonomous interplay of companies and a mutual limiting of spheres of interest through competition. Would the ultimate result of this movement be, then, through the creation of an unregulated, universal market, an 'end of history' in the economic order?

There can be no answer to these questions without first analysing the relationships between firms and states. Two factors relating to the strategies and organizational modes of these global enterprises allow one to begin to see the issues at stake and to begin to envisage the type of response a state might adopt. Traditionally, internationalization strategies fall into two opposing types, internal and external. In the first case, companies such as IBM or Sony base their development on the mastering of technologies or products with an international vocation. The national production and sales subsidiaries seek to penetrate the targeted markets. States can close their markets in order to get back into the race and to negotiate the optimum location conditions. But they have no hold over the strategy and organization of the global enterprises.

In the second case, groups such as Saint Gobain, Alcatel, or Hoechst acquire foreign concerns that are already firmly based in their home market, which may possess some original technology but in any case allow the incoming firm to widen its commercial base or range of activities. The organization then evolves from the model of the multinational (strongly autonomous national firms in relation to the centre) towards that of the international firm (strong integration of products and technologies), or to that of the transnational firm (strong integration favoured by formalized social technologies with no pre-eminence of nationality or origin). States have legislation at their disposal which allows them to monitor foreign takeovers, and they can negotiate the conditions of possible takeovers in line with their sovereignty considerations.

The trend towards going global can be helped or hindered by the parallel integration movement of national economies in regional groups that are evolving from customs unions towards single markets. The question, as far as France is concerned, is whether a Community preference can exist in a single market or whether high-tech Colbertism can be practised in the European context. Formally it can, as long as Europe provides a market on a par with the major infrastructure projects, in which public laboratories and large firms with European bases can find opportunities to co-operate. But practically speaking, the answer is that it cannot. None of the preconditions for high-tech Colbertism is present on a European level: neither the integration of research policies, public procurement policies, or promotion of industrial champions, nor the discretionary intervention of government, nor aggressive protectionism, nor the public service ideology; and there is no élite group ready to initiate *grands projets*.

After disappearing from the national scene, such grand designs are unlikely to emerge on the European scene. By deregulating the protected sectors (such as telecoms, electricity, and transportation), by rooting out the aid awarded by states to their nationalized industries, by issuing negative appraisals of the Community aid given to ailing enterprises (steel), by criticizing the Community research and development programmes, by regarding Japanese firms as European ones, the DGIV, often with the support of the jurisprudence of the European Court of Justice, has managed to impose a liberal conception on the economic order and forbidden the carrying out of European *grands projets*. It thus potentially endangers those enterprises whose origins lay in successful *grands projets*. The case of high-definition television illustrates the need for a policy designed at the European level (norms and standards) and the inability of the Commission not only to make choices but even to stick to decisions already made. The furious battles between lobbies, the poor organization of the European Parliament, and the conflicting ideologies of the British and French are leading to a state of total paralysis. Once it became obvious that the European Commission could not decide or implement what was already decided, the main question for the French was: how to act in high-tech sectors without fear of Brussels intervention?

Sector-based policies, therefore, for reasons pertaining to the sociology of the state–industry relationship, cannot, with the exception of *grands projets*, have a bearing on the specialization and strategies of major concerns, either public or private. These *grands projets* cannot come to fruition within 30 to 50 years and within a context of border controls, due to the confusion between the roles of the regulator, the operator, and the industrialist. It follows that in an open economy the only state action which has any significance is one affecting the firm's environment. Nevertheless, important advantages persist for national champions that have managed to go international. From 1985 to 1990 notably, France has both consolidated its traditional international presence (through operations by Rhône-Poulenc, Saint Gobain, Pechiney, Air Liquide, and Lafarge), and attempted some daring manœuvres, some of which have already succeeded, such as those pulled off by Alcatel Alsthom. The current wave concerns the agro-food sector and services, and it is destined to be extended to distribution, computer services, telecommunications,[10] the hotel industry, and tourism.

Might not the shareholding state be tempted to regain the power lost by the industrial state? There again history has been a deciding factor. The state can appoint a chairman, accept or postpone an investment, act upon the shape of a group. But it has no substantial bearing on its strategy. For evidence of this, one need only look at the major operations of the decade:[11] the transfer of Thomson's medical electronics; ELF's American foray; the consent wrung from the state in the ITT/CGE affair, and the indiscriminate public support for Honeywell's, Zenith's, and RCA/GE's operations. The only case worth noting in which the state offered resistance to a public industrial group (Saint Gobain/Générale des Eaux) was more a matter of political jockeying than pursuing strategic objectives. In 1991–2 Prime Minister Cresson's massive restructuring plans in the electronics and nuclear sectors fell victim to the nuclear lobby and to obstruction from heads of nationalized industry who would have been difficult to dismiss.

Having failed to serve the designs of governments, nationalizations and privatizations have had one eminent virtue: the renewal and consolidation of French capitalism. State property has served as a defence against takeover bids, allowing a weak group with questionable technological advantages such as Thomson Consumer Electronics to absorb American, German, and British firms, with no threat to itself and allotting no other role than that of passive financial backer to the state. It has also allowed the French electronics groups, especially Bull and Thomson, to record, over a long period of time, results that were consistently weaker than those of their competitors. Finally, for national groups, it has removed the worry of indebtedness. Of course, too heavy a debt places a burden on profits and competitiveness, but, being underwritten by the Treasury, the international financial market opens up to these groups at a more attractive cost. The French government's signature is an excellent one.

The relevant strategy for the future is not one aimed at specialization, at defending the Frenchness of the groups, but at the creation of an economic and institutional environment conducive to their growth. France has just taken a decisive step in that direction by downgrading the concept of the strategic enterprise. Bull, after being the vanguard of the French computer industry and after unsuccessfully attempting to fight under a European banner, entered IBM's orbit in the name of anti-Japanese competition.

Does this mean that the nationality of capital or the will to keep leading firms under national control is in vain? The answer cannot be affirmative. If one cannot influence specialization by defending domestic capital, there is no reason to favour, through a passive attitude, foreign takeovers justified by the peculiar fragility of a national capitalism that is bringing about the change-over from a public administered economy to a privatized market economy.

The collapse of the rational, equitable national state, due to the effects of integration, decentralization, and domestic crisis, leaves open the question of the future of the public and nationalized sector. Does it have a future, a legitimacy, or even a specificity left? If not, what are the probable courses of action open to it?

There are two conflicting conceptions of national industry. In the first, only the nationality of the capital is important. It guarantees the national character of the power centre and ensures a total control of manpower, technologies, and markets. The role of the Gaullist state, faithfully followed in this respect by the various governments of the Left, has always been to promote national champions, even when the latter have massively delocalized their research and production centres, and have devoted their energies to financial operations alone. In this case the state is the travelling salesman of the so-called 'national' groups, and the vigilant protector of their national 'patch' in order to ward off foreign investors and purchasers.

In the second case, only the territorial criterion is really important. What is favoured is the quality of the jobs created, the localization of research centres, the advantage gained by the consumer from reinforced competition; in short, everything that contributes to developing a high-added-value activity on the national territory. The nationality of capital is considered secondary. But this conception of sovereign customer does have its limits. Some goods remain sovereign, such as those produced by the defence industry.

Neither of these two models functions as such in practice. The fact remains, nevertheless, that if the national interest and the interests of the national industrial group do not happen to coincide, the state must review its priorities, and encourage localization across the national territory. Above all, it must provide the most conducive physical and intellectual framework for the development of a highly developed capitalist economy based on choice and requiring large quantities of skilled manpower. The state may favour a foreigner setting up a company against the will of the national champion when the latter chooses to invest abroad to open up new markets.

3. THE STATE AS A SHIELD OF NATIONAL CAPITALISM

Regardless of the acceptance by public élites of the new industrial context, three factors combine to call into question the unconditional support of the state for nationalized concerns: European legislation regarding public aid, budget constraints, and the nationalized sector's loss of legitimacy.

On the subject of budget constraints, we need only remind ourselves that even when the French government was most determined to be generous in its aid to nationalized firms (1981–5), the total funding (48.7 billion francs) was lower than the cumulated losses (67.155 billion francs).[12] Since then priorities have changed, and capital endowments from budgetary sources have progressively decreased (9.66 billion francs from 1988 to 1990 out of a total increase of 104 billion worth of capital).[13] The policy of competitive deflation, the burden of the public deficit, and the choice of a policy geared towards competitiveness (tax cuts, freezing of fixed charges, and a drop in interest rates) have brought about a reduction to a strict minimum of budgetary endowments and a policy of reserving them for those firms which can demonstrate their need for substantial and risky investments (Thomson, Bull, and Air France in 1991). It is true that taking over the debts of those firms affected by the crisis has contributed to an improvement of their balance sheets (12 billion for Renault and over 9 billion for Usinor-Sacilor). All European governments are facing a budgetary squeeze. On the one hand, they are losing fiscal revenues for the sake of European integration (harmonization of VAT and zero taxation on capital revenues). On the other hand, they are paying huge amounts of money for past and current deficits and they face growing demands in the educational, social, judicial, and police sectors. The budgetary squeeze solution is very difficult because citizens reject any new taxation, and due to the Maastricht Treaty (EMU) governments have to limit their deficits and debts. The French situation is not the worst. But in terms of priorities, capital allocations for nationalized firms are not essential.

By signing the Single Market Act, and by giving up the control of its foreign trade policy (such as Japanese quotas in the car industry), France has not only underlined its firm commitment to Europe, it has also implicitly accepted the sovereign consumer model. The Renault case illustrates this turning-point. In order to recapitalize the firm, France has undertaken, via the European Commission, to submit all state funding of nationalized industries to strict profitability conditions. In order to remove any trace of implicit state aid form capital increases underwritten by the Government, Sir Leon Brittan, Vice-president of the Community, requested and obtained that the state must set itself quantitative criteria of profitability identical to those obtaining in comparable private businesses in the same sector. The Renault precedent was then immediately used against Bull. It is surprising that a Socialist government did not move to defend the notion of nationalized industries as a public service. Had it lost faith in them?

But matters are not so simple. They are three conflicting European orientations: liberal, organized market, neo-Colbertist. Each decision is the result of a bargain and a compromise. The balance of power between the Commission, the Council, and the nation states is not stable. The issue of trade policy depends heavily on American demands and Japanese compliance, and each country refers to Europe in reviewing its internal policies. The main result of this set of choices and constraints is that France no longer believes in the nationalized firms as a tool of industrial policy and is losing faith in a Euro-Colbertism.

In partially privatizing *Crédit Local*, the Socialist Government even threw in the ideological towel by admitting that the operation would reduce risk and enhance profitability. It is true that short-term economic prospects favoured the move, but the admission sounded more like a confession. A state threatened with impoverishment through loss of tax revenue at a time when spending demands for its traditional functions (education, law and order) are on the increase, no longer considers public sector industries as priority candidates for funding and acknowledges that private shareholders are the *sine qua non* for effective financial management.

It is this context which prepared the way for the incredible inventiveness of the lucky victims of the 'Neither (nationalization) Nor (privatization)' policy of governments between 1988 and 1993. Indeed, how can one defend national capital and recapitalize national companies, without new budgetary resources so as to respect the directives from Brussels without completely destroying what is left of socialist ideology? The response was found in financial ingenuity embedded in poor rhetoric on the French mixed economy. Other than allocations of capital from budgetary sources and the cancelling of debts which already existed, three main techniques were used to facilitate the financing of nationalized companies: 'false' capital; the transfer of equity; and the floating of subsidiaries on the stock exchange.

'False' capital comprises certificates of investment, unlimited duration bonds and new profit-sharing bonds. Rhône-Poulenc has especially distinguished itself in this difficult art, which consists of offering attractive returns and fiscal advantages against the absence of a right to vote linked to the possession of only a fraction of total capital. The transfer of equity has usually been restricted to operations which combine the recapitalization of public banks and financial support for industry. We may distinguish three forms: the transfer of equity from the Treasury to a public company (shares of Roussel Uclaf were given to Rhône-Poulenc and then to Crédit Lyonnais on the occasion of Rohrer Inc. being bought out); exchange of shares (UAP/BNP, Renault/Volvo) which permitted increases in the Cooke ratio; facilitation of international alliances (the transfer of Altus Finance, a subsidiary of Thomson, to Crédit Lyonnais in exchange for a stakeholding in its capital). The last technique is floating a subsidiary on the market to raise capital, which was notably the case of Pechiney International when it bought back American Can.

For three years these solutions were preferred to the early 1980s suggestion by Michel Rocard to offer up to 49 per cent of the capital of nationalized companies to private interests where profits were being made (this was done when he was Prime Minister by the Decree of 4 April 1991) or to create holding companies capable of raising capital for their industrial subsidiaries. Finally, the state capitalists, acting like private capitalists, rediscovered what Berle and Means at the beginning of the 1930s called 'legal devices'.[14] These were a group of techniques which enabled a shareholder to reduce his stakeholding while keeping control of a company. There is nothing reprehensible about the state behaving as an inventive capitalist. None the less, there have been several consequences. One can postpone state bankruptcy by pushing the current techniques to their logical limits. However, one cannot prevent the development in certain cases of a saturation of false capital or even dangerous links when ill-prepared banks accumulate industrial shareholdings without being capable of supervising their holdings properly (Crédit Lyonnais).

The shareholder state exists, but by weakening the Treasury in order to support public investment banks, it is limiting its capacity to apply direct influence. If the state continues to be a major shareholder, the decisions taken today by insurance companies such as UAP, AGF, and others are singularly capitalistic strategies, as the surreptitious attempt to renationalize the Société Générale demonstrated.[15] Thus the state, which did not have an investment strategy and could use its shareholdings for diverse political reasons (macro-economic balance, industrial strategy, social regulation, distribution of political benefits), is finding itself increasingly playing the role of guarantor in the last resort to national capital, since the management of public shareholdings is increasingly the business of private centres of power.

The financial structure of French capitalism is becoming more and more fragmented: it has borrowed from the German bank-industry model (Crédit Lyonnais-Thomson, linked to the control of public investment funds), from the Anglo-American public company model which rests upon a dynamic financial market (Alcatel-Alsthom, Générale des Eaux), or even the Japanese model of financial archipelagos (the flexible grouping of BNP/UAP/Suez/ Générale de Belgique).

4. CONCLUSIONS

If the case presented is valid, industrial policy and a specific role for public companies would have to be consigned to the realm of ritual incantation. In this context, the French state would be called upon to play three roles: advocate of national interests within European and international institutions; implementer of policies designed to improve the environment of firms so as to promote the creation of added value on French territory; ultimate protector of national capital.

This idea of the state as protector means that companies will not be left to the mercy of foreign predators. They will also be able to benefit from such protection for some time and on a contractual basis. One may try to outsmart Brussels but one cannot do so without costs and still continue to fulfil commitments. Nationalized companies benefit by their status, but it must be stressed that if the Rocard plan of allowing 49 per cent of a public sector company to be sold to the private sector is fully implemented, private investors will have their say on investment, profitability, and employment levels. One wonders whether a government, which despite every-thing continues to believe in the virtues of industrial intervention, is well advised to let public control slip when the actions taken by Brussels will clearly be more effective in future. There is no doubt that the combined action of the external regulator (Brussels) and internal private investors will lead to conflict with the will of the state, which might like to continue an industrial gamble which threatens the profitability of the group.

The coming of a Balladur Government in 1993 meant that a different hypothesis may come true. Rather than confining itself to privatizing 49 per cent of companies in the competitive sector to meet the needs of industrial groups and the stringent state budget, the state could find new resources by partial privatization of public service monoplies such as EdF, France Télécom, SNCF, or Air France and exploit this opportunity to revive the promotion of a shareholding democracy by introducing clauses limiting the number of shares sold and votes linked to them. This would have a threefold attraction. It would create new sources of finance, dis-cipline the state by forbidding it to compel these companies to support hopeless causes, and create a strong external pressure for the modernization of the management of these companies.

With hindsight 1982–3 marked a threefold break with what had been accepted in France as industrial policy:

- the transition from an economy of administered financing to a market economy (the state as macro-economic actor);

- the transition from sectoral to territorial policies based on the attractiveness of certain areas (the state as meso-economic actor);
- the transition from the shareholder-state in national champions to state-protector for worldwide champions in the process of being privatized (the state as a micro-economic actor).

Notes

1. Preceded in 1991 by the publication of a document expressing the DGIII's doctrine regarding the Community's industrial policy.
2. Report of the Competitiveness Policy Council quoted in *Le Monde*, 1 Apr. 1992.
3. 'Industrial Policy', *Business Week*, 6 Apr. 1992.
4. 'Économie de financements administrés' in French. The economy of administered financing is not a state-oriented or a state-led financial system because there is no sectoral industrial orientation. It is a system where the money supply and the interest rates are regulated.
5. Solemn commitment given by F. Mitterrand in his 'Letter to the French' that if re-elected President in 1988 he would neither proceed with new nationalizations, nor with additional privatizations.
6. R. Penaud and F. Gaudichet, *Sélectivité du crédit, financement, politique monétaire* (Paris, 1985).
7. E. Cohen, *L'État brancardier* (Paris, 1989).
8. The Compagnie du Midi was a huge conglomerate with interests in fine wines, insurance, real estate, etc. As the ownership of this conglomerate was very fragmented, the Italian Generali Group bought shares at discount prices during the crash without any organized reaction.
9. See E. Cohen : *Le Colbertisme 'high tech'* (Paris, 1992).
10. In two years France Télécom bought into the Argentine and Mexican networks, making a remarkable breakthrough in mobile telecommunication.
11. E. Cohen and M. Bauer, *Les Grandes Manœuvres industrielles* (Paris, 1985).
12. E. Cohen in P. Birnbaum (ed.), *Les Élites socialistes au pouvoir* (Paris, 1985).
13. H. Bentegeat, *L'Expansion*, 25 Jan.–7 Feb. 1991.
14. A. Berle and G. Means, *The Modern Corporation and Private Property* (New York, 1932).
15. In this case, the Socialist Government which was seeking to recapture

influence over the privatized Société Générale bank failed in using UAP as a tool because the man in charge, a socialist, Jean Peyrlevade, decided that this move by the shareholder state conflicted with his policy.

2

Germany: Challenges to the Old Policy Style

JOSEF ESSER

The Federal Republic's economic and social system faces immense economic, social, and political demands. These may be encapsulated in phrases like 'third technological revolution', globalization of production, and internationalization of markets (triadization versus Europeanization), as well as the integration of East German into West German capitalism. What I want to do here is to analyse the reaction of the German economy to these challenges and to ask if there are dramatic changes of the relationship between the private economy and the state.

But let me start with the argument that the relationship between the private economy and the state cannot be accurately described in such terms as 'national champion' or 'nationalized firm' in Germany. For one thing, a very internationally competitive sector of key industries exists, which includes the motor vehicle, machinery construction, chemical, and electrical equipment industries. Around these sectors many small and medium-sized subcontractors are grouped. This competitive sector has always been present on the world market and has been able to maintain its European as well as global position of leadership.

A politically regulated sector also exists, in which market competition is limited in the interests of political or social goals, through state stipulations, regulations, or intervention. The legitimacy of these political regulations is derived from the specific German social project of the 'social market economy'. These types of politically regulated enterprises can be found in the services sector (transport, postal services, telecommunications, energy supply, banking, and insurance), while some industrial sectors (coal, steel) were only subject to such regulation during the immediate post-war years.

Since then, however, these latter sectors have been completely exposed and unprotected in international competition (steel) or are regulated at the European level, such as coal (in part steel) and agriculture. Since the mid-1980s, vehement political discussion regarding order of and competition in this sector has broken out. The demand for *deregulation* has been increasingly debated within the conservative–liberal government coalition of the CDU/CSU and FDP. It is remarkable in that it was not so much the deregulation policies applied in the USA and Great Britain that have given rise to this conflict about the future direction—although these are permanently quoted as shining examples by neo-liberals—but rather the new internationalization of the finance and service markets, the development of the European Common Market, as well as new technological–economic developments.[1]

In the first part of my analysis, I shall discuss the historical and conceptual reasons why a 'social market economy' has developed since the Second World War, with its mix of market-oriented self-regulation and political regulation. In the second part I shall briefly discuss the internationally competitive sector of key industries, which is supported by banks, trade unions, and the state, and then describe their global market adaptation strategy. It is important to note that this sector has increasingly concentrated its activities on the growing triad markets of Western Europe, the USA, and Japan/South East Asia during the 1970s and 1980s. Furthermore, these enterprises considered themselves decreasingly as national or European enterprises and increasingly as triad enterprises or as 'global players'. The third part deals with the politically regulated sector and the way in which the previous deregulation policy in the areas of telecommunications, rail and air traffic, and the power industry have changed the structure of political regulation in Germany.

Finally, I shall look at the way in which the reunification process, particularly the attempts to preserve or to rebuild a competitive industrial structure in East Germany, has influenced 'model Germany', for a long time such a successful state. My argument here is that failed attempts to re-industrialize East Germany by 'creative destruction' and radical privatization led to a broad social and political consensus that government support and intervention would be necessary for a long time, and that the market could not achieve the economic and social integration of the two Germanies.

Until now reunification has not brought changes in the relationship between economy and state worth mentioning. On the contrary, after initial neo-liberal soul-searching, an attempt to transfer the West German 'social market economy' to East Germany is now being made with the consequence of massive de-industrialization of East Germany, a high unemployment rate there, and an enormous rise in the German state debt. This has led to bitter conflicts within the political class and between the social actors of West German corporatism.

1. SOCIAL MARKET ECONOMY AND POLITICAL REGULATION

The West German economic system can be characterized as a 'mixed' economy, made up of both a self-regulated and a politically regulated sector. For historical and party-political reasons, the term 'social market economy' has been accepted for this German model of welfare state capitalism.[2]

Even though during the first post-war years the political parties came to a relatively speedy agreement concerning the state organization of the FRG, a basic difference did exist relating to the future form of economic and social order. Two opposing models for reconstruction were in competition with each other: the modified liberal social market economy, advocated by the CDU/CSU, and 'liberal socialism', which was endorsed by the SPD. In 1949, with the victory of the CDU/CSU in the first German election, the social market economy was adopted, with the major occupying power, the USA, also intervening in favour of this model. Finally, the political and economic reality of the Soviet occupation zone discredited socialism in West German eyes and the economic upturn in the FRG, which considerably increased living standards during the 1950s, was attributed to the social market economy. In addition, it was advantageous for the CDU to integrate the widespread anti-capitalistic and anti-monopolistic sentiments prevalent after the war within their conception of the social market economy, and to establish this as a third way between *laissez-faire* capitalism and state socialism. In the light of this development, the SPD gave up its opposition by adapting the Godesberg Programme of 1959, and since that time the social market economy has become the uncontested economic and socio-political model, first of West Germany and then a united Germany.

The conception of the social market economy originated from the Ordoliberal school of thought, just as in the 1930s the Freiburg School of Economists (Walter Eucken, Franz Böhm, and others) developed as a reaction to the world economic crisis and expansion of a socialist economy in the Soviet Union. This school recognized the structural deficiencies of the market economy's competitive order and therefore demanded a strong state. This state could then organize competition to prevent the emergence of monopolies. For individual citizens, the negative effects of the process of the free market economy would be corrected or diminished through state policies, social policy, and structure policy to seek a synthesis between economic freedom and social justice. Because an order for competition would not be automatically achieved but had to be institutionally secured, state intervention in the economic order was justified. Naturally the state's economic and socio-political measures would be limited to providing a framework for economic order, while the economic processes were to proceed independently. Only in exceptional cases, such as the avoidance of monopolies, could state intervention in the economic process be justified.[3]

Until the early to mid-1980s, there existed a broad consensus regarding the need to combine private and political regulation. *Macro-economic regulations* by fiscal, financial innovation, and trade policy are an integral component of this type of economic and social policy. This is supplemented by *micro-economic regulation* of enterprises, which seeks two goals. The first is carefully to steer socio-economic structural changes, so that there will not be any ruinous consequences for those affected or for society in general. The second is to prevent the private formation of monopolies, and detrimental competition as far as prices are concerned in those sectors that have strategic importance for the national economy.

2. POLITICALLY SUPPORTED INTERNATIONALIZATION OF KEY SECTORS

The key exporting sectors of the German economy, which comprise the engineering, motor vehicle, chemical, electrical, and electronic industries, steel, optical electronics, and mineral and plastics-processing, have often been described and analysed, so they can be dealt with briefly.[4] The internationalized sectors are interlocked with each other and operate in close co-operation with many competitive and technologically efficient small and medium-sized firms. The private and public service sectors, which are made up of banking, insurance, marketing, engineering, science, and research enterprises, are functionally subordinated. Beside these factors, an efficient and flexible internally and externally organized education, continued education, and training system should be mentioned.

There have often been references to the major German banks, whether private or public, which play an important role in the long-term financing and viability of these export-oriented industrial strategies. Nevertheless, it would be wrong to characterize the relationship between German industry and finance capital as the major banks playing the dominating role over industry. It would also be wrong to consider the banks as controlling the private sector's structure and investments within the German economy.[5] Even in lending, the banks are unable to exercise such a dominant position, primarily because the large industrial firms have succeeded in substantially raising their self-financing capability and in reducing the debt they owe to the banks. What remains is the dependence on credit of small and medium-sized firms. But the latter are also in many ways dependent on the big industrial firms; so it would make more sense to speak of the dominance of the large banks and of big business firms over the small and medium-sized firms.

In addition, shareholdings in industry, presence on supervisory boards, and proxy-voting rights are not a good indicator of the power of the banks in Germany. First, property rights and personal influence factors are quantitatively not as considerable as is usually asserted. Second, a presence on a supervisory board has not been translated into control of the business policy of the executive board of the firm. Naturally the banks exercise influence through their presence on supervisory boards, but in the sense that information is exchanged and common strategies are discussed in the forum of the supervisory board between representatives of the banks and those of the executive board. This is a form of mutual dependence. In exceptional situations one can point to the strong position of a bank, but one should not generalize from that to the majority of situations. Finally, it would also be an exaggeration to attribute to the German banks a general planning and economic guidance capability greater than that of the firms in industry. It is true to say that the tight intertwining of universal banks and industry—more than elsewhere—has led to a highly organized system of capitalist production and reproduction. And it is also true that the German banks are involved in the long-term aims and strategies of industrial firms. However, first, such a structured relationship does not alter the fact that this banking–industry complex is dependent on the changeable and uncertain economic developments in the capitalist international market. Second, such collective organizational capacity is limited by the ability of the large industrial firms, through self-financing possibilities, to emancipate themselves from their house banks. Related to that is the increasing competition among the banks themselves; and such competition will further increase rather than decrease because of the globalization and liberalization of financial markets.

Instead of speaking of the overarching planning capacity of the universal banks, it is more accurate to say that certain industrial firms have long-established and stable relationships with certain big banks; and these connections compete with other bank–industry connections. With the concept of financial groups in mind, it is not so important to ascertain on whose initiative (i.e. of a bank or a firm) the group has come into being and how and why it functions; nor is it particularly important to answer the question of who dominates whom in the bank–industry relationship. What is important to bear in mind is that individual German firms, or groups of them, have for some time resorted to the practice of building strong linkages with financing sources, such as house banks or a group of them; linkages that are, moreover, resilient and hold firm through thick and thin, in bad times as well as in good ones. Such financial groups share a common interest or at least interests that run in parallel, which make them stand out from members of other financial groups or other autonomous firms not organized in financial groups. But conflicts of interests do exist within these groups; intra-group co-operation can resolve them or overcome them over a period of time, reflecting bargaining relationships within the financial group.

On the whole, West German industry has the organizational capacity to co-ordinate and take important decisions relating to the changing competitive conditions within the global economy. This is, firstly, supported by co-operative partnerships with trade unions.[6] Secondly, this is complemented financially and legislatively by state policy, which supports the 'private industry policy' of enterprises through tax reliefs, subsidies, investment aid, provisions for infrastructure, social support via structural adaptation, regional aid, etc.[7] There are many state or semi-state actors which take part in state industrial policy, which is subordinated to the demands of global competition: the Federal Ministries for Economy, Finance Research and Technology, Defence, Postal Services and Telecommunications; the respective ministries at the state level; affected communities; science and research institutions at the federal and state level; chambers of industry and commerce; chambers of handicrafts; state banks or the federal-owned Kreditanstalt für Wiederaufbau (Credit Institute for Reconstruction). When there is deliberation about what the appropriate strategy should be, most importantly when the Federal Ministry for Economics voices its concern on market grounds to the most intervention-friendly ministries (Research and Technology, Postal Services and Telecommunications, Defence), discussion within the complex institutional network is more than likely to proceed in a co-operative and consensual manner. Intense conflicts seldom occur. This is most probably due to the private economy's relevant interests regulating themselves prior to the political decision-making processes.

We are familiar with the successful rationalization, modernization, diversification, and internationalization processes of the key sectors of the German economy in the 1980s.[8] There is no systematic difference in Germany between the 'management of growth', the 'management of decline', or the 'management of innovation' industrial policy. West German industry is trying to reconcile the new demands of globalization and internationalization, as well as the so-called 'third industrial revolution', with the past corporatist political model. In the centre stand private enterprises and alongside stands an institutionalized network of subsidiary 'services', of banks, science and research, trade unions, and the federal government.

What must remain open here is how long this narrow corporatist alliance will remain in the interest of securing Germany's leading position in the world market. This is because the current debate on the high costs of locating production in Germany have reflected the fact that German industrial trusts, large banks, and insurance brokers are continually forced to internationalize their production locations and market strategies. (Important examples are firms like Siemens, Daimler Benz, the chemical giants Bayer, Hoechst and BASF, Deutsche Bank, Dresdner Bank, Commerzbank, Westdeutsche Landesbank, Allianz, or Bertelsmann in the media sector.) They have 'triadically' shifted their efforts toward the regions of Japan/South-East Asia, USA, and Western Europe.[9] The dynamics of development and the power relations within this capitalistic centre of the world economy will not only decide if an independent European model for growth and social project will be brought about at all. They will also decide if the strong German economic enterprises will remain tied to the present 'German model'.

3. POLITICAL DEREGULATION OF THE 'PROTECTED' SECTORS

In 1957 a law was passed (modified in 1973) against the limitation of competition. This law distinguishes two areas, which are partially removed from market competition and subject to political regulation.[10]

3.1. Regulated Basic Industries

Sectors such as agriculture, mining, and partly steel were in practice regulated before the establishment of the FRG, partly to ensure security of supply, partly to ease the effects of the changes in certain regions and sectors. They impinge much less today on the German economy or the deregulation debates because of their economic decline or integration in international agreements (EC policy).

3.2. Regulated Infrastructure Enterprises

This concerns enterprises such as energy supply, rail and air transport, the postal service, and telecommunications. Many are in part the property of the state (rail, post, Lufthansa), because it is thought that due to the high expenditure for investment and the lengthy turnover periods for capital, they would not be manageable within the private sector. Access to markets, prices, or tariffs are subject to political regulation, in order to prevent damaging price competition and to allow those participating in the market in all regions similar competitive conditions. According to the social market economy, the state regulated sector should be guided by underlying business and market-oriented principles. Structural adjustments to changes in the market, rationalization measures, and employment reductions have to a large extent occurred similarly to the market regulated sector.

Energy Supply This sector comprises the generation, distribution, and use of electricity, gas, and nuclear power, employing about a quarter of a million people. The most important actors are some large enterprises, like Rheinisch-Westfälische Elektrizitätswerke (RWE), VEBA, Ruhrkohle AG, Ruhrgas AG, Bayernwerk AG, Hamburger Elektrizitätswerke (HEW), as well as Siemens with its nuclear energy subsidiary KWU.[11] They are partly private firms, partly cities and states that have significant shares in these enterprises, which means that appointments to political sinecures and the proliferation of clientelist networks often occur. It is argued that a fair price energy supply which is sufficient and satisfies the needs of the consumer cannot be guaranteed by market competition alone.

Communications State regulation in this sector had already been emphasized prior to the 1 July 1989 law on the PTT structure by the post and telecommunications policy of Deutsche Bundespost (DBP). The DBP was the only operation with comprehensive public communications networks and telecommunications services. Entirely private institutions, that were to be linked to a public network, had to allow access to the DBP. As the network manager and supplier of communication services, the Bundespost was obliged to offer each interested party a connection to the public network and to offer all services in all locations under the same conditions. Similar stipulations apply to the postal service. The DBP also was of central importance to procurement policy. The Bundepost obtained its equipment from a few large German electrical firms such as Siemens, Bosch, AEG or SEL (now Alcatel), in relation to which it was the dominant customer. Foreign manufacturers were practically excluded from this exclusive cartel of suppliers on the German market. The DBP hardly had any research capacity at its own disposal. That meant that for the development of the telecommunications sector, it relied on the research and development services of the electronic trusts. They could cover their costs from the sales price.[12]

Transportation   The regulated transport industry has approximately half a million employees. Included are the government's own Deutsche Bundesbahn (DB), the German Federal Rail System, the government's Deutsche Lufthansa (DLH), the German airline, as well as the mostly private road transport of goods and inland shipping. The transport sector is one of the most extensively regulated in the FRG,[13] whether it be prices, quantities, or quality, or whether it be measures which influence which parties can act as suppliers. The DB has a monopoly of the rail network; activity within this network, even if undertaken through other suppliers, is only possible with the DB's permission. The case is similar with air traffic. The air routes and who has access to them are decided by the Federal Transport Ministry. The charges are also decided by the Ministry. Inland flights are almost entirely reserved for state-owned Lufthansa. International air traffic can only be regulated bilaterally between the respective governments in the absence of multilateral agreements. There are detailed regulations in the agreements concerning landing rights and regular services, prices, and the division of capacity between the national airlines. Just as in the cases of the postal service and telecommunications, these extensive regulations and the natural monopoly of rail system and airline (Lufthansa) are justified in the name of the common good, the regional or sociopolitical equality of all citizens, and the danger of ruinous price competition as well.

4. CORPORATIST DEREGULATION POLICY SINCE THE MID-1980s

The expert opinion of the government's federally appointed Economic Advisory Committee opened its evaluation in 1985 with a new political deregulation debate that until then mainly remained ideological. This committee gives its views each year on overall economic development, as well as being politically expedient, taking up fundamental economic and socio-political questions. Above all, general technological advances and the related economic potential for innovation with possible new markets for growth, have been brought into the discussion as an argument for dynamic competition through the policy of opening up markets.[14] Additionally, after the ratification of the European Act, beside the technological-economic requirements, there has been an increase in references to the demands and opportunities of the new European Common Market.

Although the conservative–liberal government coalition has been put under pressure by this public debate over deregulation, especially by the liberal-market oriented coalition partner of the FDP, a rather conservative, cautious, and pragmatic deregulation course has been conducted. There are many interests permanently involved in the work of the social market economy and in the corporatist-oriented economic, social, local, and regional components of the German political system. These interests are closely connected to the two large parties of the CDU/CSU and SPD, and through the policy interdependence between the federal, state, and community organization, as well as the powerful social interest groups. According to these social and political actors the 'German model' until today distinguished itself internationally through its conspicuous economic success and social stability. Furthermore, effectiveness as well as stability are thought of as two sides of the same coin: a lasting economic modernization which is generally accepted due to its success, which is itself due to its general acceptance. The political and organizational resources of the social market economy have sufficed up to the present to make this demanding equation work. Why should it be challenged if no real problem exists?[15] This may change in the 1990s, principally because of the re-integration of the former GDR and new world-wide demands. These factors, however, have not yet had much effect, so any radical changes to this model would have had no political chance of adoption.

The 1989 successful restructuring of the telecommunications sector provides an example of this cautious, pragmatic, and corporatistically arranged German deregulation policy.[16] The state monopoly in the postal service and telecommunications has traditionally been considered sacrosanct. But fundamental and world-wide technical, economic, and regulatory changes in telecommunications have also led to a questioning in West Germany of this 'natural monopoly'. Neo-liberals have urged, following the example of the USA, Great Britain, and Japan, the privatization of West German telecommunications.[17] The conservative–liberal government has not followed this advice, although the liberal coalition partner, the FDP, has vehemently advocated this course of action. However, out of concern for the international competitiveness of the German economy, the federal government has recognized the necessity to rethink the traditional structures in telecommunications. In providing the infrastructure for modern telecommunications through the creation of an Integrated Service Digital Network (ISDN), the DBP performs a vital technological function for the modernization of the economy. To carry out this pivotal role, it was argued that the DBP might have to be restructured in order to allow for quicker responses to technological, economic, and political changes.[18]

An inquiry into the necessary structural changes was started in 1985 with the creation of a high-ranking advisory body, the Government Telecommunications Commission. Its members were selected in corporatist fashion and comprised important representatives of the business associations, one representative of each political party, and one representative of the postal trade union. Three academic consultants in telecommunication technology, law, and business completed the membership. The hearings and the decision-making process lasted over two years. In the end the commission succeeded in creating a broad consensus about the future of the German telecommunications regulatory system which became the basis of the structure of the Postal Service Law of 1 July 1989.[19]

It is remarkable that a consensus was reached that did not involve the privatization of the telecommunications system, despite manifest differences in interests within the commission between the telecommunication manufacturing industry, the data-transmitting industry, users of telecommunication services and the main association of the fitters of leased lines and telephones. Public responsibility was separated from the entrepreneurial functions and transferred to a restructured Ministry for Postal Services and Telecommunications. This Ministry is in charge of central regulation in this sector. The German postal service has been divided into three relatively independent state companies for the postal service, the postal banking service, and telecommunications. Cross-subsidization will be permitted from profit-earning telecommunications to the loss-making postal service but only for a transitional period. Telekom has retained the network monopoly and is solely responsible for the extension of the ISDN. Communication services of all kinds and user equipment can be offered by private enterprises, which compete with Telekom in the market.

With this liberalization of services and user equipment the central demands of the private economy have been fulfilled. At the same time, as a state enterprise, Telekom retained the central technological-political function of expanding the ISDN and standardizing the technological norms for all participants. The interests of the Federal States were also preserved; without their consent, no legal changes to the organizational structure and functions of the German Bundespost are possible. The states' interests were safeguarded because they keep the network and telecommunications monopoly of Telekom under surveillance, to guarantee a common, federal-wide communications and information infrastructure.

The *commercialization* of Telekom was also to be further pressed ahead through restructuring. In order to be able to raise enough funds for expansion of the ISDN (which according to current estimates is DM 300 billion by the year 2030), Telekom must act in the market like a private sector services enterprise. Management adopted the goals and methods of business cost accounting and profitability, as far as public service law allows. The consequence was a loss of jobs by rationalization and new working conditions. For this reason, the German postal trade union, the Deutsche Postgewerkschaft, and the postal civil service organization, the Deutscher Beamtenbund, were involved in the negotiations and eventual compromise. First, the German postal trade union was going to mobilize its members against the restructuring of the Bundespost, but then it accepted 'soft deregulation' as a lesser evil than privatization.

A new debate on the complete privatization of Telekom has nevertheless ensued. Now it is argued that because of challenges posed by a completely altered and increasingly competitive world market Telekom must position itself as a global, high-tech service provider in a key technology area for virtually every high-tech industry, in chip manufacture, opto-electronics, or software developments, and that strategic alliances with foreign partners must extend its current activities to the global stage. Therefore, if Telekom would no longer be subject to public service law in matters of wages, employment status, and working conditions, it could become increasingly flexible in terms of the market. This discussion is occurring in a familiar setting. The opposition SPD party must be involved in order to achieve a two-thirds parliamentary majority, which would be necessary to remove the Bundespost's constitutional status as government property. The Federal States must become involved, since otherwise they could exercise a veto in the Bundesrat. Finally, the postal unions and the postal service officials must also agree, since both the SPD and CDU/CSU would not have been able to stand up to any resistance from the postal employees.

A bill providing for privatization of Deutsche Telekom, the postal services and the Postbank in February 1994 met with little resistance in the German legislature as all parties gave their basic approval to it and the trade union reduced its opposition after its failure to persuade the SPD opposition to reject privatization. This bill followed two years of negotiation between the government, the opposition, the federal states, and the trade unions.

The law, which is expected to come into force at the beginning of 1995, will turn the three public services into joint-stock companies. Starting in 1996, Deutsche Telekom is expected to sell on the stock market an initial tranche of shares representing 25 per cent of the company's equity. However, as a result of demands made by the SPD and the trade union, a state-owned holding company will be created to keep a share of the three companies temporarily. In the case of Deutsche Telekom, the holding company will retain a majority ownership until 2000. The state is expected to remain the sole shareholder of the postal services as long as they continue to report losses. The holding company will also retain 12.5 per cent of the Postbank with another 12.5 per cent held by the postal services. There are conflicts in interpretation of the power of this holding company. Deutsche Telekom will also have to accept the creation of an 'infrastructure committee' made up of officials from the federal government and the states. This follows demands by the SPD for some continued state supervision. The party and the states want to ensure that the private companies will not neglect infrastructure investments in less populated areas. The refusal of the SPD to accept a deadline on the monopolies enjoyed by Deutsche

Telekom and the postal services led to a compromise; they will now end on 31 December 1997. This date coincides with the European Union voice communication liberalization. However, the formula also allows Germany to keep the monopoly on its telephone infrastructure and postal services after 1997, depending on liberalization at the European level.

Telecommunications is so far the most remarkable example of governmentally negotiated and politically implemented deregulation in Germany. To what extent the established national interest coalitions will split in this sector cannot yet be completely answered. The strong tendencies toward more extensive international competition are none the less clearly recognizable, not least because of the new order envisaged at the EC level.

In order to extend the process further, a deregulation commission was established in 1989 after the model of the government committee on telecommunications services. This committee concentrated on the possibility of deregulation in the transport, energy supply, expert advice, job centres, and artisan areas. The commission published in 1991 its final report and made its recommendations for deregulation, but a wide-ranging political discussion did not reach any definitive conclusions; though, for example in the field of energy supply, extensive suggestions to break up cartels have been formulated. The federal government is rather cautious when dealing with this domain. Only on the basis of a report by a working party of government representatives recommending which deregulations might be adopted would the government take an initiative.[20]

This, of course, does not mean that the established energy and transport cartels, criticized by the deregulation commission, would not have been either broken up by other developments or forced to adapt to the new international demands. Energy supply and Lufthansa demonstrate that the enterprises—as has been usual for quite a while in Germany—are carrying out their own strategies for restructuring. I shall use Lufthansa and the largest energy supplier REW as examples to demonstrate this private rather than politically organized adaptation to new international demands, before briefly considering plans for the restructuring of the German Bundesbahn.

Lufthansa, despite frequent announcements by the Federal Finance Minister, will probably not be privatized. Hitherto, all attempts in this direction have failed due to resistance of some Federal States.[21] Above all, the Bavarian CSU has led, and is still leading, industrial-political opposition to privatization in the debate. The state of Bavaria is the centre of the German aerospace industry, dominated by MBB, now merged with a Daimler-Benz subsidiary called German Aerospace (Dasa). The German component of the European Airbus programme is also concentrated in Bavaria. It is feared in Bavaria that privatization of Lufthansa could undermine a hitherto close relationship between Lufthansa, Airbus, and German Aerospace, which is arranged through Federal purchase guarantees. Similar structural–political standpoints have been adopted by the states of Hamburg and Bremen, which also possess shares in German Aerospace.

Despite this, the restructuring of Lufthansa is well under way. High losses, increased pressures relating to costs of the liberalization and deregulation of European air traffic, as well as sharpened competition from the USA and the Far East are the reasons for its Board of Directors submitting a first restructuring programme in 1991 and a second one in 1992. This is gradually being implemented in consultation with representatives of the personnel. The central business sectors—freight, technology, and airline transport as independent profit centres, sales, cost accounting and product management—would be under the one roof of the Lufthansa holding company. The status of the workers as civil servants would gradually cease, starting with flexibility in the contracts for management employees. In a new mode of bargaining the public service trade union ÖTV and the minor important white-collar union DAG accepted the reduction of employment by about 15 per cent, from 48,000 (1992) to 40,000 (end of 1993). They also agreed to wage cuts of DM 500 million. From 1992 to 1994 productivity rose about 15 per cent and productive capacity was 10 per cent higher.[22] Although depoliticization of Lufthansa is going very successfully, one unsolved problem remains. Who has to pay the bill for a special old-age pension fund, which is a privilege of all employees in German public service: deregulated Lufthansa or the federal government? Finally, the process of international concentration has involved Lufthansa in trying to build strategic alliances with United Airlines of the US and Varig in South America.

REW and other German energy suppliers were forced to adapt their internal running under pressure, especially from the EC

Commission, which would radically change the way the industry operates and reshape its relations with both consumers and suppliers. The main elements of this EC reform plan include increasing transparency of utilities accounts, achieving greater access for non-utility power producers to grid systems. Third Party Access would give greater scope for large energy users and distribution companies to deal directly with competing power producers. This would end privileged relationships between national utilities and local suppliers of fuel and equipment, and change pricing structures for consumers.[23]

In fact, the result will be a reduction in the high electricity prices in Germany. But the firms think they are only able to guarantee an inexpensive and sufficient supply of energy for all regions and all customers if prices are regulated and they have the backing of the local, state, and federal governments. Only the Ministry of Economy is unsuccessfully fighting for more liberalization of prices, but strong opposition within the Cabinet has blocked its attempts for financial, ecological, and regional reasons.[24] But again we can identify specific and decidedly market-oriented firm strategies in the new context shaped by the EC's proposals. REW's answer is that outwardly, co-operation will be sought with foreign energy producers (e.g. Electricité de France) by means of joint ventures or strategic alliances. Secondly, the diversification of the petrochemical sector will be intensified. Thirdly, REW is one partner in a planned telecommunications consortium which initially plans to offer fixed-wire services to corporate clients. The other members of the consortium are Mannesmann, the main competitor to Deutsche Telekeom in the German mobile phone market, Deutsche Bank, Germany's largest bank, Energieversorgung Schwaben, another German energy supplier, and the French firm Cofira.[25] Inwardly, each business sector would be split into profit centres, which would independently operate their own markets and use their own business-related cost-benefit strategies. The public shareholders did not question this strategy, nor was it opposed by the employees or their unions.

Finally, we consider the plans to convert the German Bundesbahn into a corporation which will remain in the government's possession. In addition, reunification has also put pressure on the rail system for adaptation, due to increased financial losses and international competition. The integration of the East German Reichsbahn with the Bundesbahn will be very expensive because of the civil service status of their employees.

A government commission for the rail system has been appointed and has made the following suggestions for remodelling the rail system. First, the Bundesbahn and Reichsbahn will be combined in the Deutsche Bahn AG and get the status of a joint-stock company. Second, under this government-owned holding company, three independently operated enterprises for passenger transport, goods transport, and the rail infrastructure will be formed. Third, civil service status will be revoked for new employees; wages and working conditions will become more flexible. Fourth, regional rail traffic should be managed under the authority of the Federal States. Trade unions, Federal States, and opposition parties have indicated their general agreement and in the beginning of 1994 this deregulated and partly privatized Deutsche Bahn AG was established by the main actors in the German neo-corporatist system.

5. RE-INDUSTRIALIZATION IN EAST GERMANY: A FUTILE SEARCH FOR 'INDUSTRIAL CORES' IN THE EAST

On 3 October 1991, the Federal Republic of Germany and the former German Democratic Republic became one state. A unification of the two societies, however, has not yet been achieved. In the new German state, two societies exist side by side, with different economic, social, and cultural structures. Whether, how, and when this real unification will take place, and its consequences, are unpredictable. It is estimated it will take ten years or more to revitalize East German industry, so it would be fruitless to speculate about a stable model there in industry–government relations or what influence this could have for 'model Germany'. But the political decision of a sudden integration of the Eastern economy into the Western structure has hastened the destruction of this economy so that for the next four years the division between the two parts will become more rather than less pronounced, threatening German stability.

6. THE PRIMACY OF POLITICS IN REUNIFICATION

Improvisation and short-term crisis management on the basis of a 'radical simplification of problems' was inevitable.[26] The great consensus principles of the political and social élites in West Germany were: firstly, the political collapse should not bring about economic chaos such that most of the ten million citizens of East Germany would flee westwards. Secondly, and more importantly, they were united in the belief that the established and efficient FRG, with its political and institutional framework, its existing power structures, and its network of interests, should not be put at risk or even questioned in a constitutional debate with unpredictable outcomes. This fundamental consensus rests on the deeply rooted tradition 'of a society which had in the past been fragmented regionally, religiously, and socially, that the constitutional consensus is negotiated amongst important corporate actors'.[27]

Without much discussion, the integration of the GDR into the federation of West Germany according to Article 23 of the Basic Law was adopted. This decision meant a radical and swift transformation of the political and economic structures of the former East Germany into a social market economy, parliamentary democracy, and a federal structure. The alternative path of a gentle and slow transition, as is attempted at present by the other East European countries, was not taken. It is worth mentioning that this *Anschlusspolitik* was supported by the economic and technical élites of East Germany as well as the great majority of its people. Everybody was hoping for a fast increase in wealth and an improvement in efficiency.

So the 'Economic and Social Union' of 1 July 1990 was the result of primacy given to political considerations. Economists, industrialists, and the Bundesbank had warned against such a step and its economic and social consequences. But they too accepted political factors such as the migration from East to West Germany and the risks to the political and economic system of the FDR. Economic and monetary union set the agenda for the transformation of the East German economy, which was exposed unprepared to a competitive world market and pushed to the periphery of the dominant and dynamic West German economy.

7. ECONOMIC AND SOCIAL CONSEQUENCES OF UNIFICATION:
   DE-INDUSTRIALIZATION AND HIGH UNEMPLOYMENT

Government economists saw the structural weakness of the East German economy mainly in three fields:

1. Lack of competition, a policy of no redundancy and frequent periods of enforced idleness in factories, caused by shortage of parts and materials, had led to a situation of permanent over-manning in industry.
2. Since economic resources were channelled by state directive, a structure had developed in which production did not follow consumer demands.
3. Because of its isolation from world markets, production was not sufficiently specialized, and a great deal of machinery and parts came from East Germany's own sources. East German firms had not made sufficient use of division of labour.

According to these experts' findings, a programme of 'creative destruction' would result in industries which were not overmanned in comparison with those of their western counterparts and would lead to diversification and specialization.

Critics of the unification policy were warning that the crash programme of hard and fast structural change into a market economy would bring about a long-lasting crisis in the East German economy. They claimed that this economy had consider-able industrial production potential, a developed training system, and qualified skilled workers, as well as a broadly based research and innovation potential, all worth keeping. They could have been used in the process of adjustment and modernization by way of massive transfers of capital and technology. Instead, the trans-formation currently taking place created a situation where this potential was destroyed and where any possibility of development was seriously put at risk.[28]

Three years after unification, destruction, and de-industrializ-ation the East German economy is in full swing and shows no sign of coming to a halt. Further, since the industrial structures in East and West Germany are largely similar, it is mainly the West German firms with their greater competitiveness which profit from unification. They have simply expanded their capacity and all but taken over the market of the former East Germany. Industrial output there fell by two-thirds between 1989 and 1994; manufacturing industry reduced its jobs from about 3.2 million in 1989 to 700,000 by 1994; about 2 million people in industry lost their jobs and a quarter of the working population were unemployed. Experts compare the industrial base of East Germany with those of developing countries like Honduras, Tunisia, or Sri Lanka.[29]

So far this process of de-industrialization has not been offset by new businesses and sufficent new investment. Without taking into account the activities of the Treuhandanstalt in privatizing and modernizing former state plants, the number of newly founded businesses from 1990–3 was about 440,000 (with about 3 million jobs), but many of these quickly closed down. Most of them have been in the service sector, in retail and handicraft, and they have not contributed to the reconstruction of manufacturing industry. Investment by West German industry has so far been limited and rarely takes place in key areas of the economy like construction of plants and machinery, electrical engineering, chemicals, and vehicle manufacture, but rather in the building industry, oil refining, and food processing. On the other hand, the West German banks have already expanded, but they are criticized for being too cautious. Generally, private enterprise prefers to sell western-produced goods to East Germany and, more importantly, Germany is only one of many investment areas for increasingly global industrial enterprises.

Inevitably, this process of de-industrialization has already produced much open as well as hidden unemployment in East Germany. More than 1 million have migrated to West Germany; more than 400,000 work as daily commuters in the west; many take part in training and retraining programmes or work short-time officially (which means in fact not at all), but are counted as employed because they receive state-financed short-time salaries; more than 500,000 took early retirement. Only about 1.2 million are left as the officially registered unemployed.[30] However, the victims of the process of massive de-industrialization are unequally distributed over the area, both socially and regionally. As we observed during the 1970s and 1980s in West Germany, a more extreme version of a social and regional division of society is developing.[31] Will it be possible to create a modern and competitive industrial structure which will endure? If the shipbuilding industry in Mecklenburg-Vorpommern is not made viable, if mechanical and electrical engineering in Brandenburg and the chemical industry in Sachsen-Anhalt cannot be saved, then the north–south divide in East Germany will be a lasting feature, because Saxony and Thuringia with their traditionally diversified industrial culture will be in a better position to survive under the new capitalist conditions.

8. ECONOMIC AND SOCIAL MEASURES FOR THE RE-ESTABLISHMENT OF SOCIAL UNITY

The economic and social policy aimed at reintegration of the former GDR into the West German system divides into three parts. The Treuhandanstalt's function was to privatize and/or make viable the former nationalized industries. Special government programmes, tax measures, and promotion measures, which have already been successfully practised in the FRG, have helped the restructuring process. Labour market measures are designed to soften the impact of the necessary redundancies and to improve the qualifications of the labour force.

The Treuhand was attempting to privatize or restore the 9,000 national enterprise properties and combined collectives with financial support from the German budget. The Treuhand had largely autonomous powers to decide which of the units was to survive, whether and how they were divided up, whether and at what price and to whom they were sold, and what happened to the profit from the sales. As the Treuhand was not a public company in German law, the right of the trade unionists to sit on the administrative council did not legally exist. Nevertheless, the Federal Government, under continued pressure from the unions, agreed to a minimum co-determination, although the unions were not kept sufficiently well informed and they complained, too, that the fifteen regional offices of Treuhand which privatized smaller and medium-sized businesses were difficult to control.

In keeping with neo-liberal ideology, the Treuhand at first declared it their priority to privatize so-called competitive and abolish non-competitive businesses. It did not feel responsible for structural, industrial, or social policy. With such scorched-earth policies, however, it soon made enemies not only among the East German population but also among the political representatives of communes and governments of the new Länder. Likewise the trade unions demanded in mass demonstrations that businesses should be made viable rather than abolished or privatized at all costs, in order to rescue, as far as possible, the industrial base of East Germany. In the spring of 1991 the Bonn government compelled the Treuhand to change its priorities: firms, even if not yet viable, were to be saved rather than liquidated. Furthermore, structural, industrial, and labour market aspects were to be considered before decisions on the future of plants were made. The prime ministers of the new Länder gained far more influence when plant closures and mass redundancies were threatened. Whilst the Treuhand officially still has sole authority for deciding the future of firms, and whilst the state governments alone are responsible for the structural, regional, and social consequences of Treuhand policies concerning the labour market, the new Länder economic councils, entitled to early information on imminent closures, have brought about a new corporate system of co-operation between the Treuhand, governments, unions, and communes.

So the radical privatization strategy of the Treuhand has already been abandoned. The danger of the total de-industrialization of East Germany has led to a broad social and political consensus that government support and intervention will be necessary for a long time, and that the market cannot achieve the economic and social integration of the two Germanies. It was merely the scale of the government intervention which was disputed. Should there be a shift to a systematic and comprehensive industrial policy with the creation of government-financed industrial holding companies, as the trade unions, the SPD, and some employers believed? Or would it be enough for there to be a mixture of state participation and private and public bank participation in the so-called 'structure participation trusts' of distinct regions, as the CDU/FDP Government and most business associations believed? As a result of this dispute a compromise was achieved: Treuhand, together with political and social actors in the concerned regions, had to define so-called industrial cores which had to be protected and which had to be subsidized in its efforts for revitalization and modernization.

So far the results of the privatization and rescue policy of the Treuhand are difficult to evaluate. Progress has been made in the dismemberment of the vast industrial and commerical combines, and instead of 9,000 there are now about 13,500 enterprises. By December 1993, 97 per cent had been privatized. Only 6 per cent of the buyers came from foreign countries. The new owners promised to invest about DM 182.4 billion and to protect about 1.5 million jobs.[32] The Treuhand ran up debts of about DM 275 billion. But nobody is able to say today whether these new private companies will be able to help revitalize the economy in East Germany. First, many of these new units have a possible future only as subcontractors for West German and large multinational companies, and so far only modest beginnings for such co-operation exist. Secondly, many of these privatized firms have been bought by West German competitors, which may simply close them to reduce competition.

So far, Treuhand has not been able to create modern, competitive industrial cores in East Germany. Although it tried hard, together with the Land governments and private buyers, to rescue the ship-building industry in Mecklenburg-Vorpommern, the chemical industry in Sachsen-Anhalt (Leuna-Werke, Chemiekombinat Bitterfeld-Wolfen), the motor industry in Thuringia and Saxony (Volkswagen/Mosel and Opel Eisenach), the steel industry (Eko-Stahl, Eisenhüttenstadt) in Brandenburg, the opto-electronic industry in Thuringia (Jenoptik, Jena), and the micro-electronic industry in Saxony (Siemens, Dresden), all these 'East German champions' are only viable with large subsidies from West German taxpayers. It is difficult to see how these firms could survive in the face of growing competition world-wide in these sectors. Additionally, it remains an open question whether and how these enterprises may function as cores for a regional, self-sustaining economy in the East.

As I mentioned earlier, it has always been part of the political philosophy of the social market economy that economic moderniz-ation should be supported and aided by a system of public credits and guarantees, tax relief, and programmes for weak regions, har-monized between the Federation and the Länder. Therefore it was to be expected that such programmes would be extended to East Germany. However, all these are single programmes and measures, not parts of an integrated, fully harmonized plan. Although it is not yet clear whether these programmes will eventually contribute to the restructuring of the East German economy, their main result so far has been an enormous rise in the German state debt. The Bundesbank and Economics Ministry have both demanded a lowering of financial involvement at all levels in West Germany, of state subsidies and promotion programmes, as well as higher indirect taxes. All this means that social and political stability in the new FDR is endangered.

9. CONCLUSION

The Federal Republic's economic and social order faces immense economic, social, and political pressures. The German economy has reacted to a further internationalization in the already global operations of key sectors. This has occurred so far without abandoning or significantly modifying the familiar neo-corporatist model. The politically regulated sector finds itself in a partially automatic, partially politically initiated process of deregulation, 'flexibilization', and commercialization. This has been accompanied by a massive reorganization of enterprise structure, but this adaptation process followed in the well-worn tracks of neo-corporatist political methods.

Despite all the official optimism that East Germany would soon become the 'new Japan of Europe', for the moment West German and foreign goods are flooding East Germany rather than being produced there. Where new jobs have appeared, they are in the service sector, banking, and in the insurance business. After initial neo-liberal market rhetoric, the political-economic process of reunification and re-industrializing East Germany are starting to follow the old West German path and the West German taxpayer is paying the bill.

So far, there has been no need to introduce any radical policy change. This is because German capitalism in the international realm has functioned very well and the economic, social, and political costs have been successfully controlled. But this is the story of the 1980s and the beginning of the 1990s. No one knows if and for how long this success story will continue, but the new challenges make it probable that dramatic processes of adaptation are necessary. The 'model Germany' of the 1990s will be very different from that of the 1970s and the 1980s.

Notes

1. *Sachverständigenrat zur Begutachtung der gesamtwirtschaftlichen Entwicklung, Jahresgutachten 1983–84* (Bonn, 1985), 156 ff.
2. H. van der Wee, *Der gebremste Wohlstand* (Munich, 1984); C. Böhret *et al.*, *Innenpolitik und Politische Theorie* (Opladen, 1979); J. Esser and W. Fach, with Kenneth Dyson, ' "Social Market" and Modernization Policy: West Germany', in K. Dyson and S. Wilks (eds.), *Industrial Crisis* (Oxford, 1983); W. Abelshauser, *Wirtschaftsgeschichte der Bundesrepublik Deutschland, 1945–1980* (Frankfurt, 1983); H. Jaeger, *Geschichte der Wirtschaftsordnung in Deutschland* (Frankfurt, 1988); G. Thompson, 'The Evolution of the Managed Economy in Europe', *Economy and Society*, 21/2 (May 1992).
3. M. Welteke, *Theorie und Praxis der Sozialen Marktwirtschaft* (Frankfurt, 1979). See also Böhret *et al.*, *Innenpolitik*, and Abelshauser, *Wirtschaftsgeschichte*.
4. Esser and Fach, ' "Social Market" '; J. Esser, 'State, Business and Trade Unions in West Germany after the "Political Wende" ', *West European Politics*, 9/2 (Apr. 1986); E. J. Horn, 'Germany: A Market-led Process', in F. Duchene and G. Shepherd (eds.), *Managing Industrial Change in Western Europe* (London, 1987).
5. J. Esser, 'Bank Power in West Germany Revisited', *West European Politics*, 13/4 (Oct. 1990).
6. J. Esser, *Gewerkschaften in der Krise* (Frankfurt, 1982); and id., 'Post-Fordist Capitalism? Corporatism and Dualism in Britain and West Germany', in J. Clark *et al.* (eds.), *John H. Goldthorpe: Consensus and Controversy* (London, 1990).
7. See Horn; J. Esser, 'Does Industrial Policy Matter? Land Governments in Research and Technology Policy in Federal Germany', in C. Crouch and D. Marquand (eds.), *The New Centralism* (Oxford, 1989).
8. P. J. Katzenstein (ed.), *Industry and Politics in West Germany* (Ithaca and London, 1989).
9. J. Esser, 'Technologieentwicklung in der Triade: Folgen für die europäische Technologiegemeinschaft', in W. Süß and G. Becher (eds.), *Politik und Technologieentwicklung in Europa* (Berlin, 1993); *Bericht der Bundesregierung zur Zukunftssicherung des Standortes Deutschland*, Deutscher Bundestag 12. Wahlperiode, Drucksache 12/5620, 3.9.93, Bonn.

10. W. Polster and K. Voy, 'Von der politischen Regulierung zur Selbstregulierung der Märkte', in K. Voy *et al.* (eds.), *Marktwirtschaft und politische Regulierung* (Marburg, 1991).
11. R. Soltwedel *et al.*, *Deregulierungspotentiale in der Bundesrepublik* (Tübingen, 1986); and Monopolkommission, *Mehr Wettbewerb ist möglich, Hauptgutachten 1985* (Baden-Baden, 1976).
12. E. Grande, *Vom Monopol zum Wettbewerb?* (Wiesbaden, 1989).
13. Soltwedel, *Deregulierungspotentiale in der Bundesrepublik*, 192.
14. *Sachverständigenrat* (1985), 156 ff.
15. J. Esser *et al.*, *Krisenregulierung* (Frankfurt 1983); and J. Esser, 'State, Business and Trade Unions'.
16. J. Esser, 'Symbolic Privatisation: The Politics of Privatisation in West Germany', *West European Politics*, 11/4 (Oct. 1988).
17. Deutscher Industrie und Handelstag, *Bericht 1984* (Bonn, 1984); and *Sachverständigenrat* (1985).
18. Bundesminister für Forschung und Technologie, *Informationstechnik* (Bonn, 1984).
19. Regierungskommission Fernmeldewesen, *Neuordnung der Telekommunikation* (Heidelberg, 1987); Projektgruppe Universität Frankfurt, '*Stück für Stück verkauft': Umbau der Bundespost—Folgen für die Beschäftigten*, ed. Deutsche Postgewerkschaft, Bezirk Hessen (Frankfurt, 1988); Grande, *Vom Monopol zum Wettbewerb?*
20. Jahreswirtschaftsbericht 1992 der Bundesregierung, *BT-Drucksache 12/2018*, 30 Jan. 1992.
21. Esser, 'Symbolic Privatisation'.
22. '*Eine Minute vor zwölf*': Lufthansa-Chef Jürgen Weber über die aktuellen Ergebnisse, seine Privatisierungsstrategie und den Ärger mit den Amerikanern', *Wirtschaftswoche*, 48/11 (11 Mar. 1994).
23. F. McGowan, *The Struggle for Power in Europe: Competition and Regulation in the EC Electricity Industry* (London, 1994).
24. 'Widerstand im Kabinett gegen Rexrodt-Plan', *Süddeutsche Zeitung*, 28 Jan. 1994.
25. 'Monopole unter sich: Großkonzerne drängt es in die Telekommunikation', *Wirtschaftswoche*, 48/12 (18 Mar. 1994).
26. G. Lehmbruch, 'Die improvisierte Vereinigung: Die dritte deutsche Republik', *Leviathan*, 18 (1990).
27. Ibid., p. 463.
28. G. Sinn and H. W. Sinn, *Kaltstart Volkswirtschaftliche Aspekte der deutschen Vereinigung*, Tübingen, Mohr, 1992; U. Voskamp and V. Wittke, 'Aus Modernisierungsblockaden werden Abwärtsspiralen— zur Reorganisation von Betrieben und Kombinaten der ehemaligen DDR', *in Berliner Journal für Soziologie*, 1, no. 1 (1991).
29. D. Kampe, *Wer uns kennenlernt gewinnt uns lieb. Nachruf auf die Treuhand*, Berlin, Rotbuch, 1993.

30. *Sachverständigenrat zur Begutachtung der gesamtwirtschaftlichen Entwicklung, Jahresgutachten 1993/1994*, Deutscher Bundestag 12, Wahlperiode, Drucksache 12/6170 (Bonn, 1993).

31. Esser, 'State, Business and Trade Unions'.

32. *Sachverständigenrat*, 1993, pp. 86 ff.; *Frankfurter Rundschau*, 10 Jan. 94.

3

Britain: The Spectator State

WYN GRANT

Of the countries studied in this book, Britain is the one in which the transition from the old conception of a 'national champion' to that of the international firm has gone furthest. In part, this reflects the fact that rather than developing *grands projets*, or seeking to influence the structures and strategies of powerful industrial actors, government involvement with national champions in Britain came in the form of lame ducks which brought with them new political problems rather than opening up economic opportunities. National champions were acquired because their collapse would be economically and politically too costly (British Leyland); or they were developed as rather low-key efforts to create a British presence in technologically significant sectors which not surprisingly failed to fulfil the hopes placed in them (ICL, Inmos). The few *grands projets* that were attempted, e.g. Concorde or the Wilson government's aluminium smelter projects, were seen as offering examples of what should be avoided, and reinforced tendencies towards a more re-active industrial policy. This ultimately led to the emphasis on privatization and deregulation, given that no government-led industrial strategy seemed to be feasible. This lack of confidence in domestic solutions is reflected in the continued promotion of inward investment policies which seek to encourage the entry in particular of Japanese firms to compensate for and correct inadequacies in British management.

It should be emphasized that it is not being argued that Britain should have attempted to pursue 'national champion' policies. Such policies embody implicit 'think big' assumptions. They come from an era when economies of scale were emphasized, and diseconomies of scale little emphasized. They belong to a Fordist age of mass production and mass consumption, before the application of computer technology in manufacturing transformed the production process, and before more affluent consumers increased the opportunities to serve niche markets with high value added products. The 'national champion' seems like a dinosaur from another age when Soviet economic planning was at least in the back of some analysts' minds as having something to offer (the classic and disastrous example of this is the Muldoon 'think big' strategy in New Zealand). Advocates of national champion policies confused the effect of success with its cause. As Kay notes, 'the larger relative size of American and Japanese companies in many sectors . . . is the *result* of their greater success, not the *cause* of it . . . the evidence does not exist that there are unexploited scale economies in many sectors of European industry'.[1]

One of the fundamental problems with 'national champion' strategies is that they create an imbalance of information and expertise between government and the firms with national champion status. This enables the firms to exploit the imbalance of knowledge by demanding levels of assistance which are not really justified, but which government has no effective means of checking. These difficulties are particularly acute in a system of governance such as that of Britain where generalist civil servants run industry divisions, and where there is little interchange of personnel between government and industry. For example, Abromeit's work shows that this was a serious problem in the case of the steel industry.[2]

1. THE MAJOR ACTORS

Given that British government's role in relation to industry has often been that of a 'spectator' or 'auxiliary' state, exposing British firms to greater international competition and encouraging them to develop an international orientation (a policy that goes back to the formation of ICI in the 1920s), the government apex of the triangle of institutional relations is less important in Britain than it has been in other countries. The principal ministry dealing with industry in Britain, currently the Department of Trade and Industry, has been through a succession of internal and external reorganizations, often dictated by political expediency (e.g. limiting the responsibilities of

Tony Benn) as much as by any sense of what the role of such a ministry ought to be.

At the beginning of the 1990s, the DTI had at its head a minister, Michael Heseltine, who believed that there was a role for an industry ministry, and thought more systematically than most of his predecessors about what the role of such a ministry ought to be. He was, however, severely limited in what he could achieve by both the general assumptions of government about its proper role in the economy, and the constraints placed on public expenditure. Whenever the DTI takes a serious interest in questions of industrial strategy, one can be sure that the Treasury will wish to become involved in questions of industrial policy. Thus, when industrial policy moved to the centre of the political agenda in the 1970s, the view quickly developed in the central finance ministry that 'industrial policy would be safer in Treasury hands'.[3] Even when government is performing its more familiar roles of a spectator or undertaker, it is the Treasury that has a determining influence, in conjunction with the central bank, on such key economic policies as exchange rate and interest rate policy which shape the conditions under which firms have to operate and make their strategic decisions.

The policy triangle should really have the financial institutions at its apex in the British case. London is one of the great three financial sectors of the world, and the financial services sector exerts considerable economic and political influence within Britain. The received conventional wisdom is that this has been harmful to manufacturing industry. It is argued that the lack of close bank–industry links on the German model means that the financial sector lacks an understanding of the problems and needs of industry. There is an active stock exchange dominated by institutional investors who are interested in short-term portfolio management. Companies are judged in terms of their dividend performance and other short-term indicators. Financial institutions do not intervene to correct the problems of companies exhibiting poor performance, but tolerate an actively hostile takeover market as the preferred solution to such problems. One consequence of these arrangements has been that 'the relative cost of capital for long-term R&D projects has been about 60 per cent higher in the UK than in Germany'.[4]

The real losers from these arrangements are small and medium-sized firms reliant on overdraft finance and oriented to the domestic market. Large firms fund most of their investment out of retained profits and have their own treasury departments who can select between a variety of products offered by the financial sector. Their boards often include non-executive directors whose career experience has been in the financial sector, for example directors of clearing banks. These links, and the role of London as an international financial centre, make it easier for those firms who wish to internationalize to do so. The side of the triangle linking industrial firms and financial institutions is better developed in Britain than is often assumed to be the case, but it is developed in a way that suits the objectives of large firms with global ambitions.

Our theoretical understanding of the firm as an actor is poorly developed. A variety of insights are available from economics, economic history, business history, organization theory, business studies, and even political science, but the task of integrating these insights into a political economy of the firm has scarcely begun. Pending the commencement of this task, one or two useful general statements can be made about large British firms. First, they are generally internationally oriented or, if they have not been in the past, are becoming so. Second, they are usually more well disposed to the process of European integration, and in particular to economic and monetary union, than the British Government. Such a stance is consistent with their international orientation. Third, they are acquisitive, often preferring to expand their geographical base of operations through the purchase of existing companies rather than the construction of their own plants. This behaviour is consistent with their domestic experience of an active takeover market; forming an international acquisitions team is an obvious step for large British firms. Fourth, they are politically sophisticated, being far more advanced than, for example, German firms in the development of their own high-quality government relations functions. This reflects their experience of a 'company state' in which intermediary organizations between business and government have generally been weak.

Some large firms, the privatized public utilities, are subject to regulation by specialized public agencies such as OFGAS and OFTEL. Some firms, notably British Gas and British Telecom, consider that the regulatory regime is so severe that it constrains their freedom of operation to such an extent that many of the advantages of privatization in terms of management autonomy are lost. The broader issue here is the displacement of a notion of public interest defined in terms of some set of economic or social goals by an emphasis on championing the rights of consumers rather than producers. Consider, for example, the electricity industry. The original objectives of the nationalized industry centred around the concept of security of supply, which meant maintaining capacity which was used infrequently in order to ensure that industry had an uninterrupted supply of electricity. Pricing policies followed in the first decade of the industry's history could be said to have underpriced electricity and hence to have subsidized energy-intensive industries. Even when pricing policies were reformed, much of electricity policy was driven by a need to secure a use for the output of the politically sensitive coal industry. Under privatization, major electricity users are complaining that they have been disadvantaged. The political context of regulation ensures that considerable attention is given to the impact of the pricing regime on domestic users, rather than any consideration of the relationship between energy prices and industrial competitiveness.

When the relationship between the major actors in Britain as a whole is examined, what is striking is their relative isolation from one another, and the tenuous nature of the connections between them. The inadequacies of British business associations and the relative weakness and policy shifts of the DTI mean that the relationship between government and industrial firms has been weakly developed and characterized by mutual misunderstandings. The closer relationships between the Ministry of Defence and the defence industries only serve to highlight the general difficulties of the relationship. Although the financial sector and industry are not so far apart as is often assumed, and to some extent share a belief in a strategy of acquisitive internationalization, the nature of their relationship is much more distant and unproductive than those to be found in Germany and Japan. The relationship between government and the financial sector has, if anything, been deteriorating, as the Bank of England has to some extent lost its traditional intermediary role, and a succession of City scandals have increased political pressure for more effective regulation of the financial sector. Indeed, it is interesting that the debate sometimes compares what is perceived to be the relative ineffectiveness of regulatory institutions in the financial services sector with the more vigorous regulation of privatized utilities. There may be a sense in which Britain is moving more in the direction of a 'regulatory state' in which government's role is seen as being to provide consumer champions to check the otherwise unfettered operations of firms oriented towards an international market.

Any study of government–business relations in Britain tends to lead to a mood of scepticism, if not pessimism, and it is too easy to assume that relationships are so flawed that the only option is to rely on outside management expertise to revitalize British industry while British firms scour the world for new markets. Some government interventions have been successful, but they have been of an indirect character. ICI was created with government encouragement out of a fragmented and uncompetitive British chemical industry and has developed into one of the leading world chemical companies, with an impressive record of innovation and product development. No doubt this is in large part because of the internal culture of the company, with a strong emphasis on investment in research and development, combined with an ability to produce unorthodox leaders like Sir John Harvey-Jones at the time they are needed.

Government treated ICI as its 'chosen instrument' in the chemical industry, at least until the 1980s when the relationship broke down amid criticisms by Harvey-Jones of Mrs Thatcher's policies, and a lawsuit brought by ICI against the government (which it won). Before these unhappy times, 'a distinctive feature of ICI was its willingness to accept quasi-public responsibilities'.[5] At the time of the post-war Labour government, one minister commented that it was easier to get co-operation out of the ICI than out of the nationalized electricity industry.[6] For its part, ICI benefited from having a substantial portion of its post-war investment programme funded by government assistance, notably through the regional development programme, although its capital-intensive activities created few jobs. The relationship between government and ICI seems to have been characterized by a mutual trust and understanding which was generally absent in government–industry relations in Britain.

ICI was not unique, as in many ways BP functioned as a 'chosen instrument' rather similar to ICI, despite its half ownership by government for much of the twentieth century. In this case, there was an implicit political bargain between government and the firm. The Admiralty secured a supply of (very) cheap oil for its ships. Government granted favours to BP as its chosen instrument in the oil industry. For example, Harold Wilson recalls in relation to North Sea oil, 'British Petroleum had been given a special position in tapping and marketing, in effect as a chosen instrument on behalf of the British Government'.[7] Both BP and ICI have experienced difficulties in the 1980s and early 1990s, and both have made different responses, ICI splitting into two companies, and BP staging a boardroom revolt against its chief executive after an unpopular attempt at internal reorganization. Both companies are clearly moving away from their status as national enterprises to becoming international firms which happen to have British roots. Even where national enterprises have been successful 'chosen instruments' in the past, this does not offer a model for the future.

2. THE EMERGENCE OF THE GLOBAL FIRM

'National champions' were usually set up to operate in their own domestic market and, where possible, to export. The logic of an increasingly internationalized market demanded, however, that national champions transform themselves into multinational companies. Thus, 'despite its status as a nationalized industry, Thomson has increasingly become a genuinely multinational company, in effect an "international champion"'.[8] For companies that failed in their efforts to internationalize production, such as British Leyland, this was a reflection of, but also aggravated, more fundamental failures. 'The collapse of the Italian deal and the closure of Seneffe [in Belgium] had a quite disastrous effect on Austin Rover's exports volumes.'[9]

'National champions' have, therefore, had to internationalize in order to succeed. However, they may be relatively late players in a process that has been under way for some time. Some existing multinationals have themselves been undergoing an important transformation. They have realized that the logic of economic globalization requires a move away from the 'traditional' home-based model of the multinational company towards a more stateless form. The major features of the traditional model are a large headquarters in the home country with business being conducted in its language; board members and shareholders coming from that country; finance and research and development being located in the home country; branch plants elsewhere carrying out what are essentially assembly-type operations. Global companies have a small headquarters staff which could be located anywhere, provided it is near a major international airport; shareholdings dispersed across a number of countries, with multinational boards; business conducted in English, and accounts denominated in dollars or D-marks; dispersal of research and development and financial control.

Companies such as ICI have deliberately set out to internationalize their boards and shareholdings in an effort to transform themselves into global operations, a change perhaps exemplified by the ICI's case when a board meeting was held for the first time in New York. Companies like ICI, however, remain identifiably British, but that cannot be said of companies like ABB, formed from a merger of the Swedish company ASEA and the Swiss company ABB. The company is highly decentralized, with only one hundred people in the Zurich headquarters. The shares of its two parent companies are traded on stock exchanges in Austria, Denmark, Finland, Sweden, Switzerland, the United Kingdom, and the United States. As constituted in early 1993, its board included three Swiss, three Swedes, two Germans, and one American. It was subsequently reorganized to eliminate country directors with responsibilities for plants in ABB's three main countries of operation, Sweden, Switzerland, and Germany, and the number of Swiss directors was reduced to one. The company's chief executive argued that country directors were sometimes too parochial in their outlook, and that nationality was no longer a relevant criterion for board membership. The new structure had three regional directors for Asia, Europe, and the Americas, reflecting what the company saw as the emergence of three regional trading blocks, and the need for a global player to have a presence in each of them. Its chief executive claimed, 'we have global co-ordination, but we have no national bias. The 100 professionals who happen to sit in Zurich could just as easily sit in Chicago or Frankfurt.'[10] Business is done in English, and the books are kept in dollars. Companies such as ABB do not just regard themselves as responding to changed circumstances, but also as catalysts acting on the change process: 'we do change relations *between* countries. We function as a lubricant for worldwide economic integration.'[11]

Many forces have contributed to economic globalization, such as improved and less expensive rapid means of communication both of information and of persons. Deregulation of financial markets is both a cause and consequence of globalization. Whatever its original causes, the process has now acquired a momentum of its own. There are, of course, still many barriers to a genuinely international economy, ranging from non-tariff trade barriers to differences in national customs and tastes. A shortage of genuinely global managers who can 'sort through the debris of cultural excuses'[12] remains a constraint on the emergence of truly stateless companies. Even so, globalization is now so far advanced that it represents a serious challenge to national policy strategies, and to the domestic policy communities and networks which help to make such strategies effective.

Compared to companies such as ABB and ICI, which have had the autonomy to pursue self-conscious policies of internationalization, many former national enterprises in Britain have had to make relatively late adjustments to an increasingly internationalized economy. Such enterprises were used to responding to domestic policy priorities, and were accustomed to operating in a relatively protected market in which either there was no direct competition, or in which potential competitors faced a variety of entry barriers. It is therefore not surprising that not all national enterprises found the transformation to being an international firm an easy one, and that the results have been mixed. A contrast is drawn here between British Airways, which has made a reasonably successful, if yet incomplete, transition; and British Steel, which has encountered more serious difficulties.

2.1. British Steel Corporation

The post-war history of the British steel industry is so well known that it is necessary only to summarize the highlights (if they can be so termed) here. After an interwar policy based on protection and state-sponsored cartelization, the industry was nationalized by the post-war Labour government as one of the 'commanding heights of the economy'. The 1951 Conservative government de-nationalized the industry, but disposing of the companies to private owners was not straightforward, and one very large company, Richard Thomas and Baldwins, remained in public ownership when Labour returned to office in 1964. The renationalized British Steel Corporation inherited an industry which was technologically backward by international standards and had too many small and outdated plants. Peter Walker took the 'courageous' decision to authorize a major investment programme in the industry, an implicit premiss of which was that many of the older plants would close, and production would be concentrated in a relatively small number of plants. The downturn in demand brought about by a mixture of the world economic crisis and increased import penetration intensified the pressures for rationalization, and the process of retrenchment was begun by the Labour government. The Thatcher government inherited an industry that had been making losses for years. A cut of over a quarter in productive capacity was announced in December 1979. By the late 1980s BSC had returned to profit, allowing the government to prepare it for privatization in 1988.

Steel has been the ultimate symbol of heavy industry, the perfect setting for Stakhanovite feats of production, the epitome of Stalinism. Latter-day Stalinist imitators such as Prime Minister Muldoon in New Zealand have seen steel as a cornerstone of their industrial strategies. Developing countries have seen steel as the first stage on the road to industrialization. Hence, world steel supply has increased at a time when demand has been falling. There has been a long-run structural fall in demand in response to the declining steel intensity of the economy. Other products such as aluminium and engineering plastics have substituted for steel, while those industries that continue to use significant quantities of steel (for example, motor vehicles) have learnt to use it more economically. Those industries which continue to use significant quantities of steel (e.g. construction) are often extremely vulnerable to economic downturns, giving the steel industry a highly cyclical character. Making use of new technology such as electric arc furnaces, using scrap metal as a feedstock, and mini mills have increasingly challenged the old steel producers. They already dominate the market for lower-cost carbon steel mill products in the US, but using a newly developed technology, the thin slab caster, they have started to enter the sheet market, which accounts for 60 per cent of total industry shipments in the US.

Against this background, can a privatized company succeed where a public corporation failed? The privatized company has, of course, certain advantages. It has inherited a slimmed-down industry with relatively modern capital equipment with most of the debt acquired to finance the investment written off.

After a period in the late 1980s when it was seen as a symbol of Britain's industrial resurgence, British Steel's performance in the early 1990s was very disappointing, although understandable against the background of serious overcapacity in the European steel industry of at least 15 to 20 million tonnes even at peak output levels. These problems have been exacerbated by reduced demands for steel from Western Europe in Eastern Europe and the former Soviet Union, and a significant rise in imports from Eastern European producers eager to obtain foreign exchange. In 1991–2 British Steel reported a trading profit of £17 million compared with £323 million in the previous year, which became a loss before taxation of £55 million after charging exceptional items of £100 million largely related to the costs of closing the Ravenscraig plant.

Some of these difficulties are a by-product of a persistent recession, but British Steel also has more fundamental problems. It remains highly dependent on a British market which accounted for 54 per cent of total deliveries in 1991–2, and which is characterized by a weak manufacturing sector, although even in the British market competition drove its market share down from 64 per cent in 1990 to 55 per cent in 1991. British Steel's strategy within Britain is to concentrate production at two sites, Llanwern–Port Talbot in South Wales and Teesside. In this way, it hopes to gain the economies of scale it needs to match its largest continental rivals, Usinor Sacilor in France and Thyssen in Germany. Only Usinor Sacilor had a larger output among European companies in 1990 (16.5 million tonnes for Usinor Sacilor against 13.0 million tonnes for British Steel).

British Steel's main strategic response to its weaknesses is, however, to internationalize to overcome its dependence on the British market. The limits to the success of this strategy are emphasized by the fact that 52 per cent of turnover by destination was to the UK market in 1991–2, with 31 per cent being obtained from the rest of the EC. Indeed, the internationalization strategy has encountered a number of obstacles. A joint venture plan with Bethlehem Steel of the US, under which British Steel would take over and reorganize the US group's subsidiaries which make structural and rail steels, foundered in the face of opposition from the United Steelworkers' union. In Europe, British Steel has concentrated its acquisition efforts on Germany. British Steel denied that it had made a bid for Hoesch, acquired by Krupp in 1991, although it admitted that there were talks about collaboration. British Steel did succeed in purchasing the Troisdorf works from Klöckner, as well as a flat products service centre (Degels GmbH), but has been less successful in efforts to move into the new German Länder.

In some respects British Steel is as much constrained by its shareholders as it was by government. Because of their near monopoly of much of the relevant information, BSC was often able to run rings round the generalist civil servants supervising it from the sponsorship division. Abromeit concluded from her study of British Steel that there was 'a definite superiority of the nationalized industries' managements over the supposed controllers, who lack real power'.[13]

One of the fundamental problems that British Steel faces is that it is perceived as a yield stock (high income unit trusts, for example, often have significant holdings). 'It takes courage to disrupt the dividend flow when that would undermine the whole rationale for investors.'[14] British Steel continued to pay dividends against a background of losses in 1991/2. 'This reflects the continuing intention to seek to provide shareholders with a flow of income and to use the financial resources of the Company to support dividend payments during this recession.'[15] 'In the longer term, however, there can never be any real sense in paying dividends out of capital unless the objective is to wind down the business.'[16]

Shareholders' perceptions of what the company's priorities ought to be are also affecting its internationalization plans. The chief executive in 1991, Sir Robert Scholey, indirectly blamed British Steel's shareholders for the company's failure to move into East Germany. He noted that 'British Steel cannot do what it wants'. Its institutional shareholders were unhappy if profits failed to appear and share prices fell. 'Life would be easier if we had Deutsche Bank behind us.'[17] Although it was noted earlier that the financial sector in Britain was generally favourable to internationalization strategies, this depends on its assessment of the likely success of a particular company's strategy succeeding in terms of maintaining profits and dividends.

That is not to say that privatization has not made any difference. The decision to close Ravenscraig, built as part of a national industrial strategy, would have been very difficult to implement if British Steel had still been publicly owned. Although a number of decisions made by British Steel—such as the closure of the Clydesdale steel works—undermined Ravenscraig's viability, it is difficult to see how it could have survived in an integrated European steel market characterized by a combination of over-capacity and price competition.

If the steel industry still has national champion status, it is in Scotland, where an attachment to heavy industry as the core of a successful economy remains, even though an independent Scotland might hope to base its future on such sectors as electronics, food processing, and financial services. Within the UK as a whole, steel has moved from centre stage as a political issue, and there is a sense in which BP, which had a more distant relationship with government, is still perceived as more of a national champion than British Steel.

2.2. British Airways

Governments across the world have had a substantial involvement in their civilian airlines. The symbolic importance of a national 'flag carrier' is illustrated by the fact that one of the first actions of a new state is often to set up its own airline, as in the case of Croatia. In Europe, most national 'flag carriers' have either been publicly owned or have had substantial state shareholdings. Britain's leading airline was publicly owned until British Airways was privatized in 1987.

The performance of British Airways before privatization was less than satisfactory. It often gave the impression of a business oper-ated for the benefit of its staff, with customers being regarded as an unfortunate nuisance. Up to the early 1980s, BA was 'not a good performer' when compared to other international airlines.[18] 'Up to 1980–1, BA's costs were significantly higher than they need have been. Better management, better utilization of inputs and less politi-cal pressure could have resulted in costs being lower.'[19] The most significant improvement in performance actually occurred before privatization, after Lord King became chairman in 1981 and assembled a new management team.

An essential component of the strategy of the privatized BA has been to develop into a global airline. Indeed, it ranks first among world airlines in terms of scheduled passengers carried, although eighth in total size. Although BA is no longer formally a national enterprise, it is often treated as such in practice, although it considers it has faced 'considerable and sustained opposition from various sources principally representing vested interests'.[20] More competitors have been allowed to operate into its home base at London Heathrow, with the number of carriers using the airport growing by 17 to 87 in 1991. However, enough of the bilateral route agreements survive to give it a virtual operating monopoly on a number of international routes, or at least to share such routes with other national airlines. 'BA now operates in a relatively protected world, the result of Britain's cozy air treaty with the US. That has helped make transatlantic routes provide 50 per cent to 75 per cent of BA's total profits.'[21] This means that BA has been able to approach its globalization strategy with a measure of caution. 'Although we remain committed to the concept of a global airline, and while we believe our long-term future may be bound up with world-wide alliances, we are in a position of strength which many would envy. We will not act in haste and repent in leisure.'[22]

BA has faced many frustrations in its attempts to build a global airline. For all the emphasis on deregulation in the civil aviation industry and on an 'open skies' policy, many barriers to market entry remain, not least control of airport landing slots and gates. 'Governments are closely involved with the allocation of routes, the licensing of airlines, the setting of fares and airports policy ... moves towards liberalization are being made in many countries, but progress is slow and patchy.'[23] Many countries place restrictions on the ownership of domestic airlines by foreign companies: there is a 25 per cent limit in the United States. In Germany, a consortium of banks own 51 per cent of Deutsche BA so that it qualifies as a German airline. Foreign airlines cannot provide domestic services between American cities.

The US air travel market accounts for around 40 per cent of global air traffic. Access to this market is therefore vitally important for an airline following a global strategy. An alliance between BA and United Airlines of the US collapsed in 1989. A proposal to set up a joint venture airline to be known as Sabena World Airlines, with partners Sabena and KLM, was abandoned in early 1991. Merger talks between BA and KLM broke down in 1992 over the issue of the size of the share each company would have in the merged airline. BA did obtain a 24.6 per cent stake in USAir Group Inc., the fourth largest airline in passenger number terms in the United States. Three BA representatives sit on the USAir board. Unlike the alliance with United, the arrangement with USAir does not give BA significant access to the important Pacific Coast market. The deal does give BA access to the USAir hub in Pittsburgh, with some USAir flights into Pittsburgh sharing coding with transatlantic flights operated by BA. However, the shared coding arrangements which facilitate passenger transfer and hence boost bookings suffered a setback in November 1993 when BA was given permission by the US government to expand its code sharing services by only 60 days compared with the usual 12 months. Sixty days is considered to be an inadequate basis for airline planning, and the UK aviation minister, Lord Caithness, described the decision as a 'provocative act quite contrary to our agreement with the US'.[24] The British government gave notice that it would withdraw permission for two American flights a week to use Heathrow unless BA's code sharing agreement was renewed before January 1994.

BA has made some progress towards its goal of becoming an international airline. It has acquired 25 per cent of the Australian flag carrier, Qantas, with the remaining shares to be sold to the public. This deal does not, however, give BA any significant share in the major and growing North Pacific market which remains a significant gap in its global strategy. Forty-six per cent of its turnover by original sale in 1993 was still in the UK, emphasizing that, as Lord King has stated, 'the catchment area for BA is this little island'.[25] In terms of staff location, BA still looks very much like a British rather than an international company, with 87 per cent of its staff in 1992 employed in the UK. According to the Chairman, Sir Colin Marshall, BA's vision of the future remains one of a globalized industry, evolving in a similar way to many other industries with 'relatively few very large global partnerships, with a strong presence in all of the key markets, and many, much smaller airlines operating in specific geographic or market segments'.[26]

3. CONCLUSIONS

The policy of the British government towards economic globalization in the 1980s and 1990s can been characterized as one of 'welcome'. A neo-liberal 'spectator state' has exposed businesses to the international market. Privatization has enabled former 'national champions' oriented to the domestic market to follow strategies of internationalization, although these have been more successful in some cases than in others. What is clear is that domestically oriented policy communities based on a stable set of relationships favouring particular domestic actors, notably equipment suppliers, have broken down. For example, in the electricity industry:

The generating boards, distribution boards, the coal industry, and the power plant construction industry formed self-contained, yet overlapping, circles of influence within the overall ESI policy sector. The strong links between these groups created a powerful interest in the status quo, while new technologies or ideas which threatened the interests of those within, such as renewable generating technologies . . . remained out in the cold.[27]

Such well-integrated policy networks do not disappear overnight. In the case of the electricity industry, the need to preserve some kind of market for British coal to facilitate the privatization of the industry did have some influence on the conduct of policy after privatization, although not enough to save the coal mining industry from drastic rationalization. Some of the 'outsiders' remain relatively weak actors. The Combined Heat and Power Association has received financial assistance from the DTI to develop its EC level activities, and is working with the European Commission to develop an EC-level organization. Even so, the potential of privatization to transform relationships is illustrated by the case of telecommunications, where a 'club' of equipment suppliers kept out new entrants.[28]

As well as having the effect of breaking up established policy communities, and exposing industry to international competition, government policy has also placed a considerable emphasis on attracting Japanese inward investment to Britain. Thirty-nine per cent of Japanese direct investment in the EC in the post-war period has gone to Britain.[29] In motor vehicles in particular, it has been evident for some time that 'Britain's role in the international motor vehicle industry could be that of the major European production platform for Japanese cars'.[30] Oliver and Wilkinson go so far as to suggest that 'British industry is undergoing a fundamental transformation, the nature of which is neatly captured by the term "Japanization"'.[31] They argue that this 'is not simply a matter of implementing total quality control and just-in-time (JIT) production processes—it entails the adoption of particular work practices and personnel and industrial relations systems as well'.[32] Work undertaken by Cardiff Business School at automotive component plants suggests that there has been some successful adoption in Britain of Japanese practices in terms of team working, production organization, and lean supply chains. It was found that 'some UK suppliers are achieving impressive levels of productivity with disappointing quality . . . and others high levels of quality with relatively low productivity. None of our UK sample achieves both at the same time.'[33] A more sceptical report conducted for the Department of Employment by Industrial Relations Services argues that Japanese working practices produce resentment among workers which could lead to future industrial relations problems. The report found 'little evidence that Japanese-style international competitiveness can be achieved in Britain by copying some, or even most, Japanese working methods'.[34]

The notion of Britain offering an EC manufacturing base with an enterprise economy, open markets, and low tax rates is now being extended to other Far Eastern countries. The Invest in Britain Bureau 'has focused on the economically significant Asian neighbours of Japan, the "Four Dragons"—Singapore, Korea, Taiwan, Hong Kong'.[35] This does not mean, of course, that more traditional sources of inward investment have been neglected. The US remained the major provider of inward investment projects and jobs in the early 1990s; Britain has been the destination of 37.5 per cent of all US inward investment in EC countries in the period from 1951 to 1990. Britain was also the principal destination for German foreign direct investment in 1990.[36]

Although Britain's inward investment promotion efforts emphasize its attractions as a manufacturing base within the EC, Britain has not been an enthusiastic proponent of the integration process beyond the creation of an internal market. The European Commission and leading member states such as France, Germany, and Italy have been seen as unduly influenced by notions of social partnership which could undermine Britain's commitment to a deregulated economy and reintroduce corporatism through the back door. If one regards state aid to industry as one of the products of corporatism, there is some support for that view:

in 1981 of the big four economies, Germany, UK, and France all gave approximately the same aid to manufacturing . . . with Italy much higher. By 1988 the divergences had become greater. The UK was clearly the lowest (3.2 billion ECU) followed by France (4.7 billion ECU), i.e. the underlying trend for both is well below the 1981 figure allowing for inflation. Germany had climbed steadily to 7.8 billion ECU . . . Italy stood at 9.8 billion ECU in 1988, i.e. around three times the level in the UK.[37]

In so far as the Community pursues a vigorous competition policy and attempts to reduce state aids, its actions are compatible with the policy perspective of the British Government. In practice, however, the application of the state aids policy often depends on a political bargain within the college of commissioners, while even a vigorous competition policy may be less welcome if it threatens the interests of British firms. The one *grand projet* that promotes European integration and that has been supported by the British Government, the Channel Tunnel, has been approached in terms of private sector funding. It should also be noted that large-scale infrastructure work of this kind has been a key policy concern of the Round Table of leading European industrialists.

The EC is only a regional structure within a global economy, and a central theme of this chapter has been the development and importance of the global firm. Some firms may even be assuming a stateless character, although Hu argues that 'global companies are far from being international, multinational or transnational when it comes to their locus of ownership and control'.[38] What is clear is that firms like ICI have embarked on a deliberate strategy of internationalization which reduces their dependence on their home base. Chemicals is a sector in which internationalization has been relatively advanced throughout the twentieth century. 'Trends in the internationalization of industrial activities are not uniform but tend to vary by industrial sector.'[39]

In a phase of internationalization in which the development and application of new production technologies is of key importance in securing competitive advantage, 'companies now interact on a global scale through a wide range of external alliances—e.g. joint ventures, subcontracting, licensing, and interfirm arrangements'.

The OECD forecasts that joint ventures 'will be a popular choice for multinational firms in the 1990s . . . Joint ventures allow more rapid market access than exports and have lower costs than foreign investment.'[40] Joint ventures provide many of the advantages of merger without its disadvantages. A company does not lose its identity or its control of its assets, but is able to benefit from pooling those assets with others. It is possible to be involved in a large number of joint ventures simultaneously covering different markets and products. Such special-purpose arrangements can help manufacturers to fill gaps in their market coverage and seek manufacturing cost efficiencies. New forms of external competition can encourage joint ventures. According to information provided by a major motor vehicle manufacturer, the emergence of Japan as a leading car producer 'has irreversibly shifted the "balance of power" and joint ventures between competitors that were unthinkable a decade ago are expanding yearly'. The motor industry has become 'a global village with a spider's web of collaborative arrangements'.[41]

Where do such developments leave the nation state? For a spectator state such as Britain, they represent the logic of market forces. The role of the state then becomes to encourage leading British firms to internationalize, to ensure that barriers to their global operation are reduced as much as possible, and to offset the deficiencies of the domestic economy by encouraging inward investment. The one role of the state that has grown in the 1980s and 1990s is that of regulation, reflecting a shift from the protection of producer interests in public sector enterprises to safeguarding domestic consumers under privatization. Regulation may yet be further strengthened in the financial services sector, as the limits of self-regulation become more apparent.

The most difficult agenda item for nation states in the 1990s is how can a globalized economy be matched by adequate political structures that can control any self-destructive financial crisis, and also provide some minimal degree of protection for consumers and workers? In so far as there are effective political structures above the nation state, they seem to be developing at a regional level, notably the very mixed success represented by the European Community, but also regional trading blocs such as that in North America. Yet 'most corporate decisions are taken within a global frame of reference and are based on diverse relationships between multinational firms.'[42] To match this complexity, and to be able to influence it, what is needed is not a revival of the heroic entrepreneurial state of the early post-war years, but the further development of effective regulatory co-operation at an international level to match the integrative efforts of firms and the consequences of financial globalization.

Notes

1. J. Kay, *1992: Myths and Realities* (London, 1989), 26–7.
2. H. Abromeit, *British Steel* (Leamington, 1986).
3. E. Dell, *A Hard Pounding: Politics and Economic Crisis 1974–76* (Oxford, 1991), 90.
4. N. Crafts, 'Reversing Relative Economic Decline? The 1980s in Historical Perspective', *Oxford Review of Economic Policy*, 7 (1991), 81–98, 94.
5. J. Turner, 'The Politics of Business', in J. Turner (ed.), *Businessmen and Politics* (London, 1984), 1–19, 12.
6. P. M. Williams, *Hugh Gaitskell* (Oxford, 1982), 133.
7. H. Wilson, *Final Term* (London, 1979), 217.
8. A. Cawson, K. Morgan, D. Webber, P. Holmes, and A. Stevens, *Hostile Brothers: Competition and Closure in the European Electronics Industry* (Oxford, 1990), 263.
9. K. Williams, C. Williams, and J. Haslam, *The Breakdown of Austin Rover* (Leamington, 1987), 85.
10. W. Taylor, 'The Logic of Global Business', *Harvard Business Review*, Mar.–Apr. 1991, 91–105, 105.
11. Ibid.
12. Ibid. 94.
13. Abromeit, *British Steel*, 292.
14. *Financial Times*, 12 Nov. 1991.
15. *British Steel Report and Accounts 1991/2*, 3.
16. *Financial Times*, 12 Nov. 1991.
17. *Financial Times*, 28/29 Dec. 1991.
18. M. Ashworth and P. Forsyth, *Civil Aviation Policy and the Privatisation of British Airways* (London, 1984), 46.
19. Ibid. 49.
20. *British Airways Annual Report and Accounts, 1992/3*, 2.
21. *Business Week*, 24 Aug. 1992.
22. *British Airways Annual Report and Accounts, 1991/2*, 2.

23. J. Vickers and G. Yarrow, *Privatization: An Economic Analysis* (Cambridge, Mass., 1988), 344.
24. *Financial Times*, 18 Nov. 1993.
25. *Financial Times*, 22 July 1992.
26. *British Airways Annual Report and Accounts, 1992–3*, 2.
27. J. Roberts, D. Elliott, and T. Houghton, *Privatising Electricity: The Politics of Power* (London, 1991), 43–4.
28. Cawson *et al.*, *Hostile Brothers*, 114.
29. *Invest in Britain Bureau Annual Report 1991–2*, 10.
30. W. Grant, *The Political Economy of Industrial Policy* (London, 1982), 96.
31. N. Oliver and J. Wilkinson, *The Japanization of British Industry* (Oxford, 1988), 2.
32. Ibid. 4.
33. Andersen Consulting, *The Lean Enterprise Benchmarking Project* (London, 1993), 19.
34. *Financial Times*, 19 July 1993.
35. *Invest in Britain Bureau Annual Report, 1991/2*, 8.
36. Figures from *Invest in Britain Bureau Annual Report, 1991/2*.
37. Commission of the European Communities, *Second Survey of State Aide in the European Community in the Manufacturing and Certain Other Sectors* (Luxembourg, 1993), 16.
38. Y.-S. Hu, 'Global or Stateless Corporations are National Firms with International Operations', *California Management Review*, 34 (1992), 107–26, 114.
39. Organization for Economic Co-operation and Development, *Globalisation of Industrial Activities* (Paris, 1992), 12.
40. Ibid. 14.
41. *Financial Times*, 13 Sept. 1991.
42. OECD, *Globalisation of Industrial Activities*, 12.

4

Italy: The Crisis of
an Introvert State

PATRIZIO BIANCHI

1. NATIONAL ENTERPRISES AND ECONOMIC INTEGRATION

The term 'National Enterprise' refers to companies which operate at the global level but have strong roots in the national society; it might also be argued that they are companies which are fully integrated in the global economy but have a special duty to defend specific national interests. This definition assumes that the economy is globalized but the polity is still fragmented among nation states.

In a closed economy, the state is supposed to control market forces by imposing institutional barriers to entry and controlling concentration among domestic firms. Public intervention protects domestic firms against international competitors, which can be assumed to be more efficient, and regulates to prevent monopolization of the market, to protect consumer interest and to avoid the establishment of an economic power capable of dominating the government itself. In a fully open economy, firms are supposed to be free to move, without any institutional constraint, in order to locate their activity according to relative cost advantages. In this case, the nation state does not control either barriers to entry or the concentration of the domestic market, and the market is supposed to be self-regulating. Institutional constraints are ineffective and nation states lose the legitimation which results from representing collective interests. In a closed economy, the market is restricted to the extent of the state's sovereignty; in an open economy, the market is globalized and the nation states' sovereignty is dissolved. In both cases, economy and polity tend to coincide.

The transitional case, such as currently obtains in Central and East Europe, moving from a closed economy to an open economy,

is quite different. The nation state is still relevant but firms rooted
in its history and institutional context have to compete in both the
domestic and foreign markets with firms flying other flags. Thus,
when countries tend to open their economy to international trade,
competition among companies also involves conflict among states.
If we assume that firms operating in different states have different
efficiency rates, the process of economic integration alters not only
the power relations among firms but also the power relations
among states. Therefore, the process of opening up the market has
been carefully regulated by the governments of countries having
weaker firms in order to avoid the collapse of the national
economy. The sudden opening of a market could drastically reduce
the internal price to the international level. We assume this to be
lower because domestic producers who have been protected for
many years are less efficient than the international market leaders.
Domestic prices become more favourable to consumers but domestic producers are ruined.

Until the Single Act came into effect, the EC had been essentially
a customs union in which governments collectively guided the
process of internal opening of the economy by promoting adjustments in their own national productive structures relative to those
of the partner countries. With the Single Act, a process of integration was relaunched which reversed traditional procedures of
institutional harmonization, necessary to guarantee the transition
towards an economic union, by giving priority to competition.
Public institutions no longer confine themselves to protecting specific interests but also have the role of defining policy in the larger
market, so that a close interrelation among public and private
institutions becomes the principal condition for having firms which
are strongly rooted in a local context but are able to act in a global
market.

In this new context, the position of Italy is particularly difficult.
Italy has had an extremely rigid public institutional structure
incapable of managing the adjustments of a productive system
characterized by a strong public presence in industrial activities, a
small number of large firms which are strictly family-owned, highly
fragmented industry, the complete separation between banks and
firms, limited financial market activity, and finally increasing per-
meation by political parties of all the industrial and financial activities of the country.

2. ITALIAN NATIONAL CHAMPIONS

Today, Italian industry is still characterized by a few large national enterprises, of comparable size to the international leaders. A growing literature has noted the positive role of the industrial network of Italian small and medium-sized firms. Nevertheless, Italy has only a few national leaders listed among the 500 largest industrial corporations in the world.[1] The US still has the largest number of companies in the list (164), followed by Japan (111). The EC as a whole has 130 companies, and by adding the EFTA companies the European firms total 169. Nevertheless, European countries have a very different industrial structure. Britain has 43 large national companies: 14 super corporations (companies ranked among the 200 largest corporations) and 29 large companies. France has 12 and 18, Germany hosts 21 and 9 super and large corporations. Italy has only 6 super corporations and one large enterprise. (See Table 4.1.)

TABLE 4.1. *The Italian companies listed among the 500 largest industrial corporations in the world (1990 sales in US$ millions)*

A	B	C	D	E	F	G	H	I
7	11	IRI	61,433	419	2	Metal	1	1
13	15	Fiat G	47,751	303	9	Motor V.	5	2
18	28	ENI	41,762	130	41	Oil ref.	5	3
85	85	Ferruzzi	13,972	44	165	Food	7	3
165	170	Pirelli	8,463	68	101	Rubber Pr.	4	2
179	198	Olivetti	7,549	(4)	na	Computers	7	1
359	350	EFIM	3,800	(37)	na	Metal	32	13

A: rank 1990
B: rank 1989
C: corporation
D: sales 1990 in US$ millions
E: employees (thousands)
F: rank employees 1990
G: main sector of activity
H: rank in the world industry
I: rank in the EEC industry

Source: *Fortune*, 29 July 1991.

These super corporations are as follows:

IRI (Istituto per la Riconversione Industriale), a publicly owned financial holding company, controls industrial enterprises in some heavy industries (such as steel, plant engineering, railway and underground transport systems, shipbuilding); other industries such as electronics, data processing and software production, aerospace, food processing and distribution as well as the companies supplying network services (telephone and telecommunication, radio and TV broadcasting, air transport, ship transport, motorway construction and management). This conglomerate also owns three of the largest Italian banks. In terms of sales, IRI jumped to seventh largest in 1990 from eleventh in 1989, and in terms of employment IRI is the second largest industrial holding company in the world. After a long period of losses, IRI made a profit in 1989, but went badly into debt in the early 1990s owing to political interference. It concentrates its activities in Italy, essentially because it has been considered by the government and by parliament to be an instrument for creating employment and industrial activity within the country. In 1993 IRI started a new stage of internal reorganization, based on the privatization of banks, and public utilities and the dismantling of collapsing activities, such as the firms involved in steel production.

FIAT (Fabbrica Italiana Automobile Torino) Group is an enterprise controlled by the Agnelli family. FIAT Group is the fifth largest company in the motor vehicles industry world-wide and the second in Europe, but it also operates in the aerospace and weapons production sectors, in telecommunication, in electronics, food and beverage production, newspapers, and insurance. In the 1980s, the Fiat Group developed a strategy of diversification, especially allied with French groups, although an attempt to enter the beverage sector in France was blocked by the French market leaders. FIAT has since concentrated upon automobile production, launching a new model produced entirely in a new plant in southern Italy. To sustain the huge investment plan, FIAT launched a recapitalization programme. For the first time in its history, the Agnelli family shared its control with other partners, Alcatel, Deutsche Bank, Mediobanca.

ENI (Ente Nazionale Idrocarburi) is a publicly owned enterprise operating oil refining and distribution and basic chemical production. The group is quite profitable, listed as fifth largest in the world and third in Europe in its sector. ENI holds a monopoly position in gas distribution and a very dominant position in oil refining and distribution in Italy. In 1989 ENI and Montedison (owned since 1989 by the Ferruzzi family) started a joint venture to create a national champion in the chemical sector; this joint venture failed and ENI acquired the control of ENIMONT (now ENICHEM), which is the largest chemical producer in Italy. The management of this joint venture was investigated because of a huge bribe to induce the government to dissolve the agreement. The dramatic suicide of the Chief Executive of the group and the imprisonment of most of its top managers involved in the Tangentopoli affair, induced the government to replace the management of the group; ENI is running a massive privatization plan, to concentrate group activity on the oil and gas refining core.

Ferruzzi, ranked at 85, is a family group, traditionally working in the grain trade. Ferruzzi enjoyed spectacular growth in the 1980s. It became the European leader in some food processing and agriculture sectors through acquisitions and join ventures. In 1990, after its unsuccessful joint venture with ENI, it sold its basic chemical production to the state but retained the innovative plastics production (Himont). Ferruzzi runs its industrial activities at the international level both directly and allied especially with French groups. Prior to its 1993 financial collapse, it was listed at 7 in the world and 3 in Europe in its sector. The group collapsed in July 1993 and its family management was tried for corruption. The previous Chief Executive—Gardini—who led Ferruzzi to the position of second largest private group in Italy, committed suicide in the summer of 1993. At present, the group is run by managers, appointed by banks, under the supervision of the court.

Pirelli is a family-owned company and a national leader in rubber and tyre production; it is listed fourth largest in the world and second in Europe in the sector. After Pirelli failed to take over Continental in Germany, the old family leader, Leopoldo Pirelli, left control to new management.

Olivetti is controlled by the De Benedetti family. It is seventh largest in computer production on the global market and it is listed by *Fortune* as first in Europe. The De Benedetti Group also operates in industrial equipment (tobacco and food processing machinery) and in newspapers. The group has tried a wide strategy of financial diversification, by entering into the food processing industry, motor vehicle parts and component production, publishing houses. Most of these attempts were not successful and the group is refocusing its activities on its core business. At the international level De Benedetti has a wide network of industrial and financial alliances. It failed to take over the Belgian SGB Bank.

New leaders emerged in 1980s, such as Berlusconi (television, advertising, publishing, building and real estate, supermarkets) and Benetton (clothing and footwear production and distribution) but they are still not ranked among the largest global corporations. The Berlusconi group enjoyed very rapid growth in the late 1980s, expanding its business from television to advertising agencies, from publishing houses to retailing. Berlusconi was closely connected with the Socialist Party, but after the collapse of this party, he became a leader of right-wing coalitions. He has invested abroad through his television and advertising network. He has incurred huge debts and the group is considered very fragile. This contributed to his entering the electoral arena at the head of a new party, Forza Italia, which formed the spearhead of the right-wing alliance that won the 1994 general election, with the result that Berlusconi became Prime Minister.

The dominant role played by the largest public and private groups in the Italian market is even more evident if we consider the 25 largest industrial firms based in Italy. Table 4.2 shows that apart from those controlled by foreign firms, they are often subsidiaries of the 'Big Six'.

3. INTERNATIONALIZATION AND CORPORATE GROWTH

So Italy's large industrial groups, owned either by the state or by families, are concentrated in a few specific sectors. The recent process of diversification, both in products and markets, having been largely unsuccessful, most of these groups have concentrated their activities on their traditional core business. Nevertheless, since the late 1980s, the major Italian groups have attempted to gain control of big European firms. Except in the case of Ferruzzi, which operated in France through a solid network of local alliances, all

TABLE 4.2. *The twenty-five largest firms based in Italy in 1990 (sales in LIT billions)*

	Firm	Sector	Parent company	Sales
1	Fiat auto	Motor V.	Fiat	22.938
2	SIP	Telecom.	IRI	16.718
3	AGIP P	Oil D.	ENI	14.151
4	SNAM	Gas	ENI	9.559
5	AGIP	Min.	ENI	8.439
6	IBM	Elect.	for.	7.595
7	ILVA	Met.	IRI	7.313
8	Iveco	Motor V.	Fiat	5.364
9	Esso	Oil D.	for.	5.315
10	IP	Oil D.	ENI	4.999
11	Alitalia	Transport	IRI	4.434
12	Alenia	Aersp.	IRI	3.677
13	Praoil	Oil D.	ENI	3.622
14	Autog. VW	Motor D.	for.	3.598
15	Montedipe	Chem.	ENI	3.267
16	Rinascente	Distr.	Fiat	3.046
17	UNIL+IT	Chem.	for.	3.000
18	RAI	Telecom.	IRI	2.993
19	Standa	Distrib.	Ferr (Berlusc.)	2.623
20	Ford IT	Motor D.	for.	2.538
21	Olivetti	Electr.	De Benedetti	2.496
22	Publit.	Advert.	Berlusconi	2.483
23	Tamoil	Oil D.	for.	2.302
24	Renault	Motor D.	for.	2.167
25	ISAB	Oil D.	for.	2.101

for. = foreign

Source: Mediobanca, Le principali società Italiane (Milan, 1991).

the Italian groups have endured notable failures. Let us touch on three cases which illustrate the difficulty large Italian groups have had in their attempts to become European leaders. In all three cases, the national leader Italian firms underestimated the reactions of the takeover 'victims', supported by close relationships with their national financial systems and with the national authorities that supported the resistance to attempted Italian takeovers.

3.1. Olivetti

In 1989 Carlo de Benedetti tried to take over the Société Générale du Belgique (SGB), a financial holding company which controls an important part of Belgium's financial, insurance, and industrial activity. This move on the part of the Italian entrepreneur caused SGB to seek the help of the French Group Suez, which entered the struggle as the 'white knight'. This intervention brought about the rearrangement of the Belgian group under the auspices of the French group and excluded the Italian group.

3.2. Pirelli

In 1991 Pirelli attempted a takeover of the German firm Continental. The merger of the two firms would have created a new European leader in tyre production. Once again, after an initial phase of shareholding penetration by the Italian firm, the management under siege responded by launching a search for financial support. Here, in traditional German banking style, the Deutsche Bank was successful in preventing the Italian group from acquiring Continental.

3.3. FIAT

In 1992 the Agnelli Group, after having had a long alliance in the foodstuffs sector with the French corporation BSN, tried on its own to take control of Exor-Perrier, the leader in the mineral water and beverages sector, as well as being the owner of vast real estate properties. In this case, also, the reaction of the national firms, and above all of BSN itself, enabled Nestlé, with the decisive help of the Suez Group, to acquire the industrial activities of Perrier, causing the retreat of IFI–Agnelli.

The failure of this process of European growth through international takeovers of French, Belgian, and German firms illustrates how a system with only a few big groups, strongly backed by a strictly controlled financial system, is not capable of effectively acting at the international level when the system regulating European oligopoly is still being redefined. These three cases must, above all, be seen in the context of the restructuring process that has involved Italian firms in the past decade. The recent wave of mergers and acquisitions has been essentially devoted to reinforcing Italian medium-sized enterprises on the domestic market, not strengthening national enterprises on the international markets.[2]

TABLE 4.3. *Mergers and acquisitions in Italy*

	Intragroup	External minority	External majority	Total
1983	91	61	115	267
1984	126	118	180	424
1985	148	153	268	569
1986	189	185	290	669
1987	393	440	500	1,333
1988	375	439	500	1,314
1989	508	682	727	1,912
1990	605	710	698	2,013
1991	382	482	477	1,341
1992	447	361	354	1,162
Total	3,264	3,631	4,109	11,004

Source: Banca Dati, Laboratorio di Politica Industriale. Table 'Repartizione Annuale Delle Acquisizioni-Tipologie Aggregate', *Acquisizioni Fusioni Concorrenze* (Giugno, 1992), n. 1, Nomisma, Bologna, June 1992, p. 53; June 1993, p. 76.

TABLE 4.4. *Mergers and acquisitions by dimension (proceeds from sales in LIT billions)*

Buyers	Acquired companies				
	>1,000	500–1,000	<500	Foreign	Total
>1,000	2.11	0.00	8.84	13.26	24.21
500–1,000	0.63	0.21	2.11	1.05	4.00
<500	4.84	0.84	32.84	10.95	49.47
Foreign	3.58	0.42	14.32	4.00	22.32
Total	11.16	1.47	58.11	29.26	100.00

Source: Banca Dati, Laboratorio di Politica Industriale. Reproduced on p. 69 in *Acquisizioni Fusioni Concorrenza* (Giugno, 1992), n. 1, Nomisma, Bologna.

Beginning in 1983 (as Tables 4.3 and 4.4 show) there has been growing merger and acquisition activity, mainly among Italian medium-sized firms operating largely in the same sector, capable of reaching sufficient scale to survive on the domestic market and launch international activities. Yet, the international operations conducted by Italian firms remained limited in the period following 1987, while the acquisitions of Italian firms by foreign firms has increased noticeably (see Table 4.5).[3] When examining Italian acquisitions abroad, however, one notes the strong reorientation of the Italian acquisitions towards countries of the EC after 1987, in particular towards France. Direct investments in France by Italian firms have also increased in the past few years, which confirms the growing attention France has received even on the part of medium-sized groups.

Acquisitions and sales of public companies have also been limited. With the exception of a few cases, the activities of public companies in the entire period have been horizontal acquisitions and sales by Italian private companies to consolidate specific productive activities. Table 4.6 shows that acquisitions have been greater than sales in the last few years as well. These were direct operations among owners without the mediation of financial markets, so that from 1983 to 1991, less than 3 per cent dealt with firms listed on the stock exchange.

TABLE 4.5. *International mergers and acquisitions involving Italian firms*

	Foreign acquisitions		Italian acquisitions		Domestic acquisitions	Total transactions
	In Italy	By European companies	Abroad	In Europe		
1983	16	7	11	9	75	102
1984	56	31	7	6	109	172
1985	62	29	19	9	176	257
1986	55	36	34	21	192	281
1987	106	76	77	56	294	477
1988	132	97	66	49	278	476
1989	187	121	74	57	439	700
1990	174	129	83	53	409	666
1991	94	62	94	68	276	464

Source: Banca Dati, Laboratorio di Politica Industriale. Reproduced on p. 71 of *Acquisizioni Fusioni Concorrenza* (Giugno, 1992), n. 1, Nomisma, Bologna.

TABLE 4.6. *Mergers and acquisitions involving state-owned companies*

	Majority share operations		Minority share operations	
	Acquisitions	Sales	Acquisitions	Sales
1983	14	3	13	2
1984	11	8	16	12
1985	24	19	24	13
1986	18	19	17	4
1987	43	23	44	27
1988	26	15	60	47
1989	45	37	96	61
1990	45	23	113	67
1991	28	25	87	52
Total	254	172	470	285

Source: Banca Dati, Laboratorio di Politica Industriale. Reproduced on p. 75 in *Acquisizioni Fusioni Concorrenza* (Giugno, 1992), n. 1, Nomisma, Bologna.

To sum up, in the 1980s reorganization *within* the Italian industrial system took place through a wave of mergers and acquisitions. Notwithstanding this, the process did not alter the basic characteristics of the industrial and financial system.

4. OWNERSHIP AND CONTROL OF LARGE ENTERPRISES IN ITALY

The most striking aspect of Italian industrial structure is that the basic rules created to face the 1930s slump have provided the framework for Italian society for half a century. The banking system has been ruled by the 1936 law, which established that deposit banks cannot control industrial activities. The state-owned firms, established as a temporary expedient in 1933 to rescue collapsing firms already owned by the banks, have directly managed basic public utilities and, to a large extent, the industrial system. A variety of public-based bodies, created by the Fascist regime to manage every specific aspect of Italian economy, survived it.

At the end of the Second World War this imposing structure regulating a closed economy was not dismantled but redirected to support the economic exposure to competition of a fragile and protected economy. The result was that this vast organization of banks, firms, and public companies gave rise to the new political class, first associated with centrist governments and later with centre-left governments. A system of social regulation developed, based partly on the exclusion of the Communist Party and therefore on the impossibility of an effective alternative to the governmental bloc, and partly on the creation of a vast network of social consensus through public intervention that acted to isolate and minimize each particular conflict by absorbing the social costs.

This vast public presence, however, proved beneficial to the development of the small nucleus of big private firms. This was not only because it initially furnished raw materials and investment goods at low cost to favour the international competitiveness of the Italian manufacturing firms. It guaranteed a decent infrastructure to the country, for example the network of highways that greatly helped the automobile industry. It also furnished a social buffer during the recurring crises, absorbing firms on the verge of collapse. It carried the cost of restructuring because it supported relocation in the Mezzogiorno by subsidizing new investments by large private companies.

This was why the regulatory structure of the economy remained in force for such an extended period. Despite many adjustments over the years, it remained marked by:

1. the separation of banks from firms;
2. the weakness of financial markets;
3. a large presence of state-owned firms not only in the provision of services but also in numerous industries;
4. a small number of large, family-owned firms and the absence of companies controlled by non-owner managers;
5. a vast number of small, highly localized firms;
6. a marked difference in the processes of growth between southern and northern Italy.

These characteristics, which became clear in the 1930s and were subsequently confirmed, engendered relations among firms and between firms and the state which were different from those traditionally present in Anglo-American capitalism, but also remote from those associated with German capitalism.

Thus, a mechanism for regulating relations between public and private firms was created that balances the two blocs of the Italian large-scale industry, each of these strictly regulated within its own boundaries by rules which have been well consolidated over time. The public firms and the banking system were increasingly controlled by the government parties and the appointments made by the government were shared out to maintain the party balance within the political coalition. On the basis of this principle, the president of IRI has always been chosen by the Christian Democratic (DC) Party and the members and the executive board were shared among the coalition parties. On the other hand, ENI was considered the property of the Italian Socialist Party (PSI), with a politically balanced board selected in the same manner. These systematically corrupt links were exposed by the Tangentopoli scandals.

In addition to these public firms and to a vast public administration there are approximately 50,000 public bodies, created in large part in the 1930s and still in existence, to regulate a heterogeneous range of activities such as opera houses, ports, and banks. This breath-taking proliferation is due to the fact that these bodies, even though they are public, are not regulated by the same laws governing the civil service in matters of administrative control and pay. Their heads are directly nominated by the government or the regions, so these bodies have allowed penetration by the political parties to many aspects of daily life in the country.[4]

The large family businesses are strongly interconnected, creating closed coalitions that permit an individual family to control vast groups even when they possess minority shareholdings. An important example is Pirelli. The Pirelli family has a minority share (5 per cent) but exercises control with the Tronchetti-Provera and Orlando families; on the other hand Orlando controls the Socièta Mobilare Italiano with the decisive help of Pirelli.

The case of Montedison demonstrates how difficult it is in Italy to delineate the forms of ownership and control of managerial capitalism. Montedison was born in the early 1970s from a merger of Montecatini, a traditional leader in the chemical sector, and Edison, an electrical company that after the nationalization of its activities in this sector in 1961 had plenty of capital to invest. Edison had previously diversified into various activities, among which was basic chemical production, and it later assumed control of the old chemical and mining firm. The Montedison group changed ownership several times. It was first acquired by the state, then reprivatized with the assistance of the dominant family firms. In the late 1970s the management had tried to become independent of this strict family ownership, creating the possibility for Montedison to become a public company. This aim rapidly disappeared because Montedison was acquired by the Ferruzzi family with the help of Mediobanca. In the course of the subsequent reorganization, it sold off Standa, the leader in commercial distribution in Italy, to Berlusconi and the group's basic chemical activities in a joint venture with ENI. The failure of that operation allowed the sale of the basic chemical production activities to ENI and left the specialized chemical activities and the diversified activities to the Ferruzzi family, which, as we have already mentioned, lost control of the firm in the financial scandal of 1993.[5]

The failure of the 1989 Montedison–ENI ENIMONT project was only one example of joint ventures between public and private firms to create national enterprises capable of operating on a global level. In 1989 the IRI group, that owned Italtel, and IFI–FIAT, that controlled Telettra, decided to launch a joint venture, called TELIT, that would have been the national champion in the telecommunications sector. The agreement failed to share control between public and private shareholders. The cause of these failures is that the two areas not only have different decision-making models but also have different schemes of internal regulation, so that every attempt to create a new, mixed firm of large enough dimensions to become a national champion, gets bogged down when it comes to deciding what the command structure of the company will be. The public component wants to re-establish the principle of interparty distribution that thrives in public industries and the private partners seek to reassert the family coalitions of control that flourish in the private sector.

Even in such a rigid ownership organization, there are opportunities for the growth of a variety of manufacturing firms, not only in traditional but also in innovative sectors. None the less, the ownership structure of the new groups remains the traditional system of family control, as has been demonstrated in the cases of Ferruzzi, Benetton, and Berlusconi, in which new dynamic organizational structures continue to be controlled and managed by family-owned groups.

5. THE REGULATION OF THE FINANCIAL SYSTEM

The Italian banking system is in large part owned directly by the state (almost 90 per cent of deposits). The deposit banks, which are largely public bodies, with their top management appointed by the government, are not allowed to act as investment banks by acquiring the control of industrial activities, and the international operations of the Italian banks are still very limited. The Italian banking system has therefore traditionally been divided into deposit banks, which finance short-term activities of businesses, and the special credit institutions, which finance long-term investments and provide credit for the productive system.

The Italian banking system is among the least concentrated in Europe. In 1991 there were over 1,000 ordinary banks with over 19,000 branches. However, such fragmentation did not encourage dynamic internal competition because until 1990 the Italian banking system was rigidly governed by local oligopolies. The situation was strictly regulated by the central bank, which only rarely authorized the opening of new branches; in particular the vast network of local banks, savings banks, and rural banks was constrained to operate exclusively at the local level.[6]

In connection with the realization of the Single Market, the 1990 Amato Act outlined the way in which the Italian banking system might be reorganized. The law allows the banks which are already public bodies and the savings banks which are public charities to transform themselves into joint-stock companies and therefore to sell part of the shares, to merge with other banks, and to acquire other banks.[7] None the less, there is strong resistance to change. Many concentration plans among big banks, like the constitution of regional groups of savings banks, failed because these institutions represent the crucial instruments of economic control by political parties at the local level or within industrial sectors. Therefore, mergers would have disrupted political power relations among parties and interest groups at both the local and national levels.

However, an important change in the rules was the liberalization of the opening of bank branches, which brought about a dynamic response from the minor banks, previously limited to operating at the local level in nearby markets. In a single year this brought about a large increase in the number of branches and a significant increase

TABLE 4.7. *Organization of the Italian banking system*

Bank category	1990		1991	
	No. of banks	No. of branches in Italy	No. of banks	No. of branches in Italy
Istituti di diritto pubblico (owned directly by the Treasury)	6	2,449	3	1,246
Banche di interesse nazionale (owned by IRI)	3	1,459	3	1,657
Banks organized as joint-stock companies	106	3,981	136	8,730
Banche Popolari Cooperative (banks organized as co-operatives)	108	3,290	103	3,432
Casse di Risparmio e Monti di Credito (public banks spending at local level)	8 4	4,695	47	2,055
Casse Rurali e Artigiane (very small local banks)	715	1,792	708	1,901
Foreign banks	37	50	38	52
Istituti di Categorie (2nd level bank activity by category)	5	5	5	7
Totals	1,064	17,721	1,043	19,080

Source: Banca D'Italia, *Annual Report, 1991* (Rome, May 1992), 294.

in competition on the local level (from 17,000 to 19,000). Another significant provision was the possibility of reorganizing the banking structures as multi-functional groups, capable of providing a variety of financial services.

This reorganization of the banking groups, in conjunction with the restraint imposed by the EEC on subsidies to firms, limited the function of the public industrial credit institutions, which had financed industrial investments and now became above all instruments for the distribution of public subsidies to firms in crisis and for investments in the Mezzogiorno. On the other hand, it has to be noted that the Italian stock market is not large enough adequately to exercise control over business behaviour. There are

226 companies listed on the Milan Stock Exchange and of these, 95 belong to 10 groups, accounting for 80 per cent of the total capital quoted. They are either state-controlled or closely controlled by family concerns, so that hostile takeover operations are very difficult. Furthermore, the 'Big Six' groups account for two-thirds of total capitalization, controlling 83 out of 226 firms listed on the Milan Stock Exchange. In 1974 a Commission for the control of the stock market (CONSOB) was created. This commission could only partially regulate the exchange that was itself marginal to the industrial development of the country. Only since the mid-1980s have laws been introduced to regulate insider trading and takeover bids.

6. PUBLIC INTERVENTION

Since the end of the Second World War, the Italian government has provided subsidies in order to promote underdeveloped areas, encourage innovation in small and medium-sized firms, induce large firms to reorganize their plants and, in very extreme cases, has helped firms avoid bankruptcy. In the case of institutional monopoly, the Italian choice has been to contract out public good production and distribution to public-owned firms. Thus, the central or local public administrations are the regulators and the state-owned firms are the regulated agents.

The basic justification for providing industrial assistance was that Italian firms suffered from financial disadvantages because of the rigidity of the Italian banking and financial regime. They had trouble getting loans for innovative investments or for investing in less-favoured areas. The only innovation considered was the acquisition of new machinery. The aid was given to individual firms as a discount on the normal rate charged by the banking system. Thus, subsidies paid to the individual companies to acquire new machinery are a form of compensation for higher interest rates paid to a very rigid oligopolistic banking system, which is able to discriminate according to the size and location of the companies.

After the industrial slump of the 1970s, massive intervention was provided to favour the reorganization of large enterprises (Law 675/1977) and to promote research and development activities

(Law 46/1982). Both of these laws went into operation many months after approval, because of the opposition of the EEC Commission. Tables 4.8 and 4.9 show the great disparity in matters of subsidy between Italy and France, Germany, and the UK.

The European Community authorities considered most of the Italian laws devoted to assisting private and public firms as infringements of article 92 of the Treaty of Rome and re-examined all the intervention programmes. Only specific aid given according to the Community rules was accepted. Since the late 1980s, the Commission has developed control over financial transfers from the state to public companies, requiring that state-owned firms reimburse the government for subsidies they have received and pay fines to the EEC.[8]

This high level of aid testifies to the fact that a rigid, central bureaucracy provides subsidies to compensate operational disadvantages, simply because it is not able to manage a real institutional transformation of the country. More evidence of this rigidity is given by the public aid supplied to the Mezzogiorno. The central government has for decades given public subsidies to relocate in-

TABLE 4.8. *Subsidies distributed by national governments*

	Total subsidies		To manufacturing industry		To manufacturing industry minus steel and ship building	
	% of GDP	ECU per employee	% of value added	ECU per employee	% of value added	ECU per employee
Italy (EC est.)	5.66	1,357	16.72	6,226	15.8	5,951
Italy (Bank of Italy est.)	4.26	1,022	10.97	4,086	10.1	3,084
France	2.68	792	4.93	1,649	3.6	1,223
Germany	2.53	761	3.03	982	2.9	940
UK	1.79	396	3.81	971	2.9	757

Note: Subsidies to manufacturing industry do not include contributions to agriculture, fishery, transport, or coal where subsidies are given because of Community rules.

Source: Commission (1989c). From Bianchi, Patrizio, 'Industrial strategy and structural policies', in Cowling, Keith, and Sugden, Roger (eds.), *Current Issues in Industrial Economic Strategy* (Manchester: Manchester University Press), 203.

TABLE 4.9. *Legal disputes between Italy and the EC over the application of Laws 675/1977 (on subsidies for industrial restructuring) and 46/ 1982 (on subsidies for industrial innovation)*

Sector	Outcome
Fashion	
textiles clothing	1
footwear leather	1
Electronics	
computers and micro-electronics	2
appliances	3
Steel	5
Chemicals	
man-made fibres	1
secondary	3
Mechanical engineering	3
Paper	
mass	1
special	3
Food and drink	3
Cars	4
Car parts	3
Aerospace	5
Environment	5

Key:
1 national subsidies forbidden
2 national subsidies allowed
3 national subsidies allowed, notification to EC required
4 national subsidies allowed only in situations specified by EC
5 national subsidies allowed only with Community programmes

Source: Bianchi, Patrizio, 'Italy', in Cowling, Keith, and Sugden, Roger (eds.), *Current Issues in Industrial Economic Strategy* (Manchester: Manchester University Press), 188–94, 192.

dustrial plants in the southern regions of the country. Money was given by the national government to individual companies through the banking system to acquire machinery, without any attention to creating the context that is the precondition of successful industrialization. The result has been that a large proportion of firms have failed, especially in southern Italy, where the infrastructure is lacking and firms are isolated in a poor local context. Thus, the national government's intervention has weakened the regional governments and the new structural approach proposed by the Community is also not working. The Integrated Mediterranean Programmes, which require the active participation of the local authorities, are not working, so the EC Commission has redirected grants from southern Italy to France.

Italian industrial policy has been used as a buffer during times of international crisis and as a way to compensate for weaknesses in the domestic industrial and financial system. The completion of the Single Market, the enforcement of articles 92–4 (concerning state aid) and of article 90 (regarding public companies), and the reorientation of structural policies, are forcing the Italian government to face the crucial aspects of industrial strategy managed by the government. In this context, the most significant new element is the creation of the High Authority for Market Competition, to act as the national antitrust authority (Law 287 of September 1990). This antitrust authority was born after an extremely lengthy debate, because for years it was argued that it was unsuitable to place limits on business activities in a small country like Italy. In fact, the Italian Authority was established thanks to the prompting of Community Regulation 4064/89, which placed concentrations having an important European character under the control of the Commission, leaving to the national authorities those concerning local interests.

7. POLITICAL CRISIS AND INDUSTRIAL RESTRUCTURING

Change was for years blocked by the state, which protected the productive system's inefficiency, resulting in an industrial structure that had a final escape mechanism in the state. At the beginning of the 1990s this stalemate finally broke for four reasons:

1. The fiscal crisis of the state made its role as buffer difficult to perform without evaluating the efficiency of the productive system as a whole; for example, the cost of labour in Italy tends to be the highest in Europe, essentially because of the fiscal burdens to cover health insurance and pension funds.
2. The growing influence of the political parties in the management not only in the central and peripheral administration but also in the public firms and in the myriad public bodies (from pension funds to opera houses) increasingly paralysed the economic and political life of the country.
3. The EC imposed limits to the growth of the public deficit; in particular, its vigilance in matters of subsidies and public transfers to the firms became more stringent as part of the Completion of the Single Market Programme and as a prerequisite to the Economic Union Agreement.
4. Last but not least, the end of Cold War made explicit the exhaustion of the internal political model based on the stability assured by Christian Democrats–Socialist Party Alliance, creating the conditions for a fundamental reorganization of the relations existing between private and public firms in Italy.

A serious political crisis gathered momentum in the spring of 1992 with the resignation of the President of the Republic. The result of the April 1992 elections was severe political fragmentation, exacerbated by a series of arrests for corruption of politicians in the North and an explosion of Mafia crimes in the South.

In a macro-economic situation in which Italy was diverging from the EC and in a very fragmented internal situation, the Amato government—which only took office in July 1992 with a slender parliamentary majority, but was strong through the absence of any plausible alternative—launched a series of important measures which tend to interfere directly in the regulatory mechanisms of the Italian system. The following government, chaired by the Governor of the Bank of Italy, Carlo Azeglio Ciampi, implemented a strong stabilization programme to reduce the public deficit, to curb inflation, and to reorganize the public administration. In September 1992, the Italian lira was devalued by one-third, but inflation remained at 4.5 per cent; the government reduced the huge public debt and started a serious programme of privatization.

On the privatization of public firms and of public bodies in charge of specific services, the Amato Government proposed the transformation of IRI, ENI, and also ENEL (electrical energy), INA (social security), and the state railway company, into joint-stock companies. Their boards of directors, generally held to be dominated by political parties were abolished, and the management pending reorganization and sale was entrusted to three temporary administrators. The principal effect of this transformation is that control passed directly to the Treasury, eliminating that of other ministries and in particular the Ministry of State-owned companies. At the same time, the Amato Government liquidated EFIM, one of the major state-owned holding companies, controlling arms production and light machinery, that had accumulated huge losses. The end of special intervention in the Mezzogiorno was declared, abolishing the Ministry responsible and redirecting the distribution of subsidies to areas less favoured by the EC directives.

The first privatization programme launched by the Ciampi Government in February 1993, based on a French-style model, was stopped by the scarcity of large groups, the rigidity of banking systems, and the narrowness of the financial market. A fierce debate occurred between those sustaining French-style privatization, led by a 'stable core' of national enterprises, and those who considered the Italian firms incapable of offering a stable basis for growth. A privatization programme led by Mediobanca, and its allies, such as Fiat and the large family firms, would result in a further concentration of the Italian economic and political system, without the capacity to provide resources for relaunching industrial activity of the public sector. This position asserts that public banks have to be sold to private savers, usually investing in public bonds, in order to create the conditions to enlarge the Italian financial market, to establish new independent financial groups, and to create the conditions for modernizing the Italian economic system. After a dramatic contest between the Minister of Industry and the President of IRI, the privatization of the Credito Italiano, one of the largest Italian banks, owned by IRI, was based on a public offer to private shareholders. Its success demonstrated that a new phase of Italian economic life may be beginning.

Furthermore, the elimination of the *scala mobile*, the automatic adjustment of wages indexed for inflation, and the abandonment of wage negotiations for three years were demanded of the unions in

July 1992. The Amato Government also committed itself to reforming the health care system, pension plans, the social security system, to outlining the reform of local finance, and to boosting the stock market, all within three months. Such an ambitious programme of action was possible because of the serious internal political crisis, coupled with external pressure from the EC Commission on Italy to respect her obligations under the Maastricht Treaty.

8. CONCLUSIONS

The difficulties in establishing international champions result from the defensive regulation of Italian capitalism. After the war Italy was able to achieve industrial growth, while maintaining unaltered the arrangements that in fact had sustained the country for 40 years. The political system acquired control of the huge state apparatus inherited from the Fascist government and was able to establish a model of defensive regulation, in agreement with the group of large private firms, based on three supports:

1. a banking system strictly controlled by the state, which operated as a financial intermediary to guarantee liquidity without controlling the firms;
2. an industrial system composed of three segments which barely communicated with each other: the state-owned companies, under the control of the government parties; the large companies, controlled by a limited number of powerful families through a system of interlocking holdings; a vast number of small and medium-sized firms which were family-run;
3. widespread public intervention to sustain industry, through subsidies for localization and restructuring, and to assist small firms; and special interventions favouring firms in crisis, including the acquisition of bankrupt firms by the state.

Crisis overwhelmed this system of defensive regulation for three reasons:

1. because its cumulative cost swelled the public deficit, generating inflation and therefore elevating the costs of production within private industry;
2. the political system was no longer able to play its part in this regulation because it was fragmented and delegitimized;

3. the completion of the internal market and, to an even greater extent, the process of economic globalization, no longer permitted defensive action on the part of the internal economy through non-tariff barriers, and forced the Italian companies to face firms of larger dimensions and greater efficiency on the international market directly.

Undoubtedly EC regulation of the movement of capital and the control of state aid have induced the government and Parliament to introduce new laws which have partially modified the previous situation. None the less, the principal effect of 1992 was that it highlighted the inadequacies of the internal regulatory system in a phase of economic globalization. The government used, above all, the pressure from the EC to promote rapid reform to achieve a convergence with other EC countries in matters of inflation and the deficit, and to legitimate and impose new economic policies which would otherwise have been unacceptable.

There certainly are Italian companies which have positions of leadership in specific areas and in specific industrial products, but we cannot assume that they can become international enterprises, because the system of regulation of Italian capitalism was turned inward and was not prepared for the international projection of national production. Furthermore, from 1987 to 1992, in the years of intensive international restructuring, in which the rules governing the behaviour of the European oligopolies were redesigned, the internal crisis of the Italian political system exploded and made the development of national strategies for international economic growth extremely difficult to carry out. After 40 years, Italy is rapidly changing and so is the regulatory framework, but creating the preconditions of an effective market society is at the centre of a severe political struggle.

Notes

1. *Fortune*, 29 July 1991.
2. The data bank organized by Nomisma Research Institute, Strada Maggiore, 44, Bologna, has analysed almost 12,000 operations (transactions) from 1983 to 1993 involving Italian companies. The results are reported in *Acquisitions, Fusioni, Concorrenza*, Biannual Report on Mergers and Acquisitions in Italy (Bologna, June 1993).

3. Here one should note the many acquisitions realized in the foodstuffs sector by foreign national enterprises. Especially in the sectors of pasta and mineral water, the European leaders BSN and Nestlé have conducted a systematic policy of taking over family-owned firms, acquiring control, but maintaining the original brand names.

4. S. Cassese, *Le Basi del Diritto Amministrativo* (Turin: 1989), 104–70. See also S. Cassese, *Il sistema amministrativo italiano* (Bologna: 1983), 262.

5. On the history of Montedison, see R. Amatori and B. Brezza (eds.), *Montecatini 1888–1966* (Bologna: 1991).

6. In every city there was a strict oligopoly, formed by the local savings bank, which operated as the city treasurer and universal bank for the local small industrial and commercial firms, and by one or more national banks, usually operating as treasurer of the national public administrations and as agent of the big national firms, and even more as a source of subsidies and assistance distributed on the basis of national laws concerning aid for businesses.

7. Among the savings banks and public banks 80 have become corporations. Twenty-four mergers have been approved by the Banca D'Italia which involve banks controlling approximately 21 per cent of total loans and 65 banks have exchanged minority holdings amounting to approximately a quarter of all loans. The principal operation dealt with the merger between the Cassa di Risparmio di Roma, the Banca di Roma, and the Banca di Santo Spirito which was already owned by IRI. (Banca D'Italia, *Relazione Annuale* (Roma: 1992), 295.)

8. e.g. in the sale of Alfa Romeo to Fiat, IRI did not take into account the accumulated debts of the corporation to it. The EEC held that this amounted to assistance and required restitution to the Italian Government. Similarly, the public steel works ILVA, after having received a recapitalization on the part of IRI following significant losses, had to sell several activities to be able to repay the transfers which the EEC considered to be subsidies.

PART II
FIRMS AND THEIR INDUSTRIAL SECTORS

5

The European Electricity Industry and EC Regulatory Reform

FRANCIS McGOWAN

The transition from national to international champion has proved to be a particularly difficult process for the electricity supply industry (ESI). Not only has the industry been organized as a *natural* monopoly with associated rights and duties but it has also been treated as a *national* (if not a local) monopoly, conceived very much as operating within, rather than across, frontiers. The need to meet all a country's power requirements, to offer a universal service, and to serve as a basic infrastructure have reinforced the national focus. This sovereign status has been strengthened by the need to act as a strategic support for other national enterprises, ranging from high-technology engineering industries to declining mining companies. In effect a bargain has been made between the electricity utilities and their governments which has swapped the commitments of the industry on issues of public service and industrial support for considerable autonomy in both day-to-day conduct and strategic planning within those nationally formed constraints. International contacts, where they have taken place, have been literally or metaphorically at the frontier, whether in the form of mutually beneficial trading arrangements or in extremely high technology and speculative research (ad)ventures.

Over the last 20 years, however, the prevailing regime in the sector has begun to fray as the performance of the industry has deteriorated, prompting some mainly outside the industry to reconsider the robustness of its existing structure and conduct. That process of reassessment has accelerated over the last 5 years, leaving the European ESI (indeed, the industry globally) in flux. The mix of technological, organizational, and political factors which underpinned the old model has changed, and the industry's future has been a focus for debate. In some cases this debate has brought into question both its national and natural monopoly status. Elsewhere, the outcomes appear to be less radical, at least so far.

As the system has come under wider challenge, a key role in the debate over the future of the industry has been played by the Commission of the European Community (CEC). After decades of being excluded from scrutinizing, let alone regulating, the conduct of the industry, the CEC is now actively intervening in many aspects of the sector, with a primary interest in applying the not always convergent logics of integration and deregulation. The growing regulatory role of the Commission, particularly in the areas of competition (the main focus of this paper) and environmental policy, has evolved rapidly but not without a struggle. Its attempts to reform the regime prevailing in the sector have been resisted by most governments and utilities, who have sought to maintain the existing balance of power in the industry (or at least contain the extent of the changes). However, regardless of whether the Commission achieves all its objectives, it has proved itself to be an important influence upon the sector, at least partly responsible for the increasingly international orientation of some utilities.

In this chapter we review the emergence of the ESI as a set of national champions and the factors which may be pushing it to become an international (or at least European) industry. In particular we note the way in which the utilities have had to shift from being 'immovable objects' and consider how far the proposals for change, particularly from the CEC, are indeed 'irresistible forces'. After considering how the industry came to enjoy its special status, what factors have undermined its performance, and what changes have been considered, we concentrate on the cases of Britain, France, Germany, and Italy (the largest industries in the Community) to explore how the technical and organizational characteristics of electricity supply were interpreted in different national settings, how relations with key supplier industries evolved, and how these national factors affected the process of change in recent years. Turning to the internationalizing pressures in the sector and particularly the debate within the Community on reorganizing the industry, we conclude by considering how far the industry is undergoing a fundamental transformation institutionally and geographically.

1. THE DEVELOPMENT OF THE ESI IN THE COMMUNITY

For much of its history, the ESI has been able to benefit from a virtuous circle of improving supply technologies and increased demand. The size of plant steadily increased, as did the thermal efficiency with which heat is converted to electricity. As a result, the cost of electricity declined throughout much of this century. Lower costs and falling prices encouraged greater use of electricity against its competitor fuels. Demand was also fuelled by the diffusion of new appliances and applications. The evolution of structure and control in the industry in Europe has generally sought to exploit such technical developments, which generally involved capital intensive technologies and large financial requirements (even the relatively low investment needs of recent years still average £3–5 billion annually for the countries examined here). In order to reap the benefits of these improvements, utilities consolidated horizontally and vertically; the number of utilities has decreased in almost all countries over the last century. The growing concentration of the industry has for most of its history been accompanied by higher public participation, whether at a national or a local level.[1]

Historically, institutional changes have followed the paths of incremental development or fundamental reform. In both cases, they have been brought about largely as a response to obstacles to the full attainment of the benefits of technical change or to unevenness in the allocation of those benefits (because of shortcomings in the performance of incumbent utilities). These changes have led to an apparently wide variety of national regimes for the industry in terms of structure and conduct as well as in terms of technology and fuel choices, and owe much to variations in geography, economic development, resource endowments, and political culture. However, the apparent diversity across the industry largely reflects alternative ways of arriving at largely similar objectives. There are many common features across all systems, particularly in the trend towards consolidation and public participation. In every case, the degree of *de facto* centralization and integration is much larger than structures portray. None the less the particular structures in each country and the underlying reasons for those structures are significant, especially when further reform is under discussion.

It is possible to identify three structures followed by Community industries. There is a cluster of utilities which are largely publicly owned, centralized monopolies created between the 1920s, when the Irish Electricity Supply Board was founded, and the 1970s, when the post-revolution government in Portugal nationalized its industry. Included in this group are countries such as Britain and France, where although separate entities existed for some activities (principally distribution), there was *de facto* integration with the powerful transmission and production firms. Other countries have a largely decentralized structure but with public ownership dominant in the system. The Danish and Dutch systems are the exemplars of this structure. In both countries the industry is made up of transmission companies owned by production companies which are in turn owned by distribution companies: in Denmark the distributors are a mix of local authorities and co-operatives and in the Netherlands the industry is purely municipally based. In a few cases, private companies make up the bulk of the industry, though even in these cases there is a significant public element. In Belgium and Spain, state-owned utilities have increased their role in the industry's operations. In Germany, local and Länder governments either run utilities in their own right or own significant stakes in ostensibly private firms.

In those countries with significant energy resources or engineering industries, utilities, whether private or public, tended to buy nationally. The reasons for this lie in a mixture of factors, including the possibility of supplier cartels agreeing not to compete in home markets, government pressures on utilities, and the utilities' own preferences for technical and security of supply reasons. Above all, however, the cost plus nature of the industry meant that there was little incentive to do otherwise. The monopoly structure of the industry was not generally challenged by tough regulation; public ownership and the generally weak controls on nationalized industries were seen as sufficient to protect the public interest, while in private systems the level of regulation was weak, certainly nothing equivalent to the legalistic structures developed in the US, reflecting both the closeness of the utility to national interests and the capture of those interests by the utilities (whose shareholders often included the major industrial and financial players in the economy).[2]

In international contacts, utilities have generally enjoyed good relations, often sharing more in common with each other than with their governments, suppliers, and consumers. Until the last few years, there was no semblance of competition for supply, internally or internationally (beyond occasional rivalries for large customers to locate in their territory). This co-operation has extended to joint ventures (in areas such as advanced nuclear technologies), joint representation (in international technical and promotional bodies such as the International Union of Producers and Distributors of Electricity—Unipede) and to trade. The latter has been a feature of the industry for much of this century, with utilities willingly co-operating to exploit joint resources such as rivers for hydroelectric development, to take advantage of different patterns of demand and powerplant capacity, thereby optimizing their national systems through co-operation, and to assist each other in the event of an emergency. Loose co-operative organizations such as the Union for the Co-ordination of Production and Transmission of Electricity in Western Europe and Nordel in Scandinavia have been formed by utilities to facilitate trade. Such trade has always been carried out by utilities alone, however, and scarcely challenges their autonomy (for example in the area of investment). The utilities have retained their national monopolies, arguing that the need to ensure security of supply and the technical stability of the system requires that trade be conducted on this basis. Pooling sovereignty in long-term decisions, let alone permitting direct competition for customers from inside or outside the national system, would undermine the benefits of the integrated ESI.[3]

In the last 20 years, however, the conditions which underpinned the successful development of the industry have changed and the international harmony amongst utilities also came to be tested. In terms of the performance of the industry, the virtuous circle turned vicious. Energy crises and economic recessions played havoc with input prices and demand. The technical economies which had delivered ever lower costs of production began to be exhausted, as the technical limits of larger plant were reached and their operational limitations emerged. Not only did the benefits of larger plant diminish, but the costs of that plant, either through longer construction times or poor load factors, were greater than anticipated. Yet utilities continued to plan for bigger plant on the basis of the historic trend for large increases in the rate of growth of demand. As a result, in a number of countries there was substantial over-supply. The utilities' decisions in this area were often unpopular. Not only did they often require higher tariffs, but they often involved environmental problems. Siting of new plant became more difficult and the selection of nuclear technologies was particularly opposed. Controversies in this area inevitably undermined the image of the ESI as acting in the public interest. Environmental concerns played a major role in criticisms of utilities' bias towards large supply-side technologies, rather than towards renewable forms of energy and/or energy efficiency, and have undoubtedly played an important role in many countries' reform debates.[4]

The idea of the utility acting for the public interest was also undermined by government's use of the industry. Throughout the 1970s and early 1980s, governments intervened in the ESI's decision making far more than in previous decades. In many countries, the utility was used as a part of the public sector to control inflation (through price controls) and public expenditure (through financial controls). The utility's traditional role as a purchaser of local fuel and plant was exploited more by government (though it might be agreed that the previous exploitation only became more blatant as international fuel and equipment markets developed). The extent and nature of government intervention varied from country to country, but in many countries the government's use of the industry for its wider objectives effectively compromised the utilities' task of providing cheap and relatively efficient electricity supply.

In a sense therefore, the implicit contract between the ESI and government broke down or was seen to be doing so in many countries. As a result, there was growing criticism of the utility's conduct and its relationship with government, as the traditional models of control and influence were seen to be failing. It would be wrong to suggest that the overall record of the ESI dramatically deteriorated in this period; in most countries a high standard of service and relatively low electricity prices prevailed. None the less, where there were shortcomings (whether technically, organizationally, or politically rooted), these were often ascribed to a more general malaise in the regime which underpinned industry.

In some countries, the collapse in energy prices in the mid-1980s exacerbated the utilities' position. Although the price of certain internationally traded fuels fell dramatically, utilities were not always able to take advantage of them (because of obligations to local suppliers or government fiscal requirements). The collapse in prices, and its roots in the apparent oversupply of most fuels, had a number of effects. It exposed the utilities' position in protecting national fuel industries, in some cases leading to trade tensions with potential exporters. On the demand side, large consumers in particular began to place more importance on price than security of supply, and a number questioned the value of their existing supplier's monopoly. The fall in energy prices weakened the scarcity culture which had dominated energy policy in the 1970s, fostering the perception that energy was just another commodity and that the energy industries were not 'special cases'.

Just as the mix of criticisms has varied from country to country, so have the types of reforms proposed to address the problems of the industry (though often there is more than one motivation for change). Claims that the public ESI has failed have been strongest in those countries with neo-liberal governments (principally the UK and to a lesser extent Portugal), though they are not unique to them, as the debate on privatization in countries such as Ireland and Italy demonstrates. In the context of neo-liberalism, it is hardly surprising that the industry came to be regarded as part of the privatization/deregulation agenda. Ideas of market liberalization and structural change which were applied to other regulated industries were considered for the energy sectors, including the ESI. The types of restructuring include internal reorganization, the introduction of competitive mechanisms into the industry, and privatization. Elsewhere, the reasons for reform are focused on factors such as the need to secure operational efficiency (France and the Netherlands) by rationalizing the structure of the industry or to contain environmental problems (Denmark and Germany) by fostering energy efficiency or renewable energies, though in each of these cases the changes have not challenged the basic structure of the sector. There are those countries where the debate on reform is a matter of struggle between government and industry, whether privately or locally owned (Spain and the Netherlands). Finally there are those where the reforms are at least partially motivated by the prospect of a more European electricity industry (Belgium and Spain).

2. UNITED KINGDOM

The UK electricity industry consisted of a mixture of municipal and private utilities until 1947. However, government attempts to improve the co-ordination of power station operation and investment created a state transmission company in 1926. Over the following 20 years, there was considerable debate on the future of the industry, as many shortcomings in operation and variations in performance and price persisted. Such considerations, as well as broader strategic concerns, led to the nationalization of the industry in 1947. The system consisted of a single production and transmission company—a body which was to become the Central Electricity Generating Board (CEGB)—and twelve distribution companies in England and Wales.[5]

The industry's operations were overseen by the Treasury and the Ministry of Fuel and Power (later, the Department of Energy). The Treasury in particular has been important in determining the general regime within which the industry operated, generally as part of a wider system of controls over nationalized industries. Indeed, over the post-war period, the government extended a system of controls over the public sector as a whole covering issues of productivity as well as investment and finance.

However, there were other ways in which government and industry interacted. The immediate task for the new nationalized industry was reconstruction, both of itself and of the economy as a whole, in the wake of the war. Equally important, however, was its role in supporting the national coal and power equipment sectors, a function which persisted over the next 40 years (extended in the 1950s to nuclear power). For the most part the CEGB was a willing partner, even pushing for reorganization of the local equipment manufacturing industry to meet its needs better.[6] There were good reasons for maintaining such support from the industry's vantage point: it was able to maintain fuel supplies, and it was able to exercise considerable influence over the design of plant as well. However, the relationship between the utility and its suppliers was underpinned by government concerns and on occasions direct pressure.[7]

In the 1950s and 1960s, the UK ESI functioned well, certainly better than the pre-war patchwork of private and municipal utilities.[8] Though the first decades of nationalization were marked by some tensions between government and the industry, the performance of the UK industry deteriorated in earnest over the 1970s and 1980s due to a combination of shortcomings in the industry's own conduct and government interference. Arguably, what happened was that the industry was allowed autonomy where government should have intervened and government interfered where utilities should have been granted autonomy. Utility performance was particularly poor in the areas of technology selection and investment management. Its venture into large-scale power generation in the mid-1960s proved highly problematic, though not as disastrous as its subsequent management of nuclear power investment and the promotion of the Advanced Gas-cooled Reactor (AGR). Its management of new power station construction in the 1970s led to serious delays in completion, partly because of constant re-specification of plant. Its forecasting methodologies were also severely criticized in the 1970s and 1980s. Yet in these areas, the industry was able to pursue its own agenda with relatively little government control.[9] Government intervention was more to the fore in enforcing onerous procurement obligations on the industry. Plant orders were brought forward by the government for regional employment reasons. The coal industry was protected by government pressure on utilities to buy at prices well above those on the world market. The government, moreover, used the system of financial controls and performance scrutiny variously to control inflation or to raise government revenue.[10]

Given this record, it is perhaps not surprising that the industry was considered to be ripe for reorganization when privatization was announced in 1987. In contrast to other privatizations such as British Airways, British Gas, and British Telecom, the management of the CEGB were unable to ensure that the industry retained its existing structure in the private sector, nor was there much support from outside the industry for the CEGB. If anything, many, particularly in the environmental movement, hoped that privatization might lead to a more accountable industry. At the same time there was increased pressure on the government from its own ideologues to move towards a more competitive market structure in the sector.

Privatization of the industry entailed the splitting up of the CEGB into three and then four companies (initially two generators and a transmission company, though the impossibility of selling nuclear stations to private investors meant that the government had to retain them in the public sector and split generation three instead of two ways). The regional distribution companies were able to lobby for their existing status. The industry was to be scrutinized by a competition-oriented regulatory agency—the Office of Electricity Regulation—modelled on similar organizations established in the wake of utility privatization.[11] In effect, the industry was shaped into a structure and mode of operations quite different from that in place anywhere else in the world; the industry was vertically disintegrated and competition rather than long-run planning would be the guide to its conduct.[12]

The system is in its infancy but already it has had a dramatic effect on the industry. There has been severe rationalization of employment and a dramatic reorientation of priorities away from long-term planning towards short-term profit maximization. Links with plant and fuel suppliers have been radically restructured as the industry has chosen to diversify in terms of sources (foreign suppliers) and resources (fuels and technologies). Capital intensive technologies such as coal or nuclear power plant have been rejected (along with the industry's substantial long-term research and development programme) and there has been a rush to invest in gas turbine plant. There has been a move towards importing fuels, notably coal, and power equipment. Financial rather than electrical engineering has been the defining characteristic of the new industry.

The new regime has led to some surprising developments. The most remarkable has been the apparent failure of the new regime to deliver lower-priced electricity to British consumers, the principal 'overt' reason for the policy (as opposed to the 'covert' political and fiscal reasons).[13] Other notable changes include two linked phenomena: the interest of the electricity companies in diversification both in terms of international markets and new activities, these latter a function of regulatory changes in other utility industries; and the emergence of the industry as a target for other companies engaged in diversification.[14] Aside from the fact that production companies have moved into the business of direct supply and distribution companies have become generators, almost all the companies have sought to move into other energy and even other utility activities (such as gas supply and telecom services), taking advantage of previous reorganizations in the UK economy, as well as more predictable moves into contracting and retailing activities. A few companies have also sought to invest in foreign electricity ventures, primarily but not solely in non-EC countries which are themselves engaged in privatization. Equally significant have been the moves in the opposite direction. A number of apparently 'independent' power generation projects in the UK are effectively consortia of foreign electricity companies, while other entrants into the industry include some of the largest energy consumer companies and the gas and water industries. As a result there has been a considerable blurring of the boundaries between the electricity industry, consumers and suppliers, and other utility industries.

Unsurprisingly, the government has heralded the experiment as a great success and a model for the rest of the world and other network industries.[15] To some extent the model is being considered by other countries with governments of a neo-liberal bent (New Zealand, Argentina, Sweden) and also by the EC Commission, which has seized on the emergence of an alternative structure in its own reform proposals (see below). However, while a few countries appear to be emulating the experiment, most countries are wary of, if not hostile towards, the British experiment. That attitude has probably been increased (and perhaps the government's enthusiasm tempered) by the repercussions of the privatization. The 'dash for gas' (the rush to invest in gas-fuelled power plant), with the increased imports of coal on the one hand and the subsidy of the nuclear industry on the other, led to a dramatic decline in demand for British coal. While this process had been underway for some time (and the rationalization of the coal industry for even longer following the 1985 miners' strike) the announcement of a major closure programme (involving 30,000 jobs and 30 million tonnes of coal) provoked an unexpectedly vociferous reaction from British public opinion, calling into doubt the survival of the government. However, although the decision prompted a wave of public sympathy which obliged the government to review the policies which led to the decision, the policy was upheld in the subsequent White Paper.[16] (Rather ironically, the government invoked environmental benefits—of burning less coal—as one of the reasons for the restructuring of energy balances.)

3. FRANCE

The French industry followed a similar path of reorganization in the wake of the war and for broadly similar reasons. Electricité de France (EdF) was established in 1946 by creating a single nationalized and vertically integrated utility out of the patchwork of municipal and private utilities that had previously supplied power to France. Other power producers exist, notably the publicly owned coal company CdF and the company responsible for managing the hydroelectric resources of the Rhone Valley, the CNR.[17] Responsibility for the industry has been shared by the Ministry of Industry, within which the Directorate for Energy resides, and the Ministry of Finance. The former has been responsible for the strategic development of the industry and the latter has scrutinized price setting and borrowing. Both ministries are members of the nationalized industry's board of directors. For more than 20 years, with some breaks, the formal mechanism which has mediated relations between EdF and the government has been the planning contract. Under this system, the utility negotiates a range of performance objectives with the government. In return it gains a framework within which it can plan its future development.[18]

However, the freedom within limits which the planning contract offers is not the most important dimension of EdF's autonomy. More generally, EdF has maintained a more or less equal relationship with the government (even being referred to as a state within a state). One reason for this has been the cohesion of the French technocracy, reinforced by the practice of *pantouflage*, the transfer of high civil servants to state industry. As a result of this great homogeneity in the group of high civil servants and senior management in the public energy firms, there has been a close relationship between the government and the nationalized industries, particularly for those firms which were subject to planning contracts.[19]

The strength of EdF—and the balance of power in its relations with government—is undoubtedly best illustrated by its development of a massive nuclear programme.[20] Throughout the post-war period, EdF has been one mechanism for the government's strategic concerns in this area. However, far from being a pawn of policy, EdF has been successful in changing the direction of that policy. Although the early phase was marked by efforts to develop a truly French national champion, in 1969 the French government approved a switch, in line with EdF's wishes, to American nuclear technologies. It was then able to use its position in the French industry and economy to develop successfully a major nuclear investment. The first priority in launching this programme was to ensure that the nuclear power plant supply industry was built up to the level of scale and efficiency necessary to see through such a programme. This meant close work with the power plant manufacturers, though as with the UK, EdF already enjoyed close links with suppliers and had sought to encourage their rationalization in the 1960s.[21]

While the ESI in France has encountered many of the same problems confronted by the British industry, it has been much more resilient than its British counterpart. Over the last 10 years it experienced major financial problems over the costs of its controversial nuclear investment programme, which itself led to the creation of a massive surplus of capacity over demand. Yet in no case were the shortcomings in performance effectively exploited by the industry's critics, while opposition to the programme on environmental grounds was effectively overcome by the mid-1980s. The institutional relations between the utility and government clearly operated in favour of EdF, permitting it to neuter the function of control which the administration should have exercised. Instead the government has tended to focus on controlling the company's financial position (on one occasion refusing the utility its contractually agreed price increase). Even here, however, it might be argued that EdF could maintain its autonomy as reflected in its nuclear investment programme, which has left the company with debts of over £20 billion.

During the Chirac government there was an attempt to restructure the company, and many believed that the move was in preparation for privatization and possibly greater competition. However, the government's commitment to restructuring was rather half-hearted and the debate within EdF nipped in the bud. Some ideas of reform have permeated the company, however, as demonstrated by the series of potentially important internal reorganizing, involving the removal of a tier of administration and a sort of competition by comparison amongst production centres. The company's willingness to restructure within the system indicates a recognition that further productivity growth will not be met by simply resorting to technical fixes such as the nuclear programme, and that other mechanisms for improving performance will have to be found. Such reforms are unlikely to challenge EdF's central role in the industry, at least in the short term, however. The Balladur government has not included EdF in its privatization plans, while the Mandil report, prepared for the government at the end of 1993 to consider liberalization, stopped well short of any British-type reform. It remains to be seen whether these moves mark the sum total of the Balladur government's interest in the energy sector.[22]

The extent to which EdF has been able to retain its central position in the French industry and to resist radical reform has kept it to the fore in defending the traditional utility model, particularly *vis-à-vis* the EC. This has not prevented EdF from adopting a highly internationalist strategy, however, for example by promoting exports of power to neighbouring utilities and by engaging in foreign ventures including the construction of power stations in other Community countries.[23] None the less, while the company is prepared to take advantage of reforms in other countries, it remains opposed to any challenges to its own internal status.

4. ITALY

The Italian electricity industry was one of the last in Europe to move to the structure of a vertically integrated publicly owned utility. The industry had retained a structure of over a thousand private and locally owned utilities until the early 1960s. The state holding company IRI had built up an interest in power production from the 1930s onwards (rationalized into a single company, Finelettrica, in 1953) and there had been discussions of nationalization in the past, but the private companies (which included some of the most important industrial firms in Italy) successfully resisted change.[24]

When it came, nationalization was a controversial political act. It was one of the conditions set by the Socialists for entering the government (though the policy was also supported by left-wing Christian Democrats) and was seen as marking a new phase in Italian economic planning.[25] The programme was challenged by many in the industry (leading to a court case in the EEC) and an outflow of foreign capital.[26] Yet, beyond the rhetoric, the objectives of nationalization were relatively modest and primarily focused on rationalizing the conduct of the industry and co-ordinating the development of future investment. The government created a single company, Ente Nazionale per l'Energia

Elettrica (ENEL), to bring about greater coherence in the planning investment and construction of power plant (though a number of industrial self-producers and municipal suppliers survived). It was not intended as a national champion in the same way as other Italian public enterprises or even other European electricity companies. It was formed outside of the two major state holding companies IRI and ENI (both of which had interests in electricity) and was forbidden from engaging in the subsidiary and diversification activities of those companies.[27]

Its links with government have been primarily with the Ministry of Industry. Regulation of investments was carried out by the Interministerial Committee for Economic Planning (CIPE) and of prices by the Interministerial Committee for Prices (CIP), and its operations were intended to fit in with an overall National Energy Plan. In common with other EC states, the industry was expected to support local manufacturers (there was relatively little indigenous fuel capability). While at times, ENEL appeared more willing than other nationalized industries to look for outside sources to encourage price competition, for the most part it supported the various suppliers which were clustered round the IRI structure.[28]

The Italian electricity industry has encountered particular problems in the last ten years. While ENEL may have been intended as an efficient public utility developing national infrastructure and maintaining supply demand balances, it was grafted on to a chaotic political structure. Positions at the head of the company have had to be determined by political considerations; appointments have had to reflect the balance of power in coalition governments.[29]

It is hardly surprising that ENEL has been used as a mechanism for pursuing government policies. It has been expected to keep price increases down for counter-inflation reasons, but in contrast to other utilities who faced this obligation it was not accompanied by support in investment. Instead, ENEL has had to borrow for investment, adding to a debt burden at least partially the result of the need to compensate previous owners. Financial problems have been compounded by the difficulty in getting new plant constructed. Nationalization was meant to smooth the transition of the Italian system away from hydroelectricity to thermal power stations. In practice, however, while formal approval of investment has not proved a problem, obtaining permission to build new power plants has been extremely difficult, given the ability of local environmentalists to oppose new construction. While this has been a problem for all utilities, in Italy the problem has been particularly difficult to overcome. As a result, the company has had to rely on imports of electricity from its neighbours to meet its needs.[30]

Some of these problems have been addressed by the government in recent years. Price increases to cover costs have been approved and attempts to streamline power plant construction have been made. The government has also sought to reform ENEL itself. Since the mid-1980s, the government has established a number of commissions to reform the structure of the industry. The results have been modest (mainly confined to encouraging independent power production). More recently, the economic and political crises facing Italy have spilled over into the electricity sector. In summer 1992, the Amato government announced that ENEL would be included in a wide-ranging reform of the Italian public sector, though that programme is itself under question, at least partly because of the high debt burden of the nationalized industries (including ENEL).[31]

5. GERMANY

Although it has undergone various changes in the last hundred years, the structure of the German electricity industry has been remarkably stable. The industry developed on the one hand by industrial companies generating power for their own needs or as a by-product of their activities, and on the other by municipal authorities developing power capabilities for lighting and subsequently public supply (and so able to exploit rights of way). The structure of the industry inevitably gave rise to conflicts and at times led to debates on the industry's nationalization. Common interests between the private owners and the local and Länder elements in the industry, however, prevailed and ensured the continuation of the status quo. This coalition (though at times shaky) has also been maintained for much of the post-war period, whenever reform of the industry has been considered.[32]

The German electricity industry was shaped by pre-war legislation and agreements. The Energy Act of 1935, which recognized the principle of local monopolies in exchange for security of supply, was the main legal instrument followed by a series of demarcation arrangements which divided the country into a set of fiefdoms. The legislative structure and the demarcation agreements effectively created a multi-tiered industry characterized by three types of utility: the *Verbundunternehmen*, those companies with considerable production and transmission capacity, responsible for supply within a region and interconnected with each other; the *Regionalunternehmen*, which focus primarily on distribution activities, often embracing rural areas; the local utilities, often municipal companies, or *Stadtwerke*, with distribution and, in many cases, some production capabilities. In addition, there are some companies which are predominantly production-only utilities.

There were several hundred local utilities, just over 40 regional utilities and 8 interconnected utilities in the pre-unification Federal Republic. The structure in the former East Germany (or Democratic Republic) was characterized by a more segmented structure, with transmission, production, and distribution largely separate.[33]

The structure of ownership adds further complexity to the industry. There are a range of companies with public, private, and mixed ownership, and there are ownership linkages between these companies. The Verbundunternehmen have shareholdings in a number of the regional and local utilities (and to some extent in each other). Moreover, the shareholdings in the Verbundunternehmen are often held partly by local and Länder government. Public ownership was manifest at all levels of government. The Federal interests were largely through its shares in industrial conglomerates such as VEBA and VIAG. Throughout the industry, however, a key role has been played by banks either as shareholders or as lenders.[34]

The rather decentralized structure of ownership in the industry and the federal structure of the country has left government with fewer direct controls over the industry. Thus, while the government authorities play an important role in setting the agenda, particularly in areas such as investment controls, price setting, antitrust policy, and environmental protection, the policies are largely carried out (and are open to interpretation) by the local or Länder governments. Investment control has been exercised through the 1935 Act which gives public authorities an opportunity to vet new capacity plans. Price control is outlined in the Federal Tariff Ordinance, which sets the broad criteria by which tariffs are set and changed, but considerable scope for interpretation is given to utilities and scrutiny is carried out by Länder governments. Antitrust controls over the industry have been relatively weak—the 1957 cartel law granted the electricity sector an exemption from the general provisions of antitrust, though some restrictions remain (see below).[35]

Although economic regulation is relatively light, there are some important government policy interventions in the sector, relating to nuclear power and the environment. Indeed, of the four countries examined, Germany has had to adjust to pressures for environmental protection the most. The 1976 Atomic Law sets out the framework for licensing nuclear power plants and appraising their operations, but like other federal legislation, it is administered by Länd authorities and has been interpreted in different ways according to their political complexion. The federal law on environmental controls was established in 1982 to control emissions from power stations which it was feared were contributing to acid rain and forest damage in Germany.[36]

Relations between the utilities and their suppliers are formalized for the purchase of coal. The centrepiece is the 'contract of the century', an agreement made in 1981 to ensure a market for German coal which obliges the utilities to buy and burn German coal, supplemented by the *Kohlepfennig*, a levy on electricity prices designed to cover the costs of that purchase obligation. Links with equipment suppliers are less blatant, though the near absence of any imports suggests that preference exists, with Siemens and the German subsidiary of the then-Swiss power equipment supplier Brown Boveri particularly privileged.

The German industry has faced a number of problems over the last 10 years, though in many respects they have been mediated by the ability of the utilities to pass on the burden of such problems to consumers. However, increasingly, larger consumers have sought to circumvent these costs. A particular problem has been that of the support for the German coal industry. When the agreement was originally designed, the low level of international trade in coal along with high coal and oil prices, rendered it of mutual benefit to both industries. Since the mid-1980s the agreement has been necessary because of the high cost of German hard coal relative to other fuels and sources of coal. Although there has been considerable pressure inside and outside Germany to reform the mechanism, it survives, not least because of supply security and social concerns within Germany, and because the utilities are able to pass on cost.

The cost plus nature of the industry has also moderated utility resistance to greater environmental protection. Throughout the 1980s, the German power producers had been engaged in a heated debate with government and environmentalists over the issue of controlling emissions from power plants, primarily regarding SO_2 and NO_x. Eventually the German ESI agreed to one of the toughest environmental regimes in the Community, though to some extent this was a painless commitment for the ESI as it was able to pass on much of the costs of control to the customer. More generally, there has been considerable political opposition to the investment strategies of the large utilities and greater interest in energy efficiency and renewable energy. The actual effects of this debate have been modest: in this respect, as in many others, the big utilities still dominate the system, paying lip service to these objectives not least to counter any further moves by local municipalities to establish their own utilities (though the financial problems of local governments have restricted their ability to do so).

The most telling example of the power of the major utilities was seen in the wake of unification. An attempt to create a new industry structure in the former East German region—backed by the Cartel Office—was successfully resisted by the Verbundunternehmen, the largest three of whom were able to take over the industry and remake it in their own image (claiming that they were the only ones able to make the financial commitment of several billion pounds needed to upgrade the industry).[37]

The industry has traditionally been hostile to greater competition, successfully resisting or neutralizing earlier attempts to liberalize.[38] At the end of 1993, however, the government announced its intention to open the sector to greater competition (a decision which was paralleled by a more supportive approach to the Commission's attempts to liberalize the sector at a European level). There are grounds for believing that this effort will be more successful, not least because many of the large utilities appear to support competition themselves. A number have already engaged in cross-border co-operation with utilities in Sweden and Spain, and they clearly believe that they are likely to be the beneficiaries of this process. However, the move towards a more liberal system is likely to be gradual, given the sensitivities in other parts of the industry.

6. INTERNATIONALIZATION OF THE INDUSTRY

However large or limited the scale of reorganization under consideration within countries, it is clear that the attempt to keep that decision an internal one is becoming harder to sustain. After many years in which international contacts were characterized by cooperation, national industries began to clash over the terms of trade and access to markets. Such disputes have given the European Commission an opportunity to intervene in the industry, proposing policies which would radically restructure the sector. A partially related development has been the growing internationalization of the industry. A number of utilities are looking towards foreign ventures either as a preemptive strategy (to anticipate challenges from new competition) and/or as a means of diversification.

To understand the nature of the changes within the Community's industry, it is necessary to examine the changing significance and character of trade in electricity. In 1970, only 3 per cent of EC member states' electricity needs were imported (either among members or with neighbours outside the Community). In 1989, imports accounted for nearly 7 per cent of requirements. More importantly, whereas in the past most countries' trade positions were broadly in balance (either within or between years), now some countries have become net importers or net exporters. Countries such as Belgium and France have emerged as substantial exporters as a result of over-investment in nuclear power plants; while others such as Italy, because of rising demand and/or problems in being able to build new capacity, have turned to imports as a medium-term solution to their power needs. This switch away from a situation where countries imported as much as they exported to one where some countries were net exporters (for reasons of technology choice) while others were net importers (for reasons of poor planning and other difficulties) has begun to affect the way in which electricity trade is treated. The change in the character of trade has coincided with (and arguably has resulted from) the problems of the 1980s and the increasing divergence in the performance and prices of utilities. There has been increased tension between the utilities and between them and their customers over the trade issue.[39]

The major dispute among the utilities occurred in the late 1980s between Spain on the one hand and France and Portugal on the other. Portugal sought to buy power from France, but the cost which Spain sought to charge to act as an intermediary was considered to be exorbitant. For more than two years, the industries and governments of the three countries were locked in argument over the issue. The problem was only resolved when Community intervention was threatened. The row between utilities and their customers arose in a number of cases, as certain large consumers sought to look for supplies from abroad, an idea which was fiercely resisted by local utilities. The principal dispute arose in the mid-1980s, when a number of large industrial consumers, primarily in Germany, sought to import power directly from France. They had to pay relatively high prices for German utility power. In opposing these proposals, the German utilities argued that it would present major technical problems, and raise the cost of ensuring secure supply. As it turned out French utilities were prepared to sell directly, but not before they had challenged the protectionist attitude of the German utilities. In the period 1986–9, relations between the two industries and the two governments were tested by French complaints over the subsidy and protection given to the German coal industry. Although the matter was resolved in a Franco-German understanding on energy co-operation, it showed once again both the fragility of relations between utilities and provided another opportunity for the Commission to intervene.[40]

7. THE ROLE OF EUROPEAN COMMUNITY

The Treaty of Rome applies, by implication, to the ESI, since the industry is not explicitly exempted in its provisions. It is true that the electricity industry has often been regarded as a special case both in economic theory and in national policy practice. The near monopolistic characteristics and the close links with public authorities was (and still is) reflected in exemptions from national monopoly laws or in direct public ownership. None the less, there are key principles enshrined in articles of the Treaty of Rome which could be applied, particularly the articles on freedom of movement and competition (notably under articles 30, 37, 85, 86, 90, and 92 of the Treaty).[41]

Given the potential of the Treaty to deal with the industry, what has been the impact of Community law and policy on the sector? Until recently, very little. Other issues took precedence in Community deliberations. Moreover, the energy sector as a whole was one in which member states sought to maintain their autonomy, while public utilities as a whole were even more closely protected than other industries. Given that the ESI straddled both areas, the sector's organization and conduct were not up for debate by the CEC. In the 1960s, the Commission reviewed the issue of the monopolistic character of the industry, but while it recognized the potential for abuses of market power both within member states and between them, it shied away from action. The Commission stated that it had not received any complaints and did not think that trade in power would grow until 'co-ordination at European level of the national development programmes in the electric power sector is achieved'.[42] In other words the approach was to leave member states to determine the pace and nature of change in the industry as they thought fit.

In the 1970s, the Commission sought to influence decisions in the industry, but its efforts were made in the context of the prevailing debate on supply security which aimed to diversify sources of supply and reduce dependence on imported oil in power generation. The use of gas and oil was limited in 1975 (though the restriction was largely honoured in the breach), while various incentives for coal, nuclear, and renewables were also devised. There was also an unsuccessful attempt to break the links between utilities and their suppliers of equipment, for competition and technology reasons. This failure was symptomatic of a much wider inability to secure greater integration of Community markets as a whole.[43]

It was only in the mid-1980s that the Commission demonstrated both the willingness and the competence to challenge the national utilities which had previously been effectively protected from Community purview by member states. The new initiatives occurred in the context of developments on environmental policy and the debate on the Internal Energy Market.[44] In both respects, the Commission acted as a regulator, a role which has proved more effective than its earlier attempts to sponsor comprehensive energy policies.

The Commission's role as an environmental regulator developed in response to the problem of acid rain when, on the basis of German support, it was able to establish its leading role in regulating emissions from the 1980s on. It was able to consolidate its role as environmental regulator in the wake of the Single Act and the Maastricht treaties (though on policy initiatives in other energy issues, such as the greenhouse effect, it has proved difficult to secure agreement).

The Internal Energy Market initiative was launched on the back of the revival of the Commission's authority following the signing of the Single Act, the renewed commitment to a Single Market and, arguably most importantly, the Commission's increased readiness to apply competition law to the Community economy. This increased activism on antitrust affected public enterprises and public utilities in particular. In cases concerning the telecommunications and transport industries, the Commission effectively established precedents for action in the energy industry.[45]

The legislative onslaught followed the success of the Single Market initiative. The original Cockfield paper on the internal market did not touch on energy directly, aside from its proposals on harmonizing taxes and standards and liberalizing equipment procurement (the latter programme, designed to break the traditional links between national suppliers and utilities, was fiercely but unsuccessfully resisted by the utilities).[46] By 1988, however, the Commission published its proposals for an internal energy market. It was clear that the most significant changes were planned for the ESI. At the core of its critique of the ESI was the industry's organization. This, it was argued, acted as a barrier to trade and competition. According to the Commission, it felt 'a change in the operational (as distinct from the ownership) system would be conducive to further opening of the internal market'.[47] The analysis and Commission's initial proposals for trade and transparency were fiercely debated within the industry, with the trade issue the major area of concern. Many utilities expressed doubts both on the technical feasibility of some options and whether they would improve upon existing arrangements for trade (though inevitably, such arguments also reflected their own concerns at loss of autonomy).[48]

The Commission's first practical step came at the beginning of 1989 in its proposed package of directives covering the transparency of electricity prices, investment co-ordination, and trade amongst utilities. In effect, the Commission developed an incremental policy which it hoped would culminate in a fully integrated EC electricity market. Initially, the Commission wanted to establish the right to trade between utilities across the Community. All power-producing utilities (as distinct from distribution utilities) would be able to trade with one another. Behind this seemingly unobjectionable proposal is the problem of transportation of electricity between two countries by an intermediary (such as France, Portugal, and Spain). The Commission believed that clarifying the terms for such inter-utility trade would encourage its development. For the longer term, the Commission proposed two other measures. It sought to increase price transparency for customers to enable them to compare their prices with the objective of encouraging greater competition. It also sought to foster greater co-operation in the industry by seeking to ensure greater energy investment co-ordination, with the aim of creating an EC electricity system. In practice this would mean that a country planning new capacity would more fully assess the potential for obtaining that capacity from trade rather than engaging in new construction.[49]

The proposed directives met with mixed success. In debating these measures, member states and the industry were keen to ensure that it was left entirely separate from more radical changes in the structure of the industry. After much debate the legislation on transit and transparency was passed, confirming the EC Commission role in this area. However, a number of amendments to the transit directive restricted the scope for using it as the basis for more radical trade arrangements. Moreover, the proposal for greater co-ordination of national investment programmes was scaled down. The proposed reform to existing rules in this area (which had been scarcely used since their introduction in 1973) was dropped, with the Commission securing member state commitments to ensure that the existing rules would be pursued more vigorously.

Given the slow progress of the other initiatives, and the degree of controversy they provoked, the second stage of the programme—moving towards greater competition on a Community basis—was handled very carefully. The Commission established two working groups (one government-based and one industry-based) to investigate the pros and cons of competition in the industry. Within those groups, the balance of opinion was against change, though the presence of the governments of Britain and some other states (principally Ireland and Portugal) on the government inquiry and their utilities and some industrial consumers on the technical committee meant that the Committees were unable to present a unanimous rejection of further liberalization. However, both the industry pressure group Eurelectric (speaking for its 'continental members' and not for the British industry) and the public enterprise pressure group, the Centre for European Public Enterprises (CEEP), were vigorous in challenging Community action in this area.[50]

As a result of lobbying by opponents of the policy and the uncertain balance of opinion within the Commission, the proposals for further liberalization were steadily watered down over the course of 1991. In particular, plans to use article 90 to break the utilities' exclusive rights (paralleling developments in the telecommunications sector) were put on the shelf and the Commission proposed its liberalization under article 100A. Instead of forcing the issue (and risking a conflict in the courts and pressures on the Commission), it sought instead to secure agreement by majority vote. This decision apparently reflected a compromise both between the directorates involved and within the Commission, where it appears Sir Leon Brittan's readiness to tackle the issue was not, as in many other cases, shared by other Commissioners. The proposed directive set out two key tasks: the promotion of competition which would be put into operation at the levels of generation, transmission, and, within limits, final consumers and the creation of greater transparency and the unbundling of integrated utilities.[51]

Competition in generation would require harmonizing access conditions and a licensing procedure to be made clear to all and applied without discrimination. The proposal made provision for security of supply (up to 20 per cent of needs could be produced using indigenous resources) and limited priority could be given to the use of renewable, waste, and cogeneration sources. To ensure that production capacity is adequate to meet demand there would be for each grid a regional review of future trends in supply requirements sufficiently long-term to identify any future shortfall. This would serve as a framework for buyers to determine their needs, whether by own investment, or long- or short-term contracts. Competition in transmission would also be allowed.

The key element, however, was that of third party access (TPA) competition for end users. This would allow generators to sell their power to a range of potential customers, not just the local utility, and would permit consumers and distributors to purchase from a wider range of suppliers. For this to work the legislation requires that producers and consumers have access to the networks of distribution and transmission companies on fair terms and within the limits of available transmission and distribution capacity. As noted, this access would in the first instance be limited to larger consumers (i.e. those with annual consumption of over 100GWh/year) and larger distribution companies (or consortia). The implementation would be the responsibility of network operators.

In order that existing utilities did not abuse their position in the system, particularly in competitive situations, the directive also proposed that the utilities increase the transparency of their operations. Production, transmission, and distribution activities would each be carried out in separate divisions with separate accounts based on standard commercial practice. On this basis it was hoped that it would be possible to ensure that there would be no discrimination. The other element of transparency would relate to the operation of the terms and conditions of system use in TPA transactions. The utilities would have to outline the use made of transmission capacity and the criteria behind charges for using the system. There would also be a requirement for reports of quality of supply and service.[52]

The proposed directive therefore envisaged a gradual development of competition in the industry. It also emphasized that regulation was to be kept to a minimum and that implementation of the proposals would be left in national hands. These proposals failed to gain acceptance in the Council, however, only surviving because of the support of the UK and some other states.[53] Following further consultations—and the proposal of major amendments by the European Parliament—the Commission made further amendments to the proposals. These included the strengthening of public service obligations (countering the pro-competitive bias of previous versions) and rendered the question of competition for final users subject to a more negotiated procedure.[54]

The prospects of the directive were at the time of writing unclear but it is likely that some form of compromise allowing a more limited form of competition will emerge. The Commission is pursuing a case through the European Court to tackle the trading monopolies of utilities in a number of member states, while an article 90 action is still possible.[55] In any case, it appears likely that the Commission will remain an important factor in the European industry. On a number of occasions (notably during the UK electricity privatization) the Commission was able significantly to shape national plans. Such initiatives are likely to continue.[56]

Moreover, there are a number of developments which suggest that the shape of the industry itself is becoming more European. While the spate of national reorganization plans clearly owes a lot to the interest of the Community, the most interesting cases are those involving cross-border alliances or even mergers. In addition to the British and French activities noted earlier, there are instances where the privately owned utilities in Germany, Spain, and Belgium are buying stakes in each other. These appear to be alliances designed to preempt or at least adjust to Community intervention. In that sense these developments are bringing about a more European industry, even if it is not the one which the Commission has for the most part been aiming for.[57]

8. CONCLUSION

The European ESI is facing a challenge to its traditional pattern of organization of vertically integrated monopolistic industries operating in the public interest and often within public ownership. In each of the cases we have examined, the utilities have historically enjoyed monopoly rights to supply power to customers. Competition has been non-existent, reflecting a belief that centralizing and co-ordinating electricity supply was the best means of ensuring low cost and secure provision. Even in a case like Germany, where private companies apparently play an important role, the close links between government and the utilities has ensured that similar monopolies exist. In return for this right and considerable autonomy in their day-to-day operations and strategic planning, the utilities have been largely loyal purchasers of fuel and equipment from local sources. While there have been some key differences between the major countries, notably in the relative strength of the utility and the government, there has been considerable similarity in structures.

Across the Community, the relations between utilities and governments have come under strain, however, and new solutions have been proposed. Whereas historically the utilities have in many respects looked more like each other than their national systems, in this period of change, national characteristics have come to the fore. In Britain, poor utility performance and a neo-liberal government converged to create a completely new structure for the industry. In France, the utility has been able to resist most pressures for change though in part by devising its own reform. In Italy reform has been on the agenda for many years but has been effectively halted by political inertia and financial problems. In Germany, some reforms have taken place but without really challenging the structure of the industry. In these cases, unless the forces pushing for change are particularly strong (as arguably they were in the case of the UK) the prevailing regime can largely neuter the reform process, or at worst accommodate it within the existing rules of the game.

What is less clear is the extent to which these national regimes can continue to prevail. Will the national monopoly be eroded and the natural monopoly with it, as the proposed reforms of the Community appear to indicate? There is considerable opposition to these measures, but though the final outcome remains uncertain, changes are taking place, most notably in the internal and external orientations of the industry (often beyond the countries examined in this study). Internally, the reforms are strategic actions, as national industries seek to protect themselves from competition and takeover in a more open Community industry. In this sense the reforms might be seen as a last-ditch effort to maintain the national industrial structure. Internationally, the reforms can also be seen as strategic or preemptive, mirroring moves towards transnational ventures in sectors such as air transport and telecommunications (not to mention numerous industrial sectors).

It should be noted that the international and internal reforms are not unique to the Community. While only a handful of countries are pursuing the root and branch reorganization characteristic of the British model, there is a much broader trend towards private participation in the industry, whether through increasing access for independent power generation or in transferring publicly owned utilities to the private sector. In many developing countries these reforms are a matter of necessity: debt-ridden governments need to find some means of meeting rapidly growing demand and international advisers and lenders are pushing ideas of privatization. In industrialized countries, the policies and the motivations are a more complex mix of ideological (primarily pro-competition) and pragmatic (primarily financial constraints) concerns.

Thus, while true globalization of the industry is not possible given the limitations of networks and technology, there are some trends towards Europeanization in the operation of the industry and of broader internationalization in the corporate strategies and ownership intentions of a number of European utilities in both the Community and in the rest of the Continent. The cross-ownership stakes of Spanish with German and Belgian utilities, the ventures of EdF, the attempts by ENEL to construct power plant outwith its frontiers and the diversification spree of the British utilities, are all manifestations of this trend.

It is possible that the final outcome of such ventures will be a handful of major European utilities with interests spreading well beyond the Community and the Continent. Such a development, however, would require a weakening of the current protectiveness of most governments and utilities. A high premium continues to be placed upon security of supply and sovereignty and most of the ventures described above are for the moment rather limited in their scope. There will have to be a further erosion of the traditional preoccupations and concerns of the industry if it is to become more malleable, or at least less immovable. The policies of deregulation proposed by the Commission may not be an irresistible force, but they may contribute to the steady whittling away of the nationally based and monopolistic industrial structure which has prevailed for nearly one hundred years.

Notes

1. No general histories of the European electricity industry exist; most are confined in terms of geography and/or the time examined (of which the most notable is T. P. Hughes, *Networks of Power* (Baltimore, Md., 1983)). A useful conceptual treatment of the industry is provided in

J. P. Bouttes and P. Lederer, 'The Organization of Electricity Systems and the Behaviour of Players in Europe and the US', paper to the conference 'Organizing and Regulating Electric Utilities in the Nineties' (Paris, 1990).

2. On the pattern of regulation, see D. R. Helm and F. McGowan, 'Electricity Supply in Europe: Lessons for the UK', in D. R. Helm, J. A. Kay, and D. Thompson (eds.), *The Market for Energy* (Oxford, 1989).

3. Some details of the workings of European electricity trade are provided in International Energy Agency, *Electricity in IEA Countries* (Paris, 1985).

4. On the flagging performance of the industry as a whole, see P. Joskow and R. Schmalansee, *Markets for Power* (Cambridge, Mass., 1983).

5. The best and most comprehensive account of the pre-1980s electricity industry can be found in Leslie Hannah's history of the industry, *Electricity before Nationalisation* (London, 1979) and id., *Engineers, Managers and Politicians* (London, 1982). See also M. Chick, 'Competition, Competitiveness and Nationalisation, 1945–51', in G. Jones and M. Kirby (eds.), *Competitiveness and the State: Government and Business in Twentieth Century Britain* (Manchester, 1991).

6. See A. J. Surrey and J. C. Chesshire, *The World Market for Electric Power Equipment: Rationalisation and Technical Change* (Brighton, 1972) and B. Epstein, *The Politics of Trade in Power Plant: The Impact of Public Procurement* (London, 1972).

7. See F. McGowan and G. S. MacKerron, 'Contractualisation in the Electricity Supply Industry', in A. Harrison (ed.), *From Hierarchies to Contracts* (Newbury, 1993).

8. The first post nationalization inquiry—the Edwards Committee—emphasized the improvements from the pre-war industry: see R. Pryke, *Enterprise in Practice: The British Experience of Nationalisation over Two Decades* (London, 1971).

9. For a useful critique of the electricity industry, see Monopolies and Mergers Commission, *A Report on the Operation of the Board of its System for the Generation and Supply of Electricity in Bulk* (London, 1981). On the specific issue of the AGR, see H. Rush, G. S. MacKerron, and A. J. Surrey, 'The Advanced Gas-cooled Reactor: A Case Study in Reactor Choice', *Energy Policy*, 5/2 (June 1977).

10. See A. J. Surrey, 'The Nationalised Energy Industries', in J. Gretton and A. Harrison (eds.), *Energy UK* (Newbury, 1986).

11. See F. McGowan, 'Electricity: The Experience of Offer', in T. Gilland and P. Vass (eds.), *Regulatory Review 1993* (London, 1993).

12. See J. Roberts, D. Elliot, and T. Houghton, *Privatising Electricity: The Politics of Power* (London, 1991); and J. Vickers and G. Yarrow, 'The British Electricity Experiment', *Economic Policy*, 12 (Apr. 1991).

13. On the consequences of the new systems see House of Commons Select

Committee on Energy, 'The Consequences of Electricity Privatisation'; and G. Yarrow, 'British Electricity Prices since Privatisation', *Studies in Regulation*, 1 (Oxford, 1992).

14. On these issues, see F. McGowan, 'The Consequences of Restructuring Electricity Supply in Anglo-Saxon Countries', paper to Coped Conference, Beijing, May 1992.
15. See the Conservative Party Manifesto for the 1992 General Election.
16. See Department of Trade and Industry, *The Prospects for Coal: Conclusions of the Government's Coal Review* (London, 1993).
17. See J. Virole, 'Electricité de France', in V. V. Ramanadham (ed.), *Public Enterprise* (London, 1986); and N. Lucas and D. Papaconstantinou, *Western European Energy Policies* (Oxford, 1985).
18. On planning contracts and their precursors, see S. Estrin and P. Holmes, *French Planning in Theory and in Practice* (London, 1983). On the details of the current contract between EdF and the government, see International Energy Agency, *Energy Policies in IEA Countries 1991 Review* (Paris, 1992).
19. The author is grateful to Dominique Finon for many helpful discussions on French electricity. On the question of EdF's autonomy see also J. Hayward, *The State and the Market Economy* (Brighton, 1986).
20. S. D. Thomas, *The Realities of Nuclear Power* (Cambridge, 1987).
21. Epstein, *The Politics of Trade*, 11–13; and J. H. McArthur and B. R. Scott, *Industrial Planning in France* (Boston, Mass., 1969).
22. *Le Monde*, 10 Nov. 1993.
23. According to one report, EdF expects to allocate 50% of its investment to foreign projects by the end of the century, *FT Energy Economist*, Oct. 1992.
24. On IRI's electricity interests see K. Allen and A. Stevenson, *An Introduction to the Italian Economy* (London, 1974), p. 228. On its poor record in electricity supply, see M. V. Posner and S. J. Woolf, *Italian Public Enterprise* (London, 1967), p. 67.
25. See R. King, *Italy* (London, 1987), p. 34.
26. Allen and Stevenson, *Introduction to the Italian Economy*, 99.
27. S. B. Clough, *Economic History of Modern Italy* (New York, 1968), 339.
28. Surrey and Chesshire, *World Market for Electric Power*, 3.
29. Lucas and Papaconstantinou *Western European Energy*, 166 ff. on appointments.
30. L. de Paoli, 'Organization and Regulation of the Italian Electricity System', *ENER Bulletin*, 9 (1991).
31. On the decision to privatize and the wider economic problems see *The Economist*, 14 July 1992, p. 79.
32. Though equally the impetus for nationalization was weak: see K.

Hardach, *The Political Economy of Germany in the Twentieth Century* (Berkeley, Ca., 1980), 34, on Weimar and 142–3 on post-war German debates on nationalization as a whole.

33. F. Tjon and R. Zuhlke, 'The Future Energy Economy of East Germany', *ENER Bulletin*, 10 (July 1991).

34. On the linkages between sectors and particularly the role of the financial sector, see R. Ziegler, D. Bender, and H. Biehler, 'Industry and Banking in the German Corporate Network', in F. N. Stockman, R. Ziegler, and J. Scott (eds.), *Networks of Corporate Power* (Cambridge, 1985).

35. Helm and McGowan, 'Electricity Supply in Europe', 250–1.

36. S. Boehmer-Christiansen and J. Skea, *Acid Politics* (Brighton, 1991).

37. S. Boehmer-Christiansen, 'Taken to the Cleaners: The Fate of the East German Energy Sector', *Environmental Politics*, 1/2 (Summer 1992).

38. S. Padgett, 'Policy Style and Issue Environment: The Electricity Supply Sector in West Germany', *Journal of Public Policy*, 10/2 (1990).

39. See L de Paoli, 'Electricity and the Single European Market', *Energy Studies Review*, 1/3 (1989).

40. See D. Finon, 'Opening Access to European Grids—In Search of Common Ground', *Energy Policy*, 18/5 (June 1990).

41. On the possible application of Community law to the sector see L. Hancher and P. Trepte, 'Competition and the Internal Energy Market', *European Competition Law Review*, 13/4 (1992).

42. Commission of the European Communities, *Second Report on Competition Policy* (Luxembourg, 1973).

43. F. McGowan, 'Conflicting Objectives in EC Energy Policy', *Political Quarterly*, special edn., 'The Politics of 1992' (Dec. 1990).

44. Commission of the European Communities, *The Internal Energy Market* (Brussels, 1988 (COM (88) 238)).

45. J. E. de Cockborne, 'Liberalising the Community's Electricity Market—Should Telecom Show the Way?', *International Business Law Journal*, 7 (1990).

46. See F. McGowan and S. Thomas, 'Restructuring in the Power Plant Equipment Industry and 1992', *World Economy*, 12/4 (Dec. 1989).

47. COM (88) 238, p. 15.

48. See e.g. the report prepared by the German electricity industry association, VDEW, *Der Europäische Strommarkt* (Frankfurt, 1988) defending the *status quo*. This was of course before the recent switch in favour of competition by some of the larger utilities.

49. Commission of the European Communities, Draft Council Directive concerning a Community Procedure to Improve the Transparency of Gas and Electricity Prices Charged to Industry End Users (Brussels, 1989 (COM (89) 332)); Increased intra Community Electricity Exchanges, a Fundamental Step towards completing the Internal Energy

Market and Proposed Council Directive on the Transit of Electricity through Transmission Grids (Brussels, 1989 (COM (89) 336 SYN)); Draft Council Regulation amending Regulation no 1056/72 on Notifying the Commission of Investment Projects of Interest to the Community in the Petroleum, Natural Gas and Electricity Sectors (Brussels, 1989 (COM (89) 335)).

50. *Agence Europe*, 10 and 12 Apr. 1991.

51. Commission of the European Communities Proposal for a Council Directive Concerning Common Rules for the Internal Market in Electricity (Brussels, 1991 (Com (91) 548)). A good summary of the proposals is given in Y. Capouet, 'Completion of the Internal Market in Electricity and Gas', *Energy in Europe*, 19 (July 1992). See also 'EC Energy Break-up plan Tabled in Brussels', *Financial Times*, 16 Oct. 1991.

52. N. Argyris, 'Regulatory Reform in the Electricity Sector', *Oxford Review of Economic Policy*, 9/1 (1993).

53. At the 30 November Council Meeting, the proposals apparently only just survived the opposition of member states: see 'EC Energy Plans Survive Row', *Financial Times*, 1 Dec. 1992.

54. See Commission of the European Communities, Amended Proposal for a European Parliament and Council Directive concerning Common Rules for the Internal Market in Electricity (Brussels, 1993 (COM (93) 643)).

55. See e.g. the treatment of this issue by the Commission's Competition authorities. See Commission of the European Communities, *Twenty-First Report on Competition Policy 1991* (Luxembourg, 1992).

56. See Commission of the European Communities, *Twentieth Report on Competition Policy 1990* (Luxembourg, 1992). For a recent instance of this intervention, see *Agence Europe*, 5 (Aug. 1992) on Commission action on the French and Italian industries.

57. At times, the Commission has seemed more interested in the European-ness of the industry than the degree of competition within it. One of the key estimates of the benefits of integration is premissed on increased co-operation amongst utilities rather than increased competition. The idea of co-operation also seems to permeate the Commission's proposals for European-wide infrastructures. The proposals were presented in Commission of the European Communities, *Towards TransEuropean Networks: For a Community Action Programme* (Brussels, 1990 (COM (90) 585)).

6

Aerospace Companies and the State in Europe

PIERRE MULLER

Over the course of the last decade the aeronautical manufacturing sector in Europe has undergone a series of fundamental transformations. The 'explosion' of the civilian market and the rise of Airbus,[1] the end of the cold war, and the search for the resulting peace dividend, the emergence of new political, economic, and industrial strategies, have completely modified the environment in which European aerospace manufacturers operate. Indeed, in this sector—as in others—we are in the process of experiencing the end of the post-war period. In such a context of change, it is hardly surprising that the position of publicly-owned industries should be completely altered. In reality, in this key sector we are witnessing nothing less than a genuine revolution in the very idea of nationalized industries. These changes have had effects on three different levels, corresponding to the three major hypotheses put forward here:

1. Firstly, these companies are becoming increasingly autonomous from the governmental bodies and public policies which have existed in the aeronautical sector. It is as if the centre of gravity of the systems of action which bring together—in different ways in each country—companies and governments, is shifting in favour of the former, which are thus becoming the major actors and the place where the transaction between the market and the product takes place. This has meant that instead of acting according to a logic under which a company's actions were integrated within an overall state-determined strategy (which, moreover, was not exempt from contradictions), the situation has become one in which the company itself is now the principal actor in the system. Meanwhile, each national public policy has given itself the sole objective of contributing to a growth in its company's market share.

2. At the same time, we are witnessing a multiplication of alliance strategies between European companies which have resulted in an increasingly complex web of co-operative and competitive relationships, to the point where one can see a real problem of company identity emerging in the firms concerned.

3. Finally we can note some surprising convergencies between the policies implemented in this sector, despite the fact that these interventions had previously emerged in very different politico-industrial cultures. It seems that we are beginning to be able to discern the profile of a European model of national enterprise—within which its public or private status no longer has much importance—reinforced by the establishment at Community level of a form of 'neo-liberal interventionism' that combines both competition policies and respect for the free market on the one hand, with aid for the construction of a powerful European industrial base on the other.

In order to evaluate the extent of these changes, we need to return briefly to the importance of historical factors before presenting the new situation of the 1980s which, in turn, has led to the transformation of state–company relationships.

1. THE WEIGHT OF HISTORY

The relationships between European companies in the aerospace sector and their respective states have both some common traits and other characteristics which remain specific to each country.

1.1. Industries Under the Influence of the State

The most important facet of the aeronautical industry is the importance of the military factor. In France, the army is virtually the origin of the development of the aircraft industry in the sense that it was the military, the principal clients of the newly formed manufacturing companies, which imposed their technical choices and vision of how the market should be divided up so as to prevent any possibility of a monopoly being created. The nationalizations of

1938, together with those of the immediate post-war period, intensified this model of state–industry relations.[2]

However, this hold on the industry by the military is not a phenomenon restricted to France. Similarly, the restoration of the German aeronautical industry in the 1930s fitted in directly with Hitler's military projects. In the minds of senior military officers, the programmes for civil aircraft construction were above all a means of keeping an eye on the technology so as to maintain the capacity of research groups and the means of industrial production during times of peace. It was precisely this situation which justified the strategic character of the aircraft industry, as much in France as in Great Britain or Germany. In the minds of all politicians, regardless of their ideological stances, the maintenance of a sufficient industrial base, if necessary through public subsidies, was always a fundamental objective.

European aircraft industries therefore share a common characteristic, linked to their history and the way they were established. Until the end of the 1960s, these were armaments-based industries in the sense that their modes of operating, the choice of products manufactured and the nomination of industry leaders were all very largely in the hands of their respective governments. In his book on the relationship between the British aircraft industry and the state, Keith Hayward highlighted the dependence of the former upon the latter: 'To a large degree . . . the British aerospace industry as a whole has depended on Government. Few other industries can . . . claim a comparable depth and variety of experience of Government involvement in their affairs. The liaison has grown and expanded since the early days of aviation, when military interest first precipitated the relationship, to include all phases of manufacturing and virtually every aspect of aerospace technology.' The author, revealing the similarities between his diagnosis and that of the French equivalent, then added: 'Governments have been concerned not only with setting overall strategic objectives for the industry, but also with the minutiae of design, development, and production.'[3]

During the immediate post-war years, this system reached its apogee. At that time, both British and French ministries published a series of specifications through which they hoped to see the needs of national carriers covered (BOAC, BEA, Air France). In 1943, the British government, in the hopes of returning Great Britain to her place in the civil aviation market, set up an advisory committee under the chairmanship of Lord Brabazon. The 'Brabazon Committee' produced its report in 1945 in which it defined nine specifications for aircraft types whose construction the state ought to aid financially. The Comet and the Viscount were products of this committee's reflections.

In France a 'prototype policy' was pursued, consisting of financing the development and construction of numerous prototypes in order to maintain diverse research efforts by constructors, mass production only occurring later. This policy organized the renaissance of the French aircraft industry under the shelter of public procurement. As regards the air force, this policy enabled the launch of a succession of fighter aircraft by Marcel Dassault (Ouragan, Mystère, Mirage, etc.). In the civil aviation sector, this policy produced the launch of the Caravelle in 1951. Nevertheless, if one looks at the detail, it is noticeable that the armaments-based logic took relatively different forms in each of the countries involved. These differences are the result of both national traditions and the impact of the Second World War.

1.2. Three State–Industry Relationship Models

At the end of the war the British aircraft industry was extraordinarily powerful. It was capable of designing and building entire civil and military aircraft. It was in the vanguard of technological development, ahead of even the American aircraft industry in certain fields such as jet propulsion. This meant that it could attempt to play a leading role on its own, and that it was not going to be prepared to relinquish this role without a fight. However, in order to preserve this technological leadership, those in favour of public intervention had to organize and mobilize themselves against the Treasury, which had always remained very sceptical as regards the use of public funds on the aircraft industry. All this meant, contrary to the situation in France, that state aid to the industry was always a subject of political controversy.

Immediately after the Second World War, aircraft construction policy still depended upon the Ministry of Supply. However, in 1951 the Conservative Government, supporting their arguments with evidence of the relative failure of the programmes drawn up by the Brabazon Committee, looked to reducing the financial involvement of the state, without going as far as abandoning the idea of steering the development of British civil aviation, notably through applying pressure to airlines to 'buy British'. The consequence of this policy emerged in 1959, when serious tension came to the surface between the Ministry of Supply, responsible for civil aviation manufacturing, and the Ministry for Civil Aviation, in change of policies concerning the airlines.

Following this clash, the functions of the Ministry of Supply concerning civil and military aviation were transferred to a new ministry, the Ministry of Aviation (1959). This period, which corresponds to a return to a system of public 'launch aids', is a sort of golden age for public intervention in aeronautical affairs in Great Britain: reunited under the same ministerial department, the aeronautical sector as a whole became a formidable pressure group. The return to power of the Labour Party in 1964, however, modified the contours of the system of state–industry relations, without fundamentally challenging the principle of state aid to civil aviation programmes. The Ministry of Aviation, seen as the exclusive spokesman for the industry, became integrated within the Ministry for Technology in 1966. More widely, the 1965 Plowden Report put the accent upon the necessity for a more commercial approach to state aid for civil programmes. Of course the major trauma for the British civil aviation policy was the Concorde programme. As difficulties ranging from leadership conflicts to the shocking loss of expenditure control came to light, the image of the civil aviation industry deteriorated to a point where it became synonymous with a black hole into which public money disappeared. In interministerial discussions, the Treasury began to get its way more often, and this is certainly one of the major explanations for the British withdrawal from the Airbus programme in 1968.

The French aircraft industry in 1945 was in a paradoxical situation: its factories and equipment had been destroyed and it suffered from technological backwardness linked to the hibernation of researchers during the war. As a result, immediately after the *Libération* a frenzy of research projects and prototypes occurred. Not all of these were very realistic, but they enabled France to recover its position as a major power in aviation within ten years. It was during this period that the relationship between the state and the industry emerged in a most spectacular manner.

The French model is characterized by the central role of the Ministry of Defence which has had power over this entire industrial sector. Beginning with the launch of the Caravelle, the Ministry of Transport, through the General Secretariat (from 1976 Directorate General) for Civil Aviation and its responsibilities for airlines, became more important in decisions concerning the launch of civil aviation programmes. However, this role remained minor until the launch of Concorde, and it was not until 1976 that the Ministry of Transport became the body genuinely in charge of aircraft manufacturing. This situation is due to the manner in which technical expertise was located in the French aviation sector. This gave a special place to the corps of engineers involved in arms development because there was a concentration of strategic expertise in the hands of a socially homogeneous group capable of mastering most of those in positions of administrative and industrial responsibility. The strong cohesion of this state–industry system has been a result of this period and contrasts with the uncertainty of its British and German counterparts.

In many respects the comparison between the German aeronautical policy and that of France and Great Britain reflects the relative weakness of this sector in Germany: immediately after the war the German aeronautical industry no longer existed. Its leading specialists were 'headhunted' by Allied countries. In addition, a part of the industry's potential was in East Germany and therefore unrecoverable. Until the end of the 1960s the German industry had to be content to produce under licence aircraft designed by its former enemies.

When, in 1968–9, the German so-called 'grand coalition' government began to invest large sums of money in the Airbus programme, this was with the aim of re-establishing an industrial base in the civil aviation construction market, even if this objective was somewhat overshadowed by the more global aim of reinforcing links between France and Germany. Moreover, the German aeronautical industry remained for a long time divided into many different companies, none of whom apparently made much in the way of profits. The conflicts over the construction of Transall, the Franco-German military freight plane, which had led to the establishment of two production lines in Germany, and the problems of the association between VFW and Fokker which blew up over the

VFW 614 fiasco, are further evidence of German weakness in aircraft manufacture.

These three countries therefore represent three different models of the armaments strategy. In France the model was at its 'purest' due to the role of the *Armement* engineers. In Great Britain, if aviation policy was seen as a strategic field, as borne out by the existence for a long period of a Ministry of Aviation, the policy was not promoted by a group that was as coherent or powerful. As for Germany, the aeronautical industry enjoyed no particular prestige, and only the need to rebuild an industrial sector befitting the economic power that Germany had become, justified intervention by the federal government. Nevertheless, despite these different conditions, all three countries went on to encourage in a similar manner the establishment of a public industrial development champion in the aeronautical sector.

1.3. Concentrations and Nationalizations

Public intervention in the aerospace sector has taken two successive forms in the period since the Second World War.

The first, until about the middle of the 1960s, corresponded to a logic of market sharing. It consisted of maintaining the potential for research and production sufficient to face up to possible military needs. In this respect public authorities looked to share out different civil and military programmes between the principal constructors. Meanwhile they hoped to encourage the specialization of research bodies. Thus in France, at the beginning of the 1960s, research and production of military aircraft went to Dassault and Bréguet, tactical missiles and military transport aircraft went to Nord Aviation, and civil aircraft and helicopters to Sud Aviation. During the same period in Great Britain, civil aviation programmes were shared out between Hawker Siddeley (Trident, the Airbus) and BAC (VC 10, Concorde).

However, in the middle of the 1960s it became clear in all the European countries that this market-sharing logic was keeping their aeronautical industries in an inferior position as regards international competition. So long as firms were working for a protected market, such an approach could still be profitable for the state. With the opening up of frontiers, though, this approach was no longer sustainable. Consequently a new logic of action developed, this time based upon industrial concentration with the objective of holding on to the industry's place in the face of world-wide competition. In some ways the same pre-suppositions (retain an industrial and technological capacity in a field seen as strategic) resulted in opposite responses. This is why at this time the race for concentration reinforced statist interventionism; in all cases mergers occurred at the instigation of states. In France, Aérospatiale was created in 1970 by merging Nord Aviation, Sud Aviation, and the rocket manufacturer SEREB. In Great Britain, British Aerospace was set up by the nationalization of Hawker Siddeley and its merger with BAC. In Germany the federal government constantly looked to promote the concentration of its aeronautical industry using financial crises to impose alliances. In order to do so, it used the support of several key people in the industry, in particular Ludvig Bölkow, who in many respects was the federator of the German aeronautical industry due to his merger of VFW and MBB (the 'southern' and the 'northern' industry) through an alliance of German capital, the Federal Government, and certain Länder.

As the 1980s dawned the European situation had therefore become much simpler. In the three major aeronautical countries a public firm dominated the sector in a more or less clear fashion, leaving the crumbs to several private companies (Dornier in Germany, Shorts or Westland in Great Britain). Paradoxically it was in France, where this movement had begun the earliest, that the process was the least complete, since Dassault (which had taken over Bréguet) kept its independence, even if this was in the form of a private armaments manufacturer.

2. THE NEW FACTORS OF THE 1980s

As of the 1970s the system founded upon military procurement relations was progressively brought into question. This evolution can be interpreted on several levels, but it is clearly the development of the Airbus programme which marked the introduction of the logic of the market, reinforced by the round of privatizations in Great Britain and in West Germany.

2.1. Airbus Changes the Nature of the Problem

Four European countries are linked in the Airbus programme: France (through the company Aérospatiale) with 37.9 per cent, Germany (DASA) with 37.9 per cent, the United Kingdom (British Aerospace) with 20 per cent, and Spain (CASA) with 4.2 per cent. Over the last 20 years the Airbus programme has enabled Europe to regain its position in the world civil aviation transport marketplace, previously entirely dominated by American manufacturers. Currently, Airbus is responsible for about 30 per cent of the world market, the Airbus range comprising six models of medium- or long-range, 150- to 350-seater aircraft.

In the beginning the Airbus programme developed according to the classical model: the relevant ministries defined a programme with specifications regarding the needs expressed by the airlines and technological possibilities; on the basis of these specifications tenders were put out and the response to these evaluated according to military-type guidelines. As in any venture involving co-operation, the most difficult problem to resolve was the programme's leadership. In 1967, when the strict style of military procurement continued to reign, it was decided that Sud-Aviation (which later became Aérospatiale) should be given this role for the airframe, with Rolls-Royce taking on the corresponding role for the motors. However, the airlines, doubting the credibility of the programme, refused to agree to this arrangement. By 1968 the programme was virtually at a standstill. This is when, faced with the project's loss of political, technological, and industrial direction, those responsible for the programme decided to study *in secret* a new version of the aircraft which would be better adapted to its users and likely to be equipped with an 'off the shelf' engine. It was at this moment that the decisive *rupture* with the military procurement system of reference occurred: firstly there was an attempt to follow as closely as possible the demands of the world market, without tying one's hands to the specific demands of a national carrier; secondly the military procurement-style compromise between France and the United Kingdom was criticized for blocking the development of the aircraft's configuration over questions of political and industrial leadership.

Consequently the British government, seeing the project shift away from its original specifications and the position of Rolls-Royce under threat, withdrew from the project (the United

Kingdom rejoined Airbus ten years later for the launch of the A310). Conversely, the German government was adamant that it wanted to continue the programme with France, Spain associating itself with the project subsequently. Indeed, for Germany this was a unique opportunity to make a comeback in the civil aviation market. The enterprise responsible for the management of the programme was called Airbus Industrie. Contrary to the hopes of a section of its management, Aérospatiale did not win the role of implementing this operation. The Germans, conscious of the risk of becoming locked into French industry, succeeded in getting the co-ordination of production, marketing, and test flights under the control of Airbus Industrie and not under one of its partners.

This decision was fundamental because it gave Airbus Industrie sufficient autonomy of decision making to allow it to take over the programme's leadership. Indeed, although it could have become little more than a simple sales office, Airbus Industrie progressively imposed itself on the world market as a constructor in its own right. In order to take maximum advantage of its principal resource (commercial expertise) the managers of Airbus Industrie adopted new, more aggressive marketing techniques along the lines of those of their American competitors. This is how, after difficult beginnings, Airbus came to earn itself a commercial credibility with its customers that was completely different from the traditional image of European constructors (Fokker excepted). It was this commercial success which made Airbus Industrie into the indispensable channel for all programmes of civil aeronautical co-operation in Europe, sidelining all other attempts, notably by the French. In other words, Airbus Industrie affirmed itself as the key actor in the decision-making system (especially for the launch of new versions or new models) because, through its marketing capacities, it possessed the most strategic expertise. However, in a reciprocal manner, this expertise only became strategic from the moment when a new system of norms imposed itself to the detriment of the military procurement system of reference: *the market system of reference.*

For the European managers involved in this project (and for the French in particular) this has been no less than a cultural revolution: it was discovered that there was no point in producing aircraft if the market did not want them. Commercial managers took over the leadership to the detriment of state engineers. In discussions with industrialists on the choice of equipment or on the characteristics of the aeroplane, the management of Airbus Industrie systematically ensured that their point of view prevailed because it reflected the needs of the market.

The Ariane programme is another example of this evolution towards market-led logic. Over and above its technical success (spectacular when one recalls the previous setbacks experienced by Europe's space sector) or commercial success (on 15 April 1992 the European rocket carried out its fiftieth flight since the first launch in December 1979 and had captured around 50 per cent of the world satellite market), just like the Airbus programme, the programme's progress is evidence of the transformation of the dominant system of reference in the aerospace sector. Since 1980, indeed, marketing of the launcher to other operators has been handed over to the company Arianespace, thus becoming the first company involved in space transport. Created at the initiative of the French Centre National d'Etudes Spatiales, the company is also responsible for financing launcher production.

Even if it is obvious that this company remains strongly linked to the European, and particularly French, 'space community', as the career histories of its managers testify, it is striking to note how closely Arianespace's strategy mirrors that of Airbus Industrie at its early stages. Deliberately adopting a low profile from the technological point of view, the company sets out its only objective as satisfying the market at the least cost possible. Consequently, in order better to adapt itself to the needs of its customers, Ariane 4 has six different versions weighing from 210 to 470 tonnes and can put into orbit payloads ranging from 1.9 to 4.2 tonnes. In order to keep costs down the company has set up a policy of long-term supply, ordering a series of 50 launchers from industrial companies. In 1991 Arianespace had a turnover of FF5.9 billion and a net profit of FF154 billion.

Of course, the development costs of this system of spatial transport remain the responsibility of the states within the European space agency, linked to their financial involvement on a pro rata basis,[4] the industrial shares corresponding to the reciprocal *juste retour*. Nevertheless, it is interesting to note that it is the necessity to maintain Europe's commercial presence in satellite markets, and this is now the main justification for the financial efforts made. This is so clear that of the three European space projects in operation, only the Ariane 5 rocket is not the subject of budgetary conflict, unlike the Hermes and Columbus projects. As in the case of Airbus, it is therefore commercial norms that have taken centre stage for space policies, justifying and setting which investments are made.

2.2. The Switch from Military Aeronautics towards Civil and Space Sectors

Of course, even when the military procurement logic was dominant in the aerospace sector, aeronautical programmes were supposed to satisfy certain commercial criteria. However, at the time, the market was just one constraint amongst others, coming after political, technological, or industrial constraints. For example, Concorde was built in order to compete in the long-haul carrier market dominated by American firms. However, the approach of the engineers and government officials meant that the satisfaction of the customers' needs would be achieved implicitly through the definition of the technical objective itself. Airbus and Ariane are therefore not simply programmes which, in contrast to Concorde, have succeeded in attaining a more commercial phase. They are evidence of a fundamental change in the operating procedures of the actors involved in the European aerospace sector. This change has taken shape both through the victory of marketing managers over engineers in the definition of their products, and by the transformation of the norms that structure public policies.

Subsequently this market logic has spread to other aeronautical programmes. This was the case for the Franco-American medium-range jet engine, the CFM 56. Through this programme, and as a result of contacts with its associate company General Electric, Snecma (which previously had only manufactured military engines) also discovered commercial markets. The genesis of the CFM 56 is also very similar to that of Airbus: the operation was launched initially in close collaboration between the constructor and the state; then, with the aid of some commercial success, increasingly decisions to widen the range became taken in relation to the strict commercial logic of developing the product, with the French ministry only intervening at the end as a simple provider of funds. Similarly, the Franco-Italian programme ATR (a regional transport aeroplane with 50–70 seats) was developed using criteria based exclusively upon the state of the market.

Clearly the switch to a more commercial logic has been facilitated by the increasing share of civil aviation in the plans of the
aeronautical industrialists following the emergence of a new context of East-West *détente*. This is particularly clear for Snecma, the
steady rise in sales of the CFM 56 leading the French engine
manufacturer to a situation where most of its turnover is in civil
activities. The same has occurred in Aérospatiale which, with the
enlargement of the Airbus range, in 1988 saw its civil turnover
exceed that of military sales (56 per cent in 1989). Even Dassault,
which remains a principally military constructor, aims for a civil
turnover of around 35 per cent. Overall, although the civil part of
the French aerospace industry's turnover was 30 per cent in 1982,
this went up to 44 per cent in 1987, and reached 52 per cent in
1991. Even more spectacularly, the proportion of civil production
exported has risen from 20 per cent in 1982 to 70 per cent currently. The situation is similar in Germany, where the proportion of
workers engaged in civilian production has gone up from 30 per
cent in 1970 to 70 per cent today. In terms of turnover, the
objective of Deutsche Aerospace (DASA) is to reduce its military
activities to 25 per cent of its turnover in the medium term. This
corresponds with the situation in Italy, where around 70 per cent of
turnover is earnt from civilian production. British Aerospace's situation is a little different since, although its military activities represent less than half of the group's turnover (including cars and real
estate), they exceed by far civil aviation activities. Significantly,
military sales accounted for 83 per cent of the group's profits in
1991.

Such a situation has brought about a change in the industrial and
commercial culture of companies in this sector. From the moment
military orders became less important, companies were required to
define new approaches to their markets by looking to develop their
products beyond the simple need to satisfy the demands of their air
force. Conversely, such a situation has necessarily meant a weakening in the co-ordinating role of the ministries.

2.3. The End of the 'Armament Style' and Privatization

During the 1980s changes in the industrial strategies of European
aeronautical firms went hand in hand with the types of intervention
of the governmental authorities. In Great Britain, after the double

trauma of Concorde and the bankruptcy of Rolls-Royce, it became clear that the commercial dimension of civil aeronautical programmes had to be reinforced. Since 1971,[5] following the report written by Derek Rayner, chief executive of Marks & Spencer, the Ministry of Technology had been abolished and formulation of aeronautical policy transferred to the Department of Trade and Industry (DTI). This reform marks the end, in Great Britain, of specific treatment of the aeronautical industry within the administrative hierarchy. Even if the Labour Government interlude (1974–9) allowed the return of some forms of 'armament' strategies, with the creation of British Aerospace it is far from certain that the change in the status of the industry fundamentally altered the growth of a new logic for political decision making. In any case the Conservative victory in 1979 resoundingly marked the triumph of neo-liberal ideas and led to the privatization of British Aerospace, Rolls-Royce, as well as British Airways.

In Germany, as of the middle of the 1970s, the government began to set out increasingly strict guidelines as to the commercial credibility of projects put forward by the European consortium Airbus. More generally, the public status of MBB was increasingly open to criticism: in the West Germany of the 1980s this aeronautical company was one of the 'lame ducks' living off the public purse. Consequently the German government decided to kill two birds with one stone: by selling MBB to Daimler-Benz in 1989, it privatized the aircraft constructor and combined it with a powerful industrial group enjoying a reputation for efficiency and capable of injecting the necessary capital to give Germany back an aeronautical industry worthy of its new economic status and role.

The privatizations of the 1980s did not challenge the strategic character of the aeronautical industry. Instead, governments attempted to set up powerful private champions which would guarantee both commercial profitability and industrial and technological power. These efforts, none the less, did not signal the end of all public aid, even if this aid became more indirect, such as the sale of Rover to British Aerospace at a knock-down price, the exchange rate guarantees granted to Deutsche Aerospace, or political support given by the British government for exports of the Hawk or the Tornado. In the rest of Europe, nationalized companies continue to dominate, but doubtless not for long. If in Italy the state controls 80 per cent of the aerospace sector, a vast programme of privatization of public holdings was implemented. In Spain, CASA is 98 per cent state-owned, but the possibility of its privatization is raised from time to time.

In France, even if Aérospatiale and Thomson remain public companies, the system of state–industry relations has undergone a profound shake-up. The weakening of the proportion of military programmes compared to civil production has modified the relations between the firms in the sector and the Délégation Générale à l'Armement. This body is no longer the principal decision-making centre setting the strategies of the firms, since the latter are increasingly taking into account commercial-type factors which civil servants master relatively poorly. Major strategic decisions, such as the creation of Eurocopter by Aérospatiale and Deutsche Aerospace, are based upon the firm's strategy to occupy a significant part of the world market, much more than to meet 'armaments'-based goals. Ironically, the launch of the Tiger combat helicopter has not counteracted this change in logic. For its part Thomson has multiplied its alliances and strong-mindedly pursued attempts to set itself up in the United States, without giving too much thought to the effects of its strategy for the coherence of the industrial sector as a whole.

3. TRANSFORMATIONS OF THE STRATEGIC ENVIRONMENT

Nevertheless, by the mid-1990s the revolution of the aerospace sector is not yet complete. New strategies are developing which seem to confirm the profound change in relations between states and firms from this sector.

3.1. The European Aeronautical Industry's New Situation

Within a total annual turnover of approximately US$65 billion, that is 45 per cent of the turnover of the American industry, France and Great Britain each represent around 30 per cent, while the German industry accounts for 25 per cent and the Italian 8 per cent. In 1989 the British industry employed 190,000 people, the French 120,000, and the German 95,000.

The most spectacular evolution is that experienced by the German industry, whose rise has provoked strong concern in both France and Great Britain. In 1960 the German aerospace industry employed 15,000 people, with an annual turnover of $300 million. In 1989 the employees numbered 95,000 and its turnover had reached $17 billion. Within this total the Deutsche Aerospace group (DASA) had 63,000 employees and a turnover of $10 billion. DASA, with its four divisions, covers all types of activities (civil and military aircraft, including MBB and Dornier, motors, defence systems, space). British Aerospace for its part made a turnover of $24 billion in 1990, of which $13 billion came from the aerospace part of its activities. This was more than half the turnover of the British aerospace industry.

The Italian industry has an annual turnover of $7 billion while employing about 50,000 people. It is dominated by the nationalized company Alenia, a subsidiary of IRI-Finmeccanica, the product of a merger in 1990 of Aeritalia and Selenia. It covers four fields: civil and military aircraft, defence (missiles, avionics), civil systems, and space. A second public company, Agusta (9,800 employees), is specialized in helicopters and general aviation equipment. It is a subsidiary of the state holding company, EFIM, which, in the face of sizeable financial difficulties, is threatened with closure. The Spanish industry is, also, largely dominated by a public firm, CASA, which has a turnover of $55 million and employs 9,500 people. Conscious of their weakness compared to other European competitors, Alenia and CASA have deliberately played the subcontracting card, notably with American firms, collaborating with Airbus, McDonnell Douglas, and Boeing at the same time.

In most European countries, therefore, a dominant firm is emerging which is virtually identified with the sector and in any case imposes its leadership. It may be private, as in Germany or Great Britain, or public, as in Italy or Spain, but this dominant company plays a strategic role which obviously goes beyond its strictly industrial role. Whatever their status these firms, which concentrate the essential part of the innovatory and production capacities of their respective countries, constitute formidable lobbies and exercise an important influence over political choices, especially as regards defence. Only one exception to this rule exists: France, which has seen its leadership of the sector weaken in recent years.

3.2. France Loses her Position of Leadership

Faced with all these changes, times are hard for the French industry. Previously it had occupied a central position in Europe, exercising leadership in the majority of co-operative programmes in the civil field (Concorde, Airbus), military aircraft (Jaguar, Transall, Atlantic), helicopters, and even space. During this period when the armaments logic was dominant, constant support from the state and the power of the *corps de l'Armement* gave the French policy unparalleled continuity and its industry a position that was the envy of its competitors. However, when the logic of the market began to triumph, the French model lost its effectiveness. To be more precise, the French industry has suffered from three handicaps compared to its British or German competitors:

1. Its industrial base is more fragmented, with two actors dominating the scene: Aérospatiale (an annual turnover of FF 33 billion and 33,500 employees). Thomson CSF (turnover of FF 35.1 billion), followed by Matra (FF 22.6 billion). These figures are weak if one compares them to British Aerospace, and even weaker when compared to those of Daimler-Benz. Although the merger of Dassault (annual turnover of FF 14.5 billion in 1991) and Aérospatiale is often forecast, these two traditionally rival firms have kept their independence. Deprived of export markets, Dassault has looked to conserve its research and development capacity through the Rafale fighter aircraft programme, while Aérospatiale has concentrated upon civil markets, helicopters, and space. The missile sector is also segmented, with two large operators (Matra and Aérospatiale), and now Thomson. The same can be said for the aviation equipment sector. The consequence has been that Aérospatiale's leadership is constantly contested, in the past by Dassault, and today by Thomson, whose president would like to federate the entire French defence industry.

2. French public companies, notably those involved in aerospace, suffer from chronic under-capitalization which handicaps them in developing strategies of international development. To remedy this, new partners have been envisaged, the first steps towards a partial privatization of these companies. In this respect, in July 1992 Crédit Lyonnais decided to purchase 20 per cent of Aérospatiale's capital, thereby reinforcing the company's own finances. More subtly, one senses that French firms are on the

defensive faced with the power of British Aerospace and the ambitions of Daimler-Benz. In the European debate the public status of Aérospatiale is increasingly seen as an anomaly. Likewise, British and German attacks on the status of Airbus Industrie are increasing (it is not a genuinely private firm). Moreover, the public status of these firms is often invoked by foreign governments as an obstacle to associating with companies working on defence contracts.

3. More generally, one has the very distinct feeling that the French model of state–firm relations, so effective in the past in looking after French interests, is functioning less well. German national interests, for example, are better defended by Daimler-Benz than by the state, as proven by the transfer to Hamburg of the A321 production line (and no doubt that of the A319), since the German partner has justified the transfer in the name of economic profitability, which has become the decisive argument.

3.3. The Search for Optimum Size through Alliances

The third characteristic of the current period is the search for industrial alliances so as to attain a size sufficient to take on a market that is now world-wide. On this subject some caution is advisable: alliances announced as secure have a habit of unravelling after a few months, as was the case with the attempt made by Thomson and British Aerospace to work together on missile development, and the failure of Thomson to purchase the American firm LTV.

In the civil sector, one must mention the Airbus consortium which links British Aerospace, Aérospatiale, DASA, and CASA, to which should be added the subcontractors Belairbus, Fokker, Alenia, Canadair, and other American and Japanese partners. For their part, Aérospatiale and Alenia are associated to build regional transport aircraft within GIE ATR. DASA, which was already a subcontractor to the Dutch company Fokker for the production of the Fokker 100, over the last couple of years has attempted to launch a small 100 to 130 seater twin-engined jet which would compete with the Fokker project to enlarge the F100, British Aerospace's BAe 146 range and Airbus's projected A319, a development of the A320! Not being able to launch a programme alone, and after having tried to establish an alliance with Chinese firms,

DASA has signed an alliance 'in principle' with its two partners from ATR within the framework of the Regionliner programme. This has not prevented MBB from planning the launch of a competitor to the ATR 42, within the Dornier range. Finally, on 24 July 1992, the German firm managed to buy Fokker outright. Fokker should now become one of the companies within the DASA group specializing in the production of 65 to 130 seater jets. The contributions of Aérospatiale and Alenia to the capital of the Dutch firm, thus making it a European champion in the production of regional transport aircraft, is envisaged for a later date.

If, in the civil sector, British Aerospace is relatively isolated, in the military sector it is Dassault who is going it alone against the British company, DASA, Alenia, and CASA, which are linked together in the EFA programme. However, difficulties in running this programme are such that a reversal of alliances should not be ruled out in the future. For its part, Alenia has co-operated with the private Italian group Aermacchi and the Brazilian group Embraer to build a tactical military aircraft, the AMX. In addition there is the European military transport project within which Aérospatiale, DASA, British Aerospace, Alenia, and CASA co-operate.

Not surprisingly, the growth of criss-crossing alliances in these sectors and for helicopters, aeroengines, and missiles, leads to complex situations, partners in one project being competitors in others. (See Appendix.) The incredible confusion over the European 130 seater aircraft is just one example. Nevertheless three comments can be made:

- Other than for the EFA project, British Aerospace is relatively isolated from this alliance seeking which shows up a clear Franco-German axis, to which Italian firms have tried to attach themselves. Of course this has not meant that friction has been avoided between the French, looking to maintain their leadership as much as possible, and the Germans, who would like to become a major constructor in their own right. Disputes have included aspects as symbolic as the transfer of the A320 production line. Nevertheless, the links are so strong between these two countries (Ariane, Airbus, missiles, Eurocopter) that their respective strategies are completely interwoven.
- Even if certain military markets still produce alliances imposed by governments based on 'reciprocal return' (military transport,

NH 90), these large projects no longer bear much resemblance to the attempts at industrial interventionism typical of a period when the armaments model was dominant. Now the sector is more commonly dominated by the strategies of industrial actors looking to increase their power in the marketplace through developing criss-crossing links of competition and alliance, as happens elsewhere, for example, in the world-wide computer market. In this new game, governments are more spectators than promoters. Moreover, this game is not restricted to Europe: there have also been alliances with American motor manufacturers, increasingly frenetic searches for partners in Asia (notably in the civil and motor domains), and attempts by Thomson to buy out the American company LTV.

• Finally, it is increasingly clear that one of the problems posed by these co-operation strategies is that of the identity of the entities that are being set up. Indeed, large firms such as Aérospatiale or DASA are ultimately no longer anything much more than empty shells, or rather luxury subcontractors. As such they are engaged in research on and production of products defined by entities with uncertain status, such as Airbus Industrie, ATR, or Eurocopter, but whose major characteristic is always to concentrate commercial knowledge so as to provide a better interface with potential clients. This role obviously gives these consortia a special position in the definition of the product. This is why sometimes such extraordinary collisions occur, an example being the A319, vigorously pushed by Airbus, and the Regioliner, the fruit of (possible) alliances between ATR and DASA.

4. TOWARDS NEW STATE–INDUSTRY RELATIONS IN THE AEROSPACE SECTOR

Taken as a whole the new relations between companies from the European aerospace sector and governments are expressed in three phenomena which currently mark this field of activity: the continuous drop in defence budgets and the tendency for states not to commit themselves financially, the symmetrical emergence of the firm—be it public or private—as a strategic industrial actor, and the dramatic entry—although still modest in overall terms—of the EEC in a sector from which it had previously been absent.

4.1. The Peace Dividend and Financial Constraints

Cuts in military and space budgets have hit the European aerospace industry hard. In France it has been estimated that the sector's volume of business will drop by 25 per cent between 1992 and 1994, which will obviously pose enormous problems of reconversion and excess labour. Obviously France is not the only country affected. In Great Britain orders for the Tornado fighter bomber have fallen, whilst in Germany the costs of reunification have meant that the manufacture of the Jäger 90 (EFA) seems to be in doubt, a German withdrawal bringing the whole programme under question, at least as regards its initial conception.

Of course changes in the strategic situation between East and West will accentuate this trend. The movement is very clear in the United States: the managers of Boeing are engaged in a continuous process of restructuring their military activities in order to face up to the predicted drop in orders. Most new programmes in the aerospace sector are threatened with cancellation (A12) or serious reduction in the range to be produced (B2, C17, V22). In France, even if the Rafale programme seems to have been launched in a manner that cannot be reversed, arguments over its cost that have accompanied the decision to go ahead with the project reveal just how sensitive this subject has become.

This budgetary constraint does not only affect military programmes. In the space field, if the Ariane 5 programme is to be maintained because of its commercial importance, the Columbus and Hermes programmes have been put back because of budgetary shortages. Even aid to the Regioliner programme, despite its being of vital interest to DASA, are no longer secure. In Spain the incapacity of the government to ensure a reasonable recapitalization of CASA has produced a situation where partial privatization is envisaged.

State aids to firms in the aerospace sector can take various forms, thus making their identification particularly difficult, as the controversy over Airbus has shown. In particular it is necessary to distinguish aid for research which is not linked to one particular product (research into new materials, aerodynamics, jet propulsion), from aids for launching a programme. In France practically all civil programmes (Airbus, ATR, business aircraft, helicopters) have benefited from public loans. In the case of public companies one also needs to mention capital grants, which in principle are legitimate since the state is a shareholder, but which are always suspected by Brussels of being a form of hidden subsidy. Lastly one should also mention foreign exchange guarantees, such as those accorded by the German government to Daimler-Benz when it took over MBB.

More generally, there has been a transformation in the relations between governments and firms over financial matters. It is of course over the Airbus programme that this change is at its most evident. Traditionally each constructor has attempted to obtain from its government the means to finance research and development of an aircraft (this phase can last five to six years). Even if the manner of so doing has varied from country to country, the principle remains the same: the state gives the constructor an advance (launch aid) which is to be reimbursed should the aircraft be a commercial success. In the strict sense of the term this is not a subsidy and, indeed, constructors have begun to reimburse the advances on earlier programmes.

Formally, therefore, Airbus Industrie does not receive any public aid. However, in order to launch a programme the company must ensure that all its industrial partners have obtained corresponding funds. The political decision to launch a programme is only possible when the four govermments involved have reached agreement with their respective industrialists over the financial arrangements (amount of advance and method of reimbursement). In the beginning the Airbus programme was financed 100 per cent by public funds. Since then there has been a steady decrease in the percentage of public aid, notably the French contribution (75 per cent for the A320, 60 per cent for the A340, 0 per cent for the A321—which is really only a modified version of the A320).

Two phenomena explain this steady decrease in government contributions to Airbus's financing. The first is clearly the controversy with the United States which arose immediately when Airbus became a serious competitor to the American industry. Going beyond the arguments made by one side and then the other (both parties accuse each other of subsidizing their aerospace industries, using different means), this controversy highlights the different cultural models underlying the two completely different sets of state–industry relations. In Europe, as in the US, the aerospace industry is seen as strategic. However, the debate is centred upon the *form* of these relations, notably over direct aids for development as practised in Europe. Indeed, for the Americans the system of reimbursable advances distorts competition because it transfers the risk inherent in all commercial activity from the firm to the state.

The result of the agreement reached on 31 March 1992 shows that, in the main, the Europeans have moved to meet the American arguments, accepting a limitation on government aid of 25 per cent of a programme's development costs, as well as stricter conditions for the repayment of public loans. Even if the Americans have in return accepted limits on indirect aids, the Europeans have accepted the biggest changes. This point brings us to the second phenomenon. Indeed, independent of the GATT question, if European governments have on the whole accepted the American conditions, this is due to the fact that direct financing by European states of civil aviation programmes appears to be in increasing contradiction with the new norms of aeronautical policy (the market system of reference), as well as increasing budgetary constraints.

The consequences of this trend for Europe have been a weakening of states' capacities to influence the strategies of firms in this sector. Again appearances are deceptive, since France, despite its large public sector involvement, is comparatively badly placed. The proportion of public orders in the annual turnovers of its firms ranges from 28 to 31 per cent, compared with 35 per cent for British or German firms. The consequence of the weakening of state influence is an increase in the room for manoeuvre of the firms involved in this sector.

4.2. The Growth of the Firm as a Place where Diverse Policies are Made Coherent

It is obvious that freedom from state interventionism in the decision making of firms in the aerospace sector is much stronger today, even if this industry still depends very heavily upon public funding. This is due to the fact that from now on the strategic element in aircraft manufacturing is the capacity of firms to reach an optimum point between technico-industrial constraints and the demands of an increasingly competitive and uncertain marketplace. In other words, what counts is being able to offer the right product at the right time, in the knowledge that it takes about five years to develop a new aeroplane and that this plane will need to be sold over a period of at least 20 years. The aircraft manufacturing profession has changed.

Given this perspective, the role of government ministries and agencies can only decrease still further. One could even imagine that government ministers and officials will adopt the language of the market and the norms and action which go with it. At best, government may behave like a banker, trying to verify whether the market is sufficiently reliable for loans made to manufacturers to be repayable. Under such conditions it is understandable why public expertise is becoming progressively weaker when faced with the technico-commercial expertise of manufacturers who are increasingly tempted to free themselves from state supervision, even if, as in France, this guardianship is exercised by their old comrades from the *corps de l'Armement*.

From this point of view the launch of the Airbus A321 is symbolic because, for the first time, constructors have chosen to do without public funding by financing the aircraft purely through bank loans. If one adds the fact that airlines themselves, even those that are still public, are becoming increasingly autonomous from supervising ministries, it becomes clear why the very purpose of aeronautical policies themselves is under question from certain quarters. Of course, decisions over military equipment programmes (EFA, Rafale, the Tigre, and NH 90 helicopters) remain in the public domain, as well as choices over space equipment (Ariane, Hermes, Columbus). However, even if the sector has retained some strategic aspects, at government level one no longer comes across the will to decide, in an overall manner, the conditions under which firms are to develop and the nature of products to be manufactured. The industrial actors have changed the scale on which they operate. Now they are present in several connected sectors, combine civil and military activities, and are capable of placing their activities in a world-wide context. Moreover, their freedom from political structures is very important, although this does not prevent them from having considerable political influence.

This trend is probably at its most spectacular in France, in the sense that it breaks with a very strong tradition of state interventionism. An example is Snecma and its attempt to escape from excessive dependence on Dassault's aircraft by proposing its military engine, the M88, for use on foreign aircraft, thus provoking a certain friction between the two manufacturers. In the same vein, Matra has attempted to sell its air-to-air missiles independently from markets where the Mirage 2000 has been sold. It is clear that this trend brings into question the integrating role of the Délégation Générale à l'Armement which, until recently, was the only place where attempts had been made to obtain some consistency between the aircraft, engines, radar, and weapons systems. This is what explains the surprising passivity of the French authorities who seem incapable of deciding between Thomson's strategy, which would like to impose its leadership by posing as a federator of an industry oriented primarily towards defence, and that of Aérospatiale, which defends a 'dual' strategy (civil and military) supported by a multitude of European co-operation arrangements, but which cannot go as far as admitting the necessity of taking over Dassault.

4.3. The EEC's Intervention in the Aerospace Sector

Until recently the Community's institutions had been carefully excluded from major decisions affecting aerospace. Military programmes and major civil or space programmes (Airbus, Ariane etc.) have resulted from intergovernmental co-operation. Today the situation has evolved under the combined effect of the aerospace sector's subculture and the difficulty that states are experiencing in aiding their respective industries. The intervention of Community bodies—as yet still limited but none the less real—is having an effect on three levels.

1. The first were the GATT negotiations over the refundable advances made by member states to partners in the Airbus venture. Until the present, this question had been treated in a multilateral fashion, the existence of serious conflicts between the USA and the EEC in several sectors leading the Commission to take charge of this set of negotiations as it had done in the field of agriculture, so as to achieve an agreement that would demand considerable reductions in public aid to manufacturers involved in Airbus. As we have

seen, this agreement, which effectively contributes to a retreat from the logic of public intervention, marks a sort of 'Communitarization' of the Airbus programme.

2. The second level of intervention is that of aid to research. Within the context of widespread cuts in public support to industry, aid to research and development programmes appears to be the principal domain where the close links between states and industry can continue to exist, as has occurred in the United States. It is precisely in this direction that the Community seems to be heading, since it has planned that the European aerospace sector will receive aid worth 53 million ECU within the framework of the Brite-Euram programmes. Even if these figures are not gigantic, this decision reveals the Commission's desire to take a closer interest in a sector which has hitherto escaped its attention.

3. Finally, the third level of intervention is that of competition policy. The spectacular decision to outlaw the purchase of De Havilland-Canada by the partners linked in ATR has been received as a veritable clap of thunder, symbolizing the rapid appearance on the scene of the Community in a domain which had previously been seen as untouchable. The promoters of the Regioliner partnership have not hidden their concern at this reaction by the Commission. On matters concerning military markets, article 223 of the Treaty of Rome in principle forbade the Commission from intervening. However, the Commission had already outlined its approach, in particular concerning so-called 'dual use' technology which it proposes to include amongst elements suitable for European-level control, notably over exports. Other projects exist which aim to submit public markets for defence equipment to the same transparency criteria as that of civil markets, or even for the Commission to have the right to monitor aid to research when applied to both civil and military technologies, all this in the name of competition.

5. TOWARDS A EUROPEAN VERSION OF 'NEO-LIBERAL INTERVENTIONISM'?

What should one make of this sudden intrusion by the Commission into the aerospace field? For the moment it is certain that the effects have been relatively limited. Martin Bangemann himself, vice-president of the Commission in charge of industrial affairs, has moreover sought to minimize the importance of its intervention: 'We want to be neither protectionist, nor interventionist. I really don't like the latter word and the document on the aeronautical industry does not contain it. But it is clear that it is necessary to have a framework of Community policy for all industrial activity, including aeronautics, in order that it be competitive.' Restating his disagreement with the notion of strategic industries, he also made clear his preference for general actions (training, legal framework, etc.) over sectoral ones.[6]

In reality the action of the Commission is taking place on two levels. It requires that European competition law be respected (this objective was symbolized by the actions of Leon Brittan) while the Commission is also methodically developing a quasi-industrial policy in which it aims to increase the competitiveness of European firms (the position of Martin Bangemann). However, this policy, which we have labelled 'neo-liberal-interventionist', is clearly not a return to armament-based strategies. Since the Commission is proposing to intervene over training, research, and development,[7] aircraft certification, and efforts to counter fluctuations in the value of the dollar, the Community is also looking to favour the establishment of competition regulation and to limit national aid to aeronautical programmes.

This intervention by the European Community is only at its early stages. Decisions will depend largely upon the will of the Twelve to set up a genuinely common defence policy. Nevertheless, these interventions already provide evidence of changes which are affecting firms in the aerospace sector. A European model of the national firm appears to be emerging which is increasingly private. It incorporates most of the knowledge and resources within one sector so as to confront American or Japanese competition more effectively.

Can we still talk of the European aerospace sector as a 'strategic industry'? The reply must be positive on condition that two observations are borne in mind. First, one must be aware of the spectacular changes experienced by this sector over the 1980s. Today the strategic character of a sector no longer means that the state assigns it often contradictory objectives of technological independence and the need to safeguard employment. From now on the strategic character of this sector is judged in terms of its importance to economic competition as a whole. Seen from this angle, the importance of the aerospace sector is linked both to its capacity to generate commercial profits and, more fundamentally, to its role in maintaining overall scientific and technological capacity, which of course is one of the keys to commercial success.

From the moment that the objectives of aeronautical policies became entirely identified with the search for commercial success, the public status of the firms involved was no longer seen as a favourable element by those responsible for aviation policy. The latter have preferred to encourage the establishment of powerful technological, industrial, and commercial champions, if necessary through international alliances, which, like Daimler-Benz, will have the capacity to face up to the gigantic investments required by aeronautical programmes.

The second point to bear in mind is that to attain its objective of making the aerospace sector more competitive on world markets, the state is forced to abandon most of its capacity to steer the decisions of the firms involved which, as autonomous actors in the marketplace, could lead them to choices which might eventually threaten national interests. This has been the case where McDonnell-Douglas was prepared to ally itself with the Taiwanese industry, or with Thomson in trying to create a third French missile manufacturing champion. Paradoxically, the plethora of alliance strategies that are currently being developed appear to be both a condition of maintaining this strategic industry, and a threat to each state's capacity to define its own global technico-industrial strategy.

Appendix

In helicopters, the DASA-Aérospatiale alliance has led to the creation of the company Eurocopter, controlled by a French majority, which is proving itself to be one of the world leaders in this sector. As for the military manoeuvres helicopter NH 90, this project involves the Eurocopter partners, Fokker and its Italian competitor Agusta.

The aeroengines field is also witnessing the multiplication of European and transatlantic alliances: Rolls-Royce and Turboméca for the production of helicopter engines, Rolls-Royce and BMW for the production of an engine for the possible 130 seater aircraft, Snecma and General Electric to build the CFM 56, Rolls-Royce, Pratt & Whitney and Japanese manufacturers to make the V2500 (competitor to CFM, Rolls-Royce, and Snecma's project to develop an engine for the future supersonic transport aircraft), MTU (DASA group) and Pratt & Whitney to develop a project to compete with the Rolls-Royce–BMW project.

The missiles sector is also full of criss-crossing alliances, such as Euromissile (Aérospatiale and DASA), Eurosam (Aérospatiale, Alenia, Thomson and others), and also three European firms (Aérospatiale, Alcatel, Alenia, and possibly DASA) who are joining forces to buy 49 per cent of Ford Aerospace in association with the American company Loral. Moreover, the creation of EuroHermespace and Eurocolumbus has just confirmed the strength of the links formed with Ariane. In the equipment domain there are more flexible associations such as Eurogear (landing gear) and Euronacelle.

Notes

1. P. Muller, *Airbus, l'ambition européenne: Logique de marché, logique d'Etat* (Paris, 1989).
2. E. Chadeau, *L'Industrie aéronautique en France 1900–1950* (Paris, 1987).
3. K. Hayward, *Government and British Civil Aerospace* (Manchester, 1983), p. 3.
4. Twelve countries participate in the Ariane 5 programme: France: 44.7%; Germany: 22%; Italy: 14%; Belgium: 6%; Spain: 3%; the Netherlands: 2.3%; Sweden: 2%; Switzerland: 2%; Norway: 0.6%; Denmark: 0.5%; Austria: 0.4%; Ireland: 0.2% (figures from Nov. 1991).
5. Hayward, *Government and British Civil Aerospace*.
6. Interview with Martin Bangemann, in *Air & Cosmos*, 1379, 18–24 May 1992, pp. 10–11.
7. The Commission envisages devoting up to 700 million ECU in aeronautical research over the period 1994–8.

Supplementary Bibliography

Bogdan, L., *L'Épopée du ciel clair* (Paris, 1988).
Boyne, W. J., and Lopez, D. S. (eds.), *The Jet Age: Forty Years of Jet Aviation* (Washington, DC, 1979).

Bugos, G. E., 'The Airbus Matrix, the Reorganization of the Postwar European Aircraft Industry' (Berlin, 1993).

Carroué, L., *Les Industries européennes d'armement* (Paris, 1993).

Chadeau, E., *L'Industrie aéronautique en France 1900–1950* (Paris, 1987).

Chesnais, F., *Compétitivité internationale et dépenses militaires* (Paris, 1990).

Cohendet, P., and Lebeau, A., *Choix stratégiques et grands programmes civils* (Paris, 1987).

Gunston, B., *Airbus* (London, 1988).

Hayward, K., *Government and British Civil Aerospace* (Manchester, 1983).

Hayward, K., *International Collaboration in Civil Aerospace* (London, 1986).

—— *The British Aircraft Industry* (Manchester, 1989).

Hébert, J. P., *Stratégie française et industrie d'armement* (Paris, 1991).

Muller, P., *Airbus, l'ambition européenne: Logique d'état, logique de marché* (Paris 1989).

—— 'La Transformation des modes d'actions de l'état à travers l'histoire du programme Airbus', *Politiques et management public*, 7/1 (1989), 247–72.

—— 'Airbus: Partners and Paradoxes', *The European Journal of International Affairs*, 8 (1990), 25–45.

Newhouse, J., *The Sporty Game* (New York, 1985).

Salomon, J. J., *Science, guerre et paix* (Paris, 1989).

Thiétard, R. A., and Kœnig, C., 'Programmes aérospatiaux: La Stratégie de l'organisation mutuelle', *Revue française de gestion* (Mar.–May 1987).

7

Air Transport Champions:
Still Carrying the Flag

HUSSEIN KASSIM

The support and promotion of national champions or 'flag carriers' in the air transport industry has been a key element of national aviation policies of patriotic interventionism throughout the post-war period. Under the state-centred international regime, founded on the principle of absolute national sovereignty, which has governed the industry since 1944, governments have used their powers to promote the interests of their national industries in general and those of the flag carrier in particular. At the centre of the national aviation system, the national champions of the air transport sector have been largely state-owned, protected by extensive and detailed regulations, and have derived their funds exclusively from the public purse. Within the European Union in the late 1980s and early 1990s, however, the post-war regulatory structure has been transformed and liberalized with serious implications for state sponsorship of the flag carrier and, thus, the continuation of the national champion strategy. A common air transport policy has been developed and a regulatory structure to provide for a single market in air transport services created. The member states of the EU have been deprived of their absolute rights and become subject to rules set at the European level. Civil aviation is now governed by a multilateral regulatory framework, which applies liberal rules to ownership, licensing, access, capacity, and tariff setting, and competition rules that are directed towards the prevention of restrictive practices, and the control of mergers and state aid. The flag carriers confront a new regulatory environment in which, formally at least, they cannot be protected by government policies from competition as in the past.

The revolutionary transformation of the regulatory system has produced significant changes in the industry. European flag carriers, traditionally insulated from competitive pressures, have sought to adapt to the new regulatory environment through a variety of means. These have included the consolidation of domestic markets, the forging of transnational alliances, and the making of a transition from a public service ethos and method of operation to a market-oriented outlook and competitive commercial strategy. In addition, formerly interventionist governments have in a number of cases allowed their airlines considerably greater commercial autonomy and have announced plans for the eventual privatization of their flag carrier. However, the national champion strategy has not yet disappeared. Firstly, governments have not lost their protectionist instincts and have used the means available to them to continue to support their national carriers. Secondly, the European majors have continued to draw upon the accumulated benefits of long-term incumbency and have mixed with their new expansionism strategies that are fundamentally defensive. Finally, the Commission has adopted a flexible attitude with respect to the implementation and application of EU rules, notably concerning state aids and mergers. As a consequence, genuine competition has not yet broken out in European skies and the single market, although a legal reality, is not yet an economic fact in air services.[1]

This chapter is concerned to examine the national champion strategy, the relationship between government and flag carrier, and the situation of national champions in a time of change. It will argue that, while regulatory transformation has led to change with respect to all three elements—the national champion strategy is more difficult to pursue, the relationship between flag carrier and state has been modified, and flag carriers have become unprecedentedly internationalized—change has not been radical as yet and the responses in the four larger member states have been various. The discussion that follows will begin with an examination of the post-war regime and traditional national policies. Secondly, EU action will be outlined. Thirdly, the responses of the member states and the flag carriers will be considered. Finally, an assessment of the extent to which these airlines have departed from the traditional model will be reached. Attention will primarily be concentrated on the larger four EU member states, but developments elsewhere will also be considered where instructive.

1. 'PATRIOTIC INTERVENTIONISM' UNDER THE POST-WAR REGIME

Intervention by the state in the air transport sector began with the emergence of commercial aviation in the inter-war period. Governments used the regulatory and financial resources at their disposal to safeguard their industries, in general, and to promote the national airline—the flag carrier—in particular. Only in the United States, where certain unique conditions obtained, did no national champion strategy emerge.[2] The flag carrier was typically either partly or fully owned by the state; it was usually a public enterprise, drawing its capital from state funds; it benefited from the reservation of monopoly markets, international or domestic, or a mixture of both; it enjoyed privileged access to landing and take-off slots at the country's main airports; and it was often the major beneficiary of the exclusion of civil aviation from national competition law.

Extensive state intervention in aviation was justified on a number of grounds. Firstly, it was believed that the private sector would be neither willing nor able to guarantee the provision of a reliable and extensive air services network, covering isolated regions and unprofitable routes, or perform other functions in the public interest, such as transporting post. Secondly, possession of a flag carrier acquired a particular significance and came to be symbolic of national prestige. Evidence of this fact is demonstrated by the speed with which newly independent countries sought to establish a national airline as soon as possible after liberation. The symbolic character of the flag carrier remains undiminished at the end of the twentieth century.[3] Thirdly, national airlines provided governments with an instrument with which they pursued non-aviation objectives. Air carriers were used to promote trade, to support the home aeronautical industry, to pursue the objectives of foreign and diplomatic policy, and to affect levels of domestic employment.

1.1. The Mechanisms of State Control

The nature of the international regime that governed air transport in the post-war era made possible the pursuit of the national champion strategy by governments in virtue of the absolute rights which were vested in states.[4] This enabled governments to pursue policies freely with respect to the three main types of commercial aviation, namely, international scheduled services, international non-scheduled services, and domestic services. Although the distinction between the first two has become somewhat blurred since the 1970s, international scheduled services, arguably the most basic and most important category, 'carry traffic between two or several points which remain *identical for the entire sequence of flights*, either *according to a published timetable*, or with such frequent regularity to make the sequence *a recognizable series of flights*'.[5] International non-scheduled services, including charters, are less regular and less frequent, often seasonal and directed to the needs of the leisure, as opposed to the business, traveller.

With respect to international scheduled services, governments exercised powers under a bilateral regime which grew out of the Chicago Convention and its associated Treaties of 1944.[6] The founding principle of the Convention was that each state should enjoy absolute sovereignty over the airspace above its territory. Agreement on this basic right was not inconsistent with a multilateral structure. However, at Chicago, delegates could only agree on the automatic multilateral exchange of only the most basic 'freedoms of the air', namely, the right of an airline from one country to overfly another country (first freedom) and the right of an airline from one country to land in another country for non-traffic (second freedom). A bilateral system developed after the Chicago conference, by which pairs of countries exchanged the more significant freedoms. These included the following:

- the third freedom—the right of an aircraft from one country to put down passengers, mail, and cargo in a second country;
- the fourth freedom—the freedom for an aircraft from one country to embark passengers, mail, and cargo in a second country, and carry them to the first country; and
- the fifth freedom—the right for a carrier from one country to pick up passengers or cargo in a second country and set them down in a third country.[7]

A further freedom, not traditionally granted in bilateral agreements, but significant, since it is relevant to a single market in air services, is cabotage. This is the freedom for an aircraft from one country to operate services between two points in a second country.

Bilateral agreements were modelled on the 'Bermuda Agreement', signed by the United Kingdom and the United States in February 1946.[8] These accords provided the means by which governments could exercise detailed control over the air services operating to and from their territories. First, the contracting governments agreed upon all aspects of market access. They decided how many airlines should be able to operate services between their territories and designated the companies that would be allowed to perform them. Typically, each country would name only its flag carrier for any particular route ('monodesignation') and so most routes were operated by flag carrier duopolies. Secondly, the two governments set a ratio for the sharing of capacity between each country's airline(s) on each route. Usually, the percentage share was set at 50/50, usually not in the bilateral agreement itself, but in accompanying confidential memoranda. Thirdly, the bilateral agreement obliged the designated airlines to confer with each other and to agree on the level of tariffs to be charged. Usually, these would have to be in line with the rates set by the International Air Transport Association (IATA), the trade association for scheduled air carriers, at its regional conferences.[9] The fares agreed by the airlines were subject to approval by both governments ('double approval').

The system of bilateral accords was supplemented by agreements struck between airlines ('pooling agreements') by which carriers serving a route agreed a number of operational and commercial arrangements. These included decisions on, for example, 'interlining'—the acceptance by one carrier of tickets issued by another without additional charge to the passenger—how best to spread service frequencies, and the use of technical facilities, but they also often extended to revenue sharing.[10]

Built into the bilateral system was a further mechanism that enabled governments to exercise control over home air carriers. It was a requirement of all bilateral accords that only airline companies licensed in one or other of the contracting states could be designated to operate services under the agreement. This practice was intended to prevent the use of 'flags of convenience'. Licences were granted by a government on the grounds not only that aspirant operators satisfied criteria relating to economic and technical fitness, but also that they be owned and substantially controlled by home nationals. This nationality condition or clause deriving both from the licensing requirement and from provisions included in the bilateral agreement constituted an important element in governmental control over the air transport industry, since it enabled governments to exercise jurisdiction over the right of establishment. It would later prove an important obstacle to the creation of a genuinely single European market, because it reserved traffic rights between a particular member state and a third country to home airlines only, rather than any Community air carrier wishing to operate services on such a route.[11]

Bilateral agreements were the policy instruments by means of which governments exercised control over scheduled services. The Chicago Convention also contained stipulations governing non-scheduled services, but the relevant provision was more liberal than that which covered scheduled services. According to article 5, non-scheduled flights required only unilateral permission from the state of destination. This permitted governments in Europe to pursue very different policies. Some countries, such as France, allowed relatively few such services to operate, but the United Kingdom and Germany adopted a more liberal policy regarding non-scheduled traffic to holiday destinations in Southern Europe.[12] However, all governments paid regard to the interests of their flag carrier in devising policies and taking decisions with respect to non-scheduled services, imposing conditions on the sale of charter products and denying access to charter companies where the income of the national airline would be adversely affected. Moreover, a number of flag carriers were allowed or encouraged to develop subsidiary charter companies. For example, Air France developed Air Charter, British Airways founded Caledonian, and Lufthansa formed Condor.

With respect to domestic services, governments enjoyed exclusive control over domestic services within their territory. Unilaterally, they decided the criteria for issuing licences, determined the rules for market access and the levels at which tariffs could be set. Often the domestic network would be reserved either for the national airline, as in the case of Greece's Olympic Airways, or for its subsidiary, Alitalia's ATI in Italy, for instance.

2. STATES AND FLAG CARRIERS IN THE EUROPEAN COMMUNITY IN THE POST-WAR PERIOD

Until 1987, when British Airways was privatized, all major flag carriers in Western Europe were either partly or fully owned by the state. The size and vocation of European flag carriers varied from country to country, but all, with the partial exception of British Airways, received the strong protection of their governments.[13] In France, the state has continued to own around 98 per cent of shares in Air France since just after the Liberation, despite the provisions of a 1948 statute imposing a ceiling of 70 per cent.[14] Successive governments, seeking to avoid Franco-French competition, considered deleterious to the national interest, reserved for Air France a monopoly network on major international services on transatlantic and European routes.[15] In both Germany and Italy, governments and public institutions held majority stakes respectively in Lufthansa and in Alitalia. Both flag carriers enjoyed monopolies on international and domestic networks, although Alitalia used its subsidiary, ATI, to operate internal Italian services. Alitalia's domestic near-monopoly was confirmed by the government as late as 1991.

The aviation policy pursued by the United Kingdom was unique in Europe, even before it was further liberalized by the Thatcher governments. In contrast to its Continental counterparts, the British government committed itself to a multi-airline policy on international routes, and favouring the operation of two airlines, including the independent carrier, British Caledonian. In the 1980s, the Conservative government in the UK applied its liberal market philosophy to the air transport sector. It privatized British Airways, partially liberalized the domestic market, and succeeded in renegotiating a number of its bilateral agreements with some of its European partners.[16] Moreover, in the form of the Civil Aviation Authority, it created the only independent regulatory body responsible for air transport in Europe.[17] Furthermore, the British government sought to campaign for liberalization at the European level through the European Community, arguing that the restrictive and protectionist policies that characterized the sector were, in fact, incompatible with the competition rules of the EEC Treaty. This represented a conscious strategy on the part of the British government to achieve the objective of European-wide air transport liberalization through the multilateral machinery of the European Community.

Prior to its privatization, a new chairman, Sir John (now Lord) King, was appointed to lead the restructuring of British Airways. A company that was characterized by relative inefficiency, over-staffing, and severe industrial relations difficulties was reorganized, streamlined, and reoriented.[18] It achieved substantial productivity gains and emerged as Europe's most consistently profitable airline. In contrast, British Airways' competitors suffered from the problems associated with state ownership and state control. First, states did not always prove to be generous shareholders. In France, for example, successive governments were strongly criticized for being 'parsimonious'.[19] Airline companies constituted but one among a number of state-owned companies jostling for funds, while governments faced increasing pressures to reduce their public deficits, and, moreover, airlines, like other nationalized firms, were subject to restrictions with respect to the sources from which they could raise capital. This meant that many flag carriers were seriously under-capitalized. Secondly, in their pursuit of other policy objectives, governments often imposed obligations on their flag carriers which ran counter to the commercial interests of the companies. For example, Air France was compelled on a number of occasions to purchase or operate at high cost either very old or very new aircraft manufactured in France in order to promote the home aeronautical industry. Lufthansa was obliged to provide maximum route coverage and a high frequency of services, while Alitalia was obliged to grant discounts to passengers belonging to particular social categories. Thirdly, management of these public sector companies tended towards the bureaucratic rather than the commercial. Managers tended to be drawn from the civil service rather than from the private sector and had little or no commercial experience. Fourthly, since they presided over public enterprises, airline managements enjoyed less independence with respect to important elements of commercial policy, notably personnel policy. A combination of the fact that governments were reluctant to sanction mass redundancies from such high-profile companies and the strength of public sector unions contributed substantially to the over-staffing, overly high operating costs, and low productivity of European airlines compared to their North American and South East Asian competitors.[20]

British aviation policy was unusual in a number of respects. While the British government sought to promote the cause of air transport liberalization in Europe, other EC member states remained firmly attached to the public service ethic. Moreover, the Conservative administration in the United Kingdom was prepared to allow its flag carrier to move into the private sector, a development that most other European governments could not countenance. Furthermore, while a restructured and efficient British Airways stood to benefit from increased competition in international services, its Continental counterparts still needed to undergo substantial reorganization.

3. THE POST-WAR REGIME TRANSFORMED: AIR TRANSPORT LIBERALIZATION IN THE EUROPEAN COMMUNITY

The general principles, favouring competition and free movement, that informed the treaty establishing the European Economic Community were clearly antithetical to the protectionist practices which characterized commercial aviation.[21] Moreover, at article 84(2), the Rome Treaty laid down explicit provisions for the development of a common air transport policy.[22] However, a majority of the member states, reluctant to cede any measure of their control over the industry, successfully resisted Commission initiatives to realize this treaty objective until the 1980s.[23] It was only after a series of rulings by the European Court of Justice, rejecting the argument of these member states that the competition rules of the Treaty did not apply to air transport, the commitment of the then Commissioners for Competition and Transport as well as the support of the British and Dutch delegations to apply the competition rules of the EEC Treaty to the sector, the pronouncement of the Heads of State and Government at the Hague Summit, and the general momentum mustered by the 1992 single market project, that progress towards air transport liberalization took place.[24] Action relating to other aspects of the industry—harmonization, infrastructure, and external policy—followed subsequently.[25] EC action proceeded along two main avenues: firstly, through the adoption of three 'packages' of legislative measures on 14 December 1987, 27 July 1990, and 23

July 1992 which sought to achieve in phases the liberalization of air transport within the European Community;[26] and secondly, by means of the application of the general rules of the EEC Treaty to aviation as well as the parallel development of specific rules relating to competition in the industry.[27]

3.1. The Three Packages

The staged approach to liberalizing air transport within the European Community took the form of the introduction of three packages. The first two of these sought to liberalize the provisions of existing bilateral agreements between member states rather than imposing a new multilateral structure. The changes they introduced were limited in scope to intra-EC international scheduled air services and specifically excluded relations between governments and their home carriers. They did, however, cover market access, capacity, and tariff levels.

Concerning market access, the first package introduced multi-designation for foreign EC carriers on a country-pair basis. Thus, governments could no longer restrict the number of air carriers serving their territories from other EC countries. However, access on city-pairs was restricted to routes between hub airports and an entitlement was only created where traffic reached a particular 'trigger' threshold.[28] Moreover, a number of airports received derogations. Limited fifth freedom rights were introduced and capacity controls relaxed. The traditional 50/50 sharing between air carriers of each nationality was widened to 45/55 until September 1989 and 60/40 thereafter. Finally, with respect to fares, zones were established with reference to the standard economy fare on a given route. Within these zones, airlines were allowed to set promotional fares at either 'discount' or 'deep discount' levels, subject to certain conditions relating to ticket reservation. These fares would take effect automatically without requiring explicit government approval.

The second package extended the measures introduced by the first. Trigger threshold levels for services between major airports were lowered and the number of derogations reduced. The proportion of passengers that could be carried under fifth freedom rights was extended. Capacity constraints were further eased, with movement of 7.5 per cent per annum permitted beyond the 60/40 range. Finally, the tariff zones were extended and the conditions attached to sales of promotional fares relaxed.

The third package was different in character from the previous two. Aiming to complete the single market in air services, it was more wide-ranging and radical. It covered scheduled as well as non-scheduled services, abolishing the regulatory distinction between them. Moreover, it brought the relationship between governments and their airlines within the purview of Community regulations for the first time. Most significantly, the third package included a regulation on licensing. By granting any airline carrier substantially owned and controlled by the nationals of any Community state the right to operate air services anywhere within the EC, the regulation on licensing created a genuine freedom of the right of establishment for the first time. Governments could no longer use licences as a mechanism for protecting favoured airline companies, but were compelled to permit any carrier which satisfied the European Community ownership criteria to operate air services to or from its territory.

With respect to market access, the third package permitted multiple designation on all routes throughout the EC and permitted the unrestricted exercise of fifth freedom rights. Even more radically, from 1 April 1997 full cabotage rights were to become available to all EC airlines, while in the interim carriers could exercise the freedom of consecutive cabotage; that is, they were entitled to extend existing services to serve an additional point within the country of destination. A safeguard clause was incorporated, permitting member states to limit access to designated public service routes and to airports that are congested or where damage would be done to the environment. All capacity sharing restrictions were removed, although a safeguard provision allows limitations to be imposed in the event of financial catastrophe. Finally, a system of free pricing of tariffs was introduced, under which airlines set rates according to their own commercial judgement. However, intervention is permitted where fares are excessively high or excessively low.

The three packages have successively deprived the member states of the powers by means of which they were previously able to practise policies of patriotic interventionism, although governments do retain some residual rights of intervention. Not only has this limited the policy instruments available to governments and diminished their ability to champion their national companies, but it has also led flag carriers to make thorough reviews of their operations and to adopt totally new strategies. National champions have sought alternative ways of representing their interests to the new decision-making centre in the European Community. Thus, a number of airlines, for example, Air France, have a representative permanently in Brussels, while collectively European flag carriers lobby EU institutions through the Association of European Airlines (AEA), which is regarded as one of the most effective lobbies in the EU.

3.2. The Competition Rules

The competition rules of the EEC Treaty were applied to the air transport sector by an implementing regulation in the first package.[29] Since 1988, governments and airline companies have been subject to EEC Treaty provisions relating to restrictive practices (article 85), the abuse of dominant position (article 86), the granting of exclusive rights to public undertakings (article 90), the providing of state aid (articles 92 and 93), and mergers (article 86 and later the Merger Regulation).[30] The Union's competence with respect to state aid and mergers is most relevant to the discussion here.

State Aid   The regulation of state aid is of critical importance in ensuring that genuinely competitive conditions prevail in the single market in air services. In the absence of such control, state-supported carriers would enjoy an unfair advantage over more efficient privately owned companies, which enjoyed no access to public funds. Also, rather than forcing flag carriers to become more competitive, access to state aid would permit them to continue to operate inefficiently, to ignore problems of over-staffing and to persist in providing over-capacity. Finally, liberalization of market access, capacity, tariff-setting, and licensing without regulation of state aid might well lead to a 'subsidy race' with no benefit to the customer, as had been the case in the steel industry.[31] However, the regulation of state aid in an industry where funding for the major companies has traditionally come from the public purse is a highly sensitive matter, particularly when the existence of a flag carrier is regarded as a *sine qua non* of sovereignty. This sensitivity has become even more acute since the third package came into effect on 1 January 1993, due to the fact that the establishment of the single market has coincided with the worst crisis experienced by air transport in the history of commercial aviation.[32]

Under the EEC Treaty, the Commission is charged with responsibility for administering the competition relating to state aid.[33] The specific guidelines that it follows with respect to air transport are those set out in the Second Memorandum.[34] Where financial support is offered by a government to a state-owned air carrier, the Commission must be informed. It decides by application of the market economic investor principle whether or not the operation constitutes a normal transaction between a shareholder and a company or whether it constitutes state aid.[35] If it takes the view that a private investor would have acted similarly, then the Commission takes no further action. If, however, it decides that the financial injection is aid, then the Commission can either rule that it is impermissible or that it is permitted on the grounds that it constitutes 'aid to facilitate the development of certain economic activities'.[36] The Commission has used the latter grounds to allow state-owned airline companies that have historically been poor commercial performers to allow injections of state aid on a 'one time, last time' basis where such aid demonstrably forms part of a well-defined restructuring plan. The Commission has justified its use of this reasoning by arguing that current employees should not be forced to pay the price incurred by years of mismanagement. However, it is clear that the Commission recognizes the political risk involved in taking a more inflexible stance.

Until at least the end of 1993, the Commission adopted a pragmatic attitude to the cases it considered, and it attracted criticism from a number of quarters for so doing.[37] In two instances involving Air France, the first whereby the French government injected FF2 billion into the company, and the second a complex funding operation involving the Banque Nationale de Paris, the Commission concluded that they represented normal transactions rather than state aid. However, its decision in both cases has been questioned, not least because the thoroughness of its investigation was not made public. In two further cases, concerning Sabena in 1991 and Iberia in 1992, the Commission determined that although the cash injections involved did constitute state aid, they were permissible on the grounds that they formed part of a realistic plan to put the companies on a sound footing. While the Commission's approach to the Sabena case was regarded as stringent—the Commission secured a series of undertakings from the Belgian government and from the airline—its decision with respect to Iberia was criticized for failing to extract similar commitments.

A new stringency on the part of the Commission appears to have been evident since the end of 1993. In its decision with respect to Aer Lingus, the Commission in December of that year marked a return to the disposition it adopted in the Sabena case. Dealing with two more minor issues in relation to Air Portugal (TAP), the first concerning tax exemptions granted by the Portuguese government, the second relating to the fulfilment of public service obligations, the Commission has indicated that it is likely to prohibit aid unless suitable steps are taken.[38] Evidence of a more exigent approach may be confirmed when the Commission announces its decisions with respect to its investigation of a third capital injection into Air France opened in November 1993, and to alleged state aid to TAP and to Olympic Airways into which it commenced its examination in March 1994.

Although it has been the object of criticism for its pragmatic approach to state aid, the Commission's policy of permitting 'one time, last time' capital injections, providing that certain conditions are satisfied, has been endorsed by the *Comité des Sages*, an independent *ad hoc* committee, set up to examine civil aviation in the European Union and to prepare an action programme.[39] The fate of the national champion strategy is clearly and directly related to the Commission's attitude to, and treatment of, cases involving state aid. If the Commission is faithful to this policy, the national champion strategy will no longer be possible in its traditional form.

Mergers   As with state aids, the governments of the member states have with mergers lost their autonomy with respect to an important aspect of competition policy, bearing upon the extent to which the national champion strategy can be pursued. The EU's competence over mergers has assumed considerable importance in view of the consolidation and alliance strategies pursued by many European flag carriers in anticipation of, or response to, liberalization. Two cases were treated under article 86 of the EEC Treaty, governing the abuse of dominant position, but a rather insensitive instrument. The first was the takeover by British Airways of British Caledonian in 1988, the second the buyout of UTA and Air Inter by Air France in 1990.[40] In both cases, the Commission approved the operation, subject to the respect of certain conditions laid out in a negotiated settlement with the concerned parties. In the first, British Airways undertook not to appeal in the event that the UK Civil Aviation Authority decided either to grant its route licences to other carriers or to reduce the number of slots from 35 per cent to 25 per cent of the total number available. In the second case, Air France was to sell its holding in the French independent carrier *Transport Aérien Transrégional* (TAT) to give up its rights and freeze its capacities on certain domestic routes, while the French authorities were obliged to designate independent airlines on a number of international and domestic routes.

Under the Merger Regulation, introduced as a dedicated instrument to deal with acquisitions in the single European market, the Commission has given its approval to the following: KLM's extension of its shareholding in the second Dutch carrier, Transavia; Air France's purchase of a major shareholding in Sabena; and British Airways' acquisition of TAT. British Airways' takeover of the British independent carrier, Dan-Air, did not involve an operation of Community dimension and so proceeded without requiring the approval of the Commission.[41]

4. THE IMPACT OF EC ACTION

Regulatory change has affected government policy, the state–flag carrier relationship, and the commercial character of national airlines. The gradual progression towards full liberalization, however, has given both state and airline time to adapt. A number of general developments can be discerned across the Member States, but there has been a degree of variation in response from one country to another, attributable to the ideological outlook and financial position of the government, and the commercial condition and leadership of the company.

4.1. *The Impact on the Relationship between State and National Champion*

European Union liberalization, by means both of the three packages and through the development of competition rules, has reduced substantially the capacity of the member states to protect and financially support their national champions. However, the precise impact of regulatory change on the relationship between state and flag carrier in the four larger states has varied. In the United Kingdom, the adjustment to a more commercial footing was made by British Airways prior to the advent of EC liberalization. In Germany and Italy, governments have allowed their flag carriers a substantial degree of commercial independence, although it has been alleged that both have demonstrated continued support for their respective national airlines by hesitating to allow their foreign competitors to exercise rights granted to them under the various packages. In Germany, British Airways reported a degree of bureaucratic obstruction when attempting to set up its subsidiary, Deutsche BA, in 1992, while the Italian government seems to have attempted to stall EU carriers wanting to make use of their freedoms of consecutive cabotage.

The French government has, perhaps, been the most interventionist. Not only has it engineered two cash injections into Air France and planned further capital increases, but it also played a major role in bringing about the takeover by the flag carrier of *Union de Transports Aériens* (UTA) and Air Inter.[42] Indeed, the then prime minister, Michel Rocard, claimed to have 'piloted' the operation.[43] In addition, in November 1993 the action of the French transport minister in seeking to bring an end to a strike at Air France led to the resignation of the company president.[44] Furthermore, a degree of scepticism was expressed when French authorities denied access to a foreign operator wishing to begin a service between Toulouse and Brussels on the grounds that the French airport was congested and that the environment would be adversely affected. Although governments are entitled to deny access for these reasons under provisions of the third package, some observers regard an instinctive protectionism on the part of the French authorities as providing the real cause.

Despite these obstructive attempts, governments do appear to have understood that flag carriers will shortly have to become commercially and financially self-dependent. This realization has largely come about due to EU liberalization, but growing pressures on governments of an economic, political, and ideological nature have also played a part. The clearest indication of this appreciation is the commitment made by the French and Italian governments to the privatization of their flag carriers. This is a development which would have been unthinkable even a few years ago.

4.2. The Impact on the National Champions

European Community flag carriers have responded to the challenges posed by liberalization in different ways, according to their various levels of profitability, the nature of their traditional vocation, the leadership style of their management, and their relationship with the state. However, certain common trends are discernible. National airlines have initiated restructuring programmes and adopted market-oriented management styles; they have sought to consolidate their positions on domestic markets; they have entered transnational alliances of varying degrees of closeness, ranging from joint marketing agreements to the purchase of equity shares.

Restructuring   Confronting a regulatory system that will no longer permit them to be protected or financially supported by their governments, national airlines have undertaken restructuring plans, with the aim of placing themselves on a secure and independent commercial footing. Alitalia, Aer Lingus, Iberia, KLM, Sabena, and SAS (Scandinavian Airways System) have all, in the late 1980s and early 1990s, embarked upon extensive programmes of this sort. In some cases, such as Alitalia, a new chief executive has been brought in from the private sector to overhaul the company's organization, management, and operations. In others, such as Air France, the same top management team was allowed to remain in place, but charged with the same task. Restructuring has also involved the rationalization of networks, with flag carriers shedding unprofitable routes, the reorganization of corporate structure, and the selling off of non-aviation interests, such as hotel chains and catering concerns.

A major obstacle to improving the productivity of EU flag carriers, with the exception of British Airways, has been over-staffing and high labour costs. Many of the larger carriers, perhaps aided by the recession, which has in some countries at least brought home the need for change, have been able to reach agreements relating to pay and redundancies with their unions. Lufthansa made plans for shedding 8,000 jobs, Sabena 4,000, Air France 9,000, and Iberia 3,000. Wage freezes, the linking of pay rises to increases in productivity, and early retirement have figured widely. These adjustments have not been easily achieved, however, as strikes at Air France towards the end of 1993 have demonstrated.

A further strategy by which national airlines have sought to minimize labour costs has been the setting up or expansion of low-cost subsidiaries. British Airways has adopted such a policy. It set up British Airways Regional to operate services from Birmingham, Glasgow, and Manchester, and has contracted out some services to City Flyer Express, which will fly as British Airways Express. It has also entered operations agreements with Brymon (a small independent British air carrier) and Maersk (an independent Danish air carrier). It bought out the British independent company, Dan-Air, and has sought to create out of it a low-cost carrier to operate services from Gatwick, although it has faced opposition from the unions. Elsewhere in the European Union, Iberia has expanded its use of its domestic subsidiary, Viva Air, while Lufthansa has experienced labour difficulties with its Lufthansa Express, intended also to operate as a low-cost subsidiary.

Finally, flag carriers have developed a greater commercial sensitivity. Not only have a small number introduced new fares or ticketing arrangements on some routes, but several have embarked on advertising campaigns, many have introduced customer loyalty schemes in the form of frequent flyer programmes, and nearly all have sought to improve marketing of their product and knowledge of the market through participation in computer reservation systems.

Domestic Consolidation Some EC flag carriers, such as Olympic Airways, Alitalia through its subsidiary ATI, and Iberia through Viva, have traditionally been strong on their domestic markets. A number that have been less strong domestically have sought to consolidate their national markets in order to develop 'feeder' networks to service their international flights from their hub airports. Thus, Air France acquired Air Inter in 1990, while British Airways has bought out British Caledonian and Dan-Air.

Transnational Alliances The development of transnational alliances has figured as a widespread response to air transport liberalization within the European Community. Although co-operation between airlines was not previously unknown in the industry—for example, SAS was created by and remained jointly owned by Denmark, Norway, and Sweden—the scale of partnership arrangements since the late 1980s does mark a radical departure from the traditional national-centredness of European flag carriers. The meaning of this development is ambiguous: for some airlines, it represents a desire to expand market opportunities, while for others it constitutes a defensive strategy, designed to deflect pressure for more fundamental changes elsewhere or to ensure that existing markets are guaranteed through mutual co-operation agreements.

Some partnerships are limited to joint marketing arrangements. In these, airlines seek to maximize output and network coverage through their complementary strengths in separate markets by co-ordinating their timetables. Examples include SAS's agreement with Continental Airlines. Other arrangements involve a tighter relationship, with one airline taking equity in another, or the purchasing of mutual shareholdings. For example, Swissair, Singapore Airlines, and Delta Airlines have taken token shares in one another. In these cases, a more permanent alliance is anticipated and the larger airline uses its shareholding as a means to gain access to another market.

Air France, Alitalia, British Airways, and Lufthansa, although each following different overall approaches, have all engaged in one or other form of alliance strategy. Air France has found partners in Western and Central Europe and the Americas. It has taken a 37.5 per cent shareholding in Sabena and, with the *Caisse des Dépôts* and the European Bank for Reconstruction and Development (EBRD) holds 40 per cent equity in the Czech carrier, CSA, adding to the stakes it already held in Middle East Airlines and Air Afrique. In has also entered marketing alliances with Continental, Aeromexico, and Air Canada. Alitalia, in contrast, has been a bit more reticent. It was allied with USAir until the latter reached an agreement with British Airways. It has also co-operated with Iberia and, in December 1992, it took a 35 per cent holding in the Hungarian airline, Malev. Alitalia further concluded a wide-ranging co-operation agreement with Lufthansa, by means of which it appears that the two carriers agreed to respect each other's markets.

Lufthansa initially pursued a strategy of pure independent growth. However, its policy seems to have changed and it has now taken a 26 per cent shareholding in Lauda Air, the Austrian independent carrier, in an attempt to counterbalance links forged between Swissair and Austrian Airlines. In September 1993, Lufthansa signed a co-operation agreement with Varig, the Brazilian airline and the largest in South America, and in the following month it announced a marketing alliance with United Airlines.

Of the major European companies, British Airways has pursued the most ambitious strategy and appears to be the only flag carrier seeking to become a genuinely global air carrier. In addition to its consolidation of the UK domestic market, British Airways has strengthened its presence in Europe through its acquisition of a 49 per cent stake in the French independent carrier, TAT. It has also purchased a 25 per cent stake in the Australian carrier, Qantas, and holds a 24 per cent shareholding in the American domestic company, USAir. Moreover, British Airways became, with its creation of Deutsche BA in Germany, the first airline from one member state to set up and operate a subsidiary based in another.

A number of other European majors have forged noteworthy alliances. SAS, concerned to gain access to central European hubs in order to overcome the difficulties presented by the peripheral location of its base, has taken a substantial shareholding in British Midland, one of Europe's strongest independent airlines and one based at Europe's busiest airport, namely London Heathrow. Iberia has opted to concentrate on the Latin American market; it has wound down its North American and Asian services, while taking up shareholdings in Ladeco (Chile), Aerolineas Argentinas, and Viasa (Venezuela). The Dutch flag carrier, KLM, has partnerships involving shareholdings in the US company Northwest, and the small British independent Air UK.

Alliance building by European companies, although widely engaged in, has not been unproblematic. A number of different sorts of difficulties have beset the various sorts of partnership plans. Disagreement over how profits ought to be shared (proposed merger between British Airways and KLM) and over the identity of an American partner (Austrian Airlines, KLM, SAS, and Swissair, parties to the proposed 'Alcazar' partnership) have led to plans falling through. Moreover, airlines have been obstructed by government sensitivities concerning the role of foreign shareholders in home air carriers (the US government and British Airways' plans for USAir; the Argentinian government's fears relating to Iberia's holding in Aerolineas Argentinas), have revised their plans in the light of changing economic prospects (KLM reconsidering its holding in Northwest) and have adjusted their strategies in order to focus on the health of the parent carrier (Air France with respect to its shareholding in CSA). Furthermore, difficulties concerning the modalities of a proposed merger and the operation of the new company have also led to the abandonment of projects, including the plan involving British Airways, KLM, and Sabena to create a new company, Sabena World Airlines.

5. CONCLUSION

The liberalization of air transport in the European Union has brought about a radical change in the regulatory structure governing the industry. The governments of the member states no longer have at their disposal the instruments which enabled them to pursue policies of patriotic interventionism in the past and most appear to have recognized that they cannot continue to sponsor their national airlines. Moreover, the prospect of being submitted to competitive pressures for the first time has led most flag carriers to embark upon restructuring programmes, some to enter into transnational partnerships, and a few to exploit the new freedoms offered by the single market in air services.

The extent to which the industry has been transformed should not, however, be exaggerated. First, governments have continued to be supportive of their national airlines. A majority of the member states have sought to make capital injections, some have argued for a relaxation of the new regime, and a few have used the powers granted to them by EU legislation or other methods to obstruct the efforts of foreign competitors. As far as most are concerned, the national champion concept is a long way from becoming an idea that belongs to the past. Secondly, although they may have undergone substantial changes, the national champions have not yet become internationalized champions. Despite having entered into transnational partnerships and alliances, they remain nation-based. They continue to enjoy the accumulated benefits of long-term incumbency at home and the national aviation systems, which gave them privileged positions, have not as yet been dismantled. Thirdly, the European Commission has been highly sensitive to political pressures and, despite the fact that it has signalled the need with regard to the flag carriers to 'think the unthinkable', it has so far adopted a very flexible attitude to state aid.[45] It has withheld from advocating more radical policies, such as introducing competition rules which would take into account the relative size of incumbent airlines when considering questions of market access. Until it becomes politically possible for a government to allow its flag carrier to lose its essentially national identity or for the Commission to take decisions that would have the consequence of such airlines going out of business, the national champions of the air transport sector will continue to fly the national flag.

Notes

1. For a comprehensive analysis of the state of air transport in the European Union a year after the single market in air services came into being, see the UK Civil Aviation Authority's *Airline Competition in the Single European Market*, CAP 623 (Cheltenham, 1993).

2. It is widely held that the strength of private finance, the wide dispersal of population concentrations and political cultural resistance to state interventionism enabled sustainable private air carriers to develop in the USA. Although the national champion strategy did not emerge as such, US administrations have usually sought to represent and further the interests of American companies in aviation diplomacy.

3. See Anthony Sampson, *Empires of the Sky: The Politics, Contests and Cartels of World Airlines* (London, 1984), esp. pp. 115–20, for a discussion of this.

4. For discussion of international aviation regulation, see the following: Martin, P. *et al.* (eds.), *Shawcross and Beaumont Air Law*, 4th edn. (London, 1984); National Consumer Council, *Air Transport and the Consumer: A Need for Change?* (London, 1986); Naveau, J., *International Air Transport in a Changing World* (Brussels, 1989).

5. Definition adopted by the ICAO (International Civil Aviation Organization) in 1952; citation from Naveau, *International Air Transport*, 31 (emphasis in the original).

6. The Convention on International Civil Aviation (the 'Chicago Convention') was signed on 7 Dec. 1944 and entered force on 4 Apr. 1947.

It is adhered to by the 157 signatory states of the ICAO. See Naveau, *International Air Transport*, 25–35.

7. These freedoms were defined in the Transport Agreement (the 'Five Freedoms Agreement'), one of the associated Treaties also signed at the Chicago Convention. Reference is sometimes made to the sixth and the seventh freedoms. The former refers to the freedom of an airline from one country to carry passengers from country B to country C via its hub in country A; the latter to the freedom for an airline from country A to operate services between countries B and C.

8. The 'Bermuda Agreement', HMSO, *Final Act of the Civil Aviation Conference and Agreement between the Government of the United Kingdom and the Government of the USA relating to Air Services between their Respective Territories*, cmnd. 6747 (London, 1946). It was signed on 11 Feb. 1946.

9. IATA was founded in Havana in Apr. 1945 to represent the interests of scheduled air carriers, to act as a clearing house for inter-airline debts, and to set air fares for international scheduled services. For discussion of IATA, see Doganis, R., *Flying Off Course: The Economics of International Airlines*, 2nd edn. (London, 1991), 36–41; and Naveau, *International Air Transport*, 59–66.

10. Pooling agreements are discussed in OECD, *Deregulation and Airline Competition* (Paris, 1988), 33–5. An examination of inter-airline agreements was carried out by the European Civil Aviation Conference (ECAC) in the early 1980s, whose findings are published in ECAC, *Report on Competition in Intra-European Air Services (COMPAS)*, doc. no. 25 (Paris, 1982).

11. Consider, for example, the character of a hypothetical bilateral agreement between the UK and a third country such as Zimbabwe. Such an agreement would by means of its nationality clause restrict access to routes between the two countries to British and Zimbabwean air carriers. The freedom of establishment for all EU carriers to operate from anywhere within the Union to third countries is circumscribed by the continued right of member states to conclude restrictive bilateral agreements with third countries. Arguably, this situation will only be brought to an end when responsibility for negotiating air services agreements with third countries is granted to the EU.

12. Charter services presently account for a third of total revenue per passenger kilometres within the EU. This traffic is highly concentrated between city-pairs in the north and south of Europe, with the countries of the latter seeking to promote their tourist industries. Traffic between the UK and Germany, and Spain, constitutes 75 per cent of total charter output.

13. e.g. TAP Air Portugal was charged with responsibility for linking the metropole with the colonies. Also, while Sabena (Belgium), KLM

(Royal Dutch Airways), and Luxair operated very few domestic services, domestic routes accounted for a large proportion of services operated by Olympic Airways.

14. This statute constituted the legal basis for the company's operations and remains effective in the early 1990s. Law no. 48-976 of 16 June 1948, *Journal officiel de la république française*, 27 June 1948.

15. From the early 1960s, international services were shared between Air France and UTA, while the domestic network was reserved for Air Inter.

16. The UK renegotiated its bilateral agreements with the Netherlands and the Federal Republic of Germany in 1984, Belgium, Luxembourg, and Ireland in 1985, and Switzerland in 1986.

17. For brief discussions of the role and development of the CAA, see Barnes, F., 'The Impact of Partial Deregulation in the UK Domestic Market', in OECD, *Deregulation and Airline Competition* (Paris, 1988); and Tritton, C., 'Existing and Prospective Community Law and Civil Aviation: A UK Perspective'; in P. J. Slot and P. D. Dagtoglou (eds.), *Towards a Community Air Transport Policy* (London, 1990).

18. The workforce of the company was reduced from 54,000 to 36,000, the fleet modernized, the structure of the company overhauled, and a new commercial strategy developed.

19. This was one of a number of criticisms levelled by a Senate investigatory committee in its *Rapport de la Commission de controle chargée d'examiner la gestion administrative, financière et technique de l'entreprise public Air France . . .* , Second Ordinary Session 1990–1, doc. no. 330 (Paris, 1991).

20. For a brief discussion of the relatively poor productivity of European airlines, see the report prepared by the Comité des Sages for Air Transport to the European Commission, *Expanding Horizons* (Brussels, 1994), 9–16.

21. A general commitment is made to secure the freedom of goods, workers, capital, and services. Under the EEC Treaty, member states are to eliminate barriers to trade and the Community seeks to establish conditions to ensure that competition is not distorted (art. 3); they are enjoined to abstain from measures which hinder the attainment of the Treaty objectives (art. 5); discrimination against EC citizens on the grounds of nationality is prohibited (art. 7); arts. 59–66 provide for the freedom to supply services; agreements, decisions, and concerted practices between undertakings having the intention or effect of impeding competition are proscribed (art. 85); the abuse of dominant position is illegal (art. 86); in the case of public undertakings granted special or exclusive rights, member states are not permitted to make or maintain in force any measure contrary to the rules of the Treaty (art. 90); and aids granted by states which distort or threaten competition

are incompatible with the common market (art. 92); finally, member states are required to take all appropriate steps to eliminate any agreements between themselves or with any third party that are not compatible with the Treaty (art. 234).

22. Art. 84(2) EEC reads as follows: 'The Council may, acting by a qualified majority, decide whether, to what extent and by what procedure appropriate provisions may be laid down for sea and air transport'. Art. 3(e) specifies as a Community objective the adoption of a common policy in the sphere of transport.

23. The most important of these were the Commission's First Memorandum, 'Contribution of the European Communities to the Development of Air Transport Services', *Bulletin of the European Communities*, Supplement 5 (Brussels, 1979), and Civil Aviation Memorandum no. 2: *Towards the Development of a Community Air Transport Policy*, COM (84) 72 final (Brussels), the Second Memorandum.

24. The main rulings by the Court included the following: ruling in Joint Cases 209–13/84, *Ministère Publique* v. *Asjes et al.* (1986) ECR 1425, which confirmed that the competition rules of the EEC Treaty did apply to air transport; ruling in the 'French Seamen's' case, Apr. 1974, Case 167/73, *Commission of the European Communities* v. *French Republic* (1974) ECR 359–79 stated that the sector was subject to 'the general rules of the Treaty'; and ruling in Case 2/74, *Reyners* v. *Belgian State* (1974) ECR 631–99, confirmed that the freedom of establishment provisions applied to air transport.

25. These lie beyond the scope of this chapter. For a comprehensive discussion, however, see the present author's doctoral thesis, 'Theories of Integration and their Limits; the Case of Air Transport', D.Phil., Oxford, forthcoming.

26. The first package comprised the following four instruments: Council Regulation (EEC) no. 3975/87 of 14 Dec. 1987 laying down the procedure for the application of the rules on competition to undertakings in the air transport sector; Council Regulation (EEC) no. 3976/87 of 14 Dec. 1987 on the application of article 85(3) of the Treaty to certain categories of agreements and concerted practices in the air transport sector; Council Directive of 14 Dec. 1987 on fares for scheduled air services between member states, 87/601/87; and Council Decision of 14 Dec. 1987 on the sharing of capacity between air carriers on scheduled air services between member states and on access for carriers to scheduled air service routes between member states, 87/602/87 (OJ L 374, 31.12.87). The second package included the following: Council Regulation (EEC) no. 2342 of 24 July 1990 on fares for scheduled air services; Council Regulation (EEC) no. 2343 of 24 July 1990 on access for air carriers to scheduled intra-Community air

service routes and on the sharing of passenger capacity between member states; Council Regulation (EEC) no. 2344/90 of 24 July 1990 amending Regulation (EEC) no. 3976/87 on the application of article 85(3) of the Treaty to certain categories of agreements and concerted practices in the air transport sector (OJ L 217, 11.8.90). The third package consists of the following: Council Regulation (EEC) no. 2407/ 92 of 23 July 1992 on licensing of air carriers; Council Regulation (EEC) no. 2408/92 on access for Community air carriers to intra-Community air routes; Council Regulation (EEC) no. 2409/92 on fares and rates for air services; Council Regulation (EEC) no. 2410/92 of 23 July 1992 amending Regulation (EEC) no. 3975/87 of 14 Dec. 1987 laying down the procedure for the application of the rules on competition to undertakings in the air transport sector; and Council Regulation (EEC) no. 2411/92 of 23 July 1992 amending Regulation (EEC) no. 3976/87 on the application of article 85 (3) of the Treaty to certain categories of agreements and concerted practices in the air transport sector (OJ L 240, 24.8.92).

27. Article 85(3) of the EEC Treaty, which permits by-category exemptions from the competition rules, was applied to air transport by Council Regulation (EEC) no. 3976/87. By means of this instrument, the Commission was entitled to allow such exemptions by regulation. As the regulatory framework was progressively liberalized, the rules permitting exemptions were amended accordingly. Those accompanying the first liberalization package were adopted by the Commission on 26 July 1988 and the second on 5 Dec. 1990.

28. Routes with more than 250,000 passengers or 1,200 return journeys in 1988, falling to 200,000 and 1,000 respectively in 1989.

29. Council Regulation (EEC) no. 3975/87.

30. Council Regulation (EEC) no. 4064/89 of 21 Dec. 1989 on the control of concentrations between undertakings (the 'Merger Regulation').

31. The fear of such a race was voiced by the Commission in its Second Memorandum of 1984.

32. It has been estimated that European airlines lost close to $2 billion in 1992 due to the effects of the economic recession, high operating costs, and high financial costs. See report of the Comité des Sages, *Expanding Horizons*, p. 13.

33. It is perhaps worth noting that, whereas in general DG IV (competition) assumes responsibility for enforcing the state aid provisions of the EEC Treaty, air transport is an exception in that DG VII (transport) performs this function.

34. These guidelines are currently being revised. In 1992, the Commission published a comprehensive report on state aids to the industry. CEC, 'Report by the Commission to the Council and the European Parlia-

ment on the Evaluation of Aid Schemes established in Favour of
Community Air Carriers', SEC (92) 431, 19 Mar. 1992.
35. For discussion of this criterion, see CAA, *Airline Competition*.
36. EEC Treaty, art. 92(3)(c).
37. A number of independent air carriers as well as some member states
have been critical of Commission decisions. It is believed that the
College of Commissioners has been divided on a number of cases
coming before it. See Balfour, J., 'The European Commission—poodle
or pit bull terrier?', *Avmark Aviation Economist* (Dec. 1993), 3–6.
38. See Balfour, J., 'The Control of State Aids in the Air Transport Sector',
Air and Space Law, 18: 4/5 (1993), 199–204.
39. See n. 20 above.
40. Air France already owned a 32 per cent stake in Air Inter, while UTA
owned 35 per cent. Thus, when Air France bought out UTA, it
acquired a majority stake in Air Inter.
41. Concentrations with a Community dimension, according to the
Merger Regulation, article 1(2), are those where the combined aggregate world-wide turnover of all the undertakings concerned is more
than ECU 5,000 million and the aggregate Community-wide turnover
of at least two of the undertakings is more than ECU 250 million.
42. See speech to the *Conseil Supérieur d'Aviation Marchande* by the
French Minister for Transport on 14 Oct. 1993.
43. See Senate report, *Report de la Commission de controle*, p. 215.
44. The strike had been called in response to the announcement of a plan
in Sept. 1993 to cut 4,000 jobs. This figure was to be added to the
5,000 redundancies already foreseen under the company's restructuring programme, CAP '93. The Transport Minister argued that these
further lay-offs could be achieved by non-compulsory means. Air
France's president, Bernard Attali, considered that his position had
been undermined.
45. In its report on state aid to the Council and the EP, the Commission
warned that 'one should be prepared to "think the unthinkable":
namely that flag carriers might disappear from the market'. See CEC,
'Report on the Evaluation of Aid Schemes'.

8

The Channel Tunnel:
The Problems of Binational
Collaboration

IAN HOLLIDAY[1]

By any standard, the Channel Tunnel is a major infrastructure project. Costing around £10 billion to build, and employing at the height of construction activity in mid-1990 a total of 13,500 people in Kent (8,300) and Nord-Pas de Calais (5,200), it was Europe's largest construction project at the end of the 1980s and start of the 1990s. On officially opening for business on 6 May 1994 it was transformed into one of Europe's most strategic pieces of transport infrastructure. The Tunnel substantially reshapes surface transport in north-west Europe by providing for the first time direct rail links between Britain and the Continent, as well as shuttle services for road traffic. In both the short and long terms, the Tunnel is a project with substantial regional economic—and possibly political—impacts.[2]

Yet this project, so vast in its implications for regional development in many parts of north-west Europe, was in July 1987 conceded by the British and French governments to the private sector. During an initial concessionary period of 55 years—later extended to 65 years—construction and operation of the Tunnel were made the exclusive responsibility of an Anglo-French consortium, which following selection in January 1986 became Eurotunnel. Whilst accepting that certain political guarantees were necessarily and uniquely their responsibility, the two states decreed that economic management of the Tunnel project would henceforth be undertaken by the private sector without public-sector assistance or guarantees. The official line was that should Eurotunnel encounter financial (or other) difficulties, it would not be assisted by public funds.[3]

As it has turned out, Eurotunnel has experienced a series of difficulties, many of them financial, but on no occasion has it come close to receiving overt public funding for the Tunnel project. This chapter is not, then, an investigation of state-sponsored rescue for private-sector failure, or of anything similar. Rather, it is an analysis of the more subtle and intriguing set of public–private relations which has been built around the Tunnel concession. By transferring responsibility for Tunnel construction and operation to the private sector, the two states did not terminate their association with the project. Instead, they moved their involvement into a new phase in which national policy makers were forced to operate alongside and sometimes in competition with actors representing diverse other interests.

In seeking to analyse the role played by Tunnel policy makers in the increasingly international environment in which they have found themselves in recent years, the chapter looks successively at: (i) reasons why the private-sector route was selected by the British and French governments in the mid-1980s; (ii) the division of policy-making responsibility within the Tunnel project itself; and (iii) policy-making activity around the private-sector Tunnel project. In a concluding review, it attempts to account for observed policy outcomes, noting that in the case of the Tunnel, as in other areas covered by this series of studies, ownership itself has been a less important variable than has been a variety of economic, political, and cultural factors. It also considers the roles that public authorities are ultimately likely to play in this project.

1. POLICY MAKING FOR A PRIVATE-SECTOR TUNNEL

The history of the present Tunnel project may be traced back to the early nineteenth century—possibly even to the mid-eighteenth century—during which time a variety of projects, backers, and obstacles to construction has been encountered.[4] Its immediate predecessor, launched in 1973, was a tunnel scheme which involved some private-sector finance but was fully underwritten by the British and French governments. It collapsed in January 1975 when a hard-pressed British Labour government decided that the cost of a dedicated rail link from the Tunnel to central London (then thought to be an integral part of the project) was too great to allow continuation. A fresh proposal to build a fixed link soon appeared on policy makers' agendas at the end of the 1970s. Despite the initiative being taken in 1979 by the nationalized railway companies, BR and SNCF, this project quickly developed a private-sector orientation which has not since been challenged. Policy making in the 1980s was for a private-sector Tunnel.

Reasons why the private-sector route was taken in the 1980s are not hard to find. They correspond directly to reasons why privatization emerged in other parts of the British public sector in the mid-1980s. The case of the Channel fixed link only requires additional explanation of, on the one hand, the not notably Europhile British government's decision to countenance involvement in a project with impeccably *communautaire* credentials, and, on the other, the Socialist French government's willingness to accept private-sector direction of a project for which it was jointly responsible. Standard explanations therefore comprise pressure on public finances, ideological fit, and the perceived problems of a state-funded tunnel (as demonstrated by the 1970s project). Additional explanations comprise on the one hand Thatcher's brief spate of Euroenthusiasm in the wake of resolution of Britain's budgetary dispute in 1984,[5] her more lasting desire to be considered a good European, and her permanent wish to exploit the demonstration effects of privatization (wherever they might be found). On the other hand, they comprise Mitterrand's concern to ensure construction of a fixed link on almost any terms in order to secure regional policy objectives in northern France, and his belief that any difficulties encountered by the project would not lead again to cancellation, but instead to state aid.

The project therefore advanced down the private-sector route, presenting Thatcher with a highly visible means of demonstrating to a sceptical world the validity of the horror stories she and Sir Keith Joseph had told about public enterprise in the 1970s, and the viability of the private-sector solutions they had advocated in its place.[6] The Channel Tunnel is properly viewed as part of the more general privatization drive embarked on by the Thatcher administration in its heroic, and sometimes hubristic, second term. Yet it was not only national policy makers who were involved in Tunnel policy making in the early 1980s. To begin with, a series of interests was active in the late 1970s and can take credit for relocating the project on policy makers' agendas at the start of the 1980s. Then, once national policy makers had decided to take the project in hand (and to exclude many initial interests from the developing policy network), they themselves sought to open the network to alternative sets of outside interests.

The direct trigger for national policy makers' reconsideration of the fixed link project in the 1980s was the BR–SNCF proposal to build a single 'mousehole' tunnel through which flights of trains would pass alternately between Britain and France. No provision for road vehicles was included in this scheme. Subsidiary roles were played by the European Commission and the European Parliament, both of which recognized the strong integrationist potential of a Channel fixed link, and therefore sought to promote the concept on the basis of a feasibility study conducted on behalf of the Commission. Together, these direct and indirect influences operated to bring the project to national policy makers' attention. They had little influence beyond this.

Instead, when the project was taken in hand by national policy makers, it was on the strict understanding—decreed by the British government—that a fixed link would be built and operated by the private sector, or not at all. Not only was the BR–SNCF scheme ruled out by this decree, but also the potential role for European institutions in any fixed link project was substantially diminished. In the early 1980s, national policy makers thereby established clear control over policy development, carefully regulating access to an emergent policy network which they themselves were creating. In admitting interested parties to the network, distinct criteria were, however, applied in Britain and France.

In Britain, a request was issued to private-sector interests to submit to government proposals for construction—and finance—of a Channel fixed link, and discussions with construction companies and banks became part of the routine of policy makers. In France, regional interests were seen as crucial by a government which had highly developed links into Nord-Pas de Calais (the French Prime Minister from 1981 to 1984, Pierre Mauroy, being its dominant politician), and fact-finding missions were dispatched to the region on formal and informal bases. In consequence, policy in the early years of the present Tunnel project was conducted in ways which conform very closely to prevailing national stereotypes. A clear focus on the Whitehall village in Britain contrasted with the developed centre–periphery linkages which are held to characterize the French politico-administrative system.[7]

Progress remained minimal until Thatcher's conversion to the cause in late 1984. The move from phoney to real policy making which occurred at this time is marked by a significant increase in the tempo at which policy advanced. It is also marked by clear development of the policy network in both Britain and France. In Britain, national policy makers were obliged to bring at least some regional and local representatives formally into the policy-making sphere. In France, contacts were increasingly made with potential tenderers for the fixed link concession, at both national and regional level. Yet national policy makers continued to exercise substantial degrees of control over policy making, never allowing the main lines of policy development to slip from their grasp. At the same time, they also succeeded in factoring out to other agencies aspects of policy which were uncongenial or of only peripheral interest to them. In both Britain and France, central policy makers thus left to their local counterparts the tasks of agreeing detailed local questions with potential concessionaires—a task which was pursued in many ways more vigorously in Nord-Pas de Calais than in Kent—and together the two sets of national policy makers made it a condition of project submission that tendering consortia conduct environmental impact assessments (EIAs) in line with recent EC directives. In the event, not even all of the four which were considered serious contenders actually fulfilled this condition. Eurotunnel, as it happened, did, producing a comprehensive EIA as part of its submission to the two governments.

The overall picture which emerges from a review of the early stages of policy making for a private-sector Tunnel is therefore one of substantial central control combined with an ability to displace onto other agencies aspects of policy making with which central policy makers did not themselves wish to deal. It is clear that this displacement activity exposed central policy makers to a number of risks, in that their control was bound to face increased potential challenge with expansion of the policy network, but equally evident that in the short term such a challenge did not materialize. At no stage was there ever a hint of compromise on the key political requirement—made by Thatcher—that a private-sector solution to the problem of the Channel fixed link be generated. Indeed, despite receiving advice from a panel of international banks that a fixed link could not be financed without at least some measure of public guarantee, the concession awarded to Eurotunnel is absolutely clear on this point. All public funding of the Tunnel is entirely forbidden.

As to which of the tendering schemes should be selected, it appears that there was some conflict of view between different central decision makers. Although Thatcher is said to have favoured a drive-through tunnel scheme (on the grounds of freedom of choice and general dislike of rail and the unions involved in it) and Mitterrand is said to have favoured a road–rail bridge/tunnel scheme (on the grounds that the bridge element would boost the steel industry of northern France), the project which was chosen was neither a drive-through nor a bridge-based scheme. Yet there was perhaps little surprise in the judgement delivered by a jury of British and French civil servants in January 1986. The Eurotunnel scheme which they selected was not only a good deal less risky than any of the others, it also made no more than minimal changes to the 1970s scheme which they themselves had promoted.

The decision in favour of a private-sector Tunnel was therefore certainly taken by national policy makers in consultation with outside interests, but in no sense was it controlled or even substantially influenced by those interests. Neither the more flamboyant private-sector options floated by British businessmen nor the regional and local considerations advanced by politicians and administrators in northern France held much sway over the final decision. Policy making for a private-sector Tunnel, which resulted in concession of the project to Eurotunnel, was to a very large extent conducted by the two sets of national policy makers. It is the terms of Eurotunnel's concession which next require investigation as a means of orientating discussion of public- and private-sector roles in project management.

2. PUBLIC- AND PRIVATE-SECTOR ROLES IN PROJECT MANAGEMENT

The present Tunnel project entered an entirely new phase with concession of construction and operation to Eurotunnel. By in effect privatizing the Tunnel, British and French policy makers substantially diminished the direct control which they would be able to exert over the project. Yet at the outset it must be stressed that this was the express intent of the lead influence in policy making for a private-sector Tunnel, namely Thatcher, who was convinced that the private sector would make a much better job of building and operating a Channel Tunnel than the British and French public sectors ever could. Taking the state out of detailed project management was the main objective of (British) public policy in the mid-1980s.

Central to that objective was the Concession Agreement signed by the British and French states and Eurotunnel on 14 March 1986.[8] This agreement may readily be identified as part of a boom in franchising which swept both the public and private sectors in Britain, and elsewhere, in the 1980s. Yet there is an important distinction to be drawn between the Tunnel Concession Agreement and the kinds of business franchise developed by McDonald's and Kentucky Fried Chicken in the United States and Body Shop and Tie Rack in Britain: the balance of power in each case is entirely different. In a commercial franchise, a uniform concept is systematically reproduced across a range of outlets, and substantial amounts of control reside in the franchiser. In the case of the Channel Tunnel, which is strictly a one-off undertaking, elaboration of the basic concept is determined less by the conceding authority, in this case the British and French governments, and a good deal more by the concessionaire, here Eurotunnel.

Thus, in issuing an *Invitation to Promoters* in the spring of 1985, the British and French governments laid down no more than the bare outlines of a fixed scheme. Indeed, so broad were their guidelines that they received in response a wide variety of tendered projects. Of the ten entries submitted by the deadline of 31 October 1985, four were held to be serious. Even some of these breached some of the rules laid down by the two governments. They comprised a drive-through bridge scheme (Eurobridge), a drive-through tunnel scheme (Channel Expressway), a drive-through bridge/tunnel scheme (EuroRoute), and the rail-based tunnel scheme with provision for vehicle transport on shuttles which was eventually selected. Detailed project management and planning were, then, to be handled by the successful concessionaire. This is the important context in which public- and private-sector roles in project management need to be viewed. The shift in control which it indicates is real, and may be illustrated by investigation of the regulatory activity which has been sponsored by the British and French governments.

To oversee the Tunnel project in the public interest, the two governments appointed an intergovernmental commission (IGC) and a series of subsidiary bodies to deal with technical matters on an expert basis. However, an important information imbalance which resides at the heart of this regulatory activity ensures that public oversight of the project in the construction phase is clearly constrained. In no sense has Eurotunnel got its way on all aspects of project design and development. Indeed, in the early 1990s it became so vexed at the imposition of new safety, security, and environmental standards by the IGC that it lodged a £1 billion claim against the British and French governments. Eurotunnel eventually agreed to abandon its action in December 1993 in exchange for a 10-year extension to the total concessionary period. This now runs for 65 years to July 2052. Yet the ability of the IGC to raise standards during the construction phase of the project does not alter the fact that throughout Eurotunnel has performed an important controlling function in the realm of project design.

As intended, the award of a necessarily non-patterned concession has shifted a degree of control from the public to the private sector. Here, it has not been exercised solely by Eurotunnel itself, but jointly—and sometimes conflictually—by Eurotunnel, its contracted tunnel builder, Transmanche Link (TML), and the consortium of 220 banks which came together to finance the project. It is the balance of forces within this relationship which has been crucial to project development since Eurotunnel secured its concession.

Most publicized have been relations between Eurotunnel and TML. At many stages during the construction phase of the present project disagreement between the two has spilled over into public confrontation, the basis of which may be located in the very structure of the relationship and traced back to the period after award of the concession, when a strange restructuring process was undertaken by the successful concessionaires. As has already been noted, Eurotunnel was created immediately after the concession had been secured. In effect, what happened was that the Anglo-French consortium of five banks (National Westminster, Midland, Banque Nationale de Paris, Crédit Lyonnais, and Banque Indosuez) and ten construction companies (Balfour Beatty, Costain, Tarmac, Taylor

Woodrow, Wimpey, Bouygues, Dumez, SPIE/Batignoles, Société Auxiliaire d'Entreprises and Société Générale d'Entreprises) which gained the concession formed Eurotunnel Group, the umbrella holding company which brings together Eurotunnel PLC and Eurotunnel SA, in order to place responsibility for Tunnel construction and operation in its hands. Having floated Eurotunnel off, the participating construction companies then regrouped to form the Anglo-French joint venture, TML, and in August 1986 signed a construction contract with Eurotunnel. The participating banks, meanwhile, set themselves up as formal financiers for the project, substantially increasing the size of the banking syndicate in the process.

Eurotunnel itself was thereby established as paired national enterprises, rather than as a single binational company. Officially, it operates as a binational partnership. However, the fact that its flotation in November 1987 offered twinned shares for public purchase substantially reinforced its unity and cohesion. Shares in Eurotunnel PLC and Eurotunnel SA have a separate existence only in theory. In practice, they cannot be split, but must always be traded in paired units. Eurotunnel may therefore be formally divided in the various ways shown in Figure 8.1, but in terms of its basic organization it functions as a binational enterprise.

The result of the complicated manœuvre which first established Eurotunnel was that it signed a construction contract with TML at a time of historic weakness.[9] Unsurprisingly, this contract was weighted heavily in favour of TML, and gave little consideration to Eurotunnel's interests. From the start, then, the project was contractor-driven, reflecting the balance of forces at the heart of the project in its early months. It was clear, however, that the balance of power within this important relationship would have to be altered if the Tunnel were to have long-term viability, the contractors' interest being in construction, not operation.

Such an alteration began to take place through a series of often public conflicts—some of which were discreetly mediated by the Bank of England—between Eurotunnel's British co-chairman, Sir Alastair Morton, and TML. Engaging in various degrees of brinkmanship, Morton gradually succeeded in renegotiating the construction contract to Eurotunnel's benefit. However, lengthy public disagreement between the two sides during the early 1990s indicated that the tension at the heart of the project was not easily

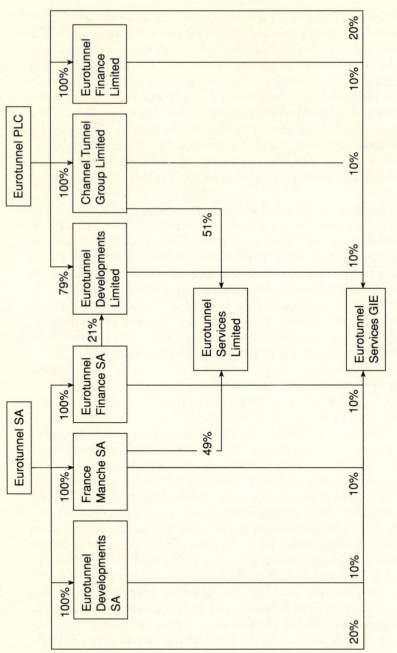

Fig. 8.1. Eurotunnel corporate structure
Source: Eurotunnel (1990).

resolved. In October 1991, TML resorted to litigation in its dispute with Eurotunnel, at stake being the by no means small sum of £800 million (at 1985 prices, £1.2 billion at 1991 prices) relating mostly to the unexpectedly high cost of installing a railway system through the Tunnel. Eurotunnel responded by taking out an injunction to prevent TML from stopping work during the period of litigation. A peace deal was finally signed in July 1993, when Eurotunnel agreed to advance TML £235 million as down payment on the settlement of its claims. This allowed an operational Tunnel finally to be handed over to Eurotunnel by TML on 10 December 1993. Once this event had taken place, it became highly unlikely that TML would receive significant further compensation from Eurotunnel.

That Morton was to some extent able to renegotiate the original contract agreed by Eurotunnel and TML reflects the changing balance of power which resulted first from Eurotunnel's public flotation in the immediate aftermath of the stock market crash, and second from completion of an operational Tunnel. Prior to the stock market flotation, Eurotunnel had relied on two sources of funds: the initial equity interest of founder shareholders, which totalled £46 million and became known as Equity 1; and £206 million of equity capital secured through private institutional placement in October 1986, known as Equity 2. Now, at Equity 3, Eurotunnel issued twinned shares at £3.50 a unit (including a tradable warrant), which were to be listed jointly on the London Stock Exchange and the Paris Bourse.

This public share issue, which was fully underwritten though under-subscribed by the public, raised a further £770 million of equity finance. It also meant that Eurotunnel had met the conditions imposed on a loan of £5 billion by the banking syndicate constructed to provide credit finance for the project. This loan included £1 billion from the European Investment Bank (EIB) secured, not (as is usual) by the recipient states' governments, but against letters of credit from the syndicate of commercial banks which is financing Eurotunnel. Its important consequence was to give Eurotunnel more room for manœuvre in its dealings with TML.

As cost projections rose, both sources of capital had to be increased. By the early 1990s estimated total financing cost to completion was £10 billion. In November 1987, it had been £4.87 billion. A £566 million rights issue was launched in November

1990 and successfully completed the following month, and increased credit facilities were negotiated. Overall, available finance rose from some £1 billion equity and £5 billion debt at the end of 1987 to £1.5 billion equity and £7.1 billion debt at the end of 1990. Of the additional loan capital of £2.1 billion raised in 1990, £1.8 billion came from the banking syndicate, with the remaining £300 million being a parallel line loan from the EIB. The unusual, indeed unique, feature of this loan is that it is not secured by letters of credit, but on Eurotunnel's existing assets. Eurotunnel's loan facility was extended by a further £700 million in January 1994, and a second rights issue was launched in spring 1994, raising £500 million. Total funding thus reached the £10 billion mark.

As its own sources of funding increased, Eurotunnel slowly succeeded in overcoming some of the power imbalance established at the start of the present project between itself and TML. Once the Tunnel had been handed from TML to Eurotunnel its room for manœuvre increased dramatically, and the prospect of TML's outstanding claims being met receded substantially.

Central to the internal politics of the Tunnel project is, however, the banking syndicate. This is the largest ever to have been assembled for a project financed entirely by the private sector. In the syndicate of 220 banks, there are 19 leading lenders, known as instructing banks, which conduct most negotiations with Eurotunnel. Within this group of 19 instructing banks, 4 agent banks—National Westminster, Midland, Banque Nationale de Paris, and Crédit Lyonnais—which were all initial sponsors of the project are distinguished. However, extensions of funding to Eurotunnel cannot be agreed by these banks alone, but instead require the support of 65 per cent of banks as measured by the value of their loans. By November 1990, two-thirds of Eurotunnel's total loan finance of £6.8 billion came from banks in four countries: Japan (23%), France (20%), Germany (13%), and Great Britain (12%). Only 2 per cent of Eurotunnel's loan finance came from American banks.

By virtue of the size and evident importance of their loan, the banks have thus become the main locus of project supervision, exercising substantial power over Eurotunnel. Nevertheless, public regulation has not been entirely undermined. In the construction phase the IGC managed to impose a series of unwelcome minimum standards on Eurotunnel. With regard to the operating phase, the

Concession Agreement contains a number of vaguely worded clauses which could be used to prevent Eurotunnel from exploiting any monopolistic position it might acquire. This represents no more than standard government procedure with regard to any commercial enterprise, but it could increase in importance in years to come. The operations of the Channel Tunnel will certainly be regulated, but the exact form and content of future regulation remain hard to judge.

In sum, some decision-making competence passed from the public to the private sector with conclusion of the Concession Agreement in the early months of 1986. This is not to argue that the passage was entirely smooth, for neither before nor after the Concession Agreement was signed did either sector have exclusive possession. It is, however, to argue that this was a crucial moment in development of the present project. In assessing this move, it should be restated that it was largely in line with British government intentions. Indeed, the remarkable aspect of British Tunnel policy making in the 1980s was the self-denying ordinance which was its major feature, and which generated this partial shift in decision-making competence.

3. POLICY DEVELOPMENT AROUND A PRIVATE-SECTOR TUNNEL

In seeking to exploit the present Tunnel project for maximum public benefit, policy makers have therefore been confronted with a central situation in which private control is far greater than public. Eurotunnel operates the Tunnel on commercial, not social, criteria and, not unreasonably, demonstrated in the construction phase of the project that its own business interests were paramount. Yet this does not mean that the efforts of state and local policy makers to draw public benefit from the project have been entirely negated. Indeed, in both Britain and France, policy makers have made progress in developing policy around the private-sector Tunnel.[10] The extent of their success has, however, been strikingly divergent.

In Britain a formal policy line of no public involvement in the Tunnel project was set in the Thatcher years and was not modified in any noticeable respect by the first or second Major government.

It was of course not interpreted by policy makers in an absolutely rigid manner, but it did successfully establish the tone of British policy making in the late 1980s and early 1990s. Eurotunnel and TML were to be treated in the same way as any other private company. Preferential treatment over and above that which public authorities would extend to any large private undertaking was ruled out.

Central to this formal policy line was extension of the self-denying ordinance—which prevents both the British and French governments from financing the Tunnel project—to encompass the provision of international rail services to the Tunnel on the British side of the Channel. By the terms of section 42 of the Channel Tunnel Act 1987, which provided British authorization for construction of the fixed link, the British government is prevented from infringing its own rules governing BR investment in new infrastructure, which state that an 8 per cent return must be demonstrated before authorization may be granted. No equivalent criterion for public funding was ever explicitly decreed on the French side of the Tunnel.

The difference between policy making on the two sides of the Channel is, however, best seen not in technical terms, but in terms of the tone of policy making set from the top of government, to which allusion has already been made. In truth the notion that international rail links on the French side of the Channel are massively subsidized in ways that ought to make an economically literate Briton wince is highly questionable. TGV-Nord has a projected return of more than 12 per cent, except for a section which has been added to take it through the centre of Lille. The difference between policy making in Britain and France genuinely does lie not so much in formal prohibitions, as in the thinking and approach which inform them. The British approach has simply been a lot more market-orientated than the French.

This does not mean, however, that contact between institutions of government on the one hand and Eurotunnel and TML on the other has been reduced to a bare minimum on the British side of the Channel. Indeed, a series of ministries has been involved in the project in recent years. Being centrally implicated (as lead department), the Department of Transport (DTp) took charge of negotiations over infrastructure links to the Tunnel, at no stage infringing either the letter or the spirit of section 42, but nevertheless ensuring that investment to the tune of between £1.7 billion and £3 billion (or more), depending on what is included, in rail links to the Tunnel was undertaken, and agreeing various changes to the road network in Kent. Central to this programme was completion of the M20, which links the Tunnel to the M25 and thence to the rest of the British motorway network. Beyond this, the most active ministry has been the Department of Trade and Industry, which played an important role in the distribution of TML subcontracting work, establishing a newsletter through which Tunnel subcontracts (and work on similar projects elsewhere in the world) were publicized throughout Britain, and operating a 'marriage bureau' seeking to develop international joint ventures that might bid for Tunnel (and other) work. At the sub-national level, Kent County Council and a number of Kent districts have sought to involve themselves in co-ordination and planning of Tunnel impacts. The most important aspects of this activity will be returned to later.

Yet despite this varied and often crucial activity, what is most noticeable at the British end of the Tunnel is the poverty of public response, most evident in the (non-)handling of the rail link issue. This has now passed through such a complex series of phases that it cannot be investigated in detail. In brief, an initial BR insistence that existing tracks in Kent would prove adequate to demand was quickly reversed, and provoked a long series of studies and announcements. Four routes were published by BR in July 1988 as the basis for consultation in Kent. Each was subsequently abandoned in the face of public outcry. In 1989 BR decided to tunnel its way under much of Kent and south London, but the projected cost of £3.1 billion proved unattractive to potential private-sector collaborators. None came forward. In spring 1990 a proposal from Eurorail (a joint venture between BR, Trafalgar House, and BICC) to build a £2.6 billion rail link provided that it was advanced £900 million in cash grants and £1.1 billion in interest-free loans by the British government was flatly rejected by the DTp. In 1991 BR's old route—now projected to cost £3.5 billion—was again rejected by the government. Finally, in March 1993 a new £2.5 billion route into St Pancras submitted by Union Railways (a BR subsidiary devised to pursue the rail link project which was separated from BR in autumn 1993) gained government support and the promise of some cash to finance domestic gains from the line.

This time consultation in Kent was successfully managed, but before long the extent of government commitment was again being questioned. Both financial and political problems could yet arise. The project cannot be completed before 2002, though 2005 is probably a more likely earliest possible date for the start of high-speed rail operations. The Kent rail-link saga is, of course, only part of a larger failure to upgrade British rail services to current European standards, and to tie British regions into an emergent European high-speed rail network.

By sticking to the entirely spurious argument of the level playing field (which certainly does not exist in the transport market), and in consequence refusing to alter its position on the provision of international rail links to the Tunnel, the British government has thus failed to perform the task which only it can perform, which is to give a strategic lead in transport matters. It is important to stress that this activity need not necessarily involve it in the expenditure of large sums of public money, but simply requires it to acknowledge the fact that a market which is heavily structured by existing policy decisions needs government to take a lead in planning future ones. Policy failure here disadvantages not only Kent but also all other parts of Britain, which are distanced from the Tunnel and from the emergent transport infrastructure of which it is a key part. There has not, then, been a sufficiently dynamic response on the part of the British government to the challenges posed by the Tunnel.[11]

In France, by contrast, from the very start the project has been managed by public authorities in a more positive manner. Given that the French policy network developed a territorial dimension as early as 1981, and that this dimension was maintained by political links embodied in Mauroy in particular, and by the kind of strong administrative links which exist throughout the French institutional system, public responses to the Tunnel were always likely to be more developed in France than in Britain. However, the difference resides not only in structural factors, but also in a distinct administrative culture, which would have found it inconceivable that a project as strategic as the Tunnel could be left largely to the free play of market forces.[12] At each stage of the project, this basic difference in approach may be seen very clearly.

Thus, on the French side of the Channel, in contrast to the British, the state has facilitated Eurotunnel's progress both by promulgating a series of decrees which eased the project's passage through the planning process, and by employing special procedures which have substantially aided both local and strategic management of the Eurotunnel project. Indeed, in characteristic ways public authorities in France have attempted to treat the Tunnel scheme as if it were a public works project. An example of such activity is adaptation to the Tunnel's circumstances of the *procédure 'grands chantiers'*. This is a mechanism devised in stages in the mid- to late 1970s by Electricité de France—a nationalized company—to manage local difficulties encountered in nuclear power station construction. Central to it is appointment of a state official to co-ordinate the activities of the project developer and those of directly affected local authorities. In the case of the Channel Tunnel, the main concerns of the procedure were fourfold: to manage housing, transport, education, health, and other problems generated by construction of the Tunnel; to co-ordinate local training initiatives; to inform local firms of opportunities created by the Tunnel; and to manage post-construction problems by retraining Tunnel workers and attending to local unemployment after 1993.

On a more strategic level, French planners have incorporated the Channel Tunnel, over which they have no commercial control, in transport infrastructure provisions stretching well into the next century. Most visible to British observers has been the decision—dated 9 October 1987—to extend TGV-Nord to the Tunnel mouth in time for the planned opening in mid-1993 (later postponed to spring 1994). TGV-Nord was officially opened by President Mitterrand on 18 May 1993, though at this time it was complete only between Paris and Arras (rather more than half its full length), the rest of the route being serviced by old track. By the time the Tunnel eventually opened the full service between Paris, Lille, and Calais was operational. Furthermore, by approving TGV-Nord as early as 1987, the French not only secured a lead in developing rail links, they also gained a head start in the development of local economic strategies. By insisting that the route pass through the centre of Lille, rather than round its perimeter as SNCF initially intended, and by putting up some of the extra funding that such an option entails, local and regional authorities in Nord-Pas de Calais have been able to set up Lille as a major development axis.[13] The TGV station in the centre of the city will now be a major interchange point for travellers from north-west Europe seeking to reach destinations south, west, and east of Paris (and for travellers making the reverse journeys). In addition, it will form the focal point of Euralille Métropole, an international business centre currently under construction in the heart of the city. Furthermore, TGV stations are being installed at Arras and at the Tunnel mouth near Calais, thereby offering the possibility of enhanced local development to these areas, and regional centres such as Dunkirk and Valenciennes will also have direct TGV services to Paris.

Equally important are plans to construct a series of motorways from the Tunnel to distant parts of France: a *rocade littorale* to take traffic north to Belgium and south to south-west France and Spain, and other motorways leading from Paris to the north-east and south-east corners of the country. Not all the thinking behind these various schemes has been strategic: an inevitable process of central–local bargaining and dealing lies behind parts of it. Nevertheless, strenuous attempts have been made by French planners to address the broad strategic issues raised by the Tunnel.

There can be, then, no justification for the contention that privatization of the Channel Tunnel was a definitive act with respect to subsidiary policy decisions. Comparison of British and French policy making around the Tunnel is sufficient to make this point. In contrast to the British response to the Tunnel, which has been to let the market decide to as great an extent as possible the wider implications of the Tunnel, the French response has sought to incorporate a conceded infrastructure project in the broad domain of national planning.

Moreover, there have been numerous developments at the edge of the present project which reinforce the argument that it is quite possible for policy to be made in a variety of ways around a project of this kind. Most notable at the sub-national level have been attempts by policy makers in Kent and Nord-Pas de Calais to profit from the increased visibility afforded them by the Tunnel.[14] These attempts have encompassed not only highly successful direct approaches to the EC for cash, but also development of a pioneering Euroregion which has secured EC recognition and now extends to cover the whole of Belgium in addition to its two founding regions. A series of development strategies has been built around the concept of the Euroregion, tourism being one affected sector.[15] Most notable at the supra-national level have been attempts by a series of transnational bodies—such as the Community of European Railways, the European Conference of Ministers of Transport, and the European Commission itself (chiefly through former Transport Commissioner Karel Van Miert)—to develop integrated transport strategies around the Channel Tunnel.

Policy development around a private-sector Tunnel has, then, been highly varied, and demonstrates that ownership itself is less important in deciding policy responses to a project of this magnitude than is a series of economic, political, and cultural factors.

4. FROM NATIONAL TO INTERNATIONAL CHAMPIONS

The 'national' enterprise which has been investigated in this chapter has in fact rarely been anything other than binational. Indeed, only in mid-Victorian times was the Channel fixed link seen strictly as either a British or a French undertaking, and then rival teams of private—not public—builders engaged in competitive tunnelling activity from the shores of Kent and the Pas de Calais. Never has the Channel fixed link assumed the status of a real national champion. Despite this, its history in the 1970s and 1980s parallels that of many other enterprises investigated in this collection, in that the policy process surrounding it has been greatly changed by the decision, on which Thatcher insisted, to open the project to private investment. The Tunnel, then, is a valid example of national enterprise faced—by privatization—with an increasingly international environment.

The main point which arises from this investigation is, however, that privatization itself is not the main issue in determining policy responses to a project of this kind. Instead, factors which are nation-specific play the major roles. In this context, the success of the distinct strategies adopted by policy makers in Britain and France requires consideration.

To the British must go credit for insisting on fixed link privatization and seeing the chosen policy line through to the completion of construction activity. Through all the difficulties the project has faced, British commitment to the terms of the Tunnel concession has been unwavering. The major success of this policy line has been the institution of Eurotunnel as project champion, able to fight for the Tunnel and to keep the project alive when in other circumstances it might have succumbed to various pressures, notably financial ones. Indeed, Eurotunnel's role as project champion could well be the crucial factor in this scheme's successful completion after a long series of failures, and should not be overlooked.[16] A public-sector project could easily have been abandoned in the face of dramatic cost increases, as happened in the 1970s,[17] or at least been subject to even greater contractor-driven cost inflation than is the case with the present project.

However, this is not to argue that the project was in all respects correctly established. Indeed, it can plausibly be held that concession of the project to Eurotunnel and its contracting-out of construction to TML left Eurotunnel in a position of weakness which led directly to major difficulties later on. Better in these circumstances would have been an arrangement which either strengthened Eurotunnel by a temporary injection of public-sector finance and expertise, or weakened TML by a division of the works contract into a series of such contracts or an arrangement which linked its revenues to the operating success of a completed Tunnel. This latter arrangement currently exists in part—for each constituent company within TML holds shares and warrants in Eurotunnel—but it has obviously not been sufficient to prevent TML from threatening Eurotunnel with financial ruin if its demands are not met. Interestingly, when work began on the £1.8 billion Jubilee Line extension to the London Underground in December 1993 contracts were deliberately split into small packages.

When all is said and done, however, the British government can justly argue that its central decision to invite the private sector to build the world's largest undersea tunnel and run a sophisticated transport system through it has been largely vindicated by Eurotunnel's success in bringing a satisfactory project to completion if not on, then at least near, time. It is true that the initial budget has been greatly exceeded, but the return on the project should still be acceptable. Comparable construction projects—such as the Seikan rail tunnel in Japan, and any number of bridge and canal schemes—have often fared far worse.

Yet despite its (qualified) success in managing the central task of establishing a viable Tunnel project, the British government has failed in other aspects of project management. As the French have ably demonstrated, it is quite possible—and, indeed, desirable—to bring a privatized Tunnel within a strategic planning framework. Such activity has been conspicuous by its absence in Britain, and has resulted in major incoherences in the developing transport network.

Indeed, a conclusion that emerges very clearly from this investigation is that the constraints imposed by privatization on French policy makers have thus far been slight, for it is their proactive stance which fits most closely with the wishes both of Eurotunnel itself and of other important actors, such as the European Commission. All are concerned that strategic management of the transport network created by the Tunnel be undertaken by policy makers, rather than be left to the operations of the so-called 'free' market. By contrast, British policy makers are increasingly being constrained to engage in strategic policy-making activity.

In these circumstances, it would seem that a kind of functional logic is developing at the heart of the present project, with the Tunnel itself likely to remain a private-sector undertaking for the full 65 years of its concession, but with important parts of the transport network of which it is but one very small, though evidently strategic, part being directed by the public sector, possibly through a range of contracts with private-sector bodies. Certainly, it seems that the British rail link saga will have to be resolved in something not vastly different from the French manner, and that a fairly similar pattern of public–private relations may develop in both Britain and France as a result. Indeed, British policy makers have already looked with interest at ways in which SNCF is allowed by the French government to call on private finance (and have learnt some lessons), and when Michael Heseltine was advised at the Department of the Environment by Peter Hall a highly visionary—and probably unrealizable—scheme to develop a new linear city around the Channel Tunnel rail link was elaborated. Beyond this, the entire British land use planning system is clearly in urgent need of reform, for its tortuous manner of dealing with major projects guarantees the injection of uncertainty and therefore risk, as is evident not only from the Channel Tunnel rail link but also from projects such as the third London airport, the M25, and Docklands. Only the parliamentary route adopted for Channel Tunnel authorization saved it from a similar fate to each of these projects.

It may then be that what is in the end most noticeable about the present Tunnel project is not the extent to which policy makers have seen control slip from their grasp—though this has of course happened—but the extent to which they have been forced to take control of aspects of the project which they would far rather, in some cases, have left well alone. This, again, is the point about functional logic. Furthermore, if such a logic does indeed exist, then it requires attention to be paid to the level at which public control can be most successfully organized. Despite substantial national resistance to the idea, it could well be that such a level is European, and that what requires elaboration in years to come is a viable European transport strategy which takes full consideration of the international environment in which 'national' projects, such as the Channel Tunnel, increasingly find themselves.

The public sector was distanced from the present Tunnel project, chiefly on the insistence of Margaret Thatcher. Yet it seems most likely that the state will have to be brought back in to various aspects of Tunnel policy making. Already the British and French states must occupy positions of project guarantors, for the Tunnel scheme long ago passed the point at which it could simply be allowed to collapse in the face of terminal private-sector problems. Such dramatic circumstances might never arise. A similar result could, however, be triggered in more subtle ways which might involve the two states—and particularly the British—in increasing their involvement in transport links to the Tunnel as a means of increasing its profitability. Furthermore, in any conceivable future, public authorities will exercise a regulatory role with respect to the Tunnel. Here, genuine uncertainty currently reigns. Light-touch regulation of a private operator is possible. However, in the Concession Agreement may be found clauses on which a more directive stance could be based. At this point, the Tunnel could be brought within the scope of public policy and set at the heart of national or (more likely) multinational transport strategies.

The present Channel Tunnel project, though placed in the hands of the private sector in the mid-1980s, could therefore find itself at least partially directed by public-sector priorities in the 1990s and subsequent decades. Such direction is unlikely to take the form of public ownership. Instead, it will most probably be the more flexible and possibly more effective direction that is available to public authorities which are freed from formal responsibilities of ownership and control, and able to engage in more subtle forms of influence. Committed to a series of strategic policy goals, public authorities can be expected to exploit the ambiguous phrasing of the Concession Agreement to mount a variety of regulatory strategies.

Notes

1. This chapter is partly based on research undertaken at the Channel Tunnel Research Unit, University of Kent at Canterbury, which was financed by ESRC (YD00250018).
2. I. Holliday and R. Vickerman, 'The Channel Tunnel and Regional Development: Policy Responses in Britain and France', *Regional Studies*, 24 (1990), 455–66; R. W. Vickerman, 'The Channel Tunnel and Regional Development in Europe: An Overview', *Applied Geography*, 14 (1994).
3. I. Holliday, G. Marcou, and R. Vickerman, *The Channel Tunnel: Public Policy, Regional Development and European Integration* (London, 1991).
4. M. Bonavia, *The Channel Tunnel Story* (Newton Abbot, 1987).
5. H. Young, *One of Us: A Biography of Margaret Thatcher* (London, 1990), 388.
6. N. Ridley, *'My Style of Government': The Thatcher Years* (London, 1991), 158.
7. H. Heclo and A. Wildavsky, *The Private Government of Public Money: Community and Policy inside British Politics*, 2nd edn. (London, 1981); F. Dupuy, 'The Politico-Administrative System of the *Département* in France', in Y. Mény and V. Wright (eds.), *Centre–Periphery Relations in Western Europe* (London, 1985), 79–103.
8. HM Government, *The Channel Fixed Link: Concession Agreement*, Cmnd. 9769 (London, 1986).
9. G. Marcou, 'Public and Private Sectors in the Delivery of Public Infrastructure: The Case of the Channel Tunnel from an International Perspective', *Environment and Planning C: Government and Policy*, 11 (1993), 1–18.
10. R. W. Vickerman, 'Transport Policy and the Channel Tunnel: UK, French and European Perspectives', in R. Gibb (ed.), *A Geography of the Channel Tunnel* (London, 1994).
11. I. Holliday, 'The Politics of the Channel Tunnel', *Parliamentary Affairs*, 45 (1992), 188–204.

12. D. Ashford, *British Dogmatism and French Pragmatism: Central–Local Policymaking in the Welfare State* (London, 1982).
13. I. Holliday, M. Langrand, and R. Vickerman, *Nord-Pas de Calais in the 1990s: A European Investment Region*, Economist Intelligence Unit special report no. M601 (London, 1991).
14. R. W. Vickerman, 'The Channel Tunnel and Transfrontier Co-operation', in R. Cappellin and P. Batey (eds.), *Regional Networks, Border Regions and European Integration* (London, 1993).
15. M. T. Sinclair and S. J. Page, 'The Euroregion: A New Framework for Tourism and Regional Development', *Regional Studies*, 27 (1993), 475–83.
16. P. Morris and G. Hough, *Preconditions of Success and Failure in Major Projects*, Technical Paper no. 3 (Oxford, 1986).
17. P. Hall, *Great Planning Disasters* (London, 1980).

9

Regulatory Reform and Internationalization in Telecommunications

MARK THATCHER

After decades of stability, the 1980s and early 1990s witnessed large-scale regulatory reform in telecommunications in Western Europe, both at national level and European Community level. The previous regulatory arrangements were crucial in the relationship between governments and public telecommunications operators (PTOs), with the latter behaving as 'national enterprises'. Over the 1980s and early 1990s, a new framework emerged which may both permit and oblige PTOs to internationalize, or at least Europeanize, by removing 'special and exclusive rights' in national markets in the EC. In examining the development of this framework, the focus of the analysis is the interaction between the changing strategies of governments and PTOs at national level, and regulatory reform at EC level.

The telecommunications sector has become a strategic economic sector: it is large and expanding;[1] perhaps more importantly, it has become an essential intermediate product for firms in a variety of economic and industrial fields, ranging from finance and tourism to manufacturing industries. The sector is also important in providing the earliest example of EC action in a network sector, and one traditionally dominated by 'national enterprises'. The decisions taken regarding telecommunications may have implications for EC regulation of other sectors such as gas, electricity, and railways. However, the analysis of the interaction of the EC and its member states can also be seen as a case study in the process of European integration and policy making. It is relevant for the ability of EC member states to maintain differing institutional arrangements and policy instruments in the light of the EC as a force for regulatory change and convergence.[2]

The chapter sets out the technological and economic nature of telecommunications and the way in which national regulatory frameworks allowed PTOs to be operated as 'national enterprises' (section 1). Then regulatory reform in four countries (Britain, France, Germany, and Italy) and their policies towards telecommunications during the 1980s and early 1990s, including at EC level, are examined (section 2), followed by analysis of EC regulatory activity (section 3). Finally, the conclusion explores the reasons for regulatory reform at EC and national level.

1. THE TELECOMMUNICATIONS SECTOR IN WESTERN EUROPE

1.1. The Nature of Telecommunications Services and Equipment Supply in the 1980s

The telecommunications sector can be divided into three subsectors, both for the purposes of analysis and for regulation. Network operation consists of the provision of the fixed line telecommunications infrastructure, the transmission of signals, and ordinary voice telephony. It accounted for the majority (75–80 per cent) of revenue in the telecommunications sector in the 1980s. 'Other services on the network' include 'VANS' (value added network services) such as fax, videotex services, electronic mail, electronic payments systems, electronic data interchange, and video-conferencing. VANS are transmitted on the telecommunications infrastructure, including the public switched telephone network and specialized networks, but most often on leased lines (i.e. capacity hired from the network operator). In addition, there are also specialized data transmission networks (such as 'packet switched' networks), mobile communications, and specialized satellite services. Thirdly, there is equipment manufacturing and supply. This subsector can itself be subdivided into customer premises equipment (CPE), which consists of terminals used by subscribers (for instance, fax machines, data terminals, and handsets) and equipment for the network, such as public exchanges and cable. The latter is not examined, as only regulation of the supply of services and CPE to final users is analysed here.

The VANS and CPE subsectors are highly diverse. Although small relative to network operation, they have grown extremely rapidly and have enjoyed remarkable technological innovation and development over the 1980s. Furthermore, they are vital to a wide range of other sectors such as computing, banking, tourism, and retailing. The conditions for access to the infrastructure are important, as CPE is attached to it and services are offered and transmitted over it. Norms and standards play a role in ensuring that different types of equipment are compatible.

The 1980s saw a more 'internationalized' environment in telecommunications. On the demand side, usage of international communications expanded rapidly, whilst the importance of multinational companies grew. Both generated a high proportion of the PTOs' revenue, and an even larger share of profits. On the supply side, large computer companies, such as IBM, began to offer services world-wide, sometimes involving use of telecommunications networks. Equipment manufacturers also internationalized, engaging in a spate of joint ventures, takeovers, and co-operation agreements.[3] Furthermore, regulatory changes took place in other countries, most notably in the US and Japan, allowing greater competition. In the US this extended to the supply of VANS and CPE, and then long distance communications including trunk, international, and satellite transmission. Moreover, telecommunications services were included in the GATT Uruguay Round.

1.2. PTOs as National Enterprises in the 1970s and Early 1980s

Before the mid-1980s, a similar pattern of rules governing the supply of telecommunications services existed in most European countries. Public telecommunications operators were state-owned organizations. The PTOs were the Post Office/British Telecom (BT) in Britain, the DGT (Direction Générale des Télécommunications) in France, the Deutsches Bundespost in West Germany, and various public bodies in Italy, of which the most important were SIP

(Società Italiana per l'esercicio telefonica) and ASST (l'Azienda di Stato per i Servici Telefonica). The PTOs were generally not firms but formed part of the national civil service, being one element in posts and telecommunications ministries, with the exception of the PO/BT in Britain (a public corporation after 1969) and SIP (a publicly owned firm and licensee).

The PTOs were given 'special and exclusive rights', generally monopoly rights of supply, under national law. These extended over network operation, and all other types of telecommunications services. The position of PTOs with respect to CPE varied somewhat, but generally they held formal monopoly rights. In practice, supply by private firms was allowed for some more sophisticated forms of equipment. PTOs also acted as regulatory bodies, issuing the few licences given for private supply, mostly of CPE, and defining norms and standards.

PTOs were 'national enterprises': they were state-owned and held 'special and exclusive rights' over supply; they were used, explicitly or implicitly, to perform a number of public policy functions rather than merely maximizing profits. They provided a 'universal public service'—the supply of the same services throughout a country's territory at the same price and under the same terms and conditions. They cross-subsidized different services; specifically, the prices of trunk and international communications were set above costs, and the profits used to cross-subsidize local communications and access to the network. Moreover, unprofitable or commercially risky services which offered technological innovation or met wider social and economic aims could be cross-subsidized. Tariffs were set to attempt to assist regional development. Furthermore, telecommunications profits were often used to subsidize loss-making postal services.

PTOs protected and privileged domestic equipment manufactures and service suppliers. Public procurement was used to support manufacturing 'national champions'. PTOs set norms and standards to favour certain suppliers, thereby creating non-tariff barriers to imports. They assisted national suppliers with research and development and exports. PTOs were also used by governments for fiscal and macro-economic purposes. On some occasions, they were used to raise revenue for state budgets. At other times, their prices were held down in order to control inflation. Their investment spending could be modified to operate 'counter-cyclically'.

1.3. Regulatory Arrangements and PTOs as 'National Enterprises'

The performance of these wider functions of PTOs largely depended on public ownership and the protection afforded by restrictions on competition. Public ownership allowed governments to use PTOs for their objectives and protected PTOs from pressures rapidly to earn large profits. A monopoly position allowed PTOs to set prices above costs for some services, without the fear of 'cream skimming' by competitors. The surplus revenue could then be used for other purposes, including cross-subsidizing other services and projects, or fulfilling wider policy aims. A monopoly position allowed the PTOs to purchase equipment from domestic manufacturers, without the fear that competitors would establish a rival network at lower cost. Regulatory powers allowed PTOs to set domestic norms to protect certain manufactures of CPE.

However, national regulatory arrangements prevented the internationalization of PTOs. European and other overseas markets for CPE and services were closed by monopoly rights. European PTOs enjoyed a protected and comfortable position domestically. Their major tasks appeared to be modernizing and expanding their networks. Their organizational status militated against internationalization: the organizational culture and remit was that of the civil service, providing a public service to domestic residents, rather than that of a commercial firm seeking overseas markets.

2. NATIONAL DEVELOPMENTS IN THE 1980s AND EARLY 1990s

2.1. Britain

Policy in Britain over the 1980s and early 1990s was centred around regulatory reforms. These were more sweeping in other EC countries and policy towards the main PTO, BT, saw a sharp movement away from the traditional 'national enterprise' approach. Two central strands can be discerned: removal from Ministers of much decision making over day-to-day regulation and the supply of services; the introduction of competition into many areas, combined with strong regulation where BT was dominant.[4]

Unlike other countries in the EC, the main network operator, BT, was 'privatized' in 1984 by the sale of 51 per cent of shares. Competition was introduced into network operation, with the licensing of a second network operator, Mercury, in 1982; the government announced in 1991 that this 'duopoly' would be ended and other firms permitted to be PTOs. Competition was allowed in CPE supply after 1981 and in VANS from 1982. Detailed restrictions on supply were progressively reduced for both,[5] and the scope of competition was extended, notably to mobile communications and satellite services. A powerful regulatory body, Oftel (the Office of Telecommunications), independent of the government and BT, was established under the 1984 Telecommunications Act. It largely replaced formal ministerial control of BT or other suppliers.

A new regulatory system grew up. Suppliers, notably BT, operated under licences, which specified rules designed to result in 'fair competition'.[6] Oftel oversaw the enforcement of licences. Its overall approach was to pursue 'fair and effective competition' and extend it as far as possible. Where this did not occur (in practice, where BT enjoyed a dominant position), its regulation of BT was more continuous and direct, including price control and targets for quality of service. After 1984, the government did not participate in BT's operational decisions, such as investment, purchasing, price rises, or employment. BT was no longer a policy instrument in the traditional sense. Instead, regulation by Oftel and competition were to yield results in terms of better services and greater efficiency.

A variety of factors were responsible for these changes. Privatization, competition, and independent regulation were part of the Conservative government's attempt to 'roll back the state' and stimulate greater efficiency. Privatization raised much-needed revenue for the government, whilst also removing BT's capital expenditure from government spending and borrowing totals. Business users, especially in the City, were influential in the early 1980s in the ending of BT's monopoly over CPE, VANS, and the provision of leased lines. Ideas over the value of competition and forms of regulation were often taken from the example of the US. International pressure for greater competition was exerted by American companies, notably IBM, and also occasionally by the US administration.[7] The head of Oftel 1984–92, Sir Bryan Carsberg, was also important in the primacy given to fair competition.

Although freer from direct government control, BT faced increased competition and tightening regulation of its prices by Oftel.[8] It adopted a strategy of improving its services in Britain, notably for large business customers; this involved higher investment, innovation in new services, and altering its organizational culture. Moreover, it brought prices closer to costs, to prevent competitors 'cream skimming' services whose prices were far above costs.

BT also sought to internationalize. It aimed to become the 'hub' in Europe for multinationals. It began to expand its sales in international markets, including offering international links across several countries and acquiring overseas suppliers.[9] But the size of activities overseas remained very limited by 1994: the purchase of Mitel was an expensive failure and the firm was sold in 1992 at a substantial loss; McCaw was a loss-making company, unlikely to produce profits for some years, and BT sold its shares to ATT in 1992; the vast bulk of BT's revenue and profits were derived from the UK market. Nevertheless, BT's long-term strategy has come to include expansion overseas.

The Conservative government strove to export the British approach to regulation to the EC. Thus it supported maximization of competition and provisions for 'fair competition', opposing the establishment of norms and standards for equipment and services which might be stricter than in Britain. This stance fitted the overall philosophy of the government, namely that the EC and Single Market should represent the lifting of barriers to competition and free trade within Europe. But it was also related to the position of British companies, and in particular BT. The latter appeared very well placed to take advantage of EC markets being opened to competition: it was freed from the 'constraints' of public ownership and its management culture was altering; it had experience of competition; its financial base was strong, having access to financial markets and enjoying high profits; PTOs in other EC countries appeared unlikely to overwhelm BT in the British market, especially as BT had rebalanced its tariffs and improved its quality of service in the 1980s, whilst BT's international services seemed highly competitive in the growing international services markets and for multinational users. Thus BT seemed to have both the means and the incentive to take advantage of reciprocal opening of markets and EC legislation allowing competition.

2.2. France

During the 1980s, France Télécom (the DGT's new name from 1988) continued to be used as an instrument for the pursuit of wider policy aims other than merely running the network. It was involved in managing and financing ambitious *grands projets*, such as the telematics programme ('Minitel'), a national cable plan, and then high definition television, as well as in providing revenues for non-telecommunications purposes (the *prélèvements* and support for French electronics firms).[10] Policy was also directed at supplying a high quality, modern network and sophisticated public services; examples included the packet-switched network Transpac and digital data transmission services. Maximum usage of public networks (rather than private networks on leased lines) was encouraged.

Pressure for regulatory reform was limited to specific fields, such as CPE supply (due to a flood of imported equipment in the early 1980s) and VANS (from business users such as banks and travel companies wishing to have a clear regulatory framework) in the early/mid-1980s. There was little support for the privatization of France Télécom, nor for competition in network operation, even under Chirac's government of 1986–8. Instead, Socialist PTT Ministers Louis Mexandeau (1981–6) and Paul Quilès (1988–91) emphasized their commitment to France Télécom as part of the *service public*, and contrasted it with the undesirable consequences of competition in the US and Britain.

Regulatory reforms were carefully tailored to protect France Télécom's position and allow it to remain a policy instrument available to Ministers. During the early 1980s, all CPE was opened to private supply; however, it had to be approved as meeting PTT-determined standards and this was sometimes used to favour French manufacturers and suppliers. Then in 1987, competition in VANS was permitted, but subject to many conditions to protect France Télécom's monopoly over network operation and to maintain maximum compatibility of equipment and services.[11]

The most thorny political issue was France Télécom's position as an *administration*. During the 1980s emphasis had been laid on France Télécom enjoying operating autonomy and behaving like a firm, albeit one offering a public service; from the mid/late 1980s, this was linked to the need to prepare France Télécom for the possibility of direct or indirect competition. But the trade unions were fiercely opposed to loss of civil service status and were able to block change under the Right. However, in 1990 reforms came under the then PTT Minister, Paul Quilés. France Télécom obtained its own legal identity and ceased to be part of the PTT Ministry. Nevertheless, despite the rhetoric, France Télécom's scope for real autonomy from the government was open to doubt. The powers of the PTT Minister were considerable: he laid down its obligations under a *cahier de charges* (licence), chose many of the members of its Board of Directors and, with the Finance and Budget Ministers, drew up a planning contract (albeit non-legally binding) with France Télécom covering matters such as the latter's investment, prices, employment, and borrowing. The Minister was responsible for regulation and no strong independent regulatory body was created.

The strategy of the French government at EC level was closely linked to its policies concerning reform of France Télécom. Under the Socialist governments of 1988–93, reforms of France Télécom were limited and the latter remained an important source of funds to support ailing state-owned firms such as Bull and Thomson. Quilès therefore sought to protect France Télécom from EC-imposed competition by attempting to retain national licensing powers and prevent the use of private networks to undercut France Télécom's public networks. He argued for strict EC mandatory standards for CPE and VANS licences, and opposed competition being permitted for data transmission networks (such as packet switching) and resale of capacity leased from France Télécom. At the same time, however, the EC also provided a useful argument for the reform of France Télécom's administrative status, in order to overcome union opposition.

But, after the return of the Right in 1993, the pace of change accelerated, as French government policy was modified and EC and domestic policy became increasingly intertwined. Longuet (once again responsible for telecommunications as Industry Minister), and many elements of France Télécom's senior management, believed that greater competition was inevitable, and indeed perhaps desirable. Thus in May/June 1993, the French government accepted EC Commission proposals to extend competition to voice telephony. The counterpart to this was an initiative to introduce more far-reaching reforms of France Télécom, notably the alteration in its *statut* to that of a limited company, possibly also including partial privatization and independent regulation. It was argued that such changes would enable France Télécom to compete effectively. As in 1986–8, there was fierce union and employee opposition. EC regulation provided the Balladur government with a powerful justification for reform of France Télécom in order to attempt to overcome resistance to change.

Reform of France Télécom and EC rules extending competition were linked to French strategies for internationalization. Before 1990, the administrative status and culture of France Télécom militated against overseas expansion and competing internationally. Reform of France Télécom and the opening of EC markets due to EC rules appeared to offer opportunities for expansion for France Télécom, due to its modern network and advanced services. Nevertheless, whilst there was greater stress on international expansion in the 1980s and early 1990s, and a number of moves were made, particularly to develop co-operation with Deutsche Telekom,[12] overseas activities constituted only a tiny fraction of France Télécom's turnover.

2.3. Germany/West Germany

Traditionally, the West German market had been one of the most closed in Western Europe.[13] The DBP (Deutsches Bundespost) exercised its monopoly over network operation, services and much CPE. However, the 1980s saw a lengthy process of regulatory reform. Competition was cautiously introduced and its scope was ambiguous. A powerful coalition of interests opposed greater competition and institutional reform, including the main trade union in the DBP, many of the Länder, elements in several political parties (the CSU, the SPD, and the Greens), the Finance and Interior Ministries, and small/medium-sized equipment manufacturers.[14] They wished the DBP to continue to fulfil its national enterprise roles, such as cross-subsidizing services for rural areas and domestic users, providing secure employment, assisting the Post and German equipment manufacturers, and contributing to the Federal Budget.

The pressures for change grew stronger in the 1980s, greatly influenced by international actors and events. Users and suppliers of CPE and services from other sectors which became related to telecommunications, notably computer companies (for instance Nixdorf), pressed for greater competition to be permitted; international firms were important in this, particularly IBM and American users. German business users altered their position, and supported some reform. The large and influential equipment manufacturer Siemens modified its stance in favour of some competition being permitted, as it sought the opening of overseas markets for its public switches.[15] The FDP, the Economic Ministry, and several prominent academic economists argued for greater competition, sometimes influenced by overseas examples, such as in the US and Japan.[16] The US engaged in powerful lobbying for competition to be permitted, and hence access for American firms to the German market.

Under these pressures, regulatory reform did take place, under Christian Schwarz-Schilling, the CDU PTT Minister from 1982 until 1993. Competition in the supply of CPE was extended in mid/late-1980s to all equipment and limited competition was permitted for some services; sometimes this was undertaken under severe international pressure.[17] However, only after the government-appointed Witte Commission published its Report in 1987 did comprehensive reform take place, with the 1989 PTT Restructuring law.

The 1989 law introduced only a limited set of changes and left many important matters to be decided by the Minister. A new body, Telekom, held a monopoly over network operation, but Telekom continued to be part of the federal administration, hence its real autonomy was unclear. Competition in all services other than voice telephony was permitted, without the extent of Telekom's monopoly being precisely defined. Provisions were made to ensure 'fair competition' in VANS, including interconnection of private networks to the public network and the requirement that Telekom pay the same charges as other bodies for leased lines. Nevertheless, some services open to competition were to be designated by the Minister as 'mandatory' ones, due to their infrastructure significance; Telekom was obliged to provide these nationally at the same tariffs but was permitted to cross-subsidize their supply from other activities. The conditions of access to Telekom's network and provisions for norms and use of 'open standards' were also left to ministerial decree. Perhaps most importantly, no independent regulatory body was established, implementation and enforcement of the 1989 law lying in the hands of the Posts and Telecommunications Minister.

Rapidly and unexpectedly, much greater changes followed in the early 1990s. The effects of reunification were an essential factor. The demands of financing the modernization of Eastern Germany's telecommunications system were enormous (an estimated DM 60 billion between 1990 and 1997). At the same time, under the 1989 reforms, telecommunications bore the costs of postal service losses as well as special government taxes. Deutsche Telekom found itself in a precarious financial position: it had to borrow large sums, was failing to make profits, and faced high interest charges.[18] There were calls for competition to be allowed in the creation of infrastructures in East Germany, the danger of illegal networks being established appeared to grow, and Deutsche Telekom seemed disadvantaged in fields in which competition was permitted. Hence the government, pressed by Deutsche Telekom's senior management, decided in 1993 to introduce far-reaching reforms with the aims of providing new capital, lighter financial burdens on telecommunications, and an organizational framework which would allow Telekom to compete effectively. Deutsche Telekom was to become a company operating under private law by 1995, enjoying great autonomy from the government; it was to be partially privatized thereafter, although the government would keep a majority stake for at least five years. An independent regulatory body would be established.

The reform process in West Germany interacted with regulatory change at the EC level. Modification of the institutional framework was influenced by EC developments. The Witte Commission's report and ensuing debate were affected by the Commission's 1987 Green Paper and the subsequent legislation.[19] More significantly, the effects of EC legislation, notably the greater competition being permitted, were used to justify the reforms of 1993. It was claimed by the Kohl government and Deutsche Telekom's senior management that in order for Telekom to face the increased threat of competition and to be able to undertake essential expansion abroad, Telekom's administrative position needed to be altered. Such arguments were part of the campaign to convince the unions and the opposition SPD (whose support was required in order to amend the Constitution, which specified that Telekom must be publicly owned). At the same time, in EC negotiations, Schwartz-

Schilling generally sided with the more 'liberal' countries, pressing for the extension of competition and minimum restrictions on supply. This appears to have been related to overcoming domestic opposition to reform and ensuring overseas markets for German manufacturers. The clearest example came in 1993, when Germany supported extending competition to network operation, which was seen as a counterpart to privatization of Deutsche Telekom.[20]

In response to the development of greater competition, the DBP/Telekom began to seek partners, including private sector and international firms, for the provision of services in Germany.[21] But, almost no overseas activities took place as the Basic Law defined the tasks and authority of the DBP and Telekom as relating only to Germany. Moreover, after 1990, Telekom's resources were concentrated on developing telecommunications in eastern Germany.

2.4. Italy

Telecommunications policy for network operation, services, and CPE supply during the 1980s in Italy had two main strands. First, continuing use of the PTOs for wider policy purposes, such as providing employment, orders to domestic manufacturers, and assisting regional development.[22] Secondly, in the late 1980s, large-scale investment to modernize the networks.

Comprehensive regulatory reform was not implemented during the 1980s. The main issue was the creation of a strong PTO: network operation was highly fragmented, with no less than six organizations responsible for different elements of the network, and acting under different administrative arrangements.[23] Nevertheless, whilst proposals were made to concentrate network operation within one organization (by transfer of ASST's services to the STET), provide greater autonomy for the network operator(s) and transform the Posts and Telecommunications Ministry into a regulatory and planning body, no decisions were made during the 1980s. It was only in 1992 that action started, involving two elements. First, a process of reorganization to reduce the number of PTOs: in 1992, ASST was separated from the PTT Ministry and became part of the IRI group; discussion then began over plans for the creation of a Telecom Italia, which would regroup all or most of the publicly owned telecommunications service suppliers. The second element was privatization: in 1992, IRI announced the sale of a 16 per cent share of STET. Privatization of the planned Telecom Italia is also being planned.

The state's monopoly over network operation was maintained throughout the 1980s and early 1990s. Competition was permitted in the supply of VANS but only under severe restrictions designed to prevent bypass of the public networks.[24] Competition in the supply of CPE was gradually extended to all equipment by the late 1980s, although the ministry remained responsible for regulation of the entire sector. No independent body was established, nor were many provisions designed to ensure 'fair competition' specified. In 1993, discussion began of further regulatory reforms which were needed to comply with EC legislation, but progress was slow, as reorganization of PTOs and their preparation for competition were given precedence.

The failure to reform the position of the various PTOs can be ascribed to opposition by the Christian Democrats to removal of the ASST from the Posts and Telecommunications Ministry, as they have close links with the ASST. However, it meant that the PTOs were ill-suited to competition: they suffer from a variety of bureaucratic restrictions, were slow to offer new services, and enjoyed little operating autonomy. Lack of investment until the late 1980s meant that public networks and PTO specialized services were underdeveloped. Furthermore, cross-subsidization between services left them open to undercutting and bypass if restrictions on VANS and use of leased lines were not tight, especially as many private networks existed. Thus the PTOs remain vulnerable, needing regulatory protection of their monopoly in order to be able to modernize, invest, and fulfil the wider uses made of them. International expansion of Italian PTOs has been insignificant and is likely to remain so until a strong PTO is created domestically. Consequently Italy sought to limit the extent of competition introduced at EC level, to ensure safeguards for PTOs by restrictions on VANS to prevent bypassing of public networks or undercutting by resale of leased line capacity, and to create scope within EC rules for national licensing conditions to incorporate the pursuit of wider policy objectives. Implementation of EC measures represents a considerable regulatory change for Italy; indeed, the extension of competition into CPE supply was implemented under EC pressure.[25]

3. THE EC AND THE REGULATION OF TELECOMMUNICATIONS IN THE 1980s

3.1. The Growth of EC Activity in Telecommunications

The period since the mid-1980s has seen a remarkable growth in activity at EC level in telecommunications. Two groups of measures can be distinguished. Firstly, those concerned with encouraging European co-operation in research and development. These have included programmes such as RACE (Research in Advanced Communications in Europe) and ESPRIT (European Strategic Programme for Research and Development in Information Technologies). They are not examined in this chapter. The second group of measures have dealt with the regulatory framework. Telecommunications were included in the Internal Market programme ('1992'); hence the provisions of the Single European Act applied, including majority voting under article 100A. In June 1987, the Commission issued a Green Paper on telecommunications. There then followed a series of legislative measures.

The main actors involved in legislation were the Commission, member states and their PTOs, and the ECJ (European Court of Justice). Users lobbied, particularly large businesses via INTUG (the International Telecommunications User Group), and were consulted on detailed technical legislation. Within the Commission, the two main Directorates involved were DGXIII (established in 1986 and responsible for telecommunications and information technology) and DGIV, the Competition Directorate. It appears that DGXIII has enjoyed close ties with manufacturers and PTOs. It generally favoured measures to protect these groups, whereas DGIV pursued a policy of maximizing competition, perhaps influenced by its Commissioner between 1988 and 1993, Sir Leon Brittan, and by the strong position of lawyers within the Directorate, focusing on certain Articles of the Treaty of Rome.[26]

3.2. The Position of 'National Enterprises' under EC Law

The Treaty of Rome contains general rules governing competition which are relevant to the supply of telecommunications equipment and services. These include: article 30, prohibiting quantitative restrictions and non-tariff barriers to intra-community trade; article 85, prohibiting anti-competitive agreements between undertakings and practices, subject only to exceptions in article 85(2) relating to beneficial effects and acceptable means of achieving these; article 86, banning 'abuse of a dominant position'; article 7, banning all discrimination on grounds of EC nationality.

Article 90 is of central importance for national regulatory frameworks.[27] Article 90(1) forbids member states from introducing or maintaining any measures contrary to the Treaty, and in particular to articles 7 and 85–94, with respect to 'public undertakings' and those enterprises to which member states give 'special or exclusive rights'. The article's scope is wide. A measure by a member state would appear to include all state actions affecting public undertakings (i.e. those over which the member state enjoys a 'special responsibility'), whatever their form. In particular, the granting or maintenance of 'special or exclusive rights' to an undertaking would appear to be covered. Such rights consist of decisions and laws by state bodies giving rights and privileges to specific undertakings (private as well as public); they include monopolies, licences, and 'concessions' of public service. Hence member states may not use 'national enterprises' to avoid other Treaty articles.

However, article 90(2) qualifies the application of article 90(1). For 'undertakings entrusted with the operation of services of general economic interest' or which have the character of a fiscal monopoly, the rules of the Treaty (notably those concerning competition) apply, but only to the extent that those rules 'do not obstruct the performance in law or fact of the particular task entrusted' to the undertaking. The scope of the exception is liable to be narrowly interpreted, including what is a sufficient 'interest' (judged by the ECJ, not the member state) whilst the exception must not harm the development of trade within the Community. Article 90(3) provides for the enforcement of article 90: the Commission ensures the application of the article, and if necessary, can issue appropriate Directives and Decisions.

Article 90 is highly relevant to the telecommunications sector. The foregoing analysis indicates the limited legal ground for 'special and exclusive rights' granted to national enterprises. In particular, the monopolies granted by national governments to PTOs are, by virtue of article 90(1), liable to scrutiny under other Treaty articles, especially articles 7, 30, 85, and 86, which constitute a formidable set of rules to ensure fair and free competition, unless and until justified under article 90(2).

3.3. The Elimination of National Restrictions on the Supply of Customer Premises Equipment

EC regulations have eliminated much of the legal scope of member states to impose restrictions on the supply of CPE. The main measure was a Commission Directive (88/301/EEC), adopted in May 1988, and known as the 'Terminals Directive'. It laid down that 'member states which have granted special or exclusive rights . . . to undertakings shall ensure that those rights are withdrawn'. Member states were to ensure that 'economic operators' had the right to import, sell, attach, put into service, and maintain terminal equipment. Member states could only refuse the right to attach and put into service equipment for which technical specifications were not laid down by the EC on 'essential grounds'. All CPE was covered by the Directive in 1990.

The main principles and aims of the Directive were not opposed within the Council of Ministers.[28] But the Commission, and specifically, DGIV, chose to issue the Directive under article 90(3); hence the Directive did not need to be passed by the Council of Ministers or require scrutiny by the European Parliament. The Commission's decision was strongly contested by several member states, resulting in the important Terminals Directive Case.[29] The case principally concerned the right of the Commission to issue the Directive under article 90(3); on this, the ECJ upheld the Commission.

However, the decision also dealt with substantive matters concerning the application of article 90. The ECJ held that the legality of 'special and exclusive rights' had to be determined by examining their compatibility with other articles of the Treaty referred to in article 90(1). It affirmed that all regulatory measures by member states which could, directly or indirectly, actually or potentially, harm trade between member states were illegal, being contrary to article 30 of the Treaty. It therefore upheld the Directive's provisions banning exclusive rights to import and market CPE. The court only ruled against the Commission on a point concerning special rights: the Directive had not specified the exact types of rights, nor the way in which they contravened provisions of the Treaty.

It is important to note that France and the other countries contesting the Directive did not attempt to utilize article 90(2) in order to justify the existence of the 'special and exclusive rights' in question. Instead, the case centred on the powers of the Commission, and whether 'special and exclusive rights' granted by member states fell under the scope of article 90(1).

Overall, the outcome of the case appears to have been favourable to the Commission, both in terms of its powers and its approach to regulation. Legal monopolies ('exclusive rights'), and to a lesser extent 'special rights' granted by member states, would appear to be contrary to the Treaty of Rome unless and until justified under article 90(2). Thus the reasoning of the case also had important implications for other areas of telecommunications and other sectors. Moreover, in deciding that competition law applied to national law and regulation concerning 'public undertakings', it greatly strengthened the role and position of DGIV in EC regulatory reform.

3.4. EC 'Re-regulation' of Customer Premises Equipment Supply

The counterpart to the lifting of many restrictions on supply of CPE national level has been the establishment of EC rules, a process frequently termed 're-regulation'. In CPE supply, EC 're-regulation' has involved three elements: mutual recognition of tests and licences; the setting of EC minimum requirements; the establishment of voluntary EC-recognized norms and standards. These rules were designed to protect the various parties involved in the sector, promote fair and effective competition throughout the EC, ensure the inter-operability of equipment, and prevent the use of licensing and testing by member states to continue special and exclusive rights in practice.

Full mutual recognition was implemented under a Directive

adopted by the Council in June 1990. Equipment tested and licensed in one member state can be marketed and attached to telecommunications networks in all member states, without any further licensing or tests. In licensing and testing CPE, member states can only insist that minimum standards defined by the EC are met. These standards consist of 'essential requirements', relating to safety, damage to the network, and inter-operability of equipment.

The principles of the 1990 Directive achieved wide support within the Council. However, there was disagreement over the scope of the application of 'essential requirements'. 'Liberal countries' such as Britain, Germany, the Netherlands, and Denmark appear to have wanted to minimize the applicability of EC 'essential requirements', whereas others, notably France, Belgium, Italy, and Spain, wanted to maximize their applicability.[30] The outcome was a compromise: the Directive would apply to mobile communications equipment but not to equipment attached to private networks, which did not have to meet the 'essential requirements'.

Although CPE had to fulfil the 'essential requirements', the EC did not attempt to impose mandatory norms and standards to meet these requirements. Different methods of doing so were possible. One method, however, was by conforming to EC-recognized norms and standards. The establishment of Community-wide standards was begun by a Directive of 1986 (88/361/EEC) adopted by the Council of Ministers under the CEPT (European Conference of Postal and Telecommunications Administrations) would draw up technical specifications for CPE. The process was very slow, and in 1988, ETSI (the European Telecommunications Standards Institute) was created; it took over the work of EC standard setting and accelerated the pace of progress. If equipment meets the standards and tests laid down by ETSI, it meets the EC's 'essential requirements' and hence can be licensed in any member state, and can be freely traded and attached to public networks throughout the Community.

3.5. The Limiting of National Restrictions on the Supply of Services

Comprehensive EC regulation of services took place in 1990, when the Commission formally issued a Services Directive.[31] Special and exclusive rights were to be abolished for all telecommunications services with the exception of 'reserved services', namely voice telephone and telex, and the telecommunications infrastructure. Separate provisions were to be made for mobile communications and satellite transmission.

From the end of 1990, all restrictions on the supply of VANS were to be ended. Member states could require VANS to be licensed but licence conditions were limited to 'essential requirements', such as the safety of the network and the inter-operability and protection of data. Services which merely involved the transmission of data, such as packet switched networks, were also to be liberalized by the end of 1992;[32] member states were allowed to impose additional licence conditions relating to availability of supply, quality of service, and measures to safeguard the pursuit of 'tasks of general interest'. Nevertheless, for all public services, any restrictions were to be 'proportional' to achieving their aims, without discriminatory effects, and most importantly, vetted by the Commission, and specifically, by DGIV. Finally, the simple resale of leased line capacity could only be forbidden by member states until the end of 1992.

The Services Directive saw conflict over the respective powers of the Council and the Commission. The Commission published a draft Directive in June 1989 and threatened to pass it under article 90(3) if the Council did not accept it. In December 1989, a compromise was reached whereby the Commission's original plans were slightly modified and were agreed by the Council. However, they were passed under article 90(3) by the Commission, and this procedure was challenged before the ECJ by several member states, including France. In 1993, the ECJ, in a ruling very similar to that in the Terminals Directive case, upheld the Commission.

There was general acceptance among member states to allow competition in 'value added services', but disagreement existed over the precise scope of competition and the conditions under which it would be permitted. Member states were divided between a 'liberal group', led by Britain, but also including West Germany, Holland, and Denmark, which largely supported the Commission's proposals, and a group of countries, notably France, Italy, Spain, and Greece, which wished to alter them. One issue was data transmission services. The 'liberal' group and the Commission wished to allow free supply of such services, claiming that this was necessary for innovation and growth. Their opponents suggested that compe-

tition would threaten the position of PTOs and prevent the fulfilment of 'public service' obligations, notably by 'cream skimming'
by private firms aiming to maximize profits; they therefore wished
'special and exclusive rights' to be permitted, including national
authorities maintaining wide powers over licensing. A second issue
was 're-regulation' at EC level. In this case, the 'liberal' countries
wished to minimize regulatory conditions governing supply, whilst
France wanted to widen their scope and specificity. In both cases,
the outcome was a compromise, with limited restrictions on data
transmission and the adoption of the Open Network Provision
(ONP) Directive on standards. Nevertheless, the conclusion was
close to the Commission's original proposals.

3.6. 'Reserved Services' and the Telecommunications Infrastructure

The 1990 Services Directive did not apply to network operation:
member states were permitted to grant 'special and exclusive
rights', including monopolies, for 'reserved services' (public voice
telephony services, plus telex services) and the establishment and
operation of fixed link public telecommunications networks. This
was important, as network operation accounts for the majority of
revenue derived from telecommunications services. However, the
limits of the exceptions granted under the 1990 Services Directive
need to be emphasized. First, in 1992 the Commission was to re-
examine all special or exclusive rights granted; second, liberalization of satellite and mobile networks would allow competing
public networks to operate; third, the Commission may apply
competition law, especially articles 85 and 86, to the behaviour of
PTOs, including in areas where 'special and exclusive rights' are
permitted. Moreover, following the Terminals Directive Case, the
legal position was not clear, as the Commission may be able to end
or restrict 'special and exclusive rights' under article 90(3), unless
member states justify them under article 90(2).

In 1990, competition in network operation had been strongly
opposed by many countries, notably France, with some support
from Germany. By 1993, this had greatly altered. The Commission
undertook its review of remaining special and exclusive rights in
1992. After considerable modifications of its original proposals

(which favoured a rapid move to allow competition in intra-EC communications), the Council agreed in June 1993 on sweeping change: from 1998, EC rules would allow competition in 'reserved services' (public voice telephony and telex services) in most EC countries,[33] ending PTO monopolies in these services; in 1995 the Commission would examine whether competition should be allowed in the infrastructure (building and operating telecommunications networks) and the use of cable television networks for telecommunications services.

The changes agreed in 1993 mean that by 1995 EC rules over competition and ending PTO special and exclusive rights may apply to almost the entire telecommunications sector. It was noteworthy in 1993 that, as for earlier EC legislation, there was little opposition by member states to the principle of extending competition.

3.7. The 'Re-regulation' of Services

The 're-regulation' of services has also involved the three elements of mutual recognition, EC 'essential requirements', and voluntary EC norms and standards. An ONP[34] was passed by the Council of Ministers in 1990. It aimed to meet three concerns: the interoperability and compatibility of different systems; prevention of PTOs using their special and exclusive rights over the infrastructure to unfairly affect the supply of other services; the effects of tariff policies on the supply of services opened to competition.[35]

The ONP Directive was a framework Directive, establishing general principles. Various Directives dealing with specific services have been issued, notably for leased lines, voice telephony, packet-switched data transmission networks, and the integrated digital services network (ISDN). Whilst each proposal has its specific features, certain elements are common. Service suppliers are given the right to connect to the infrastructure, including leased lines, and hence supply their services on it. Norms and standards, especially for 'interfaces' between the infrastructure and the service provider's equipment, are specified, so that suppliers know them and PTOs cannot manipulate them to restrict competition. Users are given rights in provision of supply, such as certain types of service being available. Perhaps most significant of all, principles for tariffs are laid down, whereby prices must be based on 'objective' criteria, notably costs.[36]

Services have to meet EC-determined 'essential requirements', which are designed to ensure a minimum level of protection and compatibility. Technical interfaces and standards were to be decided by ETSI; they were voluntary, but the Commission was empowered to make them mandatory to the extent necessary to ensure inter-operability of transborder services and improve customers' freedom of choice. A system of mutual recognition of licences was to be set up, whereby a service provider need only obtain a licence in one EC country in order to be permitted to supply in any member state.

3.8. Regulation at National Level

Permitting competition in the supply of CPE and services has altered the nature of regulation. There may be conflicts of interest between PTOs and those supplying services on PTO infrastructures, especially if PTOs also supply services in competition with private suppliers. Member states may seek to use regulatory decisions to restrict competition.

The EC's approach to regulatory decision-making has involved two related elements. Firstly, the functions of regulation and the supply of services and CPE must be separated. Both the Terminals and Services Directives specified that regulatory decisions such as licensing, the specification of technical standards, and enforcement of both, must be taken by independent bodies, separate from PTOs or undertakings involved in supplying services or CPE. This requirement was upheld by the ECJ in the Terminals Directive Case as being necessary to ensure fair competition. Secondly, decisions must be made according to public, non-discriminatory, and 'objective' criteria. All refusals of licences must be accompanied by reasons, and an opportunity to challenge decisions must be available.

3.9. Articles 85 and 86

The behaviour of undertakings is regulated by articles 85 and 86 of the Treaty of Rome, dealing with anti-competitive agreements and abuse of a dominant position. Their potential effects are sweeping, especially as regards PTOs. Agreements between PTOs and suppliers of services on the infrastructure will be covered by articles 85 and 86. Moreover, due to their size, experience, and expertise, PTOs or their subsidiaries may enjoy substantial market shares in competitive markets; their behaviour and decisions will be subject to article 86. Very importantly, supply of 'reserved services' and the infrastructure is covered by articles 85 and 86; the applicability of article 90(2) does not exclude these articles. If applied systematically, competition law could result in rulings concerning the behaviour of PTOs with respect to matters such as the range of services offered, tariffs, the terms of the provision of services and cross-subsidization between them.

In order to provide some indication as to the practical effects of articles 85 and 86, the Commission issued guidelines in September 1991 for undertakings in the sector, including PTOs. Examples of illegal agreements given included accords to divide up markets or set prices, whilst abuse of a dominant position included the refusal to supply a product or service without a legitimate reason, or practising abnormally low prices in order to drive out competition. A 'dominant position' in the sector, according to the Commission's view of the law laid down by the ECJ, covers special and exclusive rights. Furthermore, the Commission indicated that competition law applied to international agreements made by PTOs; hence the lucrative international communications business is covered. The Commission made it clear that it would scrutinize the sector case by case, to see if undertakings were following the rules of competition and whether to apply derogations to these rules, including in matters of tariffs and cross-subsidization. It also stated that interconnection of public networks and of services, and provision of better and lower cost services to consumers, were important considerations.

The law concerning the application of articles 85 and 86 is both complex and flexible: whilst anti-competitive practices are forbidden, article 85 allows exceptions if sufficient economic justification exists, and the definition of actions constituting 'abuse of a dominant position' is not always clear-cut. As the Commission's guidelines indicate, there may be a balance to be struck between encouraging competition, and other aims. Such considerations are especially important in the field of telecommunications, in which heavy investment for infrastructure is needed, with the requirement of long time horizons for profitability, and in which issues of externalities and 'public goods' arise. Finally, the relevance of articles 85 and 86 lies not only in their content but also their effects on the division of roles within the Commission, notably by strengthening the hand of the pro-competition DGIV.

4. CONCLUSION

Regulatory and institutional arrangements have been a vital element in determining the role of PTOs in Western Europe. In particular, monopoly rights and public ownership underpinned their position as 'national enterprises'. During the 1980s, PTOs in EC member states did not internationalize: their activities remained overwhelmingly nationally based despite operating in an increasingly internationalized environment in the sector. Instead, they focused on fulfilling functions within their country, such as modernizing their networks and services and performing their tasks as 'national enterprises'. Furthermore, with the exception of BT, they remained publicly owned, without even the internationalization of ownership. Only in the early 1990s did this position begin to alter, as PTOs attempted to expand their overseas activities (although these remained very small) and moves towards partial privatization were undertaken in France, Germany, and Italy.

However, the 1980s and early 1990s saw the development of a new regulatory framework at EC level which, if fully implemented, severely constrains the ability of member states to use PTOs as national policy instruments in the traditional manner. It both permits PTOs to expand in other EC countries and creates pressures to do so, by limiting the regulatory protection given to PTOs in their domestic markets. It encourages PTOs to operate more as commercial enterprises and move away from their traditional 'national enterprise' roles.

The capacity of member states to grant 'special and exclusive rights' to 'national enterprises' has been restricted and competition has been permitted in CPE and services, and may be extended to provision of the infrastructure. The ability of member states to utilize regulation to favour certain undertakings is limited by provisions concerning licensing and access to the infrastructure. EC standards and mutual recognition hinder the use of national standards as a disguised form of protection. The application of competition law may allow the Commission (and especially DGIV) to play an important role in determining the conditions for the supply of services and the operation of PTOs. Competition and competition law threaten the high profits on some services which are used to cross-subsidize other services and provide revenue for state budgets, and the ability of PTOs to subsidize domestic equipment manufacturers by their procurement policies.[37] The practical effects of these regulatory measures depends on whether and how they are implemented. However, the question remains of why the EC has been able to institute a regulatory framework reducing the ability of member states to use PTOs as 'national enterprises'.

One reason is that the Commission has been able to formulate a coherent approach at Community level. It is based on the general rule of competition, coupled with binding rules established and policed at EC level, to ensure that competition is 'fair' and that certain standards for supply are maintained. It prevents member states from distorting competition for their own policy aims and can be seen as being based on the 'logic of a single market'. Another reason lies in the legal framework of the Community. The Treaty of Rome, as interpreted by the ECJ, severely limits the ability of member states to offer special regulatory protection to selected undertakings. Furthermore, the wide-ranging scope of competition law has given DGIV an important role and power.

A third factor, however, was the interaction of policy-making at EC and national level. The principles of allowing competition and ending most national exclusive rights and privileges, and much of the proposed legislation, were widely accepted by member states. Indeed, the degree of consensus on the principles of EC regulation among member states is noteworthy, given the expansion of EC competence that EC activity represented, the contrast between the EC's rules and traditional national industrial policies, and the restriction on the ability of member states to determine regulatory frameworks at the national level. Analysis of the acceptance of EC regulation by member states must consider developments at the national level. Many of the EC's measures formed part of a process which had already begun in most EC countries. Thus, for example, competition in CPE and VANS supply had already been introduced in Britain, France, Italy, and Germany. Other modifications, such as the separation of regulation and supply and measures to encourage PTOs to adopt a more 'commercial approach' and enjoy greater operating autonomy had been introduced or were being discussed.

At times the EC provided an important useful source of support for domestic actors seeking change. This appears to have been important in Germany, to permit greater competition and the creation and privatization of Deutsche Telekom, whilst in France it assisted the long-discussed modification of France Télécom from an *administration* to a public firm. Policy making at the EC level interacted in a complex manner with policy at the national level in member states. At least two roles for the EC can be distinguished: on the one hand, the prospect of competition and the opening of national markets appeared to offer incentives and pressures for countries to reform their PTOs, in order to profit from new opportunities overseas and to be able to meet the threat of competition in domestic markets; on the other hand, EC legislation provided a powerful justification for reforms desired by national actors for reasons unrelated to the EC, such as the Right in France wishing to alter France Télécom's *statut* to make it more appropriate for an industrial and commercial organization, or the need to privatize Deutsche Telekom following the effects of reunification. Thus policy making at the EC and national levels was closely intermeshed.

Moreover, EC measures were also flexible to the point of sometimes of being ambiguous. Often they were compatible with a range of national institutional arrangements. For instance, the requirement that regulation and the supply of services and CPE be separated did not specify the institutional arrangements to achieve this. Thus EC legislation could be accommodated according to a variety of national institutional frameworks, a form of 'institutional subsidiarity'. Furthermore, national bodies dealt with licensing, offering in practice some scope for national action. The utilization of articles 85 and 86 by the Commission has been very limited thus far and their future impact has been unclear, as the law is open to wide interpretation.

Rather than opposing all EC activity, member states, with the exception of Germany, sought to obtain EC measures which were similar to their own, national regulatory frameworks, a form of 'regulatory export'. When these strategies clashed, conflict took place. Britain urged maximum scope for competition, minimum 're-regulation', and strong emphasis on 'fair competition'. France and Italy attempted to limit competition to CPE and VANS, include provisions to protect their PTOs, and ensure that licences allowed the pursuit of general policy objectives desired by national governments. Each national strategy can, in turn, be related to specific national approaches to PTOs. Two factors appear crucial in the determination of national strategies: first, the political character of governments, and in particular, their will and ability to reform the administrative and regulatory position of PTOs; second, and relatedly, the existing position and functions of PTOs, and especially whether they would benefit from regulatory reform and opportunities overseas arising from EC legislation.

Nevertheless, the extent of overall agreement on EC measures and the common directions of regulatory change in several countries suggest that common forces may have been important. The growing diversity of CPE and VANS has made monopoly supply by PTOs less appropriate, whilst their increased importance to firms has made business users an important lobby for competition. The convergence of telecommunications and computing technologies has also led to pressure for competition from computer equipment and service suppliers. New ideas concerning the value of competition and international examples of regulatory reform, together with pressure for opening of markets, especially from America, have played a part. Hence European regulatory reform must be seen in the broader context of international developments and the evolving nature of the telecommunications sector.

Telecommunications policy-making has been marked by the interaction of the EC and its member states. The EC has acted as a force for a degree of regulatory change and convergence, albeit as part of a wider process and allowing certain national differences in institutions to persist. Explanation of this process requires analysis of actors and events both at EC level, including the roles of Commission Directorates, the ECJ and EC law, and the coalitions and strategies of member states, and also at the national level, since domestic factors have strongly influenced the strategies of member states at EC level. Analysis of regulatory reform must take into account the interplay between the scope and limits of national and EC policy making, which will be explored more fully in Part III.

Notes

1. It is predicted to reach 6% of European income by the end of the 1990s; see H. Ungerer and P. Costello, *Telecommunications in Europe* (Brussels, 1988).

2. On the claims of 'new institutionalists' as to national institutions greatly differing, remaining stable, and strongly influencing policy-making, see e.g. P. Hall, *Governing the Economy* (Cambridge, 1986).

3. These primarily concerned the manufacture of public switches: see A. Cawson, K. Morgan, D. Webber, P. Holmes, and A. Stevens, *Hostile Brothers* (Oxford, 1990).

4. For an appraisal of reforms until 1988 see J. Vickers and G. Yarrow, *Privatization: An Economic Analysis* (Boston, 1988).

5 Mandatory standards for CPE were largely ended for equipment in private networks in 1987, many conditions for VANS supply were ended under the 1987 Class licence, and unrestricted resale of leased line capacity (including for voice telephony) was allowed in 1989. Nevertheless, the 1987 licence did require large VANS suppliers to register and use OSI (Open Standards Interconnection) standards, which permit the interconnection of a wide range of hardware and software.

6. For instance: interconnection between networks; no undue preference or discrimination in the supply of infrastructure, services or CPE; no cross-subsidization of services and equipment supply; see Vickers and Yarrow, *Privatization*.

7. An instance was the decision to license satellite services in 1989 in competition with BT.

8. Limits on price rises were both tightened and extended to services such as international telephony and leased lines over the period 1984–94.

9. The most prominent examples were the purchases of the Canadian CPE manufacturer Mitel in 1986, of 22% of the American cellular telephone operator, McCaw, in 1989 for £850m., and of a 20% stake in the American network operator, MCI, in June 1993.

10. See E. Cohen, *Le Colbertisme 'high tech'* (Paris, 1992).

11. In particular, large VANS needed ministerial authorization, network capacity leased for a VANS could not be used for voice telephony, and the maximum amount chargeable for merely transmitting signals was 15% of the turnover of a VANS; the use of OSI norms was encouraged and the minister was empowered to make them compulsory.

12. Examples include the creation of Eunetcom, a subsidiary jointly owned by France Télécom and Deutsche Telekom, and then an alliance with the American network operator ATT; other moves have included France Câbles et Radio taking stakes in privatized operators in Latin America and co-operation between France Télécom and the American regional Bell operator, Bell South.

13. See A. Haid and J. Müller, 'Telecommunications in the Federal Republic of Germany', in J. Foreman-Peck and J. Müller (eds.), *European Telecommunication Organisations* (Baden-Baden, 1988).

14. See S. Schmidt, 'Taking the Long Road to Liberalization: Telecommunications Reform in the Federal Republic of Germany', *Telecommunications Policy* (June 1991), 209–22, and Cawson *et al.*, *Hostile Brothers*, ch. 7.

15. Cawson *et al.*, *Hostile Brothers*.

16. Schmidt, 'The Long Road to Liberalization'; for overseas experience and the Witte Commission's reform proposals, see *Financial Times*, 21 Sept. 1987.

17. For instance, the decisions to allow the sale of modems in 1986 and to break the DBP's monopoly over satellite transmission between West Germany and the US in 1988 were the direct result of US pressure. See *Financial Times*, 31 July 1986 and 3 June 1989.

18. For instance, with revenue of DM 54 bn. in 1992, Deutsche Telekom bore debts of DM 100 bn., the servicing of which cost 12% of its income. *The Economist*, 30 Oct. 1993.

19. Schmidt, 'The Long Road to Liberalization', and Cawson *et al.*, *Hostile Brothers*.

20. See *Financial Times*, 11 Mar. 1993.

21. There was notably the creation of Eunetcom with France Télécom and the alliance with ATT; for Telekom's activities in VANS, see M. Rogy, 'Réglementation et concurrence: Effet d'expérience sur le marché allemand des RSVA', *Communications et Stratégies* (winter 1991), 31–61.

22. J. Foreman-Peck and D. Manning, 'Telecommunications in Italy', in Foreman-Peck and Müller (eds.), *European Telecommunication Organisations*.

23. In particular, SIP is a private firm, in which the state holding company STET holds a majority stake, whilst the ASST was part of the Posts and Telecommunications Ministry.

24. For instance, their usage is subject to restrictions, they require authorization from the Posts and Telecommunications Minister, and data services must transmit on the public network: see C. Picory, *Le Secteur des télécommunications en Italie* (Paris, 1991).

25. Foreman-Peck and Manning, 'Telecommunications in Italy'.

26. Cawson *et al.*, *Hostile Brothers*, 196–7.

27. For a discussion of the article, see Antunes Pais, L. M., 'L'article 90 du Traité EEC', *Revue trimestrielle de droit européen*, 27/2 (Apr.–June 1991), 187–209.

28. *Financial Times*, 28 Apr. 1988; *Le Monde*, 30 Apr. 1988.

29. Case C-202/88 *French Republic*, supported by Italy, Belgium, Germany and Greece, v. *Commission of the European Communities*, 1991.

30. *Le Monde*, 30 June 1990.

31. Directive 90/388. The legal basis for national restrictions on VANS

had already been weakened in 1985, in *Italy* v. *Commission* (Case 41/83 in 2 CML Rep 368), known as the 'BT judgment', when the ECJ ruled that regulations issued by BT under national legislation to ban telex forwarding, a type of VANS, were invalid as they constituted an abuse of dominant position under art. 86 of the Treaty of Rome. See R. Schulte-Braucks, 'European Telecommunications Law in the Light of the British Telecom Judgment', in *Common Market Law Review*, 23 (1986), 39–59.

32. Longer transition periods were allowed for certain countries with less-developed telecommunications systems.
33. Longer transition periods for countries with small networks were allowed.
34. 90/387/EEC.
35. B. Delcourt, 'EC Decisions and Directives on Information Technology and Telecommunications', *Telecommunications Policy*, 15/1 (1991), 15–21.
36. The Services Directive also prohibits all discrimination with respect to use of conditions of usage and tariffs.
37. In addition, a Directive in 1990 applied measures designed to ensure 'fair competition' in public procurement to previously 'excluded sectors', including telecommunications.

PART III

THE EUROPEAN COMMUNITY'S STRATEGIES AND CONSTRAINTS

10

European Community Regulation and National Enterprise

STEPHEN WOOLCOCK AND HELEN WALLACE

While the reach of EC regulation covering 'national enterprise' is being extended as a result of the internal market programme and the application of Community powers in areas such as competition policy, the grip of Community control will continue to vary across all aspects of EC regulation. Why is this the case?

The European Community is having an increasing impact on the operations of national enterprises for a number of reasons. First, the internal market programme is striving to remove many remaining barriers to market access within the EC, such as national technical standards and national public procurement practices, not to mention the liberalization of a number of regulated sectors, such as financial services, telecommunications, and energy. Second, and equally important, the European Commission is pursuing a competition-based policy. This includes: efforts to reduce national subsidies, including the provision of capital for public enterprise; merger policy, including controls on EC-wide oligopolies; the progressive application of EC competition provisions to public enterprise and regulated sectors of the economy such as energy. At first sight this seems like an over-ambitious programme, but on many of the issues concerned the Commission is not seeking immediate full implementation of EC powers but to put down markers for future more wide-ranging regulation. In the short to medium term it will be obliged to continue to exercise restraint when enforcing the rules in order to avoid direct confrontation with national governments. This means that national industrial identities, national preferences and national structural features will not be removed overnight. It also means that EC rules will continue to be applied flexibly in order, for example, to take account of the structural problems caused by economic recession or adjustment difficulties.

Policy-led initiatives in the shape of the internal market programme and proactive competition policy represent only half of the picture. Market-led factors for change have done as much, if not more, to limit the options for national industrial policies. Throughout the 1980s there has been a progressive growth in cross-border direct investment into the EC and within the EC. This has largely taken the form of cross-border acquisitions and mergers as companies have sought to gain access to what were previously relatively closed markets by acquiring a local presence.[1] This investment has undermined the viability of national champions in the sense that it has challenged the national champions on their home markets, which were previously kept as their exclusive preserve by means of national standards, procurement, or competition policies. The increase in cross-border investment has led to Europe-wide restructuring in which national champions have been forced to transform themselves into 'multinational champions' operating across the EC and global markets. There has, of course, been a connection between these market-led developments and the EC's internal market programme. The internal market programme complements market-led factors, and above all has made access to previously closed markets seem credible and thus encouraged firms to investment where they would previously have feared to tread.[2]

We must therefore also look at the impact of EC regulation on these 'multinational champions'. If competition is taking place on a Europe-wide basis national regulatory authorities can no longer be effective in regulating the activities of companies. This is, for example, one reason why EC merger control was introduced in 1989. Furthermore, 'multinational champions' are not above receiving support from national governments even if they operate across the EC. This makes the need for EC control over national subsidies even more important because without some European level discipline ex-national champions operating across the EC would be able to distort competition and bring pressure on national governments to provide support or see important investment directed elsewhere.

There is, however, one important respect in which the EC has little impact on 'national enterprise'. This is that the structure of corporate governance or ownership of companies which enables close identification between the stakeholders in a company (investors, employees, etc.) is unlikely to be significantly affected by EC regulation. For various reasons there are national differences in the form of industrial finance and structure of companies. In some countries such as Germany and to a lesser extent most other Continental EC member states, there is a fairly close identification with the long-term interests of indigenous companies. In most cases these are national companies. In other countries, such as Britain, the relations between companies and stakeholders are much more at arm's length. This means that there is a qualitative difference between the degree to which stakeholders identify with the interests of particular companies. A high level of identification could be seen as the *de facto* maintenance of a 'national enterprise'. This chapter therefore considers the impact of the EC on the firm–finance side of the 'iron triangle' referred to in the Introduction. It argues that even if the internal market weakens the link between government and firms by reducing the discretionary power of government to assist companies, companies may still retain a strong national identity by virtue of the relationship between the firm and its funders and other stakeholders.

1. THE INTERNAL MARKET PROGRAMME

By the end of 1993 all but a few of the 282 measures listed in the 1985 Cockfield White Paper were adopted by the Council. Many of these measures still remain to be implemented in national legislation. In some cases implementation is not due for a number of years. Although implementation remains uneven across the EC, with some countries, such as Denmark, maintaining rates of implementation of around 90 per cent and other countries, such as Italy, performing less well, progress has been made in recent years.

Even after the internal market measures have been implemented in national legislation it is still necessary to ensure they are effectively enforced. The European Commission has limited resources and simply will not be able to monitor enforcement of all directives in all the member states. The EC's policy is increasingly to aim for decentralized enforcement. This means that national authorities as well as the EC will monitor enforcement, but more importantly it means that enforcement will also depend on companies or individuals taking legal action, and on co-operation between the national and Community authorities and between the national enforcement bodies. From early 1992 the focus of attention shifted from adopting EC directives to finding ways of ensuring they were effectively enforced. In early 1992 the Sutherland Committee, chaired by ex-Vice-President of the European Commission, Peter Sutherland, was asked to examine the implementation issues. The Sutherland report highlighted formidable challenges in enforcement: for example, the difficulty in having a clear view of what is going on when there are literally thousands of pieces of national implementing legislation being enforced within different national administrative and legal settings. Sutherland made a number of recommendations, including the measures to promote transparency in enforcement procedures, the promotion of co-operation between national enforcement bodies, and a greater awareness of the opportunities of seeking redress against unfair or discriminatory practices under EC law.[3] The European Commission picked up most of these during 1993.

The impact of the internal market measures on national enterprise will depend, importantly, on how effectively the provisions are implemented. For example, in public procurement, the effectiveness will depend in no small measure on the willingness of aggrieved tenderers to initiate court action against their potential customers. As companies are often reluctant to 'bite the hand that feeds them' with lucrative contracts, there must remain some doubt that there will be strong company-level pressure for effective implementation. Another example is that of technical standards. The internal market programme removes the possibility of precluding products which do not comply with host country standards. In order to ensure the effective application of these directives, however, there is a need for more voluntary standards. Voluntary standards agreed within CEN (the European standard committee) and CENELEC (the European standards committee for electrical and electronic equipment), facilitate testing of compliance with minimum essential requirements, even if compliance with agreed standards is not a legal requirement. New approach directives are imposing a formidable workload on CEN and CENELEC. For example, the Machine Safety Directive, which introduces mutual recognition for a wide range of machines from machine tools to hedge trimmers, brings in its wake the demand for an estimated 500 voluntary standards. If these are not agreed, certification that a

particular product meets the minimum essential safety requirements will be cumbersome and could entail courts being reluctantly
drawn into having to rule on whether a product meets the minimum requirements. In the absence of European standards there
could also be continued use of national standards, although host
countries will have to accept home country standards.

The EC has not set out to regulate or harmonize everything.
Indeed the 'new approach' was designed precisely not to do this. EC
regulation is intended to be limited to those areas in which harmonization or regulation is necessary for the removal of the remaining national barriers. Beyond this, the EC is operating on the
principle of 'competition among rules'. This means that national
regulatory policies will continue to exist. National governments are
allowed to continue to regulate as they wish, provided they meet
certain 'minimum essential requirements' and do not prevent companies operating under the rules or standards of another member
state from offering their goods or services on the national market.
Thus some quite important aspects of policy will not be subject to
EC regulation.

To sum up: Community legislation is extending its reach but
there is likely to be a lag of several years before the grip of the EC
tightens. In some cases this lag could be quite long. If past experience is anything to go by, a tightening may well be precipitated by
decisions of the European Court of Justice (ECJ). The scope for
discretionary policies to support national companies will therefore
be progressively reduced as more and more case law is developed by
the ECJ. The grip of EC legislation will also depend on how
effectively it is implemented.

2. THE REGULATION OF NATIONAL SUBSIDY PROGRAMMES

A good example of the comprehensive reach but limited grip of EC
regulation is the control of national subsidies. The original philosophy behind EC policy was straightforward: if barriers to trade
such as tariffs, quantitative restrictions, or measures having an
effect equivalent to quantitative restrictions (article 30 EEC *et seq.*),
were banned, it was also necessary to control national subsidies.
National industrial policies could otherwise simply use subsidies as

a substitute for trade barriers.[4] Article 92 (EEC) therefore prohibits aid in 'any form whatsoever which distorts or threatens to distort competition by favouring certain undertakings or the production of certain goods'. Under this all-embracing coverage, every aid scheme has to be notified to the Commission, which then has the responsibility of assessing whether they satisfy any of the exemptions to the total ban set out in article 93 (EEC). The Commission may, of course, seek modifications of the terms or conditions of any such aid in order to ensure they comply with the treaty provisions. Subsidies are permissible if they promote economic development in particular regions affected by underemployment, or when the project concerned is of 'Community interest'.

For a number of reasons these Treaty provisions are applicable but not comprehensively applied. First, the Commission has only limited resources. Only some 35 or so senior officials working on state aids policy are simply not enough to deal with all the cases notified. The centralized nature of the current enforcement mechanisms means that the burden falls onto this under-staffed bureaucracy. Second, the Commission has not always had the political clout to pursue tough policies. During the mid- to late 1970s national and regional governments introduced subsidy schemes in their efforts to deal with the implications of the post-oil crisis recession and surplus capacity. These schemes were designed to mitigate the regional and social effects of industrial restructuring as well as to support the maintenance of production. It was therefore politically difficult for the Commission simply to enforce the Treaty ban on subsidies. Many of the subsidies also flowed to companies in public ownership, such as the nationalized steel companies, so Commission attempts to reduce subsidy levels were in direct opposition to national policies. Large companies also received and continue to receive a large percentage of the total subsidies, because governments wish to avoid the political and economic costs of large-scale closures in sectors such as cars. The larger the firm the more political clout it had and the harder it was for the Commission to make any real impact on the level of aid. As a result, typically only 2–3 per cent of state aid schemes notified to the Commission have been prohibited, and there have been many instances of aid in various more covert forms not being notified at all.

During the 1980s there was a general reduction in the level of aid provided by national governments. This was mostly due to national policy decisions to cease subsidizing national champions, and to constraints on national budgets. The impact of the Commission and the treaty rules were marginal. However, national governments that wish to resist demands from sectoral lobbies for subsidies invariably used the treaty provisions as justification for unpopular policies. From a peak in the late 1970s there was a general reduction in the level of subsidies. This was so in France after the early 1980s. It was especially the case in Britain under the Thatcher governments. In Germany the level of aid actually went up during the 1980s even before the effects of German unification. Subsequently the levels of financial transfers through the Treuhandanstalt, which assumed ownership of the East German Kombinate, have been substantial and are clearly subsidies within the meaning of article 92 (EEC).[5] Levels of aid in Italy fell slightly between 1981 and 1988, but from a high level. By the end of the period they were still three times the level in Britain. Total subsidies provided to EC manufacturing industry fell from 4.2 per cent of GDP in 1986 to 3.2 per cent in 1989, but 1990 showed a slight rise to 3.3 per cent.[6]

From the mid-1980s onward the Commission redoubled its efforts to control national subsidies. As in the early 1970s it was argued that if barriers to trade and investment were to be removed by the internal market directives, national subsidies also had to be controlled. 'Without a formal and comprehensive . . . policy to control national subsidies there can . . . be no real internal market.'[7] But the limits of Commission control were again clear during the recession in the early 1990s. National governments again moved to support firms in difficulties in eastern Germany, in the steel and shipbuilding industries, automobile industry, airlines (Air France), and computing (Bull). In the face of these moves, the Commission was again obliged to show flexibility.

The Commission's approach to national subsidy schemes has generally been as follows: first focus on the area in which trade distortions are greatest or where the political resistance to controls is least; improve transparency so that everyone, including the Commission regulators, knows what is going on; then progressively introduce tougher controls; and finally, extend control to the more controversial areas. In the case of national subsidies the Commission first moved against those aimed at competing to attract foreign direct investment. In 1971 efforts were made to enhance transparency and clamp down on subsidies in core areas of the EC, i.e. locations on either side of the common borders where competition for footloose investment was most intense.[8] But the grip was still loose and it was not until 1988 that the Commission produced revised guidelines which set definitive ceilings for regional subsidies according to fixed criteria such as levels of unemployment.

During the 1980s there has been a progressive shift in the structure of national subsidies away from regional aid towards more horizontal aid. Table 10.1 shows that regional subsidies now account for only 38 per cent of all national subsidies compared to 42 per cent for horizontal aids and 20 per cent for sectoral aid schemes. In response to this the Commission introduced guidelines for subsidies for research and development in 1986. Support for R&D had long been considered, by member state governments, to be effectively outside the control of the Community even though they fell under the general ban on subsidies in article 92 (EEC). Thus even though the EC provisions were applicable to R&D subsidies they were not applied. The 1986 guidelines on R&D subsidies sought to enhance transparency by requiring reporting by national governments. It also distinguished between basic R&D where an aid intensity of 50 per cent was possible, i.e. 50 per cent of investment could be covered by aid, and applied R&D where the aid intensity diminishes the closer the development comes to developing products for the market.[9] The Commission has also introduced guidelines for environmental aid with a maximum level of subsidy of 15 per cent of total investment. Export subsidies are, of course, prohibited within the EC and are controlled on extra-EC trade (supported by national export credit agencies) by OECD agreements.

Over time the Commission has moved into more and more controversial areas. One such controversial area has been the control of the subsidy element of capital provided to public enterprise. According to the latest Commission survey of subsidies such subsidies account for 7 per cent of total national subsidies for manufacturing. In reality the level could be much higher, depending on how one defines the subsidy element in the provision of public capital. As with other forms of aid the Commission first sought to increase

TABLE 10.1. *State aid to the manufacturing sector, 1988–90: breakdown of aid according to sector and function*

Sectors/function	B	DK	D	GR	E	F	IRL	I	L	NL	P	UK	EUR 12
Horizontal objectives	76	59	29	81	28	66	50	30	39	77	17	45	42
Innovation; R–D	13	35	12	1	9	17	4	4	8	35	1	8	10
Environment	0	4	2	0	1	0	0	0	1	2	0	2	1
S.M.E.	25	1	7	10	5	11	8	10	21	31	0	12	10
Trade/export	14	8	2	22	1	36	38	6	2	1	0	15	11
Economization of energy	6	10	3	0	1	1	0	1	0	2	0	0	1
General investment	12	0	0	10	5	1	0	2	8	4	1	9	8
Other objectives	6	0	2	37	6	0	0	7	0	0	14	0	5
Particular sectors	4	38	11	5	67	25	9	15	0	11	78	20	20
Shipbuilding	1	32	3	3	10	4	0	4	0	7	27	7	5
Other sectors	3	6	8	2	57	21	9	11	0	4	51	13	15
Regional objectives	21	3	61	15	5*	9	42	55	61	12	5	34	38
Regions under 92(3)c	21	3	9	—	—	5	—	4	61	12	—	25	8
Regions under 92(3)a	—	—	—	15	5	4	42	51	—	—	5	9	30
Berlin/92(2)c			52										
Total	100	100	100	100	100	100	100	100	100	100	100	100	100

* Subdivision not available.

Source: European Commission.

transparency.[10] Commission efforts to enforce these provisions faced stiff opposition, especially from France and Britain, which opposed the increase in the Commission's power and competence, but the Commission's position was upheld by the European Court of Justice (ECJ).[11] The ECJ's decision opened the way for guidelines, issued in 1990, based on the 'market economy investor principle'. According to this the degree of subsidy is determined by the difference between 'market economy principles', i.e. what the market would charge for capital and the terms on which the state provides the capital. The difficulty is, of course, that there is no clear-cut definition of what a 'market rate' is. Private companies may make strategic (loss-making) investments in the hope of long-term gains. This is, after all, what many successful companies do. Should public enterprise be prohibited from making such strategic investment? If so, would they ever be able to compete internationally with, for example, Japanese companies which often enter markets by adopting loss leadership policies? Had the national governments not provided capital for Airbus, which made a very large operating loss to start with, it would certainly never have competed with Boeing.[12] On the other hand, capital restructuring programmes are a notorious way of providing covert subsidies for public enterprise, and public enterprises will always tend to be ultimately 'bailed out' by government, so the market has no real sanction. The difficulty is compounded by the fact that national or regional governments do not always notify the Commission when they provide new capital for public companies. Hence the Commission's attempt first to improve transparency.

With regard to sectoral aid schemes the Commission has been more active. Many of these were introduced in the late 1970s when the steel, shipbuilding, and petrochemical industries were suffering from acute surplus capacity. After a lag, EC-wide measures began to have a real effect in reducing the level of competing national subsidies. This was especially the case in the steel industry, during the early 1980s, where the Commission had more extensive powers under the Treaty of Paris (ECSC), for example to set production quotas, than under the Treaty of Rome. Sectoral aid schemes in other industries, such as shipbuilding and man-made fibres, were less effective. Even in the late 1980s steel (4 per cent of total aid) and shipbuilding (5 per cent) still accounted for a large part of the aid given. The impact of the recession in the early 1990s has forced the Commission to work for a further steel restructuring plan. As a decade before, the battle was over how to get a balanced reduction in surplus capacity across the EC when some steel companies were in receipt of state subsidies and others not.

3. MERGER CONTROL

The development of EC merger control policy provides some important markers for future regulation of enterprises within the EC. The Treaty of Rome (unlike the Treaty of Paris) contained no provision for (pre-) merger control. At the time there was simply no perceived need for such a power. For one thing the scale of cross-border mergers and concentrations was limited, and for another the predominant view at the time was that what was needed was greater concentration, in order to reap economies of scale, not more or 'effective' competition. The Treaty did provide for the control of restrictive trade practices and the abuse of a dominant market position, articles 85 and 86 (EEC), but competence for merger control remained with the national authorities.

Not all member states of the EC had merger controls. Britain was the first to introduce them (1965 Monopolies and Mergers Act) followed by the Federal Republic of Germany (1973 Gesetz gegen Wettbewerbsbeschränkungen), and France, which developed much weaker provisions during the 1970s. The other countries generally had no formalized general merger control, at least until recently, although most had provisions concerning the media and banking. Without going into great detail, one can distinguish between two basic approaches to competition policy: the public policy and the competition-based approaches. The public policy approach provides significant discretionary powers for public authorities, usually the government of the day. Competition-based approaches distinguish between the assessment of competition, usually carried out by an independent agency, and the assessment of public interest by political institutions. Public-interest-based policies were especially used by national governments to limit competition for national champions on the domestic markets by blocking 'unwelcome' foreign acquisitions.

As EC policy progressively replaces national policy (see below) the scope for national discretionary policies aimed at defending the home markets of national champions from foreign competition is reduced, but there is also the question of the basis for EC policy. Should it be narrowly focused on competition or should it allow a degree of flexibility? If there is flexibility, should this discretionary power be used as an instrument of European industrial policy?

The questions of the division between EC and national competence and whether EC policy should be based on public-interest or competition criteria has shaped the debate on EC merger control for nearly 20 years. Following the initial Commission proposals for an EC pre-merger control instrument in 1973, most member state governments opposed loss of competence to the Commission. There was also a division between the advocates of a competition-based policy (Germany and the Netherlands) and a public-interest-based, discretionary policy (France and until the 1980s Britain). Together these factors prevented agreement on an EC merger control Regulation. This remained the case despite decisions of the ECJ, such as the 1972 Continental Can case, which suggested that article 86 (EEC) (abuse of a dominant position) could, in certain circumstances, be applied to mergers. Repeated attempts by the European Commission to revive the proposals failed.

In the mid-1980s, pressure for an EC regulation increased in the wake of a rising number of cross-border mergers and acquisitions. In 1987 the ECJ again intervened with a decision (in the Philip Morris case). This time the ECJ suggested that article 85 (EEC) could, in certain circumstances, be used to block a merger. This resulted in industrial lobbies changing sides in the debate and opting for EC merger control provided it offered a 'one-stop-shop' (i.e. only EC controls). European and national business lobbies have long held ambiguous positions on merger control. In general terms they favour predictability and thus oppose discretionary public interest policies, but individual firms involved in mergers will generally argue that discretion should be applied, to either allow or block a bid, in order to take full account of broader 'public interests' such as the need to create or defend an indigenous industry.

After 16 years the issues of competence and the competition or industrial policy base of EC policy were finally resolved in 1989. The merger control regulation adopted in December 1989[13] resolved the competence issue by dividing powers between the Commission (Directorate General IV) and the member state authorities. EC competence covers mergers on a 'Community scale', or those above set thresholds. The thresholds were set high. Any merger involving companies with a global turnover of 5 billion ECU or more is covered. In order to avoid catching mergers of non-EC companies with minor activities in the EC, there is a further threshold requiring the aggregate turnover within the EC of each of at least two companies to be 250 million ECU. Finally, to avoid EC coverage of what are essentially national mergers, national authorities will have jurisdiction if 66 per cent of the world-wide turnover is accounted for by merged firms located in only one member state of the EC. These thresholds are higher than the European Commission wanted because national authorities resisted ceding competence.[14] However, anything above these thresholds is exclusively EC competence.[15] This means that important or 'strategic' mergers will in future fall under Community competence and be assessed by the European Commission. At the same time the level of thresholds means that EC competence is limited. Below the thresholds national merger policy applies. The ECJ ruling in the Philip Morris case does raise the prospect that actions may be initiated by companies under article 85 (EEC), thus raising the spectre of double jeopardy and forcing most cautious corporate lawyers to play safe and notify mergers to both national and EC authorities.

On the question of the criteria for assessing a merger the letter of the regulation is closer to the German competition-based than a public-interest-based system. Thus the criteria are the need 'to preserve and develop effective competition', the market position of the companies and their economic and financial power. More importantly the scope for exercising discretion and allowing a merger which does not meet such competition criteria but which might further 'industrial policy' objectives is very restricted. The regulation (article 1(b)) refers to the 'development of economic and technical progress', but immediately limits the scope for discretion by requiring that exemptions under this heading are to 'customers'' advantage and do not 'form an obstacle to competition'. Experience with the regulation to date suggests that the Commission is initially adopting a fairly permissive approach.

Of the mergers notified to date there has been only one notable case of the Commission blocking. This was the De Havilland–

Aérospatiale proposed merger, which caused uproar in France because it was seen as preventing a merger that made sense from an industrial policy/competitiveness point of view.[16] The De Havilland case is important because it is an indication of the orientation of the current Commission and its determination to use the merger control regulation. The clear signal is that EC policy on mergers will be competition-based, as it has been in the implementation of articles 85 and 86 (EEC), the wording of which is much looser. On the other hand, one must not forget that in virtually all other cases the Commission has approved mergers. In reality the Commission, as in the past, will take its time to build up an EC policy based on case law. One area in which important test cases are likely to occur is telecommunications, where EC-level restructuring is underway, with ex-national champions such as Deutsche Telekom and France Telecom seeking to co-operate in order to compete with British Telecom and other non-US carriers.

4. COMPETITION IN THE PUBLIC UTILITIES

Perhaps the last preserve of national enterprise has been in the field of public utilities. In sectors such as telecommunications, energy, postal services, and air and rail transport, the natural monopoly characteristics of the markets meant that all national governments maintained either public monopolies, in the form of nationalized industries, or regulated private monopolies. But important provisions of the Treaty of Rome, such as article 90 (EEC), have arguably always been applicable to these sectors. It is just that like article 92 (EEC) they have not been applied. All the time these industries were run as nationalized industries there was never a question of Commission intervention being politically acceptable. During the 1980s, however, things began to change as a consequence of international market developments which resulted in increased globalization and liberalization, and deregulation policies starting in the United States and followed in Britain and to a lesser extent other EC member states.

Change raised questions about how the public utilities should be regulated. Should global markets determine the services to be provided and their costs, or should there be re-regulation at an EC level in order to retain some control in order to ensure the fulfilment of objectives such as universal service? The state of flux in policy making in some public utilities opened the way to EC intervention. The objectives of the EC authorities—the pioneering work was done by DGXIII in the telecommunications sector—was to ensure that the emerging structures would not prejudice the integration of a European market or work to the disadvantage of European industry. Over and above this, there was the long-term objective of replacing nationally incompatible systems with compatible networks within the EC. These would then facilitate the ultimate introduction of common carriage and competition among providers of services across the EC.

The approach adopted by the Commission in the telecommunication sector provided a model for subsequent policies in other utilities. First, the Commission produced a Green Paper which sought to establish as broad a consensus among member states and interest groups as possible. This recommended, as a first step, the separation of regulator and operators—a move which reflected a desire to avoid both uncontrolled deregulation and continued dominance by public monopolies which set the terms and conditions of competition themselves. The telecommunications Green Paper offered the existing network operators the basic network monopoly and thus helped to ensure their support for reform. Directives were then introduced to liberalize other services such as terminal equipment, value added services, and with some delay satellite communications. A key objective here was to ensure that the existing network operators did not extend their monopoly into new areas. These principles were then consolidated in provisions such as that on Open Network Provision (ONP), on which the Commission is, with the support of the Council, to make proposals.[17]

In the case of telecommunications, the Commission even risked using article 90 (EEC) as the basis for these Commission Directives because it felt it was working 'with the grain' of market pressures. The main liberalization proposals were accompanied by flanking measures, such as work on common standards and a liberalization of (public) procurement by *all* utilities, except for airlines. In the case of telecommunications a special standards making body ETSI (European Telecommunications Standards Institute) was set up to speed the work on developing the common standards needed for network compatibility across the EC.

A crucial limitation on EC policy in such regulated sectors, to date, has been that there is no central regulatory authority. All the EC does is to limit the discretionary powers that can be used at the national level. It has not developed an EC regulatory competence with its own discretionary powers to regulate the sector concerned on a day-to-day basis. In other words, to use the British analogy, there is nothing equivalent to OFTEL (The Office of Telecommunications) which regulates the British telecommunications sector, or OFGAS, OFER, or OFWAS (gas, electricity, and water). The only instrument available which the European Commission has been able to deploy with any degree or discretion has been competition policy and in particular article 90 (EEC).[18]

Telecommunications saw a crucial test for Commission competence in this field. As previously mentioned, the Commission introduced a Commission Directive (i.e. agreed by the Commission) on the basis of article 90 (EEC) aimed at liberalizing telecommunications terminal equipment. This was challenged by France, Germany, and Italy on the grounds that the liberalization of this sector represented a policy innovation which required approval by the Council of Ministers under article 100a (EEC). The Commission maintained that the Directive was merely implementing existing Treaty provisions and therefore required no Council agreement. In an important precedent the ECJ decided to support the Commission, thus opening the way, in theory, for the potential use of article 90 (EEC) to liberalize all utilities.[19]

Once again, however, the experience of the EC shows how the Commission is constrained by what is considered to be politically expedient or feasible on the day. The Commission has since considered but rejected using article 90 in its efforts to liberalize the energy sector, because the vested interests and their reflection in member state governments were simply too powerful to be set aside by decision based on legal powers alone. Therefore, whilst the EC is encroaching on the field of public utilities, and has claimed, in theory, that EC regulation extends to all utilities, it is in reality some way from the point at which it really challenges national companies.

There is one final point on the liberalization of public monopolies that is worth considering. Liberalization and privatization have released certain companies from the 'shackles' of being nationalized industries. For example, British Airways has become an active acquirer in other countries. At the same time the loosening of national regulation has facilitated the acquisition of previously publicly owned firms by companies from other countries. An interesting example of this has been the acquisition of English water companies by the large French water companies. British Telecom is an example of another formerly nationalized company that is now beginning to move onto the international and European markets. As noted above, the ex-national champions of France and Germany are also now entering the fray. This raises important questions concerning competition policy, since a tightly regulated home market could provide a dominant private or public company with a significant competitive advantage when operating across the EC. In the absence of national regulation or trade barriers EC competition policy may be all that can prevent such firms from dominating parts of the EC market. This brings us to the question of how the EC regulates 'multinational champions'.

5. EC POLICY TOWARDS 'MULTINATIONAL CHAMPIONS'

The issues and EC instruments are in most cases the same for dealing with national champions and 'multinational champions'. 'Multinational champions' are simply national champions that have been forced or have chosen to cut loose from their national bonds and compete internationally. Unlike national champions they are generally faced with a greater or lesser degree of competition in their home markets, but they may well still benefit from support from the home state government, or even a host state government. EC policy in all the fields discussed above remains relevant to such companies. Indeed, one might argue that EC controls are even more important when it comes to 'multinational enterprise' than 'national enterprise', because the companies concerned are to a greater or lesser extent beyond the reach of national controls. Thus EC policy on national subsidies still applies to 'multinational enterprise'. National government can still provide support for indigenous firms that are competing across the EC and international markets as 'trans-European champions'. It seems likely that some of the horizontal subsidies provided for innovation or exports are used as disguised support for trans-European champions. In this sense the Commission's efforts to control R&D subsidies are relevant. The Commission's policy *vis-à-vis* public enterprise is also crucial to the operation of trans-European champions which happen to benefit from public funding, as is the case with a number of acquisitive French companies as well as some less aggressively acquisitive Italian firms. Thus the ability to provide support for outreach by public enterprises is under control of the Commission, even if that control is at present fairly weak.

The Treaty provisions on cartels article 85 (EEC) are also important, since many companies moving to establish a trans-European position are doing so through joint ventures or agreements with other former national champions. Article 86 (EEC) applied to the abuse of a dominant position. Thus moves by former public monopoly operators into competitive markets, while retaining their established dominance in a large member state, would fall under the control of the Commission under article 86 (EEC). The introduction of the merger control regulation means that mergers between ex-national champions require pre-notification and clearance by the Commission. Thus moves to establish a dominant position through mergers or acquisitions are subject to EC regulation.

The Nestlé takeover of Perrier illustrates a further aspect of Commission efforts to ensure comprehensive coverage of pan-European champions. Nestlé decided to sell certain brands of mineral water (Volvic) to BSN, in order to reduce its market share after the acquisition of Perrier and thus avoid acquiring a market dominance. But this would have resulted in two companies each holding 40 per cent of the (French) market. The Commission argued that this would have created a position of 'joint dominance' and challenged the deal. The issue here is that much of the cross-border restructuring being undertaken between national champions is taking the form of agreed 'swops' of businesses between conglomerates. Another example of this is the framework agreement between Fiat and GEC/Alsthom, the latter being a consortium of French and British firms. This agreement provides for exchanges of businesses which would enable each to focus on their core business on a pan-European basis. This type of agreement may constitute the kind of cross-border restructuring favoured by those in DGIII of the European Commission who favour strong EC industries, but it also brings with it the possibility of simply transforming the national oligopolies that supported national champions into European-wide oligopolies. Those in DGIV of the Commission seeking to defend competition have therefore argued that the Perrier case confirms that the merger regulation is applicable in such cases and should be used to prevent joint dominance being achieved.[20]

6. PUBLIC PROCUREMENT

The Commission has learned its lesson about the limitations of dependence on centralized enforcement. In many of the internal market measures it has sought to ensure that decentralized channels of enforcement exist. Public procurement is one of these.

Public procurement by central and local government, and public and private utilities, accounts for some 15 per cent of Community GDP. Of this total some 8 per cent of GDP is accounted for by purchasing which is subject to individual contracts.[21] The EC coverage of public purchasing has, in a sense, been comprehensive from the word go. The treaty provisions which prohibit quantitative restrictions and measures having an equivalent effect (article 30 *et seq.*) are, according to rulings of the ECJ, applicable to purchasing decisions which discriminate in favour of national suppliers of goods or services. In reality, however, these have never been enforced. There are many reasons for this. Among the most important is that incredulity about open EC markets has dissuaded foreign suppliers from even bidding for many contracts. Thus by and large the suppliers of power equipment have simply not bothered to bid for power station contracts because national suppliers were expected to get the orders. Without more bids for contracts from external suppliers, aggrieved firms have not emerged to challenge a decision on the basis of EC law. Indeed, suppliers have feared that such action would probably guarantee that they did not get any future orders in their national markets. 'Do not bite the hand that feeds you (or could feed you) with orders' was the guiding principle. There are, however, signs that some firms may now be prepared to initiate cases.

In addition to these barriers, the close links established between national suppliers and public purchasers have in practice meant that markets have remained national. When a national company develops the technology for a new telecommunications system or rail locomotive, often in close co-operation with the customer, it creates a national design standard which makes access for foreign suppliers more difficult. Purchasing practices also favour a supply structure in which there are two or three key suppliers. This helps to ensure some competition but at the same time enables the real benefits of co-operation between customer and supplier to be gained. The EC's case for liberalization of public purchasing is based on the view that these practices have fragmented the European market and through the creation of national oligopolistic structures made European companies internationally uncompetitive.

During the 1970s, the Commission made its first attempts at opening national purchasing to competition. Again the approach was to increase transparency as the first step towards measures with more teeth. But the three directives adopted, which covered purchasing of suppliers (investment goods) and works (construction and public works contracts) for central and local government had little impact. Markets remained largely closed, and by the time the internal market programme was launched foreign suppliers were estimated to account in total for between 4 and 0.3 per cent of public purchasing, with Germany being the most open market and Italy the least open.[22] The directives had little or no effect because market liberalization was not credible and the compliance measures were still inadequate. The directives also failed to include the utilities (power, water, telecommunications, and transport), the so-called excluded sectors, in which there was mixed public and private ownership. In the 1970s, developing EC regulation that would apply to both publicly and privately owned firms was not considered feasible. These excluded sectors accounted for nearly half of all purchasing and included some key strategic industries.

As part of the internal market programme, the Commission embarked on a second more ambitious attempt to liberalize the markets.[23] This consists of seven directives, of which all but two have been adopted by the Council of Ministers. There are strengthened directives covering purchasing of supplies and works by central and local government. There is a directive covering the excluded sectors. This has sought to overcome the problem of mixed ownership by being all-embracing in its coverage. No distinction is made between public and private ownership. The criterion used is whether the body placing contracts benefits from special or exclusive rights determined by government or public regulatory or licensing bodies. The rationale here is that if a government agency provides monopoly rights or grants exclusive rights, such as oil exploration in part of the North Sea, it can exert leverage over the purchasing decisions of the company exercising those rights, even if the latter is a fully privately owned company.[24]

Another example of how the Commission seeks comprehensive coverage is that it has also pressed ahead with plans for a directive covering the purchasing of services. This directive, which is still to be adopted, was considered necessary because of the scope for evasion without it. Most contracts cover goods and services, so that the installation of a computer system involves the hardware and software. If services were not covered, it could have been possible for EC rules to be evaded by placing orders for software with a national supplier of computers which would then itself acquire the computers needed to fulfil the task and thus simply use its own products. The one major area still excluded from EC directives is that of military systems. Non-lethal purchasing by ministries of defence is covered by the supplies and works directive, but weapons systems are not. The Commission is seeking to extend coverage to this sector. It believes that with the merging of civil and defence technologies one can no longer distinguish between the two. Thus highly priced defence contracts may result in an indirect (cross) subsidization of the civil activities of GEC or Daimler-MBB.

The EC has also introduced compliance directives. As noted at the beginning of this section, it has sought to enlist the efforts of suppliers by providing access to remedies in cases when purchasers discriminate in favour of national suppliers. In this way, the Commission is seeking to avoid the problem of over-centralized compliance and enforcement. Given that there are literally thousands of contracts placed every week which fall inside the thresholds set by the directives, this is in any case the only feasible approach. In the excluded sectors, special provisions have had to be made to help deal with the problem of mixed public and private ownership. Private utilities, such as those in Germany in particular, have argued that they are private enterprises and cannot therefore be covered by directives requiring specific contract award procedures designed for governments. The compliance directive for the excluded sectors is still to be agreed.

Once again therefore the EC rules are increasingly extensive in their coverage. The internal market programme's seven directives will cover virtually all forms of purchasing,[25] but the requirements placed on purchasers will take some time to have much effect. In the case of standardized products, such as cars or lorries, they may have an immediate effect. In other sectors, national design standards will continue to influence purchasing for years to come. In the rail sector, for example, a generation of technology and thus standards can be as long as 50 years. Where there are shorter generations of technology, such as in computing or telecommunications (2–10 years), change may happen sooner. There are also doubts about compliance. Will potential suppliers really be prepared to take their customers to court? There have been some cases, and the Commission will certainly ensure there are cases to help define the scope of the rules, but in the end markets will only be opened effectively if the suppliers want them to be opened.

7. EC-LEVEL INDUSTRIAL POLICY

In addition to the potential impact of EC regulation or deregulation on national enterprise, there is also the question of whether the EC should itself develop an active 'industrial policy'. EC industrial policy has been the subject of contentious debate within the EC for some 20 years. Its objective would be to promote European industrial competitiveness *vis-à-vis* third countries, although some (Germans, Dutch, and more recently British officials) have, of course, argued that it should simply be competition policy and that competition within the EC is the best way of ensuring international competitiveness. The more interventionist approach to EC industrial policy would, however, essentially replace the national enterprise with European enterprise and promote an identification with EC-level industry rather than national industry. These issues figure in all aspects of EC policy, notably the debate about the role of EC merger control policy. Some (French) advocates of an activist EC industrial policy have proposed that there should be general discretionary powers for the EC to use policy instruments to promote European industrial competitiveness. The so-called 'Cresson clause' (named after the French prime minister of the day) in the Maastricht treaty is an example of such a French-inspired policy. This reflects the traditionally more active French approach to industrial policy. Germany and the Netherlands have consistently argued for a non-interventionist EC approach to industry and opposed the idea of an industry chapter in the Maastricht agreement. Britain was also opposed to the chapter, but was too preoccupied with pursuing its own agenda on the EMU and social policy opt-ins and left the battle against it to the Germans, much to the unhappiness of the non-interventionist Germans. Italy and to a lesser degree Spain and Belgium supported the more interventionist French line.

The outcome of the debate was that an industry chapter was included in title XIII of the Maastricht treaty. This provides that the Community and member states 'shall ensure that the conditions necessary for the competitiveness of the Community's industry exist'. Such broad powers would provide scope for a more active industrial policy, but the likelihood of this happening was significantly diminished by the fact that, on the insistence of the Germans, unanimity will be required to implement the powers. There has never been unanimity on an EC industrial policy. At the same time the fact that the chapter exists will result in pressure to use it, so the issue is therefore not closed.

As indicated earlier, the central role of competition policy—broadly defined to include policy towards state subsidies, mergers, and pan-European agreements aimed at oligopolies—means that the Commission's interpretation of these provisions is vital to the shape of EC policy. Recent Commissioners responsible for DGIV, such as Peter Sutherland and Leon Brittan, have pursued aggressively competition-based policies, despite opposition on particular cases from the national government or firm affected, other Commissioners and, possibly, Jacques Delors. The current Commissioner with responsibility, the Belgian socialist Carol van Miert, appears to stress flexibility more than his predecessors.[26] If, in future, a more interventionist-minded Commissioner were to be appointed to DGIV, this could tip the balance in favour of a more industrial-policy-based EC.

8. COMPANY LAW AND CORPORATE GOVERNANCE

As markets for goods and services are integrated the importance of differences in the systems of corporate governance assume greater importance within the EC. This is an area in which the obstacles to harmonization are such that the EC is in effect leaving the issue to be decided by competition among rules (in this case systems of corporate governance). Competition among rules here means that companies operate under different regulatory systems, for example those regulating capital and labour markets and company law. These different national systems of rules are brought into competition through the rivalry between companies. As noted earlier, 'national enterprise' could survive the internal market in the sense that there may continue to be a close identification between some firms and their—predominantly national— stakeholders. The question of the future of 'national enterprise' then becomes whether competition among rules results in an erosion of such national ties.

The differences between forms of corporate governance can be illustrated by a brief comparison of the German and British 'models'.[27] German 'Rhineland capitalism'[28] exhibits a strong identification between the various stakeholders in the enterprise and the long-term health of the enterprise itself. There is a close identification between investors and the company because some of the largest investors are banks which also have seats on the supervisory or management boards of the company. There is an active effort to encourage employee identification with the interests of the enterprise by the promotion of consensus. This takes the form of works councils and co-determination. Even the local communities within which enterprises have plants develop a close identification with the company, which often brings important tax revenue to the local town or region. In order to retain investment the local authorities offer vocational training programmes and other forms of social and physical infrastructure.

This system of corporate governance has evolved over a long period and is largely independent of the statutory framework within which it operates. Nevertheless, it finds support from statutory provisions. Company law is 'permissive' of provisions in company articles of association which enable the management of a company to retain control. Thus limitations on the voting rights of shareholders are allowed, as are the acquisition of company shares by a subsidiary. These ensure that hostile takeover bids can be blocked. The (restrictive) regulation of capital markets also facilitates the continuation of a strong role for banks in the provision of industrial finance and helps ensure that capital markets do not exclusively serve the interests of shareholders.

The opposite end of the spectrum is the Anglo-American free market economy which places the emphasis on an open market for corporate control as well as for goods and services. Market pressures, in the shape of the demands of the shareholders for a 'market' return on capital invested, keep management on its toes and ensure that assets are effectively employed. If performance falls below what the shareholders expect, the company faces the prospect of a takeover bid by an alternative management that will make better use of the assets employed or release assets tied up in unprofitable activities, offering higher returns on capital invested. Under this system, takeover by the highest bidder becomes one of the major forms of corporate restructuring. This contrasts with the more industry-motivated and agreed takeovers and mergers which predominate on the Continent. The net effect is a system of corporate governance in which there is a low level of identification with the (long) term interests of the company as compared to the German and to a lesser degree other Continental European systems.

The national regulatory environment underpins the system by ensuring a large and open capital market which promotes the use of equity capital as opposed to debt capital as the main source of industrial finance. The interests of London as an international capital market are clearly a factor in determining the nature of regulatory policy. There are also rules set by the financial markets themselves, which penalize any company which attempts to limit the rights of shareholders for the benefit of management. In other words, defensive gambits in hostile takeover bids, which might prevent the shareholders' rights to dispose (at a profit) of their stake in the company, are prohibited at the risk of being excluded from the capital market. There is also no effort to strengthen or promote consensus within Britain through statutes, such as on employee representation; indeed, the last decade has seen an active policy of deregulation of employment markets.

The member states of the EC have an array of features which

affect corporate governance. The Netherlands share many of the features of the German system. In France and Italy, in contrast, structural features, such as high levels of cross shareholding or public shareholding and public enterprise, make for a relatively closed market for corporate control. To a greater or lesser degree Continental European countries have systems which promote or at least permit a high or modest degree of identity of common interests between the enterprise and its various stakeholders. In contrast the version of Anglo-American corporate governance employed in Britain either discourages or impedes such an identity of interests as inimical to the preferred open market for corporate control.

Faced with such differences the EC has not sought to—and is unlikely to succeed in any effort to—harmonize all aspects of company law and capital market regulation. Those measures that have been introduced have not always made much progress. This is the case where a series of company law directives have been bogged down due to differences over employee participation. The fifth company law directive, for example, which would prohibit limitations on voting rights for shareholders, has been held up because of its employee participation provisions. The alternative parallel provision of a European Company Statute has also run into similar problems. The thirteenth company law directive, which would regulate the purchasing of a company's own shares, has been held up by, among other things, British reluctance to see EC statutes impinging upon the self-regulation of takeovers by the City Takeover Panel. The second company law directive, which would limit the ability of a subsidiary to acquire the shares of its parent company, has also been held up.

Issues of company law harmonization shade quickly into wider social questions. Amongst the most controversial elements of the social dimension of the internal market are those relating to employee consultation and employee rights to information. For the Germans and other member states that regard consensus as a precondition for long-term economic prosperity, these provisions are an essential element of the effort to ensure that EC-wide competition does not undermine the established consensus. For the British (employers and government) who see any social measures as a cost and thus detrimental to competitiveness and prosperity, EC statutory provisions are highly unwelcome, hence the support for the British opt-out from the social dimension.

These political differences mean that the EC is unlikely to get very far with harmonization of company law and other policy areas which affect the nature of corporate governance. Indeed, one of the few areas in which the EC has failed to adopt internal market legislation envisaged in the Cockfield White Paper has been that of company law. Even if some of the company law directives are adopted, they are likely to be diluted and will not bring about an approximation of the different national models. With limited EC harmonization, the question becomes whether competition among rules will bring about a convergence? The kind of pressures that would bring this about would be, for example, British companies 'migrating' to other member states by seeking incorporation under a system which eases the short-term pressures on them or enables them to defend themselves against takeovers. In the United States, a high proportion of enterprises are incorporated in Delaware because it offers favourable company law and tax regimes. Convergence may also come about in the other direction with, for example, the liberalization of the Frankfurt and Paris capital markets in order to compete with London. This would create a large open capital market and would require adequate regulation.

While there are some modest signs of this kind of convergence the underlying business 'cultures' and the structures on which they are based seem unlikely to change rapidly. Companies operating under different forms of corporate governance will therefore continue to compete with a common market for goods and services. This will mean that in those countries which encourage or facilitate it, it will still be possible to have a strong identification with 'national' enterprises.

The system of corporate governance or corporate control can therefore help or hinder the continued existence of 'national enterprise' in the sense of company identification with a particular region or country. In Germany and to a lesser extent in most other Continental EC member states the system of corporate governance results in a close identification with existing German firms by the existing stakeholders who are, of course, predominantly German. In the Anglo-American world this identification does not exist.

'National enterprise' may continue to survive thanks to the links between finance and the firm, even if the conventional government–firm links are broken by EC integration.

9. CONCLUSIONS

The reach of EC regulation is becoming more and more extensive in its applicability to national enterprise but is not always actively applied. This means there remains some scope for national preferences of a more covert kind. With the implementation of the internal market programme and a redoubling of efforts by the Commission in areas such as state aid policy and competition policy, the grip of EC policy will become tighter. But the Commission, in applying competition policy provisions, will still be subject to political constraints. This is important to remember at a time when there is much imprecise debate about subsidiarity and scepticism about the role of the Commission. In a climate in which many have directed their criticism of bureaucracy at the Commission, there is a possibility that the Commission's ability to act decisively against anti-competitive practices, whether by governments or companies, may be constrained. Economic slowdown or recession has also been accompanied by a 'more flexible' approach by the Commission in some fields.

EC regulation will also be applicable to the 'trans-European champions' that are being created out of national champions. The overall orientation of the Commission's policy is therefore important. The internal market programme has led companies to believe that restructuring on an EC level is necessary in order to be competitive, but it could also mean that national oligopolistic structures are replaced by EC oligopolies. There is therefore a case for effective EC regulation to ensure that the full benefits of the internal market are achieved. Thus far, the Commission has used the limited discretionary powers it has to push a competition-based policy. Even once the internal market has been implemented and enforcement procedures are in place, there will be important aspects of 'national enterprise', such as corporate governance or business practices, which EC regulation may well not reach. 'National enterprises' will continue to exist. How far they will be circumscribed by

EC rules or overtaken by the emergence of European enterprises will depend partly on how effectively the rules are enforced. But it will also depend on how business redefines itself under the pressures of competition and the single market.

Notes

1. See Stephen Thompson and Stephen Woolcock, *Direct Investment and European Integration: Competition among firms and Governments* (London, 1993).
2. For some illustration of the importance of this 'credibility factor', see Stephen Woolcock, Michael Hodges, and Kristin Schreiber, *Britain, Germany and 1992: The Limits of Deregulation* (London, 1991).
3. See Report to the EEC Commission by the High Level Group on the Operation of Internal Market, *Internal Market After 1992: Meeting the Challenge* (Brussels, Oct. 1992).
4. In reality, of course, subsidies, in so far as they represent direct transfers from the national exchequers, tend to be more visible than other forms of favouring national industries and thus more exposed to criticism.
5. The Commission has to date adopted a permissive approach to Treuhand support. To do otherwise would risk political retribution from the Germans, who have an unprecedented task in privatizing the whole of the East German economy. In line with past policy, however, the Commission has made it known that it cannot stand by indefinitely and that there has to be a finite end to the levels of support.
6. See 'Third Survey of State Aids in the European Community in Manufacturing and Certain other Sectors' (Commission of the European Communities, July 1992).
7. See Joseph Gilchrist and David Deacon, 'Curbing Subsidies', in Peter Montagnon (ed.), *European Competition Policy* (London, 1991).
8. See Council Resolution on a *Framework of Systems of Regional Aid*. For this and all texts of EC competition policy provisions, see European Commission, *Competition Law in the European Communities*, i. *Rules Applicable to Undertakings*; and ii. *Rules and Applications of State Aids* (Brussels, 1990).
9. See Community Framework on State Aids for Research and Development, *Official Journal*, C83 (1986).
10. See Commission Directive 80/723/1980 on transparency in public enterprises.
11. The case made by France and Britain was that the Treaty of Rome (in

article 222 EEC) is explicit on neutrality toward public and private ownership, and that the Commission could not therefore intervene and seek to influence the terms on which capital is provided to public enterprise. The Commission's argument, which was upheld by the European Court, was that public capital is all right but it should not contain hidden subsidies.

12. US critics of the Airbus subsidies argue that the project overall has been loss-making as research and development costs are not covered.

13. Regulation no. 4064/89 of 21 Dec. 1989.

14. When the merger control regulation was adopted in 1989, the Commission succeeded in including in it provision for a review of the thresholds after four years. The hope was to reduce thresholds and thus increase EC competence. But when the review came in 1993 the weight of national government opposition to reductions meant that the existing thresholds had to be retained for the present.

15. The Germans fought to claw back national competence even above these thresholds, but the provision (art. 9 of the 1989 regulation) seems unlikely to be used much in practice.

16. Aérospatiale bid for De Havilland, which produces small aircraft. The European Commission ruled that this would have resulted in the creation of a position of market dominance in small aircraft and banned the merger. For its part, Aérospatiale, with the backing of the French government, argued that the merger was needed in order to consolidate the European industry so that it could compete internationally.

17. Work in the postal services sector has followed the telecoms model with a Green Paper being adopted in 1991, followed by work (nearing completion in December 1993) to define which sectors should be 'reserved' for companies required to offer a guaranteed 'universal service'.

18. The only sector in which the EC has established an independent regulatory agency has been pharmaceuticals. In July 1993, the Council adopted new procedures for drug registration, which included the establishment of a European Pharmaceuticals Agency; see *Official Journal*, OJ 214 24 (Aug. 1993).

19. For a brief summary of the issues see Woolcock, Hodges, and Schreiber, *Britain, Germany and 1992*.

20. For a detailed discussion of this point, see Joseph Gilchrist, *Anwendbarkeit der Oligopolvermutungen in der deutschen und europaeischen Zusammenschlusskontrolle*, paper for seminar of the Forschungsinstitut für Wirtschaftverfassung und Wettbewerb (e.V. Koelln, Sept. 1992).

21. See European Commission, 'Cost of Non-Europe', *Public purchasing*, 8 (Brussels, 1988).

22. Ibid.
23. See European Commission, *Action Programme for Public Purchasing in the Community*, COM(86)375 (1986).
24. The classic case of such leverage is often seen to be the Offshore Supplies Office established to 'monitor' the sale of equipment to companies operating in the British section of the North Sea. This was successful in ensuring that the majority of contracts were placed in Britain.
25. Some areas continue to lie outside EC rules, such as air transport. Here the Commission argued that there was competition, between Airbus and Boeing, so that there was no need for EC rules, but the political sensitivity of this sector was also a reason for continuing to exclude it.
26. See e.g. speech by van Miert at the Royal Institute of International Affairs, London, 15 May 1993.
27. For a more detailed treatment, see Stephen Woolcock, *Corporate Governance in the Single European Market*, RIIA Discussion Paper no. 32 (Nov. 1990).
28. See Michel Albert, *Capitalisme contre capitalisme* (Paris, 1991).

11

The European Community and the Restructuring of Europe's National Champions

ANDREW COX AND GLYN WATSON

During the 1960s the industrial policies of European governments were aimed at the encouragement of national champions of sufficient size to challenge the region's then principal competitor, the United States. Geroski and Jacquemin have described this process, and claimed that it was a policy which, by the 1970s, had resulted in a number of shortcomings.[1] On the one hand they suggest that the efficiency benefits conferred on firms by scale proved to be smaller than the conventional wisdom of the day had supposed, while on the other, these national giants enjoyed considerable (and in some cases monopoly) power within a fragmented regional market. They were to a significant degree insulated from pressure from national and non-national rivals which the authors claim retarded both the incentive to innovate and respond to change. Nor were they encouraged to leave markets in which, by strict economic logic, they could no longer compete. The privileged position enjoyed by these firms was reinforced by national governments which sought to protect their champions first by the use of tariffs and—as these disappeared over the course of the post-war period—by the non-tariff barriers which replaced them.

It is this insulation from the pressures of market changes and the threat of new competitors which the European Commission has identified as a major contributing factor in explaining the problems of sluggish growth, high inflation, and rising unemployment which

This paper provides a summary of some of the general arguments in the authors' forthcoming volume, *The Restructuring of European Industry*.

have beset the region's economies since the first oil shock in 1973. Their solution has been to complete the region's internal market. They suggest that the achievement of a truly integrated European market through the removal of all artificial barriers to trade between the EC's member states will inject a new round of competition into the region's economy, adding an estimated 5–7 per cent to output (unaccompanied by inflation) and creating up to 5 million new jobs.[2] Approximately half of these forecasted benefits are expected to come from industrial restructuring. This will occur internally, by a process of rationalization within firms and, externally, through the pooling of resources between enterprises in the form of joint ventures, mergers, and acquisitions. The 1992 project therefore reflects a belief that, in some sectors at least, there are still significant efficiency gains to be achieved from economies of scale, while the removal of all non-tariff barriers and a strong competition policy will ensure that these gains are not lost in the subsequent concentration of European capital.

Will the 1992 project have a generally beneficial competitive effect on industrial sectors in the EC? We examine the period of concentration that occurred during the 1960s and explain why the industrial policy of the day failed to deliver the benefits predicted. As a result of this failure a group of economists was employed by the Commission to analyse past policy and to predict under exactly what conditions and in which industrial sectors a further round of concentration would increase the efficiency of European firms without an attendant risk of monopolistic competition.[3] The results of this study, presented in our second section, provide a clear insight into the Commission's thinking and policy on the subject of mergers and acquisitions. Finally we use this model to look at the current round of corporate restructuring in Europe (which has been facilitated by the 1992 project) and to give an indication of its impact on the competitiveness of the European economy.

In its monitoring of European industry, the Commission has suggested the number of corporate mergers and acquisitions in the region has increased dramatically in the run up to the completion of the internal market. Not only have the number of mergers and acquisitions increased in total but an unprecedented number of these involve cross-border deals. This is seen as evidence that even before the 1992 programme was fully in place it was already starting to produce results with the emergence of streamlined EC-level champions which (over time) would take the place of less efficient, less flexible national champions. Using data drawn from a variety of sources we conclude that, while the overall levels of merger, acquisition, and joint venture have increased in the EC since the onset of plans to unify Europe's markets, the detailed picture is more ambiguous. There are differences between the degree of merger and acquisition activity by sector. Rationalization is not universal but rather is concentrated in specific industries and member states. There is also some evidence to suggest that this concentration is not necessarily in those sectors which the Commission's model suggests have most to gain from 1992. Furthermore, concentration may not be leading to the creation of European champions so much as the internationalization of leading high-tech sectors.

1. EUROPEAN INDUSTRIAL CONCENTRATION IN THE 1960s: THE CULT OF SCALE

During the 1960s the industrial policy of the EC's member states was predicated on a belief in a direct link between scale and competitiveness. National policies were directed towards the creation of super-firms to compete with the industrial giants of the US. This was combined with initiatives to break down intra-EC tariffs, so that national super-firms might enjoy a sufficiently large internal market to reap the full benefits of economies of scale. Geroski and Jacquemin have argued that this reflected an unwarranted tolerance on the part of the policy makers of the potentially adverse consequences of sectoral concentration which arise when individual firms enjoy sufficient market power to 'drive prices above the marginal cost of producing their good or service'.[4] This tolerance is attributed to a combination of three factors. First, economies of scale were believed to be both significant and applicable to most European industries. Second, it was believed that the costs of monopoly were small by comparison and in any case, third, it was believed that the new corporate champions might achieve their efficiency gains without an undue concentration of market power.

Over the course of the 1960s the structure of the corporate economy in Europe was substantially changed, principally (though

TABLE 11.1. *Output and labour productivity (sales per man) differentials between major corporations from different industrial regions*

Industrial sector	Top 5 corporations EC		Top 5 corporations US		Top 5 corporations Japan	
	Sales	Sales/man	Sales	Sales/man	Sales	Sales/man
Metals	399	90	100	100	195	195
Chemicals	145	70	100	100	42	171
Electronics (excl. computers)	119	78	100	100	164	137
Industrial and farm equipment	108	87	100	100	91	167
Petroleum refining	97	58	100	100	19	181
Food (excl. drink)	78	82	100	100	63	227
Aerospace[1]	47	114	100	100	—	—

[1] There were no Japanese aerospace corporations that made the Fortune 55 in 1991.

Source: Fortune, 29 July 1991, pp. 71–84. Authors' own calculations.

not entirely) by an upsurge in merger and acquisition activity and prompted in part by this desire to foster national industrial champions.[5] In his survey of the UK, Leslie Hannah found that between 1960–9 some 5,635 firms disappeared as a consequence of merger activity. This compares with a figure of only 5,468 for the entire period 1900–59.[6] Today, the largest European firms are of a comparable size with those in the US and both are typically larger than those of Japan. This point is illustrated in Table 11.1, which, using data drawn from *Fortune* magazine's 1991 'International 500', compares the sales differentials of some of the world's largest corporations in a variety of industrial sectors.[7] In the case of the metals sector, for example, the total sales of Europe's 5 largest firms comes to nearly four times the total of their 5 largest American rivals and two times the figure of the Japanese. The same table shows that EC firms compare favourably in terms of size in the chemicals, electronics, industrial and farm equipment, and the petroleum refining sectors as well. Of the surveyed industries, only in the food, motor, and aerospace sectors were EC national champions detectably smaller than their US counterparts and only in the electronics sector were they smaller than the Japanese. This picture is reinforced in Table 11.2. Surveying the five largest corporations in some 21 different industrial sectors, it was found that 36 per cent of them were Community firms compared to 35 per cent for the US and only 18 per cent Japan.[8] EC strength was particularly evident in building materials, chemicals, metals, mining, and petroleum refining where the majority of the top 5 global corporations were Community in origin. There are two causes for concern, however. The first is that those industrial sectors where EC firms are underrepresented globally—aerospace, electronics, engineering, computers, and pharmaceuticals—are those very sectors which are technologically advanced and require a high R&D content and which have the greatest potential for growth in the near future. The second is the degree to which ownership of the 38 firms listed in Table 11.2 is concentrated in just four Northern European countries: the UK, Germany, France, and the Netherlands. Between them these countries account for 30 of the 38.

As a consequence of national industrial policy in Europe since the 1960s, the concentration of the region's industry has increased markedly. Hannah and Kay found that between 1953 and 1978, the share of the largest 100 firms in net UK manufacturing output

TABLE 11.2. *Regional share of the world's top five corporations in a range of industrial sectors, 1990*

Industrial sector	Top 5 corporations			
	EC	US	Japan	Other
Aerospace	1	4	—	—
Beverages	2	3	—	—
Building materials	4	1	—	—
Chemicals	4	1	—	—
Computers (incl. office equipment)	—	3	2	—
Electronics	1	1	2	1
Food	1	3	—	1
Forest products	—	3	—	2
Industrial and farm equipment	1	2	1	1
Metal products	2	—	2	1
Metals	4	—	1	—
Mining, crude oil production	5	—	—	—
Motor vehicles and parts	2	2	1	—
Petroleum refining	3	2	—	—
Pharmaceuticals	1	2	—	1
Publishing, printing	2	—	2	1
Rubber and plastics products	2	1	2	—
Scientific and photographic equipment	—	4	1	—
Soaps and cosmetics	1	2	1	1
Textiles	—	—	3	2
Tobacco	2	2	1	—
Total (no.)	38	37	19	11
(% total)	36	35	18	11

Source: Compiled by authors from *Fortune*, 29 July 1991, pp. 71–84.

rose from 26 per cent to 41 per cent. A similar trend is found in Europe as a whole, where the sales of the 50 largest European firms as a percentage of industrial output increased from 15 per cent in 1965 to 25 per cent in 1976.[9] Yet the evidence presented by Geroski and Jacquemin suggests that the policy of the 1960s was somewhat misconceived. It appears that the trade-off between the efficiency gains from scale were less favourable than had been supposed and the costs of increased market concentration were greatly underestimated.

Table 11.1 also shows that while some of Europe's largest firms compare favourably with their chief non-EC competitors in terms of size, they compare badly in terms of their levels of labour productivity (an admittedly crude measure of corporate efficiency). In six of the seven sectors analysed, the labour productivity of the largest US corporations was ahead of that of Community firms. EC performance was particularly poor in petroleum exploration and refining, where productivity was only 58 per cent of the US figure. In food it was 61 per cent, in chemicals 70 per cent, and in electronics 78 per cent. Only in aerospace were European firms more efficient than their US competitors; and if the record of Europe's national champions is set against that of the comparatively much smaller Japanese firms, then the lag in labour productivity becomes very substantial indeed.

Evidence that there is no firm link between scale and the level of productivity comes from a variety of sources. One source is a study conducted by Prais comparing international competitiveness in Britain, Germany, and the US.[10] Prais found that efficiency was not necessarily the result of the size of enterprises but might chiefly be explained by differences in labour relations, training, and the availability of skilled workers. Britain was the least efficient of the economies under study but had, on average, the larger plants.[11] Large establishments, it was suggested, tended to give rise to considerable problems in industrial relations because working conditions become authoritarian and regimented, leading to employee alienation. This is reflected in high levels of industrial action and absenteeism. Prais showed that strikes tend to grow exponentially with plant size. Between 1971–3 less than 1 per cent of plants employing 100 people or less suffered from strike action in the UK. This compared to 25.2 per cent for plants employing 1,000–1,999 people; 44 per cent for plants employing 2,000–4,999 people; and 75.8 per cent for plants that employed 5,000 or more. He cited the UK motor vehicle and steel industries, where plants with 10,000–30,000 employees were not untypical, as examples of industries where difficult labour relations played a significant role in hampering efficiency.[12]

Another strand of criticism of the efficiency gains to be had from large firms comes from Jacquemin and de Jong and relates to the claim that large firms tend to innovate more than their smaller counterparts.[13] They found that many innovations originate in enterprises with less than 1,000 employees, despite their much smaller share of R&D expenditures. Another study, focusing on the experience of the UK, showed that in 1975 firms employing 1,000 or more accounted for some 96.7 per cent of gross R&D expenditure, but were only responsible for some 65.9 per cent of innovations during that decade.[14] Whilst the evidence is incomplete, not least because it cannot take account of the relative importance of innovations coming from large or small firms, it does suggest that the link between firm size and innovation is not clear-cut.

This scepticism about the advantages of scale are apparently reinforced by studies of the efficiency gains from mergers which have shown that these have often been disappointing. One particularly interesting study about the economic consequences of takeovers was carried out by Ravenscraft and Scherer.[15] This analysed the profitability of enterprises acquired as a result of so-called 'white knight' rescues. It found that target companies' pre-tender profitability averaged 0.97 per cent below industry averages. Nine years after takeover however, it was found that acquired lines of business operated 3.10 per cent below those of non-tender lines. Most of this post-takeover profit decline was found to be a consequence of asset value writeups and there was no evidence that acquirers improved the profitability of the firms they had claimed to have rescued. An important pointer to some of the potential consequences of 1992.

A different line of criticism has been developed by Michael Piore and Charles Sabel who have argued that from the point of view of competitiveness, the importance of scale is secondary to the much more relevant factor of the mode of corporate organization.[16] They claim that the present deterioration in economic performance common to most industrial countries (compared to the historically unprecedented levels of growth enjoyed between 1950 and 1973), may be directly attributed to the model of industrial development founded on the principle of mass production, with its use of special-purpose machines and large numbers of semi-skilled workers to produce standardized goods. That is precisely the model that has served as the basis for the organization of many of Europe's national champions. They advocate a return to a more flexible, craft-based mode of production and support their argument with evidence taken from a range of industries over a large number of countries. A case in point is IBM and the computer industry.[17] In the early 1960s, using the principle developed by Henry Ford with his Model T, IBM sought to make a single product, the IBM 360, that would integrate the whole market and open the way to the economies of mass production. However, the fragmentation of demand as the market matured meant that it proved impossible to maintain this position. Other producers were able to supply substitutes for 'pieces of the 360 bundle' which were cheaper, more technologically advanced, and better suited to particular uses. By the late 1970s IBM had turned its strategy on its head. Instead of supplying a mass, single, self-contained system that made it hard to attach competitors' components, IBM designed its home computer so that all producers could attach their equipment to it. The lesson from recent history therefore is that it is not sufficient to maximize scale but that firms must be flexible to changes in market conditions.

Not only have the potential efficiency gains to be achieved from scale been shown to be exaggerated by the experiences of the 1960s; it also appears that the costs (particularly those that arise from merger) were underestimated as well. In the post-war period, these costs may have been as high as 7 per cent of GDP for France and the UK, but in any case they certainly exceeded the 1 per cent estimator on which policy decisions of the 1960s were based.[18]

National super-firms therefore did not give rise to a new competitive efficiency in Europe but arguably led to the creation of a group of firms with sufficient market power to be substantially insulated from the forces of the market. As Geroski and Jacquemin put it, 'the policy may have left Europe with a population of sleepy industrial giants who were ill-equipped to meet the challenge of the 1970s and 1980s'.[19] The challenge has taken the form of a series of shocks that have buffeted the European economy since the early 1970s. The most obvious were the two oil price rises of 1973 and 1980 which led to substantial changes in the real price of an essential commodity and generated stagflation. Perhaps of more importance, however, have been the considerable changes in comparative advantage (for example in steel, shipbuilding, and textiles) caused by the emergence of the NICs (newly industrialized countries) in a number of traditional sectors, and the rapid technological advances in a number of others (particularly electronics and computers). These developments have had a global impact, but EC firms have been slow to adjust to their implications in comparison with their US and Japanese counterparts.[20]

EC firms have been comparatively slow to take advantage of new technologies as they have become available. This has led a number of commentators to talk of a technology gap developing between Europe and both the US and Japan.[21] The average age of manufacturing capital in the EC exceeds both that found in the US and Japan—a point illustrated graphically in Table 11.3.[22] In 1965 some 41.8 per cent of real gross capital stock in Germany, Italy, France, and UK was aged five years or less. By 1983 the total had fallen below 30 per cent. During the same period the percentage of real gross stock aged five years or less in the US rose from 40.7 per cent to 45.5 per cent. Only in Germany did the age of capital stock approximate that of the US. This uniquely good performance of Germany among the major EC countries is further illustrated in a survey of R&D expenditures carried out by Patel and Pavitt, who found that by the mid-1980s the Federal Republic was spending a greater proportion of its industrial output in this area than both Japan and the US. In 1985 Germany spent 2.42 per cent on R&D, compared to 2.32 per cent for the US, 2.11 per cent for Japan, and only 1.35 per cent for Western Europe as a whole. However, even German firms which are competitive in many sec-

TABLE 11.3. *Vintage of real gross capital stock in major European manufacturing countries and US, 1965–83*

Country	% share of assets aged 5 years or less			
	1965	1970	1975	1983
West Germany	49.5	45.9	41.5	39.2
Italy	42.4	34.7	36.5	27.9
France	46.4	44.4	41.8	33.8
UK	29.0	28.9	24.8	18.7
(Mean EC4)	(41.8)	(38.5)	(36.2)	(29.9)
US	40.7	47.6	43.2	45.5

Source: Cutler *et al.*, *The Struggle for Europe* (New York, 1989), 125.

tors, particularly chemicals and mechanical engineering, have failed to keep pace with the technological threshold in electronics and electrical engineering. Lags here are crucial since the application of microprocessor technologies is vital to competitiveness across all sectors.[23]

Thus there is some reason to fear that the technological stock of the EC is becoming increasingly obsolete and concentrated in medium-tech industries. This is perhaps reflected in the export performance of Europe's high-tech industries. Between 1970–85, the share of total EC exports accounted for by such goods has increased by less that 1 per cent while their share of imports rose by over 2 per cent.[24] Data collected by the Commission shows that by the 1980s EC exports were becoming increasingly concentrated in medium-tech goods in which the major competitors are the newly industrialized countries, not the high-tech goods exported by Japan.

Despite the patchy experience of the 1960s, the Commission has not lost faith in the concept of super-firms. Rather, in its attempts to complete the Internal Market, it seeks to change the environment in which they operate, thus linking the notions of competition and innovation. The existence of entry and exit barriers it is claimed can seriously reduce corporate flexibility and impede the incentives and pressures of market selection. Entry is important as both a disciplinary and innovatory force. As a discipline it is supposed to act to eradicate the abnormal profits that 'price setting' monopolists are able to enjoy, forcing such firms to minimize their costs. With respect to innovation, freedom of entry is supposed to generate new ideas, a consequence of the challenge of new competitors to which the incumbents must respond. At the same time it is argued that restrictions on the contraction and exit of unsuccessful firms have not only made them flabby but, also, impeded the progress of the new firms. This has become a cornerstone of EC industrial policy. For the Commission, the European market has been particularly affected by barriers which impede the entry and exit of firms. Motivated by their desire to foster and protect national champions and defend employment levels, member states have retarded the development of trade through the use of a series of tariff and (as these gradually disappeared) non-tariff barriers. A wide range of anti-competitive initiatives such as national product standards have played a major role in reducing the substitutability between products from different countries, increasing costs and distorting patterns of production and trade.[25] It is not therefore that super-firms do not work, according to the Commission. Rather, in some sectors, EC firms are not big enough nor do they operate in an environment which makes them sufficiently flexible and responsive to change.

The completion of the Single European Market is therefore expected to have a substantial impact on the competitive environment of European industry. Nearly half of the benefits expected from removing non-tariff barriers are anticipated to come from economies of scale and most of these from a new round of industrial restructuring. Merger and acquisition activity is likely to play a significant part in this process, as the Commission uses competition and market entry policy as a tool to create 'European', as opposed to 'national', champion firms.

2. THE THEORY OF MERGERS AND ACQUISITIONS: EFFICIENCY GAINS VERSUS MONOPOLY COSTS

Mergers and acquisitions, however, constitute only one of the strategies that firms may employ as they restructure to meet the threat of increased competition in the post-1992 environment. Before we examine the Commission's approach to mergers and takeovers, we shall briefly explain that they are likely to be so important after 1992 because it is not clear that firms, in the absence of an effective EC industrial policy, will necessarily behave in exactly the way the EC wishes they should in an open market.

The process of restructuring can involve rationalization within companies; the pooling of resources between firms in the form of joint ventures; and, more permanently, mergers and acquisitions. Internal rationalization is the process by which firms concentrate on their core activities, while at the same time trying to extend the geographical scope of them. It follows a trend begun by US firms and is supported by studies which demonstrate that profitability tends to be greatest in the main activities of firms. An article on the strategies available to firms in the Single Market cites the example of the agri-food business as one where a similar pattern of concentration and consolidation is occurring in the EC.[26] BSN of France, for example, progressively abandoned non-core activities before establishing itself in Italy and Spain in the mineral water industry (it was already the product leader in France). Similarly, Ferruzzi, the leading Italian sugar manufacturer, has extended the scope of its operations to other EC member states, specifically to France, Germany, and the UK. The European chemical industry is another useful example.[27] Many firms, however, reject internal strategies for growth in favour of external growth by merger and acquisition. The latter approach offers a number of advantages to the firm. In the first instance they obtain assets that are already working and which offer the prospect of a quick return. Second, acquisition of a competitor automatically increases the acquirer's market share and enlarges its markets, without creating additional capacity for which there might be no demand. Finally, with the integration of European markets after 1992, the merger and acquisition option also allows the firm to enter new geographical and product markets quickly, in order to exploit first mover advantage.

Mergers and acquisitions seem to be preferred to less permanent forms of external restructuring like joint ventures.[28] Whilst joint ventures promote synergies, avoid costly R&D duplication, and ensure that risks are shared, critics argue that they are often costly and cumbersome to set up and administer, that they dissipate profit streams, and, most importantly, they may erode a firm's longer-term competitive advantage by giving potential rivals access to valuable technical knowledge. Neil Kay suggests that the post-war evolution of the Japanese economy provides firms with a caution-ary lesson as to the intrinsic dangers associated with technological collaboration. Technological agreements with overseas partners, especially US firms, gave Japanese firms invaluable access to West-ern technologies after World War II. In the absence of effective barriers to imports and inward direct investment created by Japan, Western firms would have preferred to have obtained access to the Japanese market through exports or direct investment. Although the pattern of EC joint venture activity will be covered more fully in the next section, it is worth noting here that European experience tends to support Kay's reservations. Although the total number of joint ventures has risen since the publication of the Commission's White Paper, this activity tends to be concentrated in a few high-tech sectors (chemicals, electronics, office machinery, etc.). Interest-ingly, for our general conclusions, however, there tends to be a preference for joint ventures by EC firms in these industries to be with US and Japanese rather than other European firms.[29]

For the reasons already outlined, therefore, industrial restructuring—in so far as it does occur in the key industries as a consequence of 1992—is likely to proceed through an increase in European-wide merger and acquisition activity and in joint ventures with non-EC firms. For the Commission, its willingness to contemplate and even encourage this activity suggests three things. First, that the policy of encouraging national champions, so prevalent during the 1960s, did not eliminate all the transatlantic size differentials, and there is a belief in the need for 'European champions'. Second, in some areas where it failed to do so, increasing the size of Europe's firms may be able to deliver substantial efficiency gains. Third, these efficiency gains will be sufficient to outweigh the risks associated with greater market concentration. The Commission, however, is aware of some of the shortcomings of a policy aimed at fostering market concentration, especially where it is not supported by a strong competition policy. As a result, in 1989, it sponsored a study into the potential benefits of horizontal mergers which sought to develop a series of indicators that might be used to make a preliminary classification of European industries into those in which mergers—and thus concentration—are likely to have on balance beneficial effects, and those in which the overall effect is likely to be negative.[30] Four indicators were proffered: two which help to identify the industries in which the danger of a reduction in competition, with its attendant monopoly costs, are high; two in which a further concentration might produce efficiency gains.

The first of these indicators is the level of demand growth which is seen as a measure of the stage of the life-cycle of the industry. The danger of reduced competition is assumed to be greater in mature or declining industries, since in such industries firms will be eager to increase their market share to compensate for the slowing in growth. Those already in these markets, it is believed, will vigorously defend their position from the threat of new entrants, using the advantages of experience, long-standing relation with customers etc., conferred by their incumbency. Conversely, in new and rapidly expanding industries, the danger of reduced competition is held to be less. This is because a growing market attracts many new entrants acting on the perception that high profits are to be made. At the same time entry is relatively easy since incumbents do not as yet enjoy the same advantages that are to be found in old markets in terms of cost, experience, reputation etc. The second test employed to assess the threat to competition from mergers is related to the degree to which the market is subject to import penetration from countries outside the EC and particularly from the US and Japan. An industry might be highly concentrated, but this is not always a certain guide to the amount of monopoly power held by its leading firms. It is assumed that the danger of reduced competition in the EC is greater in those industries relatively closed to international competition, whether it comes from EC or non-EC sources.

Against the two measures used to assess the threat of monopolistic or oligopolistic costs, are two others used to assess the potential for efficiency gains. The first of these, the scope for economies of scale, has already been discussed. The second is the level of technological content. Mergers, it is argued, will probably be beneficial in those sectors which are highly R&D intensive, which have a certain minimum threshold scale of operation before the cost of research programmes can be recovered. Without link-ups between EC firms (in whatever form) in a range of high-tech industries, the Commission feels, European companies will be put at a severe disadvantage *vis-à-vis* their US and Japanese competitors, who enjoy large home markets in which to spread the costs of product development.[31]

These four indicators are then used by the economists to compose two classification matrices. The first combines the first two criteria and allows industries to be classified into two broad categories. First, those in which there is a danger of a reduction of competition: mature or declining industries relatively closed to trade. Second, those in which there is less apparent danger of competition, because they show strong growth or because they are relatively open to trade. The second matrix links the last two indicators and denotes those industries in which further concentration is likely to produce efficiency gains. These industries are highly technology intensive, and/or in them there are substantial economies of scale to be won. The results of these two matrices are combined in a fashion which allows industries to be classified into the four groups shown in Figure 11.1.

Group 1 is comprised of industries where it is believed that mergers bring with them the threat of reduced competition and at

LOW   HIGH

Group 1
Industries in which mergers offer little or no
prospect of efficiency gains and in which there
is a danger of reduction of competition.

- Metal goods
- Paints and varnishes
- Furniture
- Paper goods
- Rubber goods
- Tobacco
- Building materials

Group 4
Industries in which mergers are likely
simultaneously to produce efficiency
and to present a danger of a reduction of
competition.

- Cables and heavy electrical plant
- Railway equipment
- Shipbuilding
- Some food industries
- Beer
- Boilermaking

Group 2
Industries in which mergers offer little or no
prospect of efficiency gains and in which there
is little danger of reduction of competition.

- Steel
- Industrial and agricultural machinery
- Clothing and textiles
- Sawn and processed wood and related products
- Pulp, paper, and board
- Jewellery, toys, musical instruments

Group 3
Industries in which mergers offer prospects
of efficiency gains and do not present a
danger of reduction of competition.

- Advanced materials
- Chemicals/pharmaceuticals
- Computers/office automation
- Telecommunications and electronics
- Motor vehicles
- Aerospace
- Scientific instruments

HIGH   LOW
DANGER OF REDUCTION OF

FIG. 11.1 *Classification and location of industrial sectors into the Commission's groups*

Source: European Economy, no. 40, May 1989, pp. 26–32.

the same time little promise of efficiency gain. Some of the industries, like mining, have declined because the market is being eroded by competition from other materials or technologies (for example plastics are replacing sheet steel in household electrical appliances). Some other industries are mature, with a production technology that is already widely diffused. Here there are few potential efficiency gains to come from a further round of concentration. At the same time the competition faced from imports is generally low and typically less than the average for EC industry as a whole. The Commission sees little justification for merger in these sectors therefore. Group 2 industries offer few efficiency gains from merger but, unlike the first, pose little danger of monopoly costs. As with Group 1 they include industries in the mature or declining stage of their life-cycle, like steel and textiles for example, where there has already been substantial restructuring at a European level. Also in these industries the largest EC firms are at least as big as, and often bigger than, their US and Japanese counterparts. If there are efficiency gains to be had in these industries, it is suggested, rather as Piore and Sabel advocate, they are more likely to come through the introduction of flexible production techniques or through targeting of high value added niche markets, not through greater market concentration. At the same time many of the industries in Group 2 are largely open to competition from EC and non-EC producers (hence much of restructuring has already taken place) so that while mergers present no significant danger, little gain should be expected to come from them also.

In Group 4 the pressure for mergers is likely to be strong. It includes a number of industries that might expect to be greatly affected by 1992 because their markets are at present highly fragmented by the non-tariff barriers that are in the process of being dismantled by the Commission's initiatives. Many of these industries—such as heavy electrical plant and railway equipment—mainly serve public sector markets. Hitherto they have been sheltered from competition by member governments each of which has sought to support its own national champion through the partisan use of its procurement policy. Consequently, intra-EC trade is low and the number of European producers is much higher than in the US. EC firms are as a result much less efficient. At the same time there is also the danger of monopoly. These markets are already quite concentrated, and the industries mature with only limited scope for technological change—conditions ideal for the development of oligopolistic practice between firms. In a number of them also (railway equipment, for example), 1992 will do little to address the important technical barriers that have traditionally separated EC markets. A round of EC concentration may therefore simply lead to a shift of ownership patterns in this industry without leading to a fundamental rationalization of productive capacity.[32]

The Commission itself accepts that the only group where there is a clear case for an intensification of merger activity is Group 3. Demand in many of these industries is strong and growing rapidly, leading to a greater uncertainty about firms' market positions than was the case in Group 4. In these industries competition is on a world scale, as shown by the high levels of import penetration. At the same time, because these industries are passing through a phase of development in which innovation is important, R&D expenditures are higher, and the case for efficiency gains from greater scale is strong. Included in this group are many of the EC's high-tech industries: computers, telecommunications, electronics, and aerospace.[33]

This is the model at which the Commission aimed. How has EC merger and acquisition activity matched up to what was anticipated?

3. EUROPEAN MERGERS AND ACQUISITIONS SINCE 1985

Making sense of merger and acquisition activity in the EC, and in particular comparing the level in one country with that in another is, as the Commission notes, fraught with difficulty.[34] In the first instance there is a definitional problem. Even if it is accepted that a merger or acquisition has taken place if one company takes more than 50 per cent of another's share capital, how is one to assess a case where a company that acquired 30 per cent of another five years ago now acquires an additional 21 per cent? Then again it is not always easy to track such takeovers. No member state in the EC systematically monitors all takeovers. In the UK, which has a large number of publicly quoted corporations, attracting a great deal of media interest, the picture is likely to be clearer than in Germany,

where medium-sized privately owned companies, with no obligation to inform the general public of their activities, predominate.
Additionally, cross-country comparisons of the level of takeover
activity must be related to the size of an economy. Obviously, there
will be more takeovers in France than in Luxembourg. It is with
these caveats in mind that the information that follows should be
assessed.

According to the Commission's own data, based on the operation of the 1,000 largest firms in the EC, the total number of
mergers in industry has increased rapidly since the intention was
announced to complete the Internal Market. The totals rose from
117 in 1982/3 to 303 in 1986/7 (after the publication of the White
Paper), 383 in 1987/8, 492 in 1988/9, and 662 in 1989/90.[35] This
upwards trend is also evident for minority acquisitions and the level
of joint venture activity. In 1986/7 there were 117 acquisitions of
minority holdings. This rose to 118 in 1987/8, 159 in 1988/9, and
180 in 1989/90.[36] For joint ventures the totals increased from 90 in
1986/7 to 111 in 1987/8, 129 in 1988/9, and 156 in 1989/90.[37] As
the paper predicted earlier (despite sectoral variation) there was a
marked preference for merger and acquisition over joint venture
among firms as the best means to restructure their activities externally in the run-up to 1992. This is revealed in Table 11.4, which
compares the 'aversion ratios' (arrived at by dividing the number of
mergers by the number of joint ventures) for a whole range of
sectors. The data shows two things. First, firms are more likely to
opt for joint ventures as opposed to mergers in the high-tech
industries like chemicals, computers, electrical, electronic, and
mechanical engineering. Among the EC's top 1,000 companies, the
aversion ratio for these industries was 3.8 as compared to 6.4 for
the rest. At the extremes of this observation lie electronic engineering (2.7) and computers (1.2) on the one hand, and food and drink
(11.0) and extractive industries (11.7) on the other. The second
thing to note is that the preference for joint venture grows with the
degree of internationalism. Firms looking for fellow nationals as
partners are more likely to opt for merger (6.0 times for high-tech
and 8.7 for other industries) than are firms looking for EC firms to
join up with (5.9 times for high-tech and 5.7 for other industries).
What is especially clear is that firms looking for an international
collaborator are significantly more likely to select a non-EC col-

TABLE 11.4. *Community aversion ratios for industry, by sector and domain (1986–90)*

Industrial sector	National	EC	International	Total
Food and drink	13.2	16.1	4.8	11.0
Chemicals, glass, and rubber	6.2	9.1	1.8	4.8
Electrical and electronic engineering	6.5	2.7	0.9	2.7
Mechanical engineering	5.5	9.8	2.3	4.8
Computers and data-processing	3.7	0.8	0.5	1.2
Metals and metal goods	6.8	4.3	2.3	4.9
Vehicles and transport equipment	5.0	1.9	3.0	3.0
Paper and wood products	8.8	6.9	5.8	7.5
Extractive industries	11.2	12.0	14.0	11.7
Textiles	15.3	5.8	2.3	7.6
Construction	11.0	8.7	3.0	8.7
Other manufacturing	4.25	1.3	2.0	2.7
High tech total (chemicals & electrical & computers & mechanical engineering)	6.0	5.9	1.4	3.8
Total (excluding high tech)	8.7	5.7	3.6	6.4

Source: Data taken from the Commission's 20th Report on Competition Policy. The calculations are the authors' own.

laborator if they opt for joint venture in a high-tech sector. The aversion ratio among this group falls right down to 1.4, as the earlier discussion suggested might be the case.

Despite this finding, the Commission would suggest that the general upward trend of merger and acquisition activity is a clear indication that their Single Market Initiative was working and that European industry was restructuring in the run-up to 1992. As evidence in support of their claim, they would also point to the increasing number of cross-border deals (the restructuring of the 1960s occurred principally at a national level). The breakdown of national to EC to international mergers ran as follows in

1983/4: 65.2 per cent to 18.7 per cent to 16.1 per cent (as measured by number). By 1988/9 however, some 40 per cent of mergers and acquisitions among the 1,000 largest EC industrial firms were accounted for by agreements between firms of two (or more) EC member states. The total level of purely national mergers and acquisitions in the sample has fallen by 17.8 per cent to 47.4 per cent. In the UK, whose companies top the list of EC acquiring nations, in 1989 some 40 per cent of cross-border deals were within the EC as compared with only 20 per cent as recently as 1986. Moreover, 1989 was the first year that the number of takeovers by UK companies of EC competitors exceeded the number in the US.

A detailed breakdown by sectors, however, shows a more ambiguous picture of the proportion of mergers now accounted for by cross-border EC deals (see Table 11.5). The upsurge in cross-border deals was found to be much more likely in the chemicals, transport equipment, construction, electronics, and computer sectors. In the period 1986–90 the majority of mergers, acquisitions and joint ventures for textiles, mechanical engineering, metals, extraction, and paper remained purely national affairs. In those sectors where the majority of deals were cross-border in character, a sizeable number of companies (particularly in the high-tech sectors) looked for partners outside of the EC. In computers, for example, 36.4 per cent of all sampled collaborative activity was undertaken by an EC firm looking for a non-EC partner (be it national or non-national EC). The figure for electronics was 26.2 per cent. These two figures are set against an industry-wide mean of 18.6 per cent. The proportion of cross-border EC deals for these two sectors was only 21.2 per cent and 25.3 per cent respectively. These figures again compare with an industry-wide mean of 32.4 per cent. Of the key high-tech (Group 3) sectors, only in chemicals was there a marked preference among EC firms to look to Europe for firms with which to collaborate. The difference between the attitude of chemicals firms on the one hand and electronics and computer firms on the other is no doubt in part explained by the global dominance of EC producers in the chemicals industry. Four of the top five chemicals companies (the German troika of Bayer-Hoechst-BASF and the UK's ICI) are Community companies. Internationally the relative position of the EC's computer and electronics companies is much weaker.

TABLE 11.5. *Comparison of sectoral merger differentials from the mean across domains*

National		EC		International	
Sector	% deviation from mean	Sector	% deviation from mean	Sector	% deviation from mean
Textiles	+8.0	Chemical	+8.3	Computers	+17.8
Mechanical eng.	+5.9	Transport	+7.0	Electronics	+7.3
Metals	+5.6	construction	+6.6	Other	+7.3
Other	+5.3	Food	+0.3	Chemical	+4.1
Extraction	+5.0	Metals	+0.2	Mechanical eng.	+1.1
Construction	+4.8	**Industry mean**	**32.4**	**Industry mean**	**18.6**
Paper	+2.6	Paper	−0.6	Transport	−0.6
Food	+0.9	Textiles	−1.0	Paper	−2.0
Industry mean	**49.0**	Mechanical eng.	−7.0	Food	−2.1
Electronics	−0.5	Electronics	−7.1	Extraction	−5.4
Transport	−6.4	Extraction	−9.6	Metals	−5.8
Computers	−6.6	Computers	−11.2	Textiles	−7.0
Chemical	−12.4	Other	−12.6	Construction	−1.4

Source: data taken from the Commission's 20th Report on Competition Policy. The calculations are the authors' own.

Having established that with the provisions outlined above there has been a marked upwards trend in the different forms of industrial collaboration (be they merger, acquisition or joint venture) and that there is also a growing trend for this collaboration to be pan-European in scope, what implications does this have for the general efficiency of the region's industry? Is the concentration of merger and acquisition activity in those sectors that the Commission's model suggests likely to deliver the greatest efficiency gains for Europe's economy? In those key sectors, how widespread is the restructuring among EC member states? Is the restructuring through merger and acquisition universal or confined to just a few countries?

The evidence suggests that a significant proportion of the cross-border deals (involving both majority and minority acquisitions) has occurred in those industries in which the Commission's model argues there is a strong case for greater market concentration: Group 3 industries. Using data on cross-border merger activity taken from the *European Deal Review* we have tried to assess the level of activity in each of the Commission's four groups. This meant disaggregating data for some 14 out of a possible 23 categories covered by the survey.[38] Together these 14 categories accounted for two-thirds of all cross-border merger activity for the period 1989/90. This means that services (which accounted for 25.3 per cent of the EC's total) and other industries (8.7 per cent) were not placed in any of the Commission's four groups. In the case of services, they were excluded because the model was not designed to accommodate them, while in the case of the other industries they were not included because it was difficult to categorize them with any degree of certainty. The results of this process are summarized in Figure 11.2.

The level of cross-border deal activity was low in those sectors in which mergers were believed to offer little or no prospect for efficiency gain while at the same time posing the greatest danger of reduced competition. Group 1 industries accounted for 18.5 per cent of the surveyed total (paper, 10.4 per cent; construction, 7.6 per cent; and tobacco, 0.5 per cent). Activity was also low for Group 2 industries, which while not being particularly vulnerable to significant reductions in competition, offer little hope of efficiency gains from further economies of scale. Activity in this group came to 16.3 per cent of the EC total (oil and gas, 2.5 per

Group 1		Group 4	
Industry	%	Industry	%
Paper	10.4	Food	11.5
Construction	7.6	Drinks	3.1
Tobacco	0.5	Engineering	10.3
Total	18.5	Total	24.9
Group 2		**Group 3**	
Industry	%	Industry	%
Oil and Gas	2.5	Electronics	15.4
Fashion and Textiles	4.5	Pharmaceuticals	6.7
Mining and Steel	5.1	Chemicals	8.4
Packaging	4.2	Automotive and Aircraft	9.8
Total	16.3	Total	40.3

FIG. 11.2. *Merger and acquisition activity (majority and minority) in Europe, 1989–90, according to the Commission's 4 classification groups (% shares)*

Source: data taken from the *European Deal Review* 1990. Authors' own calculations.

cent; fashion and textiles, 4.5 per cent; mining and steel, 5.1 per cent; and packaging, 4.2 per cent). Activity in Group 4 industries (food, drink, and engineering) which might enjoy substantial efficiency benefits from a further round of concentration but which also are vulnerable to monopolistic practice, was significant during 1989 and 1990. Together cross-border deals in this group accounted for nearly a quarter of the total.

This means that those industries which stand most to benefit from a round of merger activity—electronics, computers, chemicals, automotive, and aerospace—are clearly those industries which experienced the highest level of cross-border deals over the period: some 40.3 per cent of the surveyed total in fact. This is clearly an encouraging sign from the Commission's point of view. Slightly less encouraging, however, is the degree to which activity of just a few member states—both in terms of which countries' corporations are acquiring and which are being targeted—accounts for the vast majority of external forms of restructuring (see Table 11.6).

Over the period 1989–90 the top five acquiring EC nations accounted for 71.27 per cent of all cross-border merger and acquisition deals in Western Europe in the electronics and computers

TABLE 11.6. *Acquisitions and mergers by national corporate location*

Acquiring and target nations	Sector			
	Electronics %	Pharm. %	Chemicals %	Auto./Aircr. %
EC acquirers				
France	17.62	15.23	12.08	11.63
Germany		13.74	17.16	17.56
Netherlands	6.66			
UK	19.39	16.56	15.31	13.33
Non-EC acquirers				
Japan				13.66
Sweden		11.59		
Switzerland	10.92		10.56	
USA	16.68	17.80	14.32	13.61
Total	71.27	74.92	69.43	69.79
EC Targets				
France	11.53	15.73	15.84	12.54
Germany	22.52	15.73	15.18	17.00
Italy	7.57	13.66	1749.00	7.96
Spain	6.85	11.59	7.92	11.91
UK	18.09	13.49	12.87	25.18
Total	66.56	70.20	69.30	74.59

Source: data taken from the *European Deal Review* 1990. Authors' own calculations.

sectors; 74.92 per cent in pharmaceuticals; 69.43 per cent in chemicals; and 69.79 per cent in the automotive and aerospace sectors. Only four EC countries—France, Germany, the Netherlands, and the UK—made significant numbers of acquisitions in the Group 3 high-tech sectors. A similar concentration among the acquiring nations is manifest when the sample of sectors is broadened to take in all deals in the region. Over the same period France, Germany, Italy, the Netherlands, and the UK on their own accounted for 88.65 per cent of all acquisitions in Europe. Indeed, France and the UK on their own accounted for 58.59 per cent. Also of concern to those wishing to see the emergence of pan-European corporations capable of competing globally was the level of foreign direct investment from the USA. In the same period the USA was the third largest acquirer in Europe, ahead of Germany and only behind France and the UK. It accounted for 16.68 per cent in electronics and computers, 18.39 per cent in engineering, 11.02 per cent in fashion and textiles, 10.38 per cent in food and food retailing, 17.82 per cent in oil and gas, 16.08 per cent in packaging, 14.85 per cent in airlines, shipping and freight, 14.32 per cent in chemicals and plastics, 18.94 per cent in paper, printing and advertising, and 17.8 per cent in pharmaceuticals. Significant Japanese investment seemed to be restricted to the leisure (10.72 per cent) and automotive/aerospace (13.66 per cent) sectors.

This pattern is repeated when a survey is made of target nations. Taken together, the UK, Germany, France, Spain, and Italy accounted for 78.66 per cent of all cross-border merger and acquisition deals in the EC. The UK, Germany, and France on their own accounted for 57.15 per cent of all deals. With respect to the Group 3 industries, the top five EC countries accounted for 66.56 per cent of all deals in electronics and computers: 70.2 per cent in pharmaceuticals: 69.3 per cent in chemicals; and 74.59 per cent in the automotive and aircraft sectors.

In the automotive and aircraft sectors over the period 1989–90 Germany, France, Italy, and the Netherlands were the chief EC acquirers but acquisitions by Japan and the US exceeded all but for those of Germany. The chief target for German companies was France, which accounted for 6 of the 14 deals that her corporations made.[39] France also proved a popular port of call for Italian firms which made five deals in the sector, including Fiat's 50 per cent acquisition of the car battery manufacturer CEAC. In the electronics and computer sectors France and the UK dominated among EC acquirers. French firms' favourite targets were in Belgium (6 deals), Italy (7 deals), Spain (8 deals), and the UK (6 deals). By far the largest of the deals during this period was the huge asset swap between Fiat and Alcatel-Alsthom, since this gave Alcatel-FACE (jointly owned by France and the US) a 75 per cent stake in the large Italian telecoms manufacturer, Telettra. The total cost of this element in what was a much broader transaction was 1.3 billion ECU. The UK's main targets in this sector were located in Germany and accounted for a third of her deals. Finally, in the chemicals and plastics sectors the main targets for acquirers were France and Italy (15 deals each) and Germany (14 deals). Germany and the UK, Europe's principal manufacturers in this sector, were the EC's chief acquirers (18 deals each).

4. CONCLUSIONS

It is clear from this brief survey of European joint venture, merger, and acquisition activity that the industrial policy of the EC is at a crossroads. This is because the EC has not been able to formulate an agreed interventionist industrial policy and has instead been forced to rely on competition and market entry to fashion more efficient EC firms. As Chapter 10 shows, there is a desire to increase the competitive efficiency of EC firms but a confusion over whether this should be achieved by means of an EC-led policy of supporting European champion firms (the French approach) or through the adoption of neo-liberal competition policies favoured by Sir Leon Brittan. Our evidence suggests that there is support for both viewpoints.

For those who favour deregulation and the ending of non-tariff barriers as the best mechanism to generate more efficient and competitive European champion firms in the world market, there is evidence that the post-1985 Internal Market is working. The Single Market initiative has assisted in an increase in the absolute number of intra-EC cross-border mergers and acquisitions and a relative decline in the number of purely national deals. At the same time these deals have largely taken place in those sectors in which the EC has felt there is the greatest scope for efficiency gains and the lowest prospects for monopoly costs. This is particularly true for chemicals, transport equipment, construction, electronics, and computers. On the other hand, there is also considerable evidence to support those who fear that the liberalization approach will lead to sub-optimal results for EC industrial policy.

If the intention of the Single Market initiative is to create an EC industrial structure broadly based on large, champion European firms to replace the existing smaller and less efficient national firms which are able to compete in world markets against US and Japanese firms, the current neo-liberal policy approach may not be successful. There are a number of reasons for this. First, while there is some evidence that pan-European mergers are taking place, this is primarily confined to those sectors previously indicated. In many other sectors—textiles, mechanical engineering, mining, metals, and paper—Europeanization is not replacing a primarily national approach to concentration and rationalization. The process of intra-EC merger activity is also primarily confined to the five largest

EC economies—Germany, France, the UK, Italy, and Spain. Furthermore, there is also evidence that the concentration of high technology and advanced industry is increasingly a northern European—UK, France, Germany, the Netherlands—phenomenon.

Finally, and perhaps of most significance, is the considerable evidence that the relatively open market entry rules in the Single Market are encouraging not so much the Europeanization but the internationalization of leading market sectors. We have mentioned examples of an increase in pan-European deals and concentration in some of the leading high technology and high potential growth sectors, which have always been desired by the Commission. However, there is also evidence that in many of these sectors—and in particular in motor vehicles, computers, and electronics—there is a tendency for the US and Japanese to be significant participants. The US is with France and the UK one of the top three deal making countries in Europe. This trend is reinforced by joint venture activity, with US and Japanese partners being significant in all sectors. All of this seems to indicate that the Single Market may be encouraging rationalization, but this may not be leading inexorably to the creation of European champions so much as to the further global concentration of ownership by major multinational companies and financial institutions (US, Japanese, and northern European) at the expense of marginalized and sub-optimal former national champions within the EC member states.

The consequence of these trends—which is clearly most marked in high technology, high growth potential sectors—could be problematic for the EC in the future. They seem to herald the further development of an industrially unbalanced Community and the creation of even larger, politically and economically uncontrollable, multinational firms. There is little doubt that these firms will increasingly be capable of challenging and shaping the economic and industrial policies of the Commission and the EC member states. They will also be best placed to take advantage of 'competition among rules'. This being the case, it would appear that the current regulatory and neo-liberal competition policy approach may well be unwittingly encouraging the development of a global economic leviathan which even a fully integrated and federal EC structure would be unable to control. This is another way of saying that the EC may have cause to think again about the political and economic benefits of a more interventionist and protectionist industrial policy, which aims at the development of truly European champions, once the results of its current approach become more apparent.

Notes

1. Paul A. Geroski and Alexis Jacquemin, 'Corporate Competitiveness in Europe', in *Economic Policy*, 1 (1985), 169–218.
2. Paolo Cecchini, *1992 The European Challenge: The Benefits of a Single Market* (Aldershot, 1992), 91–102.
3. A. Jaquemin, P. Buigues, and I. Fabienne, 'Horizontal Mergers and Competition Policy in the European Community', *European Economy*, 40 (Brussels, 1989).
4. Geroski and Jacquemin, 'Corporate Competitiveness', 172–5.
5. Ibid. 171–2.
6. Leslie Hannah, *The Rise of the Corporate Economy*, 2nd edn. (London, 1983), 167–78.
7. *Fortune*, 29 July 1991, pp. 71–84.
8. Ibid. 71–84.
9. Geroski and Jacquemin, 'Corporate Competitiveness', 172.
10. S. Prais, *Productivity and Industrial Structure* (Cambridge, 1981).
11. Ibid. 270.
12. Ibid. 59–82.
13. A. Jacquemin and H. de Jong, *European Industrial Organisation* (London, 1977).
14. Geroski and Jacquemin 'Corporate Competitiveness', 175.
15. David J. Ravenscraft and F. M. Scherer, 'Life after Takeover', *The Journal of Industrial Economics*, 36/2 (Dec. 1987), 147–56.
16. Michael J. Piore and Charles F. Sabel, *The Second Industrial Divide* (New York, 1984), 3–19.
17. Ibid. 202–4.
18. Geroski and Jacquemin, 'Corporate Competitiveness', 175.
19. Ibid.
20. Ibid. 176.
21. Margaret Sharpe, 'Technology and the Dynamics of Integration', in William Wallace (ed.), *The Dynamics of European Integration* (London, 1992), 50–68.
22. Tony Cutler *et al.*, *1992—The Struggle for Europe* (New York, 1989), 125.
23. Sharpe, 'Technology and the Dynamics of Integration', 53–7.
24. Geroski and Jacquemin, 'Corporate Competitiveness', 176.

25. Cecchini, 'The European Challenge', 24–31.
26. P. Buigues and A. Jacquemin, 'Strategies for Firms and Structural Environments in the Large Internal Market', *Journal of Common Market Studies*, 28/1 (Sept. 1989), 60.
27. Commission of the EC, *Panorama of EC Industry—1990* (Luxembourg, 1990), 39–41.
28. Neil Kay, 'Industrial Collaborative Activity and Competition in the Internal Market', *Journal of Common Market Studies*, 29/4 (June 1991), 346–62.
29. Commission of the EC (a), *XXth Report on Competition Policy* (Brussels, 1991), 231.
30. Jacquemin, Buiges, and Fabienne, 'Horizontal Mergers'.
31. Ibid. 24–8.
32. Ibid. 28–31.
33. Ibid. 29–30.
34. Commission of the EC (b), 'The Pattern of Recent Mergers and Acquisitions', in *Panorama of EC Industry—1991/2* (Brussels, 1991), 66.
35. Commission of the EC (a), p. 229.
36. Ibid. 230.
37. Ibid. 231.
38. Mark Dixon (ed.), *The European Deal Review* (London, 1990).
39. These acquisitions included the majority acquisition by MAN of the French transmissions manufacturer, Soc. Européenne d'Engrenages and Metallgeschaft's buy-out of the automotive components manufacturer Motorac.

Conclusion: The State and Major Enterprises in Western Europe: Enduring Complexities

VINCENT WRIGHT

This book has attempted to identify the factors which shape the relationship between four West European states and their major firms, in an attempt to discover whether or not that relationship has been changing under the impact of the 1980s and early 1990s.[1] The purpose of these concluding remarks is to address this issue by picking up some of the threads of the arguments deployed throughout the book and relating them to the introductory framework of Jack Hayward.

In his Introduction to this book Jack Hayward refers to five significant changes in the environment in which major European firms have operated: the loss of *de facto* monopoly or semi-monopoly, as foreign competition has permeated domestic markets; the increasing need of the firms to have recourse to the international capital markets; the growing requirement to be financially self-sustaining; the process of transnationalization in a variety of forms; the growing detachment from concepts of national interest and national identity. Yet Hayward's five changes require further elaboration and others (some of which are mentioned by Hayward later in his Introduction and by contributors throughout the book) need to be mentioned if the complex and shifting nature of the relationships between states and their major firms is satisfactorily to be explored. Factors that require some exploration include the rise of environmental concerns (giving rise to new national and transnational modes of regulation which lock states and firms into highly complex bargaining situations); changes in labour markets and labour relations, and their effects on existing policy networks as a result of their impact on trade unions; the changing management culture rooted traditionally in an emphasis on 'big is beautiful'. Six particular changes warrant especial attention: paradigm shift; definitional problems; the financial position of many big companies; Europeanization; globalization; hybridization. Many of these changes are, of course, interconnected, and disentangling cause and effect is far from easy. Many are also mutually reinforcing and are squeezing states into convergent responses. But convergence is far from complete, as pressures for change continue to be mediated through different politico-industrial cultures and institutions.

The first major change, not specifically mentioned by Hayward, was the change in the 1980s in the dominant macro-economic policy paradigm from Keynesianism to monetarism and neo-liberalism.[2] This paradigm shift was induced by structural changes in the international environment (stagflation, the decline of the USA as a financial stabilizer, growing interdependence, increasing trade competition from new nations, and by the accelerating impact of the European Community—which Hayward tends to play down), and it, in turn, triggered a breakdown or great strains in the postwar broad consensus between governments, business and labour, and the 'distributional coalitions', frequently corporatist in nature, which profited from that consensus. The new paradigm was propagated by a wide array of institutions and its adoption facilitated by significant domestic changes: the arrival of the Thatcher government in the United Kingdom in 1979; the traumatic economic U-turns of the French Socialist government in 1983–4; the economic consequence of the dramatic events in Germany in 1989–90; the collapse of the old political order in Italy after 1991. At the same time, the apologists of the established paradigm—state bureaucracies, trade unions, left-wing parties—were very much on the defensive. In other words, many of the institutional and political elements in which the Keynesian paradigm had been embedded were weakened in the four countries being studied in this book. Furthermore, changes within the state economic decision-making machinery flowed from and then enhanced the process of paradigm shift. Thus, almost everywhere in Western Europe, finance ministers increased their influence at the expense of more interventionist colleagues in industry and in regional development ministries. A further factor which contributed to the paradigm shift of the 1980s was the changing requirements of major firms—a point to which we will return.

Peter Gourevitch[3] has argued that governments have a variety of 'policy packages' from which to choose: neo-classical liberalism based on market forces; socialization and planning; protectionism; demand stimulus through deficit spending; mercantilism to aid specific industries and firms. For a variety of reasons it was the first of these policy packages which elicited the greatest support from increasingly internationalized companies which were certainly hostile to protectionism.[4] This is not to argue that a new coalition of multinationalized industrial and financial actors pressured reluctant governments into market-oriented strategies: rather they were pushing on an open door, because governments, for their own reasons, were espousing the cause of neo-liberalism. Other significant features and implications of the internationalization of industrial and financial circuits will be briefly raised later in this Conclusion.

A final factor which fed the process of paradigm shift in the 1980s was technological, the full ramifications of which cannot be underestimated.[5] Six strands of the technological revolution are worth specific mention, since they were clearly to impact upon state–firm relationships. The first was the contribution of technology to the opening up of the world's financial markets to major firms, whatever their location: liberalization and technological change were inextricably linked. Secondly, technology transformed some national natural monopolies into sectors susceptible to domestic and even international competition (telecommunications and electricity supply are good examples of sectors in which barriers have been lowered to entry), thus undermining one of the principal arguments in favour of public control. The third technological pressure concerned the changing nature of a 'strategic' industry in the perception of policy makers—a point to which we will return. Greater flexibility in the manufacturing process provides the fourth relevant technological factor. In the car industry, for instance, not only was the assembly line made more flexible, but design, marketing, and distribution could be devolved if it was more efficient to do so. It is now possible to envisage a car manufacturer that does not make any of its own cars, but which puts out to tender the various activities involved. Fifth, the very rapidity of technological change in certain industries (combined with com-

placent management) quickly tranformed several national champions into international lame ducks—the painful lesson of IBM and
of Philips. The high-tech world, with its fierce competition, lowering prices, frenetic innovations, and possible diseconomies of scale,
requires speedy and flexible decision-making processes—processes
often ill-suited to traditional state bureaucracies. Finally, in expanding high-tech sectors the growing fixed capital cost of R&D
and of capital equipment, as well as accelerating obsolescence, have
increased production risks and costs and have contributed to a
consolidation of oligopolistic structures. Corporate strategies are
more and more geared to entrenching domestic market positions,
the creation of regional core network strategies, and the penetration of new markets through mergers, joint ventures and acquisitions. This is a point which will be raised at greater length later in
this concluding chapter.

Explanations for the paradigm shift of the 1980s must be sought,
therefore, in the complex interaction of international, European
Union, and domestic pressures, and in the interplay of ideological,
financial, political, institutional, and technological elements. The
shift took place at a different time, to a different extent, and with
a differing degree of enthusiasm in each of the four countries
studied in this book. It was also legitimized by different discourses:
freedom and entrepreneurship in the United Kingdom; 'modernization' in France; 'preparing for the open market' in Italy (and Spain
and Portugal). . . . However, broad convergence in the acceptance
of the major tenets of the new paradigm was discernible across
Western Europe.

This broad paradigm shift had several policy strands which contributed to a reshaping of state–firm relationships in the 1980s:
budgetary restraint; privatization; deregulation; 'the rediscovery of
the firm' as the principal generator of a country's wealth; market-
oriented preferences and general scepticism about the efficacy of
state interventionism. Hayward, in his Introduction, tends to emphasize the first of these strands, and especially the effect on state
funding for firms (both public and private). This was of crucial
importance in France, where the centrepiece of the traditional
system was 'institutionally allocated credit' (public and private
banks and other lending institutions) rather than 'asset-based
credit' (stocks and securities), and where the financial system was
viewed as an instrument of decisive state action.[6] But the impact of

the other four strands (which are touched upon by Hayward) have been no less dramatic.

Privatization has taken many forms, and has been enacted in all the countries of Western Europe, whatever their political complexion.[7] It has become a true policy fashion, furthered by many organizations (including the OECD and the World Bank), embraced by enthusiastic coalitions in some countries, and tolerated by uneasy governments in others. For a variety of reasons—political, ideological, technological, and managerial, but mainly financial—all European states have taken the privatization path. Of the four countries dealt with in this book, the United Kingdom has been the most radical and the most enthusiastic, and has now very little left to privatize (a declining number of coal mines and an inefficient railway system are destined to be denationalized before the next general election). France, under the Balladur government, has renewed and even expanded the Chirac privatization programme—interrupted in 1988—to include strategic industries such as Elf, the oil giant, and Aérospatiale, as well as the national flag carrier Air France. However, it is worth noting that under the Socialists partial (the sale of part of the equity or of subsidiaries of nationalized enterprises) and even 'backdoor' privatization had gathered pace in the search for new capital. In Germany, the Treuhand is transferring, not always very easily, the state sector of the East to private hands, and even the controversial privatization of the country's telecommunications system is now firmly on the political agenda. In Italy—a traditionally reluctant privatizer—determined efforts are now being made to dismantle the huge state financial and industrial holdings.

Privatization has involved not only the total or partial transfer of state industrial property to private hands, it has also frequently led to foreign ownership or entry into the capital of the firm. The 1993 privatization programme in France (unlike that of 1986–8) provides for foreigners to become part of the stable core shareholders designated by the government, and French attempts to minimize foreign control by issuing non-voting equity are running into increasing difficulties.

There is a final dimension of privatization which is reshaping state–industry relations in Western Europe: the privatization of the management and logic of those firms which remain in the public sector. Public firms are expected increasingly to behave like their private counterparts, thus depriving them of any real rationale. Moreover, in their pursuit of private sector objectives, public sector managers have accentuated their demands—and, in many cases, have had them accorded—for considerable autonomy.[8]

The implications of deregulation also require further exploration. Like privatization, it is a multi-layered phenomenon, and ranges from the removal of controls (in the currency and financial markets, on prices, on planning requirements) to the reduction (at both the European and the domestic level) in the time-consuming administrative formalities which previously hampered entrepreneurial firms. The liberalization of the world's financial markets, as Jack Hayward rightly points out, warrants particular attention, especially as it coincided with the accelerating globalization of those markets.[9] Firms are no longer constrained by the capacity of the domestic capital supply, and may even issue shares in a number of markets simultaneously. Liberalization has also coincided with an increased demand for capital by major companies with global ambitions. Even the mighty Daimler-Benz, backed by the Deutsche Bank, its biggest shareholder, decided to seek full listing on the New York stock exchange—thus becoming the first German company to do so. It has plans to increase the American ownership of its shares from 3 to 10 per cent.

The liberalization and globalization of financial markets has had several important consequences for state–firm relations. In the first place, it has reduced the ability of national policies to influence the structure of the market or the behaviour of the participants, and has created 'a powerful internal dynamic . . . for policy convergence'.[10] Secondly, it has given rise to new modes of national and *international* regulatory activity. And, finally, it has an impact on the behaviour of firms. Thus, Daimler-Benz, in order to be listed on the New York stock exchange, had to strike an agreement with the Securities and Exchange Commission to reveal more financial information (the company promptly disclosed DM 4 billion of hidden reserves). More significantly, institutional investors in French and German companies may be forced to pay greater attention to the demands of international shareholders who do not share the rather benign views of their traditional institutional investors.

Linked with deregulation is 'the rediscovery of the firm' as the principal source of a country's wealth. This element has led governments—even Socialist ones—to lend a more sympathetic ear to the pleas of industry which, according to its spokesmen, was over-burdened with controls and social costs. Hence, the policies of deregulation and of the easing of the fiscal burden on firms which all governments of Western Europe have pursued. However, there has been a less palatable consequence for some major firms, as the state has come to believe that it should no longer cushion them against the rigours of the marketplace by the customary array of direct and indirect subsidies. Indeed, the statistics are eloquent on this point, since even allowing for the immense complexity of the issue and the controversies surrounding it, there has been a steady downward trend in state industry subsidies throughout Western Europe.

The final implication for state–industry relations in the paradigm shift of the 1980s was increasing general scepticism about state intervention: state officials, cushioned from the rigours of the marketplace, inevitably strike up collusive and costly relations with privileged groups; private provision is *inherently* more efficient than public goods; state intervention, with its market-distorting bias, harbours inevitable unintended and unwelcome consequences; industrial policy is a mask for politicized market distortion; selected national champions invariably turned out to be expensive white elephants or lame ducks, and so on. These contentious claims became the axioms of the dominant neo-liberals. Together with the other implications of the paradigm shift, this one powerfully contributed to a progressive redefinition of state–firm relations. It may be argued that elements of the dominant paradigm of the 1980s are now being severely questioned—facts have an uncomfortable tendency to take their revenge—leaving an uneasy intellectual void. There seems little evidence, however, of a return to the nostrums of the 1950s and 1960s.[11] In any case, many of the key elements remain and continue to structure state–firm relations and their perception.

But there are other factors, some of which are raised by Hayward, which were also combining to reshape those relations. The second major change in the 1980s was the increasing difficulty of defining a strategic firm. The great strategic industries of yesterday—the 'commanding heights of the economy'—steel, coal, textiles, shipyards—have been decimated. Defence-related industries have also lost some of their strategic status because of the political events in Eastern Europe, or, because of soaring investment costs, may join the long list of other national strategic industries which are linked to foreign ventures. Furthermore, the importance attached to the monoliths has been replaced by a greater concern for small and medium-sized firms in the discourse and policy agendas of West European governments which have come to recognize the significance of highly fragmented service industries to the economy. Matters became even more complicated with the rapid tertiarization of economies (and of foreign direct investment (FDI)). As the complementarity between commodities and services has increased, the growing internationalization of production and exchange has prompted the deregulation and liberalization of services, thus increasing their tradability. By the late 1980s the share of services in the world stock of FDI had reached 50 per cent, and services account for 55–60 per cent of annual flow.[12] In this 'knowledge-based global order' states are no longer confronting cosily settled and domestically installed monoliths which can be endowed with privileged status. It was during the 1980s that the very notion of a strategic industry came to be seriously contested, and certain voices were even heard questioning the need for a sound manufacturing base.

The problem of identifying 'strategic firms' was compounded by the increasingly diffuse nature of many major firms, as they diversified upstream and downstream and even radically moved away from their core businesses in an attempt to spread risks. A classic case is that of Ferruzzi, an empire based on a powerful family dynasty, which was built on grain after the Second World War but which, in the 1980s, expanded, with the help of borrowing, often in foreign currency, into chemicals, cement, and insurance. The controversial tale of the diversification strategies of the privatized British regional water authorities, which used their hefty profits to buy into a variety of other industries, is too well known to be recounted here. The spread of French public enterprises by the acquisition of subsidiaries (themselves with sub-subsidiaries) led to a tentacular and often bewildering process of empire building—a process much criticized by the Right.

The scale of the financial problems confronting many major firms—both public and private—as a result of the recession and of increasing fixed capital costs, represents a third important change in the international environment. Thus, by 1993 *all* European steel companies were losing money, almost all airlines were heavily in the red, and all three largest computer manufacturers—Olivetti,

Bull, and Siemens (ICL, Britain's 'champion' had been swallowed by Fujitsu)—were in financial difficulties: Bull, the French national champion, which had failed to beat off American and Japanese 'aggression' (i.e. competition), ran up losses of FF17 billion between 1989 and 1993. Several German flagship industries, such as Volkswagen and Daimler-Benz, were in trouble, as were the big Italian family groups (Berlusconi's Fininvest, Agnelli's Fiat, and the Ferruzzi empire—Italy's second biggest private industrial group—which was crippled under a weight of debt estimated at some 31 trillion lire or over $20 billion) and IRI (in 1990 an unwieldy package of 477 companies, many of which were in dire straits). In France, state firms were seeking a combined funding of over FF20 billion from the government. The financial crisis of many major firms is leading to significant restructuring processes (particularly in Italian private capitalism), to a search for new partners, and for new sources of capital (hence Daimler-Benz's recent listing on the New York stock exchange). In short, major firms not only operate in an environment which is less conducive to state manipulation, but, by their increasing complexity and vulnerability, they were less desirable objects to manipulate.

The fourth major pressure on reshaping state–firm relations has been the impact of the European Union, a factor seemingly underrated by Hayward in his Introduction. Driven by various actors—the Commission, the Court, the member states, the major private economic and industrial actors—the marketplace of Western Europe has been transformed. Crises in the monetary system should not disguise the remarkable extent of this transformation. The Union has not only become a major trade negotiator, but has increasingly redefined many of the ground rules which determine state–industry relations. Woolcock and Wallace, and McGowan in this book emphasize the impact of the European Union and point to the nature and limits of the Union's interventions. It should be noted that the Commission is locked into persistent policy schizophrenia, oscillating between firm declarations in favour of a strong competition policy and a hesitant advocacy of some European-level industrial policy, between brandishing of the stipulations of the Treaties and a politicized caution when applying them. This structural ambivalence is, of course, rooted in the differing ideological predilections of the member states and is reflected in the tension between the various Directorates General. It is manifested in competition and mergers decisions (such as the 1992 decision on Nestlé's takeover of Perrier) and state aid decisions on Air France and on Sabena, which appear to border on the incoherent. But it is worth emphasizing that the EU as harmonizer has led to the dismantling of trade barriers, and as regulator of competition policy has been intimately involved in preventing price-fixing (notably by chemical firms), in liberalizing (in telecommunications and airlines, though there is much yet to be achieved in both areas), in vetting mergers and acquisitions, and, often controversially, in controlling state aid (as major companies such as Renault, Air France, Bull, Sabena, Fiat, Rover, and Daimler-Benz will testify), and in slowly opening up public procurement policies. In other sectors it has encouraged inter-firm co-operation in major co-operative ventures. As regulator of environmental policy it is inevitably involved in pushing costly policies onto often reluctant governments and firms.

The Thatcher, Kassim, and Muller contributions to the book all point to the 'regulatory creep' apparent in Brussels. What has not been fully explored in the book is the extent to which the Union is redefining existing political arrangements (with firms such as ICI and Philips becoming powerful lobbyists in Brussels as well as in their national capitals), in altering traditional domestic policy networks, in creating incipient Europe-wide networks based on intricate multi-level bargaining, in triggering institutional change (with new mechanisms of regulation and anti-trust, and new rules of transparency), and in reshaping the opportunity structures of both member states and firms. The prolonged and acrimonious confrontations over future Union development (open or fortress, interventionist or laissez-faire, social or Thatcherite) reflect not only genuine ideological cleavages but also different calculations about the costs of the implementation of particular options. They also serve to underline the immense significance of the Union for both its constituent states and their major enterprises. In a very profound sense, therefore, we may justifiably refer to the Europeanization of major firms.

The internationalization or globalization of the major firms—the fifth major change worth emphasizing, and already touched upon—has several strands, and in analysing state–firm relations they need to be unravelled.[13] Broadly speaking, globalization refers to two distinct yet intimately interconnected processes: on the one hand, 'the emergence of global oligopoly as the most significant type of supply structure coupled with important changes in the scope and effects of international production, technology sourcing and marketing' by the major multinational enterprises, and, on the other 'the loss of many of the attributes of economic and political sovereignty suffered by an increasing number of countries even with the OECD'.[14] More specifically, however, there are significant differences in the impact of globalization according to the criteria of sales, foreign content, passive portfolio investment, the acquisition of firms or subsidiaries, share-swaps, mergers, co-operative alliances in the form of joint ventures, licensing deals, research consortia, or supply agreements—all of which link major international firms. Impact also differs according to the country or countries involved. Thus, British overseas investment rarely involves changes in management. This is not always the case with, for example, Japanese investment.

There is little argument about the rapidity of internationalization or about the reason.[15] Cross-border business has been driven by the sustained accumulation of capital both in the form of productive capacity and of liquid assets, by falling regulatory barriers to overseas investment, by immense technological change (see above), by diminishing telecommunication and transportation costs, and by freer and cheaper domestic and international capital markets. It has been facilitated and encouraged by a proliferation of agreements and treaties destined to liberalize trade. Corporate investment across frontiers grew four times faster than world output, and three times faster than world trade between 1983 and 1990, by which date 20 per cent of the world's equity transactions involved foreign investors. The 1980s also saw a rapid growth in cross-border direct investment and trade both into the European Union and within it, transforming the shape of EU trade and leading to 'the global integration of manufacturing':[16] the Union accounted for nearly half the world's foreign direct investment in the second half of the 1980s. Ownership patterns of national industry were radically altered in the process. Even the traditionally reluctant French were affected: by March 1992 31.2 per cent of quoted French shares were in foreign hands.

Internationalization has also involved the growth in numbers and size of the world's multinational companies.[17] They have not 'taken over the world's economy' as feared in the 1970s, when Howard

Perlmutter predicted that by 1985 about four-fifths of the non-communist world's productive assets would be controlled by 200 to 300 companies,[18] and when it was alleged that these 'huge, ruthless, and stateless' enterprises would be in a position to manipulate governments in a 'borderless world'. Current figures vary widely: estimates range from 20,000 private transnationally active corporations with 100,000 subsidiaries to 35,000 multinationals controlling some 150,000 foreign affiliates.[19] There is general agreement that the top 100 multinationals control roughly 16 per cent of the world's productive assets, and about 25 per cent of those assets are in the hands of the top 300 multinationals. There is no doubt, too, that in certain sectors global strategies have to be pursued by major European firms. Thus, British Telecom's move, in June 1993, to take a $4.3 billion (or 20 per cent) stake in MCI, the second largest carrier in the USA, was inspired by a desire to become a leading global provider to multinationals. Its creation of a $1 billion joint venture with MCI was designed to exploit the fast-growing market amongst multinational companies for international voice and data transmission. By so doing, it was joining battle with AT&T, the American giant. BT's American activities have pushed France Télécom and Deutsche Telekom to enter into negotiations with AT&T with a view to forging an offensive alliance.

Similarly, BA's purchase, in the 1990s, of stakes in Australia's Qantas and in the TAT, the small French carrier, as well as in USAir was part of a strategy to create a global network. So, too, have KLM's purchase of a minority stake in Northwest and its frenetic search for a link-up with other European airlines, as well as Lufthansa's agreement with United Airlines which includes code-sharing, joint-marketing, shared facilities, and frequent flier programme. Consolidation in the airline industry means that the skies will belong to a handful of big airlines, able to wage price wars with huge economies of scale and computerized reservation systems. Some national airlines seem destined to disappear. It is the automobile industry which has probably pushed furthest the process of interpenetration of firms' activities, raising complex questions and disputes within the EU over the extent of 'domestic content'.

Interesting new patterns of ownership are emerging in Europe and especially amongst the firms of the four countries studied in this book. Thus Siemens of Germany and GEC of Great Britain jointly acquired the British firm Plessey, whilst Carnaud of France and Metal Box of Britain have merged to form CMB Packaging. Cross-border raids multiplied in the late 1980s and early 1990s: between 1 January 1988 and 30 June 1992 France was Europe's most voracious predator within the EU, with 775 deals worth £37 billion. Highly profitable French firms, such as Pechiney, Rhône-Poulenc, and Saint-Gobain, as well as French banks (Crédit Lyonnais alone spent over $1 billion in foreign acquisitions between 1987 and 1991) rushed (often foolishly) into foreign expansion. Other prominent predators included the USA (886 deals worth £30 billion) and the United Kingdom (982 deals worth £20 billion). The major target—by far—was the United Kingdom (1,320 deals worth £85 billion), with France (925 deals worth £23 billion), Germany (901 deals involving £22 billion), and Spain (489 deals valued at £4 billion) trailing behind.

Raids on major national firms proliferated, often provoking major financial (and political) battles: the struggle for control of the Société Générale de Belgique in the late 1980s and of Perrier in 1992 were but two of the more spectacular confrontations between Italian and French financial interests. Even Germany—which thought itself immune to foreign predators—became the scene of such raids, and foreigners now control firms such as Feldmühle, a major packaging firm, Hoesch, the steel company, and Sabol, the country's major manufacturer of lawn-mowers. They also hold two-fifths of the equity of Veba, the second biggest generator of electricity. French banks and insurance companies have also made several forays across the Rhine: thus, in November 1992, Crédit Lyonnais, the French state bank, acquired 50.1 per cent of BFG Bank, the sixth biggest commercial bank in Germany. The alliance between the French-owned BNP (which already had a small 4.5 per cent stake in Kleinwort Benson, the British merchant bank) and Germany's Dresdner Bank, involving a 10 per cent swap of shares, represents the most ambitious cross-border linkage to date.

On a note of caution, however, it should be pointed out that networking amongst major firms is not always easy: some alliances never reach the altar (for example, the failure, in 1991, of Commerzbank and Crédit Lyonnais to forge a partnership through an exchange of shares, or the much publicized inability in 1993 of KLM, SAS, Swiss Air, and Austrian Airlines to create an alliance, in spite of 11 months of arduous negotiations), whilst many others end in acrimonious divorce.

Globalization raises some tricky political issues.[20] What is permissible in the liberalized world marketplace? States and even domestic firms remain very sensitive to certain foreign takeovers. Witness, for instance, the attitude of the market-oriented British government to foreign attempts to take over the bankrupt British Caledonian (it was quickly swallowed by British Airways which thereby consolidated its domestic market dominance), to the Kuwait Investment Office's increase in its stake in BP after 1987 (it was eventually ordered to sell two-thirds of its equity holding), or to the spate of French acquisitions in the late 1980s (the Industry Minister referred no fewer than five such acquisitions to the Monopolies and Mergers Commission). Witness, too, the Belgian government's refusal to allow British Airways to take a significant stake in Sabena. In Germany, it was a group of bankers, acting almost as a surrogate state, which effectively prevented the Pirelli takeover of Continental. How can one effectively tax multinational corporations? How can one prevent delocalization or glocalization (to coin an ugly but useful phrase)—the transfer of industry (and employment)—to cheaper foreign countries, even within Europe, as in the controversial cases of Hoover and Grundig in 1993? Is it possible to construct an effective system of lead regulation for companies operating in several countries (an issue thrown into sharp relief by the BCCI scandal)? Is it possible to control national firms with more than half their output, assets, sales, and employment outside the country (the case with the top largest British and French companies by market capitalization in 1991)? What leverage can be exerted against a foreign firm which is bringing much needed capital, expertise, and employment into the country?

More directly, in terms of the central issues raised in this volume, what is the very meaning of a national champion in an internationalized and Europeanized economy? Does a national champion deserve that status if it is owned, wholly or partly, by foreigners? Did, for example, Jaguar, the British car manufacturer, lose that status when it fell into the hands of Ford? When the Swiss firm Nestlé seized control of Rowntree did it thereby deprive it of its British national status? Is ICL, Britain's second biggest computer company, less British because it is 80 per cent owned by the Japanese (Fujitsu, the world's second biggest computer firm) and 20 per cent by the Canadians (Northern Telecom)? And, if so, how, and what consequences flow from that loss of national status—a change of ownership or of management (ICL, for instance, has retained great local managerial autonomy in spite of its change of ownership)?

Since the early 1970s, with Raymond Vernon's *Sovereignty at Bay*, to the present, with Walter Wriston's *Twilight of Sovereignty*,[21] scholars have been pointing to the erosion of sovereignty involved in the emergence of the 'stateless firm', without roots or loyalties in any national soil and with shareholding and even board members (the case of ABB pointed to by Wyn Grant in his chapter in this book) truly internationalized.[22] Have these major transnational corporations 'reprivatized' the world economy and removed it from regulation by the fragmented pattern of national regimes? And what possible control can a national state exercise over the vast internal markets of these corporations (more than a third of US trade in 1990, which amounted to $887.2 billion, was between US companies and the overseas affiliates according to a 1992 World Bank Report)? There are many who would deny the existence of 'global firms', arguing that whilst they tend to buy, produce, employ, distribute, research, develop, raise capital, and market in many countries they do so in regional clusters around a home base. Global firms 'think globally but act locally' as diseconomies of scale become apparent (bureaucratized and cumbersome decision-making processes, the demoralization of local management structures, the lack of flexible and locally sensitive management, and of knowledge of core businesses). It has been further argued that the 1990s may well witness 'the demise of size', as these costs of operating in several countries for monolithic firms become increasingly apparent. Technological change is also enabling smaller firms to secure cheaper access to sophisticated financial models and logistical techniques previously reserved for big firms. With financial liberalization smaller firms have no difficulties in raising capital on the international money markets.

A combination of these factors could, it is alleged, lead to the superseding of today's global firms by 'the virtual firm', a temporary network of companies, formed to exploit a specific market opportunity, or by 'the relationship enterprise'—a federation of strategic alliances amongst independent or quasi-independent firms, spanning different industries and countries, and held together by a set of common objectives. There would be no single home base, but multiple home bases.[23] An early sign of such a development was the IBM alliance of 1981 with Microsoft, Intel, and Lotus to develop a personal computer—the company is now working with Apple (an arch rival in the past) to develop a new type of operating software to work on both companies' machines. Other examples include the sharing of engineers by Mitsubishi and Daimler-Benz, the linking of the design operations of Boeing and three Japanese companies to build a new aircraft, the co-operation amongst a group of telecommunication firms to provide a worldwide network of fibre-optic submarine cables. At the purely European level, the examples of Airbus, and the recent merging of the guided missile programmes of Thomson and British Aerospace, spring to mind. As Pierre Muller in his chapter points out, the aerospace sector has seen 'a multiplication of alliance strategies between European companies which have resulted in an increasingly complex web of co-operative and competitive relationships'. The same may be said of the automobile industry.

Whether we are referring to the global firm or the network enterprise we are clearly pointing to two major problems for nation states—that of the blurring of the identity of major firms, and of their regulation if not control. The problem is compounded if we explore the final dimension of the changes affecting relations between states and major companies: hybridization.

Hybridization, fed by domestic diversification and internationalization, has assumed many forms—joint ventures, purchase of voting or non-voting stock, share swaps, joint research programmes —and has involved purely national, transnational, public, and private firms. It may also involve more than one partner. Thus, the French Bull group allowed Japan's NEC to take a 5 per cent stake, and has a technological partnership with IBM (which involved the American firm acquiring a 5.7 per cent stake). Hybridization may involve links between private firms in the same country, between private firms across national frontiers (a very common form), between private and public firms in the same country (for example, the ill-fated and bribe-riddled 1989 Montedison–ENI link-up to create Enimont in Italy), between public firms across national frontiers (thus, Finmeccanica, part of IRI, the Italian state holding group, acquired 45 per cent of SGS-Thomson, the French public semiconductors enterprise, whilst Air France entered into the capital of Sabena, the Belgian state airline), and even between public and private firms across national frontiers. French public enterprises have been particularly zealous predators: in 1989, French nationalized companies spent FF11 billion on British acquisitions alone. This assault provoked a hostile response from a British government which was anxious to prevent 'back-down nationaliz-ation' by foreign state enterprises. Acquisitions by French public banks in Germany also created some political unease across the Rhine. The result of this accelerating process of hybridization—domestic/foreign, public/private—is 'boundary blurring', in which policy responsibility is obfuscated, regulatory problems aggravated (note the points made by Holliday in his chapter on the Channel Tunnel), and command structures often unclear (the battle over Enimont was highly revealing in this respect).

Where do these immense changes in the international, European, and domestic environments leave the four states in their relation-ship with their increasingly diversified, globalized, and hybridized enterprises? Clearly, there has been some 'state withdrawal': as noted above, both public and private firms have gained autonomy in recent years. But in some respects the interdependence has not been lessened: rather, it has become more complex and obfuscated. This interdependence is rooted in the fact that the state relies on the enterprises as major motors of wealth and employment, whilst the firms depend on the state not only to create the conditions for a stable, open world market but in a variety of other ways. The home nation state remains the principal source of capital, management, and labour, and the major market for most firms (even the most globalized), so exchange-rate policies, general macro-economic stance and the domestic fiscal regime remain crucial for industry.[24] Its competition policy (often an indirect and disguised form of industrial policy) may also be vital in determining the rules of the game by which most firms play. Of equal importance, too, are education and training policies (Andrew Shonfield pointed to their significance more than a generation ago[25]), labour market policy and the state's attitude towards research and infrastruc-ture—a point made forcibly by Cohen in his chapter in this book. In short, the state remains the general parameter setter for most firms.

Finally, its *increasing* regulatory role (in consumer, safety, and environmental protection for example) are no less significant in determining the well-being or otherwise of industry.[26] Liberaliz-ation of certain industries has often been accompanied by increased regulation. This is notably the case in the insurance and financial services sector: the City of London, once a self-regulated 'gentlemen's club', has fallen more and more into the regulatory net of the state (particularly when it was discovered that some of the gentlemen did not behave as such . . .). Moreover, one of the paradoxical consequences of privatizing public goods has been the creation of interventionist regulatory agencies—the case of the United Kingdom, where the privatized public utilities complain bitterly about the increasingly detailed interference of their regulatory bodies. As Holliday points out in his chapter, even in an enterprise such as the Channel Tunnel—which on the Thatcher government's insistence had to be private—the potential for public regulation is enormous and probably inevitable.

In terms of its relationship with specific sectors or firms the state continues to act as *travelling salesman* (particularly in the lucrative and highly competitive defence goods industry), as *seducer* (in attracting foreign investment in ways well described by Bianchi in his contribution to this book, and well exploited by all governments), and as *advocate* (in trade negotiations, and especially within the European Union). More directly, the state continues to intervene on occasions as *shield* or *protector* of its 'strategic' (however ill-defined) industries against foreign predators. Sometimes the methods are direct (hence, the 'Club Med' group of Southern Europe, anxious to protect their local stock exchanges, are preventing, until 1999, direct access to them by foreign banks). The most direct method of protection is, of course, public ownership, for, in spite of significant privatization drives everywhere, telecommunications, airlines, electricity, gas, water, railways, and most defence-related industries remain firmly in public hands in most West European countries. Furthermore, in many privatized industries the state has retained blocking minority stakes or has reserved for itself strategic veto rights (through the exercise or the threat of the exercise of the 'golden share' or *action spécifique*), or, in the case of France, has constructed at the heart of the privatized industries a set of stable institutional investors destined to protect those industries against unwelcome foreign takeovers. Prime Minister Balladur has promised that there will be no limits on foreign stakes in future privatized industries. However, the French have generated an arsenal of other protective devices for many of their industries, including restrictions on voting rights, shares without voting rights, shares with double voting rights, and the legal structures of French companies. Moreover, amongst the most active *zinzins*, or institutional investors, are state banks and financial institutions, including the ubiquitous Caisse des Dépôts.

Germany, too, as Josef Esser makes clear, has created a complex national web of actors at federal and Länder level which links private enterprises to friendly banks, R&D agencies, trade unions, and the government. Often the combination of rules and concerted action can effectively prevent foreign takeovers, as Bianchi in his chapter admirably illustrates with the case of the battles over the Belgian Société Générale, the French Perrier group, and the German enterprise Continental which was prevented from falling into Pirelli's hands by the action of the Deutsche Bank. In spite of increasing EU pressure, domestic firms continue to be protected also against foreign competition, through subtle trade barriers and required national standards, or through public procurement policies. Thus, public procurement, which is worth some 15 per cent of the Community's total GDP, is still very closed: in 1990, only 2 per cent of big public sector contracts flowed across EC borders. Major firms—both public and private (and privatized)—remain critically dependent on state orders.

Finally, in spite of increasing restrictions imposed by the European Union, states continue to act as *cushions* for their major firms, providing them with tax reliefs, subsidies, grants, research contracts, infrastructural support, regional relief, export aid. Often the means are indirect. Thus, French Socialist governments of the 1980s and early 1990s frequently pressured state banks into recapitalizing French firms by purchasing unwanted equity in those firms (the case, for example, in November 1991, when BNP reluctantly bought 8.8 per cent of ailing Air France). In a variety of ways, therefore, the state continues to be locked into a close relationship with the major industries, and even Britain, under the market-orientated Thatcher government, was a persistent interferer in the activities of many of its major companies.

Of course, this relationship is far removed from the more heroic entrepreneurial or *dirigiste* strategies of the past. The failure of Edith Cresson's ambitious industrial restructuring proposals of 1991, the emptiness of Michael Heseltine's 1992 promise 'to intervene before breakfast, lunch, tea, and dinner' to help British firms, appear to underline the fact that the days of the activist state, selecting and promoting national champions, appear to be over. It is worth emphasizing, however, that according to the contributors of this book, such a state never really existed in Germany, made only sporadic and limited appearances in Italy and the United Kingdom, and was not entirely successful in France. We may be in danger of comparing the more modest state of today with a mythical heroic state of the 1950s and 1960s created largely by Anglo-American academics seeking a rationale for their own predilections for *dirigisme*. Moreover, as Cohen makes clear in his work (it is summarized in his contribution in this book) on France, it was not always clear in the state–firm relationship which was the dominant partner. He also points out that successful French national champion strategies—and most were not—hinged on a combination of propitious factors—political, administrative, financial, and industrial—which did not always prevail.[27]

The retention of certain traditional functions and the shift to a more regulatory mode means that the task of the state is no less pervasive and no less complex than in the past. Thus, the balancing of the conflicting requirements of different sectors in trade negotiations remains intrinsically difficult and highly controversial. And regulation of a domestic industry is an *inherently* complex and politically delicate operation, generally involving the reconciling of conflicting objectives supported by different constituencies. Furthermore, regulation of a particular sector at different territorial levels—national, EU, and international—may lock the state into the pursuit of conflicting policies.

The broad shift in the role of the state and the changing nature of most major firms have, then, *generally* involved a less direct and more regulatory relationship with major firms. But have they resulted in a change in the structure or *shape* of those relations? Jack Hayward, in his Introduction, makes a courageous attempt to capture the structure with his model of three main clusters of actors. He points out, too, that the 'iron triangle' assumes different forms in the four countries studied, and that it operates differently according to sector. The model has the advantage of quickly defining the major actors in the field, and his concession to national differences is certainly justified, for, in spite of the broadly convergent pressures of the 1980s and early 1990s, national industrial environments continue to matter. Certainly the perception of, and adjustment to, these broadly convergent pressures have been deter-

mined by persistent national differences. These differences encompass:

- the size, location, openness, structure, resources, and performance of the economy;
- the structure and size of the national financial market and the
  relationship between banks and industry (contrast Esser's account of that relationship in Germany with that of Bianchi's in
  Italy);
- the 'industrial profile' of the country—the size, position, and
  ownership structures of the major firms (Italy's small number of
  dominant family firms has no equivalent in the other three
  countries studied);
- the traditional relationship between ownership and management—whether in public or private firms—the major sources of
  capitalization for those firms, and even their accounting practices
  (a point well made by Esser) and managerial cultures;
- the nature of interest articulation and aggregation—the subject
  of extensive political science attention;
- the domestic political institutional arrangements and resources
  (centralized or federalized, focused or diffused, the extent of
  fragmentation, the degree of state expertise etc.);
- the 'cultural inheritance', the dominant economic ideology of
  major actors towards economic power, freedom of contract and
  trade, efficiency and equity, the desirability of state intervention.

In all these respects there are major differences between the four
countries studied in this book. Of course, none of the features is
immutable, and significant changes have taken place—often in a
convergent direction. But differences persist, and they continue to
shape state–firm relations and to determine responses to pressures
of those relations. Hence, the striking contrast between, on the one
hand, the continuing 'corporatistically arranged', conservative,
cautious, and pragmatic response to deregulation in Germany, and
the Thatcherite reaction on the other.

But it is not only persistent national differences that render
difficult the construction of a convincing general model of state–
firm relations. The second complication arises from the fact that
both states and major firms, as we have emphasized, function at
four different territorial levels: international, European, nation
state, local. The salience of the territorial level for firms and states

differs according to the sector and the issue raised. Moreover, each level has generated (or is likely to do so) different coalitions, institutions, and needs, boxing both state and firms into overlapping triangular territorial relations, with differing and even conflicting objectives. Thus, the British government may, as part of a wider bilateral trade agreement with the USA, penalize British Airways by opening up slots at Heathrow. It may also proclaim the virtues of competition and liberalization. But, it is equally aware that British Airways is British, and requires a degree of support. For that reason most of its privileges are protected, and the already dominant firm was allowed to swallow British Caledonian and Dan-Air, two irritating but bankrupt competitors, without any objection from Whitehall.

The third problem in constructing a general model of state–firm relations lies in the fragmentation and often internal rivalries evident at each territorial level. This is true at European Union level (where tensions between DGIV and DGXIII, pointed to by Thatcher in his chapter, are real and deep), and even more so at nation state level, where conflicts between treasuries, sponsoring ministries, and territorially based ministries are endemic. These rivalries are well known to firms which often exploit them to their own ends.

The construction of a viable model runs into a fourth problem— that of fluidity. Many of the elements which underpin the relations between state and firms are susceptible to change: the position, needs, and strategies of firms and of states are constantly being reshuffled. Thus, the free-wheeling, frenetic acquisitiveness of the 1980s which left many countries and groups with more corporate debt than was wise (the plight of the Ferruzzi empire is exemplary in this respect) has appeared to calm down somewhat in the financially more difficult years of the early 1990s. The pressure to recapitalize or to reduce indebtedness as well as changing corporate fashion have combined to squeeze companies into paying greater attention to their core businesses. The need to raise capital on the international capital markets and introduce foreign shareholders into the equity of the enterprise may have profound long-term effects—particularly in Italy and Germany. Can, for instance, the comfortable German company model, based on a broad consensus between the shareholders (which often include employees and local authorities as well as the powerfully placed banks) survive the pressures of internationalization? It is, of course, too early to predict, but the Daimler-Benz case, noted above, may well be a pointer to a future more shaped by Anglo-American-type companies which are more restless (and ruthless?) in their location strategies. At the state level, we may be witnessing a serious questioning of the wisdom of at least some of the aspects of the dominant paradigm of the 1980s. Furthermore, to reiterate a point, both firms and states are vulnerable to changes imposed by the international political environment and by international trade agreements (the completion of the GATT Uruguay round in December 1993 triggered a hectic calculation about winners and losers) or the European Union.

Finally, in exploring the nature, intensity, and structure of state–firm interdependence, we are confronted with the problematic character of the indicators of need or dependence. Thus, formal ownership provides few clues about control. It is well known that enterprises may actually gain power in relation to the state through public ownership: 'agency capture' is by no means restricted to the private sector. Major French private companies possibly enjoyed less autonomy under the Giscard d'Estaing presidency than public firms enjoy under the presidency of his successor. In Britain, as Grant indicates in his chapter, the state's relationship with the private ICI was much easier than that with the nationalized electricity company. It is clear, too, that privatized public utilities in the United Kingdom are, in some respects, much more closely controlled by regulatory agencies than they were under direct state ownership. Matters become even more complicated when we consider the question of mixed ownership or hybridized firms. Another indicator frequently used to explore the degree of dependence—indebtedness or financial need—can be equally problem-ridden, as Keynes suggested in his celebrated remarks about the relationship between bankers and their clients: paradoxically, a high level of indebtedness may render the banker the prisoner of the customer. 'Strategic value'—a third indicator—has become, as noted above, a much more difficult concept to assess. The nature of the indicators of dependence suggests that we must be wary of comparative general models, however useful they may be as heuristic devices, because apparently similar indicators may disguise somewhat different realities.

Any attempt to provide a convincing analysis of state–firm relations must begin by identifying the actors involved, their needs, and the precise nature of the interdependence. It must also explore the resources of each, the willingness to mobilize those resources, and the constraints which hamper their effective mobilization.[28] It must recognize that whilst interdependence is evident, the degree and nature of the interdependence varies from firm to firm within any particular country, that it may vary sharply from country to country, and may be reshaped over time by domestic circumstances or by events at the other relevant territorial levels. Different levels of analysis are, therefore, required. As a consequence we may be left not with a series of triangles—overlapping and complex though they may be—but a more nationally differentiated, more complicated, and somewhat shifting interlacing of relationships, and more complex taxonomies structured by the multiplicity of factors which have emerged throughout this book.

Notes

1. I am grateful to Stephen Woolcock and Wyn Grant, two contributors to this book, as well as to two anonymous referees for their comments on the first draft of this chapter. One of the latter justifiably pointed to my unacknowledged debt to the distinguished work carried out within the ESRC Government–Industry Relations Intiative. The debt was obvious and I am delighted to recognize it. Special mention should be made of Stephen Wilks and Maurice Wright (eds.), *Comparative Government–Industry Relations: Western Europe, the United States and Japan* (Oxford, 1987); Alan Cawson *et al.*, *Hostile Brothers: Competition and Closure in the European Electronics Industry* (Oxford, 1990). Mention should be made, too, of Margaret Sharp and Peter Holmes (eds.), *Strategies for New Technology* (London, 1989); Karel Cool, Damien J. Neven, and Ingo Walter (eds.), *European Industrial Restructuring in the 1990s* (London, 1992); Richard Whitley, 'Societies, Firms and Markets: The Social Structuring of Business Systems', in Whitley (ed.), *European Business Systems: Firms and Markets in their National Contexts* (London, 1992), 5–41.
2. See the excellent article by Peter Hall, 'Policy Paradigms, Social Learning, and the State', *Comparative Politics*, 25/3 (Apr. 1993), 275–96.
3. Peter Gourevitch, *Politics in Hard Times: Comparative Responses to International Economic Crises* (Ithaca, NY, 1986). See also Peter Gerlich, Erik Damgaard, and Jeremy Richardson, *The Politics of Economic Crisis: Lessons from Western Europe* (Avebury, 1989).

4. See Helen V. Milner, *Resisting Protectionism; Global Industries and the Politics of International Trade* (Princeton, NJ, 1988).

5. See esp. B. Stevens and M. Andrieu, 'Trade, Investment and Technology in a Changing International Environment', in OECD, *Trade, Investment and Technology in the 1990s* (Paris, 1991).

6. This is one of the major themes of Michael Loriaux, *France after Hegemony: International Change and Domestic Reform* (Ithaca, NY, 1988).

7. John Vickers and Vincent Wright, *The Politics of Privatization in Western Europe* (London, 1988); Madsen Pirie, *Privatisation, Theory, Practice and Choice* (Aldershot, 1988).

8. For a description of the traditional situation, see Harvey Feigenbaum, 'Public Enterprise in Comparative Perspective', *Comparative Politics*, 15, Oct. 1982, pp. 101–22; J. Zif, 'Managerial Strategic Behaviour in State-Owned Enterprises: Business and Political Orientations', *Management Science* (Nov. 1981), 1326–39.

9. See the very useful collection of articles on 'The Politics of Transnational Regulation: Deregulation or Reregulation', *European Journal of Political Research*, 19/2–3 (Mar.–Apr. 1991). See also Sarkis J. Khoury, *The Deregulation of the World Financial Markets: Myths, Realities and Impact* (London, 1990).

10. DeAnne Julius, *Global Companies and Public Policy, the Growing Challenge of Foreign Direct Investment* (London, 1990), 94.

11. This point was well made by Wyn Grant in his comments on the first draft of the chapter.

12. United Nations, *World Investment Report: The Triad in Foreign Direct Investment* (New York, 1991).

13. Marc Humbert (ed.), *The Impact of Globalization on Europe's Firms and Industries* (London, 1993), John H. Dunning, *The Globalization of Business* (London, 1993).

14. See the very useful essay by François Chesnais, 'Globalisation, World Oligopoly and Some of their Implications', in Humbert (ed.), *The Impact of Globalization*, 12–21.

15. See Keniche Ohmaie, *The Borderless World: Power and Strategy in the Interlinked Economy* (London, 1990).

16. Stephen Thomsen and Stephen Wilcock, *Direct Investment and European Integration* (London, 1993); and John Cantwell, *Multinational Investment in Modern Europe* (Aldershot, 1992).

17. John Dunning, *Multinational Enterprises and the Global Economy* (Reading, Mass., 1993); see also the very useful essay by Wyn Grant, 'Economic Globalisation, Stateless Firms and International Governance', University of Warwick, Department of Politics and International Studies, Working Paper 105 (Apr. 1992).

18. Howard V. Perlmutter and David A. Heenan, *Multinational Organisation* (Reading, Mass., 1979).
19. See e.g. the UN *World Investment Report: Transnational Corporations as Engines of Growth* (New York, 1992), 11.
20. See esp. Alan Cawson *et al., Hostile Brothers*; J. N. Behrman and R. Grosse, *International Business and Governments* (Columbia, 1990); J. H. Dunning, 'The Global Economy, Domestic Governance Strategies and Transnational Corporations: Interactions and Policy Implications', *Transnational Corporations*, 1/3 (Dec. 1993), 7–46; R. Reich, *The Work of Nations: Preparing Ourselves for the 21st Century Capitalism* (New York, 1990); S. Ostry, *Governments and Corporations in a Shrinking World* (New York, 1990).
21. Raymond Vernon, *Sovereignty at Bay: The Multinational Spread of US Enterprises* (New York, 1971); Walter B. Wriston, *Twilight of Sovereignty* (New York, 1992).
22. See also Grant, 'Economic Globalisation', 7–10.
23. See e.g. C. Antonelli, 'The Emergence of the Network Firm', in id., *New Information Technology and Industrial Change: The Italian Case* (Dordrecht: Kiuwer Academic Publishers, 1988); B. Gustafsson and O. Williamson, *The Firm as a Nexus of Treaties* (London, 1989); L. K. Mytelke (ed.), *Strategic Partnerships: States, Firms and International Competition* (London, 1991).
24. On the importance of the home base for multinationals, see Michael Porter, *The Comparative Advantage of Nations* (London, 1990). See also OECD, *Strategic Industries in a Global Economy: Policy Issues for the 1990s* (Paris, 1991).
25. Andrew Shonfield, *Modern Capitalism: The Changing Balance of Public and Private Power* (London, 1965).
26. For an especially useful collection of essays, see Leigh Hancher and Michael Moran, *Capitalism, Culture and Economic Regulation* (Oxford, 1989).
27. See also his *Le Colbertisme 'high-tech'* (Paris, 1992).
28. Stephen Brooks, 'The Mixed Ownership Corporation as an Instrument of Public Policy', *Comparative Politics*, 19/2 (Jan. 1987), 173–92.

Index